Mapping Decline

St. Louis and its suburbs, 2005.

Mapping Decline

St. Louis and the Fate of the American City

Colin Gordon

PENN

University of Pennsylvania Press

Philadelphia

Politics and Culture in Modern America

Series Editors: Glenda Gilmore, Michael Kazin, Thomas J. Sugrue

Volumes in the series narrate and analyze political and social change in the broadest dimensions from 1865 to the present, including ideas about the ways people have sought and wielded power in the public sphere and the language and institutions of politics at all levels—local, national, and transnational. The series is motivated by a desire to reverse the fragmentation of modern U.S. history and to encourage synthetic perspectives on social movements and the state, on gender, race, and labor, and on intellectual history and popular culture.

Published by
University of Pennsylvania Press
Philadelphia, Pennsylvania 19104-4112
Printed in Canada on acid-free paper

10 9 8 7 6 5 4 3 2 1

A Cataloging-in-Publication record is available from the Library of Congress

ISBN 978-0-8122-4070-2

For Ken Cmiel, Susan Schechter, and Liz Stromquist—
and for those they left behind

Contents

Maps, Figures, and Tables

Maps

Figures

Tables

Preface

In the summer of 2002, I attended an academic conference in St. Louis. Upon arrival at the hotel, I realized that the conference was not really in St. Louis but in Clayton, an inner suburb that had reinvented itself as a corporate park. St. Louis, as I discovered on my first foray east into the city, seemed to consist largely of abandoned houses and boarded-up storefronts—interrupted, only a few blocks from the Mississippi, by haphazard commercial redevelopment. This was a bad first impression (my route took me through the most neglected neighborhoods), but it stuck.

That summer, my colleague Peter Fisher and I received seed funding to begin work on a history of economic development policies in the United States, part of which would be used to learn the ropes of Geographic Information Systems (GIS) mapping, part of which would be used to delve into the historical meaning of "blight" in urban public policy. As we wrestled with the mapping, and particularly the challenge of digitizing historical sources, it became increasingly clear that we needed to start with a local case study. And, as we sorted through the legal and political history of "blight," many of the most egregious cases (that is, cases that stretched the definition of blight in order to create tax breaks or subsidies) that cropped up were in the St. Louis suburbs.

So St. Louis was an important case but an understudied one. But the first step into the archives made one thing clear: the key to the story was not just the perfidy or futility of local urban renewal efforts, but the conditions that made such measures necessary. This pushed the research in new directions and earlier into the twentieth century. What began as a place to start a national history of local economic development policies had become a research project of its own. In some respects, this would be a conventional case study of urban decline—the St. Louis chapter of a story told so masterfully in other settings (Arnold Hirsch on Chicago, Tom Sugrue on Detroit). In other respects, it was an opportunity to tell that story in a different way, employing the visual and explanatory power of GIS mapping (using census and archival data) to underscore the causal and consequential dimensions of the urban crisis in greater St. Louis and beyond.

While the archival record was complicated—spanning two states, twelve counties, and over one hundred local jurisdictions—it also proved extraordinarily rich. One of the nation's leading urban planning firms, Harland Bartholomew and Associates, did almost all of the substantive planning and zoning on the Missouri side and left behind (at Washington University) an expansive documentary and cartographic record. The Missouri State Archives maintain extensive case and evidentiary records of most of the state's key land-use cases. And other local archives—including the Western Historical Manuscripts Collection and Mercantile Library at the University of Missouri-St. Louis, the Missouri Historical Society, the St. Louis Public Library, and the St. Louis Assessor—filled in many important gaps. I owe these institutions and their archival staffs many thanks for their help and their patience.

A novice in both local history and GIS mapping, I learned not to be shy about asking for help. Alan Peters gave me a crash course in GIS and was quick to help whenever I was perplexed by hardware, software, data, or all three. Petra Noble at the National Historic Geographic Information System (NHGIS) Center in Minneapolis helped with census data. Ben Earnhart magically transformed the old ICSPR census files on St. Louis into a GIS-friendly format. Heather MacDonald helped me to access and understand mortgage disclosure data. Mary McInroy and John Elson proved invaluable guides to map and data collections at the University of Iowa Libraries. I am also most grateful to those willing to share data or shapefiles generated in the course of their own work or research; special thanks to Charles Kindleberger (St. Louis Community Development Administration), Richard Biggs (U.S. District Court, Eastern District of Missouri), Thomas Luce (Amergis), Gary Mook (East-West Gateway Coordinating Council), Dan Backowski (Ballwin), Pamela Burdt (Town and Country), Ken Yost (Kirkwood), Linda Roberts (Fenton), Frank Hill (University City), Steve Duncan (Eureka), and Matthew Brandmeyer (Creve Coeur).

I have learned a great deal from the work of others. Much of this debt is documented in the footnotes, but some is not. For conversations and correspondence and encouraging words, I thank Robert Fogelson, Amy Hillier, Meg Jacobs, Dennis Judd, Ira Katznelson, Jennifer Klein, Greg Leroy, Maire Murphy, Dave Robertson, Mark Rose, Tom Sugrue, Todd Swanstrom, and Josh Whitehead. Special thanks to Peter Fisher and Joel Rogers who, in different ways, taught me the important questions and pointed me toward the answers. My colleagues at Iowa provided a warm and collegial environment. The department staff provided invaluable assistance—even on those days I took over the conference room to color maps. And my friends and colleagues at the Iowa Policy Project and the Economic Analysis Research Network provided the persistent and pointed reminder that, as the novelist Graham Swift put it, "history begins only at the point where things go wrong; history is born only with trouble, with perplexity, with regret."[1]

This project received financial support from the National Endowment for the Humanities, the University of Iowa Obermann Center, the Robert Seilor Fellowship of the Missouri State Archives, the University of Iowa College of Liberal Arts and Sciences, and the University of Iowa Office of the Vice President for Research. At the Press, thanks to Bob Lockhart for his support (and for not blinking when I sent him a manuscript with 72 color maps), to Chris Hu for attention to the details, and to Alison Anderson for shepherding the final stages.

Introduction
Our House

The Twentieth Century at 4635 North Market Street

The house at 4635 North Market Street, on St. Louis' near northside, was built in the 1890s. Like many of the north St. Louis homes of this vintage, 4635 North Market was a simple yet substantial structure: two stories, brick from the foundation up, skylighting on the second floor. The house and its immediate neighbors were each built close to one property line of long, narrow lots (25 feet wide, 100 feet deep) that ended with a small garage on the alley.[1] 4635 North Market stands in the Greater Ville, one of a number of older residential neighborhoods in an area of north central St. Louis— running north of the rail lines that cordon off the residential southside, west from Grand Avenue, and east of Kingshighway (see inset, Map I.1). The Greater Ville (also known historically as Grand Prairie) has always been a study in contrasts. By the early years of the twentieth century, it included some of the City's most exclusive neighborhoods, including the private streets at Vandeventer Place (about eight blocks east of 4635 North Market) and Lewis Place.[2] The Greater Ville is also nestled against the City's old industrial core (running east from the riverfront along the rail beds of the Chestnut and Mill Valleys) and, in the first decades of the twentieth century, working-class neighborhoods pushed north and west along major streets and streetcar lines. At the center of the Greater Ville (just a block east of 4635 North Market) is the Ville itself, a smaller neighborhood that by the end of World War I had become the center of the northside's burgeoning but closely confined African American population.

In the early years of the century, the area surrounding the Ville was occupied largely by working-class German and Italian American families. Fire insurance plats for 1905 listed the owner of 4635 North Market as A. Blankenmeister, who sold the property to Johanna Schroek in 1909. After World War I, the neighborhoods surrounding 4635 North Market were marked by economic strife and dramatic racial confrontation and succession. White property owners increasingly sought the "protection" of race-restrictive deed covenants, and Johanna Schroek signed such an agreement in 1923. According to the 1930 census, 4635 North Market (still owned by the Schroek family) was occupied by Charles Lang (a foreman at Wagner Electric) and his wife Annie (both second generation German Americans), two adult sons and two teenage daughters.[3] As Map 1.2 (which plots racial occupancy parcel by parcel from the 1930 manuscript census) underscores, the boundaries of African American occupancy were

Map I.1. 4635 North Market Street, St. Louis. Parcel data from St. Louis Assessor, 2003.

Legend:

★ 4635 North Market

☐ The Greater Ville

☐ The Ville

assessed parcels

■ black

■ white

Map I.2. Racial occupancy in north St. Louis, 1930. Census Bureau, 15th Census (1930), reels 1238–43.

clearly defined by the borders of the Ville and the restrictive covenants that surrounded it.[4]

The racial boundary between the Ville and the surrounding neighborhoods, however, was a fragile one. The Depression devastated the Ville, as in-migration continued but economic prospects all but evaporated.[5] The population of the census tract encompassing 4635 North Market changed little between 1930 and 1950 (hovering around 11,000), but its racial composition changed dramatically. In 1940, the tract was racially split, with a slight majority of white residents. This was clearly an uneasy balance, as the growing African American population challenged the hold, and the legality, of property restrictions—including the deed restriction covering 4635 North Market. After a flurry of changes in ownership in the late 1930s, 4635 North Market was purchased by Scovell Richardson, an African American law professor and civil rights activist. With this sale (see Chapter 2) the restrictive deed agreement collapsed. In-migration during the war (summarized in Map I.3) was starkly segregated and posed an immense burden on the northside's aging housing stock. By 1950, the tract's African American population had grown by almost 4,400 while the white population fell at almost the same rate. In 1958, Richardson himself joined the exodus, selling to his neighbor at 4639 North Market. By 1970, the tract's shrinking population (now just under 8,000) was over 99 percent African American.

Over the years, 4635 North Market fell into disrepair and at its last sale (1985) was formally vacated. Today, it is an empty lot (see Figure 1.1), as are four of the seven properties fronting the 4600 block of North Market. Of the 100-odd properties running south into Dick Gregory (formerly Wagoner) Place, nearly 40 are abandoned and another 12 have fallen into the hands of the City's Land Reclamation Authority (LRA) (see Map I.1). Between 1970 and 2000 the tract population collapsed by more than 75 percent, to just over 1,900 persons; the available housing units fell by over 60 percent, to just over 1,000—of which more than a third were empty shells. The central northside, as one observer noted in 1978, featured block after block of "windowless houses, ransacked apartments, [and] littered streets"—adding that the few "strong locations" were "almost like medieval, baronial, castle strongholds in the midst of lawless savagery." Today, the Greater Ville claims the dubious distinction, among the City's 70 neighborhoods, of ranking first or second in vacant buildings, condemned buildings, and recent demolitions. The 1999 City Plan concluded glumly that

a visual survey of the neighborhood reveals a tree-lined block of stable, well-kept, two- and four-family homes followed by a block of overgrown board-ups on a one-to-one ratio with intact housing . . . Two blocks later, a once commercial area of St. Louis Avenue is now totally empty with vacated lots and derelict buildings. This trend is not specific to St. Louis Avenue; the same can be said of Taylor, Greer, Labadie, and most other neighborhood streets. For businesses, the situation appears even worse. Signs of life are few and far between the corner store board-ups and chain-link-fence-covered storefronts.[6]

Disinvestment and depopulation are so pronounced in central St. Louis that pockets of untended green have replaced much of the housing stock. A broad swath of tax-delinquent and vacant properties [see Map I.4] extends across the northside, from

Legend:

1 Dot = 25

- increase in white persons
- increase in black persons
- new housing units

tract less than 25 percent black
25 to 50 percent
50 to 75 percent
over 75 percent
★ 4635 North Market

Map I.3. Growth in population and housing, north St. Louis, 1940–1950. Calculated from Census (Bogue Files), 1940 and 1950.

Figure I.1. Aerial view, 4635 North Market. Sanborn Total Geographic Solutions, COE 5-41 (2003).

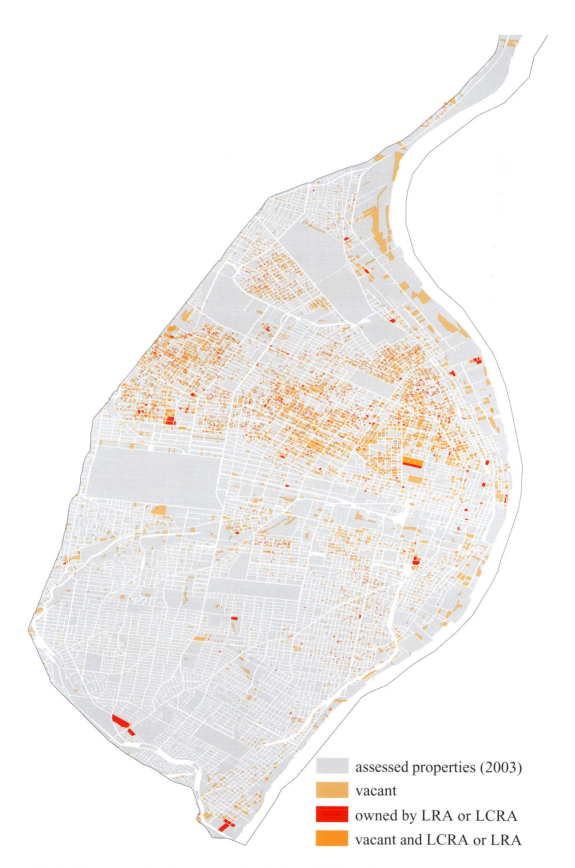

assessed properties (2003)

vacant

owned by LRA or LCRA

vacant and LCRA or LRA

Map I.4. Vacant and abandoned properties, St. Louis (2003). St. Louis parcel data (East-West Gateway).

the riverfront to the City limits. As the price of used bricks and salvaged construction metals rose in the late 1970s and early 1980s, scavengers worked hand-in-hand with conventional "slum clearance" efforts to cart off entire buildings at the rate of 5 or 10 a week. "Great neatly stacked piles of weathered red bricks stand by the railroad tracks that hug the Mississippi River," the *New York Times* noted in 1978; "It is said they are shipped to places like Savannah to restore historic buildings and to Texas to make patios for the new houses springing up around Houston."[7]

This is not a story of simply local importance or interest. This property is a part of the modern urban crisis and, like a single cancerous cell, bears all the genetic markers of the larger disease. In its lifetime, the house on Market Street confronted a series of economic and demographic crises. It was riven by the deeply racial premises of local realty and residential politics. It was caught up in a tangle of local, state, and federal policies crafted to govern the City and (increasingly but vainly) to rescue it. And just as 4635 North Market captures the logic and the consequences of St. Louis' twentieth century, so St. Louis is a telling (and understudied) setting for understanding the broader patterns of modern urban history. "St Louis is not a typical city," noted one observer in the late 1970s, "but, like a Eugene O'Neill play, it shows a general condition in a stark and dramatic form."[8]

This general condition, in St. Louis and elsewhere, is the seemingly iron law of urban decay: Rising incomes breed suburbanization. Suburbanization robs inner cities of their tax base. Inner city concentrations of poverty widen gaps between urban residents and substantive economic opportunities, and between suburban residents and urban concerns. And all of this encourages more flight, not only from the metropolitan core, but from decaying inner suburbs as well.[9] This pattern, the monotonous backbeat for most accounts of the modern urban crisis, was identified in St. Louis as early as 1919: With the unregulated and intermingled growth of commerce, industry, and housing, "partial or complete disintegration of the neighborhoods ensued," as City Engineer Harland Bartholomew observed at the time:

property values declined, the City lost tax revenue, the residents moved to more distant suburban residential districts where additional water mains, sewers, streets, pavements, transportation, gas and other utilities had to be provided, all of which represents an additional burden on the city treasury. Thus we burn the candle at both ends and seldom stop to consider that economic disaster awaits us sooner or later. We say that our cities grow, and there is no question but that American cities and towns have shown unprecedented increases in population, but do we stop to consider how large a proportion of our growth is at our own expense, a shift from one section to another—the proverbial robbing Peter to pay Paul?

Two decades later, the prognosis had not improved. "To state the condition in its simplest terms," the City Plan Commission concluded in 1936, "if adequate measures are not taken the city is faced with gradual economic and social collapse. The older central areas of the city are being abandoned and this insidious trend will continue until the entire city is engulfed."[10]

To the casual observer, this was just the market at work: The dispersal of population from the old urban core to the suburban periphery is a fairly universal pattern, accelerated in the postwar American setting by a combination of available land and general prosperity.[11] But this was hardly a level playing field, as residential opportunities were determined less by supply and demand than by the ways in which private choices were regulated, restricted, and rigged. Private real estate restrictions crowded some (in St. Louis largely African American) residents into a few older neighborhoods while effectively barring their escape to the suburban fringe. Municipal zoning replicated and reinforced this logic, creating a metropolitan centrifuge of exclusive land-use regulations that drew both private wealth and public tax capacity from the central city. Yet, because these vastly divergent opportunities were embedded in an arcane patchwork of private standards and public subsidies, the central illusion held: that individual choices and not public policies were reshaping the City and that racial segregation flowed from an unfortunate but understandable defense of private property rights.[12]

If this was a market at work, it was not only corrupt but starkly inefficient. Over time, the accumulation of individual residential choices achieved no equilibrium but only hardened patterns of residential segregation and, by robbing the central city of its tax base, encouraged even more people to escape the fiscal wreckage (baser public services, underfunded schools) left behind.[13] Over time, the City dipped below the demographic and economic thresholds necessary to sustain even basic urban activities or expectations (public transit, downtown retail and leisure, industrial clusters). As social and fiscal challenges accumulated, the City's political clout—in state and nation—evaporated. And, over time, the logic and consequences of urban decay reached inner-ring suburbs as well.[14]

The decline of the American city is arguably the most important and persistent domestic issue of the modern era. Not only is the "urban crisis" important in its own right but troubled cities hosted, shaped, and overlaid with a peculiar spatial logic so much else that was going on. Just as industrialization helped build the city, so deindustrialization contributed to its decline—a pattern of change that flowed as much from city to suburb as it did (ultimately) across national boundaries. Changes in the economy, in turn, meant fundamental changes in political and social organization, not the least of which was the slow collapse of the (largely urban) labor movement. In the American setting, all of this had a profound impact on the distribution of basic public goods and social benefits, most of which flowed from local taxes (think education) or local jobs (think health insurance).

As the process of sorting urban residency by race and class shifted political power and resources from the central city to the suburbs, it also shaped the trajectories of modern liberalism and conservatism.[15] Local land use controls and their underlying racial logic virtually ensured that the emerging suburbs would be more isolated, more homogeneous, more defensive of their advantages, and more leery of the central cities they had left behind. In the bargain, all of this helped to reshape modern American conservatism as a peculiar amalgam of complacency on the part of those now ensconced in suburbs and anxiety on the part of those (in the City or its inner suburbs) who were not there yet.[16]

The urban crisis was particularly severe in St. Louis. Large midwestern cities (Chicago, St. Louis, Detroit, Milwaukee) sat at the leading edge of urban decline, bearing the brunt of both demobilization after World War II and the deindustrialization of later years. In these respects St. Louis, whose local economy was rooted in the commerce of the Mississippi, lagged behind even its regional peers—whose economic foundations (rail in Chicago, automobiles in Detroit) at least belonged to the twentieth century.[17] Surveys and city plans, on both the Missouri and the Illinois sides of the river, suggested serious economic and demographic problems as early as 1920.[18] The looming urban crisis was masked somewhat by the universal deprivation of the 1930s and the hiccup of urban prosperity that accompanied World War II, but the postwar catalogue of urban conditions (substandard housing, physical decay) again identified St. Louis as a regional and national outlier.[19] By the 1970s, St. Louis was clearly the patron saint of the nation's urban crisis: "By almost any objective or subjective standard," the *New York Times* reported in the late 1970s, "St. Louis is still the premier example of urban abandonment in America." Even more recent and hopeful assessments of "comeback cities" routinely dismiss St. Louis as a persistent underachiever.[20]

Central city decline was inextricably linked to the political fragmentation of metropolitan areas—a problem set in stark relief in St. Louis (see Chapter 1). Missouri was one of the first states to offer home rule to its major cities, and the modern boundaries of St. Louis were sealed in 1876. This yielded an unusually longstanding and direct confrontation between the City and its suburbs—particularly those running west from the City. The latter "erected a wall of separation which towers above the city limits," St. Louis school officials noted in the late 1970s, a wall that "constitutes a barrier as effective as did those of ancient Jericho or that of the Potsdamer Platz in Berlin."[21] In St. Louis, home rule simultaneously emancipated the City and enslaved it. While the state legislature ceded more authority and autonomy to local government, it betrayed little interest in the relationship between the shape of local government and the task with which it was charged. The city of St. Louis itself is but one of *hundreds* of local political units—including suburban municipalities in the Missouri counties to the west, the old industrial and working-class suburbs (East St. Louis, Allorton) on the Illinois side of the Mississippi, the counties comprising the metro area (4 in 1940; 12 in 2000), and a welter of overlapping (school, sewer, recreation) taxing districts.[22]

Political fragmentation enabled local and parochial interests to tear the city apart and reassemble it as a crazy quilt of fiercely segregated industrial, commercial, residential, and racial enclaves.[23] Indeed, most fragments of the metropolis exist expressly to avoid the problems of urban governance or to offer well-to-do citizens a haven from them. Local government is engaged less in managing coherent economic and demographic regions than in "the art," as Myron Orfield notes, "of skimming the cream from metropolitan growth while accepting as few metropolitan responsibilities as possible." As a rule, suburbs do relatively well as havens of home rule: they are able to use their taxing and zoning powers to exclude poor residents or unwanted commercial development and to insulate their tax base from the demands made by the older urban core. Central cities (and older inner suburbs), by contrast, fare poorly: in the wake of suburban flight, their local fiscal resources cannot support the services needed to maintain both the City and its suburban fringe.[24]

The plot of this story, in St. Louis and elsewhere, is irretrievably racial in its logic and in its consequences. Throughout the twentieth century, private discrimination and public policy combined—intentionally and explicitly—to constrain the residential options available to African Americans, to confine them to certain wards or neighborhoods, and to stem what was widely perceived (in St. Louis and elsewhere) as the threat of "invasion" posed by north-to-south and rural-to-urban migration. As I trace in Chapter 2, a variety of private and public policies—including explicitly racial zoning, state-enforced restrictive deed covenants, and redlining by banks and realtors—overlapped and reinforced one another over the course of the twentieth century. In a pattern not unique to St. Louis, local reaction to early African American migration yielded restrictions and expectations that were replicated and exaggerated in the decades to follow.[25]

Again, St. Louis offers a particularly graphic and sustained version of these events, in part because the City's racial demographics were starker and simpler than those of its peers. In 1940, 99.9 percent of St. Louisians identified themselves as either black (13.3 percent) or white (86.6 percent). As the population of the City collapsed (from just over 800,000 in 1940 to less than 350,000 in 2000) and the relative size of the black population grew (from 13.3 percent in 1940 to 51 percent in 2000), the number who identified as neither black nor white remained a statistical blip: 0.2 percent in 1960, 0.9 percent in 1980, 3.4 percent in 2000. The national pattern of white flight and inner city decay, as one observer noted, could be found in St. Louis "in somewhat purer and less ambiguous form than almost anywhere else." Not surprisingly given its politics and demographics, St. Louis retained (decade after decade) its dubious distinction as one of the nation's most segregated metropolitan areas.[26]

For these reasons, St. Louis was also the setting for a string of landmark civil rights litigation. *Shelley v. Kraemer*, the 1948 Supreme Court decision that outlawed state enforcement of restrictive deed covenants, began at 4600 Labadie Avenue on St. Louis' near northside—scarcely six blocks northeast of 4635 North Market (which, as I trace in Chapter 2, was embroiled in a similar legal battle in the early 1940s). *Jones v. Mayer*, the 1968 case that finally prohibited private discrimination in real estate transactions, revolved around the practices of developers in Paddock Woods, an unincorporated subdivision in north St. Louis County. And (as I touch on in Chapter 3) another north County case, *Black Jack v. United States* (1972), was one of the key elements (alongside New Jersey's *Mount Laurel* decisions) in underscoring the discriminatory intent and implications of local zoning.

As the population of greater St. Louis sprawled west into its suburban Missouri counties, the central city—following a trajectory common to most American cities—became progressively older, blacker, and poorer. In 1956, a visiting French businessman noted that the view from Monsanto's downtown headquarters "looks like a European city bombed in the war."[27] Into the 1960s and 1970s, it became increasingly common to refer to the "bombed out" appearance of devastated inner cities. This allusion held for cartographic snapshots of urban poverty, racial segregation, fiscal capacity, crime, and private investment—all of which identified a growing statistical crater, its epicenter in the City's oldest residential wards, its edges, by century's end, circumscribing not only the bulk of the City but many of its inner-ring suburbs as well.

This process was scarcely invisible, yet, as I trace in Chapters 4 and 5, postwar efforts to save the City through urban renewal and economic development policies did little to address the problem and much to exacerbate it. Federal urban spending, funneled through local governments and only nominally public redevelopment corporations, rarely went where it was needed most. Urban renewal almost invariably looked beyond (or through) the people who actually lived in the City, resting its hopes first on luring the affluent back downtown and later on simply clearing "blighted areas" for new commercial or industrial development.[28] And such efforts were invariably dwarfed by the larger logic of federal policy, which encouraged flight and sprawl with massive subsidies for new home construction, urban expressway construction, and favorable tax treatment of commercial development on the urban fringe.[29]

This was exactly the logic and legacy of urban renewal, in its various guises and incarnations, in greater St. Louis. Under the strain of wartime growth, city leaders identified the problem as one of substandard urban housing, crowding, and an aging transportation infrastructure. The solution, as the *Post-Dispatch* summarized it in 1941, was "more traffic speed and more parking spaces."[30] But the urban highways meant to lure the affluent back downtown simply made it easier for them to leave—not at the end of the day but permanently. The focus of urban renewal shifted, very soon after the war, from housing to commercial development—that is, to "slum clearance" to pave the way for expressways, industrial or commercial sites, sports stadiums, and convention centers. Again, St. Louis set a stark example—both for its desperate (and futile) efforts to rekindle the urban economy and for its uneven (and often insincere) efforts to relocate those displaced. City officials were perpetually in hot water with federal housing programs for their haphazard relocation efforts. The City's Pruitt-Igoe towers became a case study of the social, economic, and aesthetic failure of "big box" public housing (the complex, which by the late 1960s even the mayor's office found "reminiscent of the worst nineteenth century caricature of an insane asylum," was razed in 1972).[31] And, as the surrounding suburbs assiduously avoided any responsibility for mixed income or public housing, urban renewal further transformed the border between St. Louis and St. Louis County "into a 'Berlin Wall' between city and county, the poor and the affluent, the black and the white."[32]

From the earliest efforts at residential restriction in the World War I era through the long and sorry history of urban renewal, the fate of St. Louis hinged on private property and the policies that shaped its ownership and use.[33] At the outset, these were not so much policies as they were day-to-day practices and prejudices of realtors and white homeowners. But they were formalized easily enough, and they became the ethical and effective foundation of local incorporation, zoning, taxation, and redevelopment policies in St. Louis and its suburbs. Although couched in different terms and goals, what these policies shared—across the metropolitan area and across the full sweep of the twentieth century—was the conviction that African American occupancy was a blight to be contained, controlled, or eradicated.

The intent and the effect of local public policy, in St. Louis and its suburbs, were to tilt the playing field dramatically in favor of those who were already winning.[34] The economic and locational disadvantages suffered by African Americans lengthened (in time and space) the dismal reach of Jim Crow. They undermined the legal victories of the civil rights movement, as the right to employment or education meant little in settings where the jobs had fled and the schools were crumbling. And they eroded the legitimacy of even modest efforts at redistribution or redress, as inner-city poverty was willfully misdiagnosed as a sort of community pathology, as something African Americans had done to themselves.[35]

The following chapters look in detail at the history of greater St. Louis after 1940, tracing in turn patterns of political fragmentation and political crisis (Chapter 1), real estate restrictions (Chapter 2), zoning (Chapter 3), and urban renewal (Chapters 4 and 5). Taken together, these chapters seek to explain the causes and consequences of both "suburbanization" and its conjoined twin, the urban crisis. The key, as I explore in the following pages, lies in the political history of the modern city—in the ways in which local, state, and federal policies effectively distributed people, resources, and wealth across the postwar metropolis. As a background for this story, I begin with a cursory sketch of its economic and demographic dimensions. The story itself, as I trace in the chapters that follow, rests on the tangle of public policy that shaped the fate of 4635 North Market Street, the city of St. Louis, and the wider metropolitan area.

Decline and Disinvestment: An Economic Sketch, 1940–2000

St. Louis emerged in the late nineteenth century as a manufacturing, transportation, and agricultural processing hub. Its principal economic asset was the Mississippi, and its reputation as the "gateway to the west" was rooted in the steamboat era. As a rail hub, St. Louis was eclipsed by Chicago, and its commercial focus, accordingly, shifted to the South and Southwest. By the early twentieth century, the City had claimed a fairly diverse commercial and manufacturing base. The north riverfront (North Broadway) was dominated by large lumberyards and mills, grain elevators, foundries, and a number of freight terminals. Along South Broadway there were smelters, chemical plants (including Monsanto), foundries, breweries (Anheuser-Busch) and another cluster of rail terminals. The major rail lines ran west through the City along the Mill Creek and River Des Peres valleys, both of which featured warehousing, smelting, and clay and stone industries. Downtown (east of Grand between Chouteau and Cole) was home to finance, trade, and light industry (clothing, hats, shoes). The Illinois side of the river was also a thriving, rail-based industrial district—mostly steel and metals but also boasting the massive National City packing complex. By the late 1920s, in turn, many of the City's heavy manufacturers (excepting the clay industries reliant on Missouri deposits) had migrated to the Illinois side.[36] In short, north St. Louis (including 4635 North Market) sat near the center of a thriving and diverse employment base.

Its economy still rooted in agricultural processing and transportation, the region experienced neither as dramatic a boom in the World War I era nor as dramatic a collapse after 1929 as many of its industrialized peers. But, well before the crash, municipal officials and business leaders were already worrying about the stagnation of downtown property values and the westward trend of higher assessments. "The decentralization of certain types of business is economically desirable," fretted the local Chamber of Commerce in 1931, "but for the proper welfare of the community, decentralization should take place under free competitive conditions—not under a situation where congestion, due to inadequate transportation, has placed a special handicap on the downtown central district." New economic development in the 1920s and 1930s (led by electrical supply and manufacturing firms such as Wagner and Emerson) were already pushing employment and investments to the City's western edge and across the county line into inner suburbs like Wellston and Clayton.[37]

As in the nation, the coming of World War II ended the Depression in St. Louis— although, as in many war-era industrial centers, a population boom that swamped the housing market and local services outpaced the economic boom. Just as importantly, St. Louis' economic mobilization rested heavily on sectors that would prove of little long-term sustenance to the local economy. The City got a small share of new investment in aircraft assembly and was the nation's leading supplier of ordnance for the armed forces. Greater St. Louis emerged from the war in pretty good shape, boasting a substantial (if not terribly diverse) manufacturing base and the nation's second largest rail and trucking hubs. But the region (and especially the city of St. Louis itself) was also very near the peak of its industrial growth and potential.[38]

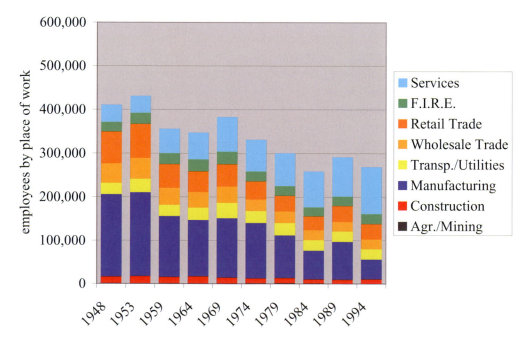

Figure I.2. Employment by sector, St. Louis, 1948–1994. *County Business Patterns*, various years.

Economic decline began in St. Louis very shortly after the war. The health of the local economy, and the relative position of St. Louis and its suburbs within that economy, reflect both conditions peculiar to greater St. Louis and national trends—including economic suburbanization, deindustrialization, and increased capital intensity. In the City itself (Figure I.2), the employment base collapsed alongside its more general depopulation. Indeed, over the postwar era, the City's share of regional employment dropped dramatically, from about half (1950) to just over 10 percent (2000) (see Table I.1). Employment in St. Louis County, by contrast, grew quickly after the war and then leveled off; employment on the Illinois side (as a share of regional employment) remained relatively stable while the share of the outlying Missouri counties (all added to the MSA after 1950) grew modestly.[39] Against national patterns of growth and decline, the region's outer Missouri counties did very well and St. Louis County held its own, but the City lagged well behind—suffering dramatically higher rates of job loss in declining sectors (manufacturing, mining) and near stagnation in growing sectors (services, retail). All of this was of enormous importance, not only to the City's larger fate, but also to those—crowded into the northside neighborhoods surrounding 4635 North Market—who lacked the freedom to move as the local employment base evaporated.[40]

Leading this decline was manufacturing, which counted almost 200,000 jobs in the City in the decade after the war, but barely half that (99,100) by 1979, and half that again (46,427) by 1994. Even as western and rural Missouri promoted itself as a haven

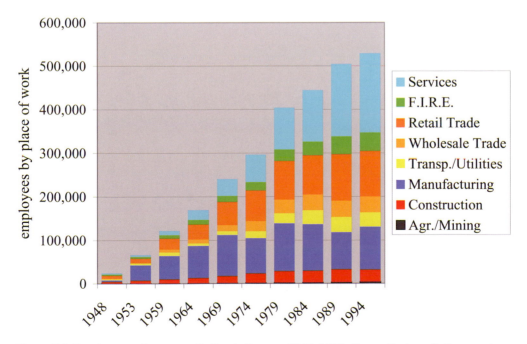

Figure I.3. Employment by sector, St. Louis County, 1948–1994. *County Business Patterns,* various years.

TABLE I.1. Metro Area (MSA) Employment by County, 1550–2000

	1950	1960	1970	1980	1990	2000
Madison	9.5	10.0	10.0	9.8	9.6	9.9
St. Clair	9.9	10.6	10.3	9.2	9.0	8.8
St. Charles	1.6	2.3	3.7	6.4	9.5	12.1
St. Louis	21.4	32.6	41.3	45.1	43.1	40.3
St. Louis (city)	50.1	36.4	24.9	16.6	13.7	11.4
Jefferson	1.9	2.7	4.0	5.9	7.0	8.0
Franklin	1.9	2.1	2.2	2.8	3.2	3.7
Clinton	1.1	1.0	1.0	1.3	1.3	1.4
Monroe	0.7	0.7	0.7	0.8	0.9	1.2
Jersey	0.7	0.7	0.7	0.8	0.8	0.8
Lincoln	0.7	0.6	0.7	0.8	1.1	1.5
Warren	0.4	0.4	0.4	0.6	0.8	1.0
			census-defined MSA			

Source: David Laslo, "The Past, Present, and Future, of the St. Louis Labor Force," in Baybeck and Jones, *St. Louis Metromorphosis: Past Trends and Future Directions* (2004), Table 2, p. 72.

from organized labor, development officials in St. Louis complained that the City was being "leapfrogged" by manufacturing firms headed farther south. Even wholesale and retail employment in the City (in a national economy increasingly dominated by these sectors) had withered by 1994 to half their 1948 levels. St. Louis County, by contrast (Figure I.4), experienced fairly steady growth across sectors.[41] The 1957 Metro-

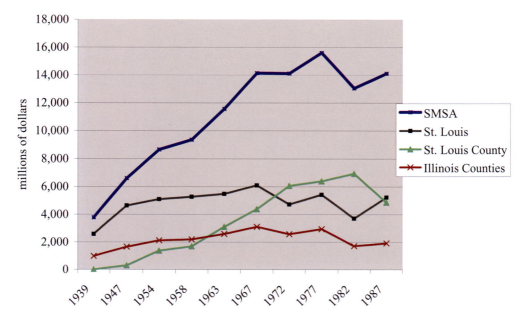

Figure I.4. Value-added in manufacturing, St. Louis MSA and selected counties, 1939–1987 (1987 dollars). *County Business Patterns*, selected years.

politan Survey noted "some movement of manufacturing, warehousing, and 'convenience shopping' away from the City's center" and had little basis for its hopeful conclusion that "the City for the foreseeable future will remain the economic heart of the metropolitan community."[42]

Much of the County's success reflected natural economic growth. As the entire metro area grew, new investment flowed disproportionately to suburbs where new industrial sites (especially along major thoroughfares and surrounding the airport, Lambert Field) were readily available.[43] But much of this success also came at the expense of the City and its industrial outposts in Illinois. Employment in river- and rail-based industry on both sides of the Mississippi lost ground steadily through the 1950s and early 1960s (see Figure I.4), while manufacturing employment in St. Louis County grew nearly tenfold over the same period—matching the City's share by the mid-1970s. Between 1963 and 1976, the City lost around 3,000 total jobs but almost 35,000 manufacturing jobs—during which time the rest of the MSA gained nearly 165,000. For their part, regional economic development officials pointed to defense contracts at McDonnell Douglas as the only sustained source of growth in manufacturing.[44] "We may well be at a kind of 'tipping point' in our economic history," the chair of the Regional Industrial Development Council concluded glumly in 1973. "We may soon be going downhill too fast to turn around."[45]

After the early 1970s, deindustrialization set in and the employment totals for the MSA and its constituent counties declined in tandem—although the City continued to count losses to poaching by neighboring counties. Wentzville (at the intersection of Highways 61 and 70 in St. Charles County), for example, developed an expansive, nearly 300-acre industrial park in the late 1960s in order to attract both new investment to the area and migrants from the City. Its biggest prize, in the early 1980s, was the relocation of the City's General Motors plant—a loss bemoaned by St. Louis officials but celebrated by the Regional Commerce and Growth Association as "retention."[46] The City (and to a degree St. Louis County) suffered a steady stream of significant plant closings that savaged employment in core sectors—including automobiles, chemicals, aerospace, and electrical goods. Local job losses (see Map I.5) were concentrated along the City's old industrial corridors, in its inner suburbs (including Clayton and the now rapidly declining industrial enclave surrounding Wellston), in suburban outposts (Fenton, Wentzville) of the automobile industry, and in the volatile aerospace industry surrounding Lambert Field.

Consider—as a stark illustration of the City's postwar woes—the trajectory of its once-thriving boot and shoe industry. At the end of World War II, the Missouri leather goods industry had an employment base of just under 45,000, of which over a third worked at 100-odd firms in the city of St. Louis (see Map 1.6). Over the early postwar era, shoe production began to migrate to smaller communities in Illinois and Missouri, offering, as *Business Week* noted, a combination of "tax-free land, free building sites, part or all of building costs, and, of course, cheaper labor with open-shop prevailing." By 1959, leather goods employment statewide had fallen to about 35,000, of which fewer than a quarter (8,331) worked in the City. Longstanding City firms (Brown Shoe, International Shoe, and McElroy-Sloan) moved production to outposts

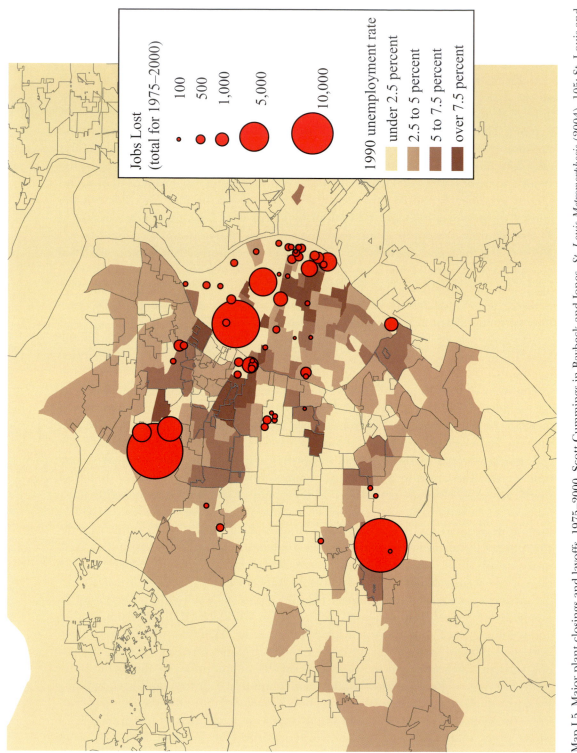

Map I.5. Major plant closings and layoffs, 1975–2000. Scott Cummings in Baybeck and Jones, *St. Louis Metromorphosis* (2004), 105; St. Louis and St. Louis County parcel data; City of St. Louis and Missouri EPA sites inventory; *St. Louis Post-Dispatch, St. Louis Business Journal.*

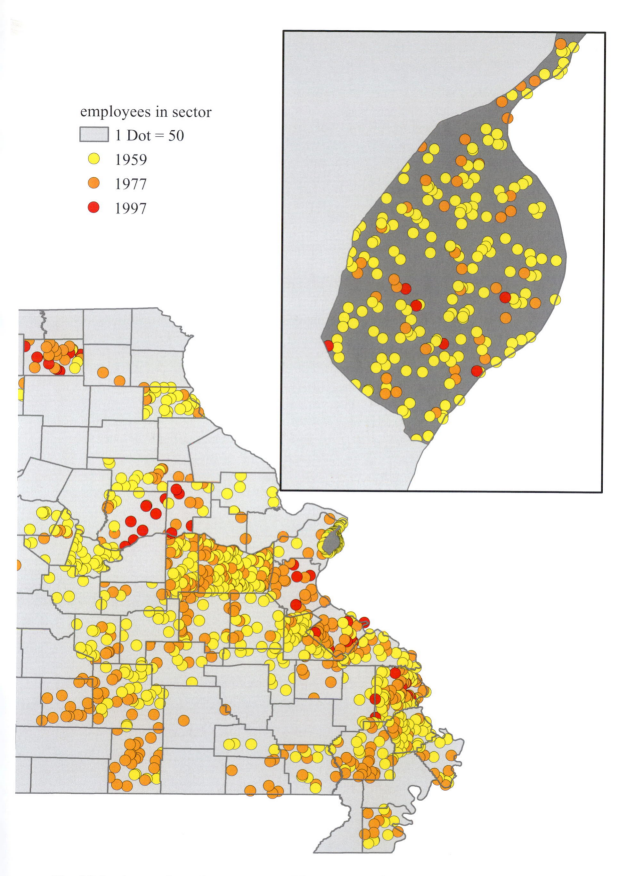

employees in sector

1 Dot = 50

1959

1977

1997

Map I.6. Leather goods employment, eastern Missouri, 1959–97. *County Business Patterns*, selected years.

like Charleston, Mount Vernon, and Vandalia in Illinois, and Franklin and Jefferson Counties in Missouri. The City's share of statewide leather goods employment fell steadily, from 40 percent in 1947 to 19 percent in 1967 to less than 5 percent in 1987. This migration was spurred by the industry, which (as the St. Louis development officials noted) seemed fixated on "one-horse towns in the Ozarks where the union movement is either weak or non-existent." And it was encouraged by local governments, who offered industrial revenue bonds and other incentives alongside a "friendly labor climate."[47] After the early 1970s, even these advantages counted little against low-wage foreign competition, and the entire domestic industry withered. Brown Shoe closed the last of its Missouri (and American) plants in 1995. By 1997, the industry claimed barely 4,000 workers statewide and fewer than 300 in St. Louis itself.[48]

Along with its industrial base, the City also lost managerial employment—a trend exaggerated by the willingness of local firms to move their headquarters out to St. Louis County and beyond even if production remained in the older industrial core. The metro area claimed the headquarters of a few Fortune 500 firms and a slightly larger share of the nation's leading manufacturers.[49] But most of these could be found in St. Louis County (especially Clayton) and points west. Beginning in the 1950s, suburban counties and municipalities used zoning (for both high-rise office towers and "campus-style" office parks) and their proximity to the westward drift of population to attract new investment and to lure companies out of the City.[50] The City could not compete, except (as I examine in Chapter 4) by offering increasingly lucrative incentives: "The city of St. Louis will be turning the corner," one observer noted in the early 1970s, "when one developer puts up a big building without a big tax write-off."[51] As of 2003, as one observer noted, the City had not broken ground for a major privately financed office building in almost fifteen years.[52]

Clayton's commercial rezoning (see Chapter 3) in 1959 attracted a number of City firms and transformed the St. Louis County seat into the region's de facto central business district. Between 1953 and 1964, Clayton broke ground on 46 new commercial buildings (during which time the City claimed only 3 new developments) and by 1966 boasted (at 2 million square feet) nearly one-third of the office space available in St. Louis itself. Brown Shoe and Standard Oil relocated to Clayton in the early- and mid-1950s. As of 1964, about a third of Clayton's business tenants were migrants from the City (a third were new arrivals to the area and another third came from elsewhere in the region). Even the federal Department of Commerce moved its local offices out to Clayton on the understanding that "by any yardstick you care to use, St. Louis County is the center of the St. Louis metropolitan region." Of the metro area's top 10 private firms in the late 1990s, only one (General American Life) maintained headquarters in the City (5 were in Clayton and 4 elsewhere in St. Louis County). By this time, the entire region was losing ground as a string of corporate mergers—McDonnell Douglas (merged with Boeing), Ralston Purina (Nestle), TWA (American Airlines), Mallinckrodt (Tyco), Jones Pharma (King Pharmaceuticals), Monsanto (Pharmacia/Upjohn)—spirited away the headquarters of local firms.[53]

Perhaps most dramatically, St. Louis lost virtually its entire retail base over the course of the postwar era—claiming over 75 percent of regional retail sales in the late

1940s but barely 11 percent by the late 1990s (see Figure I.5). Retail flight was exacerbated by a number of factors. Much more so than industrial employment or office locations, retail markets were responsive to the proximity and needs of the local population: as the more prosperous moved to the suburbs (and complained endlessly about downtown parking), stores tagged along. Initially, landmark downtown department stores like Famous-Barr simply expanded to settings like Clayton, which emerged as a major retail center in the early 1950s.[54]

In turn, local and federal tax laws created incentives to abandon downtown altogether for concentric rings of suburban malls. Beginning in the mid-1950s, federal depreciation rules encouraged new development at the expense of the renovation or rehabilitation of older commercial properties—an incentive that first hit downtown but encouraged investors to abandon first-generation shopping malls in the inner-ring suburbs too as soon as something bigger and better could be built farther out. Because Missouri tax law allowed "point of origin" cities to keep a share of locally generated sales taxes, suburbs competed fiercely (especially with the advent of tax increment financing in the 1980s) with each other for local and regional consumers. "One might say that TIF-hungry developers and co-operating municipalities are putting the cart before the horse," the *Post-Dispatch* noted in 2001, "except the horse already left for

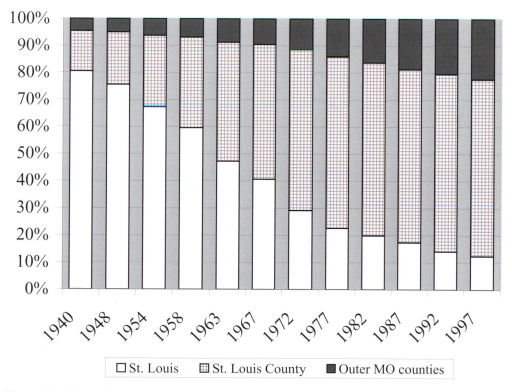

Figure I.5. Metropolitan area (Missouri counties) retail shares, 1940–1997. *County Business Patterns*, various years; ICPSR Historical Census Browser.

St. Charles County and beyond, and St. Louis County taxpayers are the ones being asked to pull a cart full of big boxes."[55]

"People Who Can, Move Away": A Demographic Sketch, 1940–2000

Certainly the most dramatic element of St. Louis postwar history is the depopulation of the City itself. The state's decision to split St. Louis from the rest of St. Louis County in 1876 effectively froze the size of the City at 61 square miles. While many cities (particularly in the west and southwest) grew by annexation and consolidation through the late nineteenth and early twentieth centuries, St. Louis entered the modern era with no prospect of expanding its borders and only pockets of undeveloped land within them. New residential development beyond the City's borders cropped up first along railroad lines. Initially an option for only the more affluent City residents, these "railroad suburbs" were made more and more accessible by private trolley and street-car lines and, after 1920, the automobile.[56] Yet, into the 1940s, few saw the suburbs—"bedroom communities" nestling against the outskirts of a vibrant urban center—as anything but a complement to continued urban growth.

All this changed dramatically in the middle years of the twentieth century. For reasons I explore in the chapters that follow, a combination of demographic change, racial restrictions, and federal subsidies made the suburbs (at least for the City's white residents) both preferable and affordable. The Federal Housing Administration, which subsidized much of the subsequent flight, concluded in 1939 that suburbanization "is not a policy, it is a reality—and it is as impossible for us to change this trend as it is to change the desire of birds to migrate to a more suitable location." Two years later, federal property assessors noted the City's slow growth and attributed it to both a "simple shift of population from the city . . . into the peripheral suburban communities . . . and, more serious, . . . the complete removal of the population itself." In 1944 the mayor's office begged a state constitutional convention to reconsider the City's 1876 boundaries: "the canker worm is in the flower and only sound and heroic husbandry can prevent progressive and disastrous decay." A 1947 pamphlet extolling the virtues of the suburbs portrayed St. Louis County as a demographic rocket and the City as a horse and buggy, rated the area's neighborhoods according to average rents, population density, and the "presence of negroes," and offered the summary assessment: "People Who Can, Move Away." For their part, some City officials whistled bravely: "St. Louis, with a colorful, historic past and a busy, variegated present, is still a city with a future," the 1947 City Plan enthused, adding that "by 1970 barely a generation hence—the city proper can have 900,000 in population."[57]

They were wrong. While mobilization for World War II temporarily reversed the City's decline, the population losses first noted by planners in the 1920s and 1930s soon returned. The City's population peaked at just over 850,000 in 1950, at which point it claimed just under half (47.9 percent) of the population of the metropolitan area. With each new census, the City's population dropped farther (750,000 in 1960, 622,000 in 1970, 453,000 in 1980, 397,000 in 1990, 348,000 in 2000) as did its share of the metropolitan area. Net migration to the region flattened after the war (and, in the

1960s, was actually negative for whites), and the rate of natural population increase (7.3 per 100) in the aging City was barely half the gap between births and deaths in the County (13.8 per 100). Such trends were suffered by many of the nation's older urban areas, but again St. Louis led the pack. The City lost an average of just over 10,000 persons a year between 1950 and 2000, during which time it plummeted from ninth to eighteenth in the national ranking of metro areas. The housing shortage of the 1940s and 1950s gave way to chronic vacancy and abandonment: by 1978, St. Louis had the highest vacancy rate (just under 10 percent) of all central cities. Of the 15 largest metro regions in 1980s, only Boston and Pittsburgh had more marginal central cities. When the City challenged the results of the 1980 canvass, census officials only rubbed it in: "If they don't wake up and acknowledge the exodus, they're going to lose it all. They ought to get out of their offices and drive through north St. Louis. A lot of it looks like a ghost town. When we come back to count in 1990, it may not even be a city. It may be a village." By 2000, when 80 percent of all Americans lived in urbanized areas and almost half of those (38 percent) in central cities, St. Louis (see Figure I.6) claimed only 13 percent of the region's population base.[58]

As important as the gross dimensions, of course, was the inexorable racial logic that earned postwar suburbanization the moniker of "white flight." Suburbanization was shaped by racial restrictions (detailed in Chapter 2) that both denied African Americans the same residential mobility and—as spatial segregation deepened—exaggerated the motives of those who wanted out. Again, this was a pattern established early in the century, cemented by the demographic and political changes of the 1940s, and exaggerated in St. Louis by the City's fixed boundaries, aged housing and industrial stock, and substantial rural hinterland.[59] Between 1940 and 1950 (see Map I.7), whites settled throughout the suburban St. Louis counties, in a few tracts surrounding

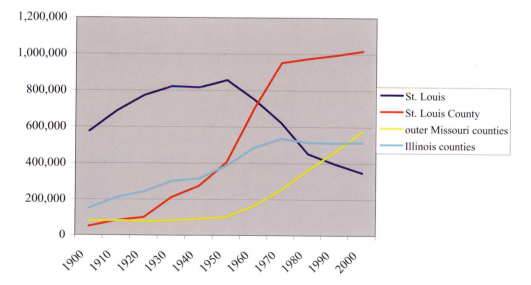

Figure I.6. Population change, Greater St. Louis, 1900–2000. ICPSR Historical Census Browser.

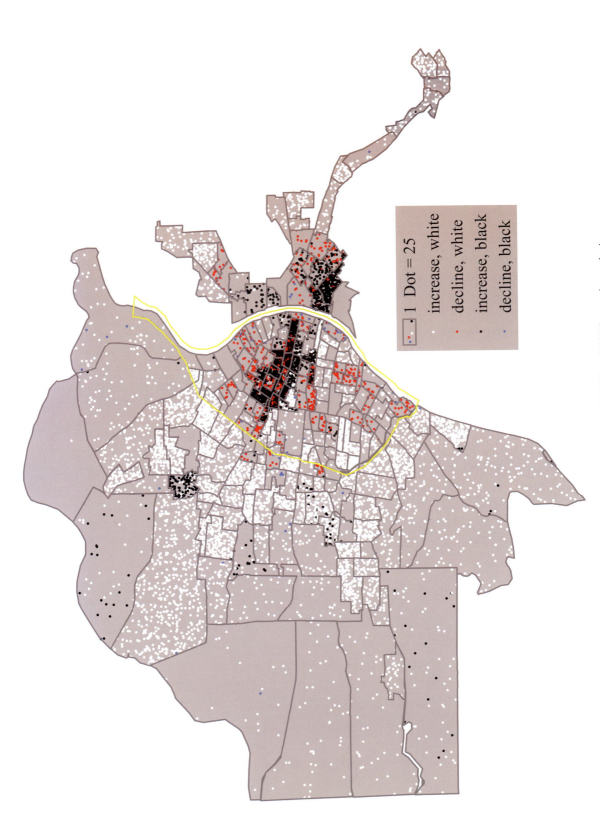

Map I.7. White flight, 1940–1950. Census Bureau (Bogue Files), synthesis of 1940 and 1950 tract boundaries.

1 Dot = 25	
increase, white	
decline, white	
increase, black	
decline, black	

Forest Park, and in the City's southern reaches. Many of these were new arrivals to the St. Louis area, but many (evidenced by the collapsing white population in many central city tracts) were moving from the City to its suburbs.[60] Blacks, by contrast, settled almost exclusively in a few northside tracts, the old industrial suburbs on the Illinois side, and scattered outposts like Kinloch in north St. Louis County.

These patterns continued in the 1950s (see Map I.8). White settlement retained its overwhelmingly suburban pattern, and flight from the City was now evident in all but a few southern tracts. African American settlement now reached the City limits along the northern border of Forest Park, concentrated in tracts being abandoned by whites. This decade also saw swaths of black depopulation, particularly in the downtown and Mill Creek tracts being "cleared" for urban renewal. Between 1950 and 1970, close to 60 percent of the (1960) white population fled the City. The same period saw a slight in-migration (about 12 percent of the 1960 population) of African Americans, although almost all of this occurred before 1960.[61] By 1970 (see Map I.9), the locus of white settlement had moved to the western reaches of St. Louis County, racial succession and white flight now reached the inner-ring suburbs (University City, Normandy, Wellston) sitting east of the City's northside, and the older northside neighborhoods were largely abandoned. The logic and pattern of racial transition reflected local demographics (race, income), local expectations, and a tangle of public policy. While blacks and whites had similar aspirations (safer neighborhoods, better schools), they faced starkly different opportunities and horizons. Neighborhood surveys in the late 1960s suggested that most blacks moved merely to stay ahead of the urban renewal bulldozer, choosing public housing, another "blighted" neighborhood, or the transitional neighborhoods spilling northwest into the County. Whites, by contrast, moved largely to escape the path of racial transition, settling in the City's southside or in the County's suburban reaches.[62]

After 1970 (see Maps I.10, I.11, and I.12), the depopulation of the City (and especially the near northside) accelerated, falling by almost 170,000 (from 622,236 to 452,801) by the 1980 census, and by more than 100,000 more (to 348,189) by 2000. By this time, whites were fleeing the inner suburbs as well, and white population growth was concentrated in the western reaches of St. Louis County and beyond. In a sense, the suburban color line had drifted west from the City limits to encompass much of near northeastern St. Louis County (Wellston, Bridgeton, Normandy, Jennings, Ferguson, Bellefontaine Neighbors) south and east of Lindbergh Boulevard (Highway 67). "Ghetto spillover," a local observer noted bluntly, "now stretches almost all the way across the county in a northwesterly direction"[63]

Not surprisingly, given these patterns of racial restriction and white flight, St. Louis remained one of the nation's most segregated metropolitan areas. The African American population in St Louis, a border and river city "northern in industrial development but largely southern in its inter-racial attitude,"[64] was already well established in 1900 (second only to Baltimore at 35,000) and grew modestly (to just under 80,000) during the "great migration" surrounding World War I (by contrast, Detroit's black population was about 6,000 in 1910 and 35,000 in 1920). During these years, the black population settled outward from the central city—north and south along the river,

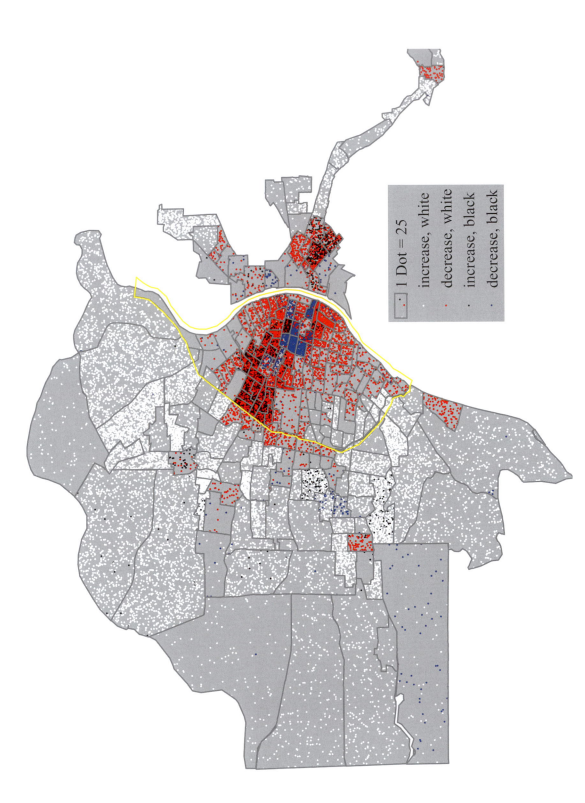

Map I.8. White flight, 1950–1960. Census Bureau (Bogue Files), synthesis of 1950 and 1960 tract boundaries.

1 Dot = 25
increase, white
decrease, white
increase, black
decrease, black

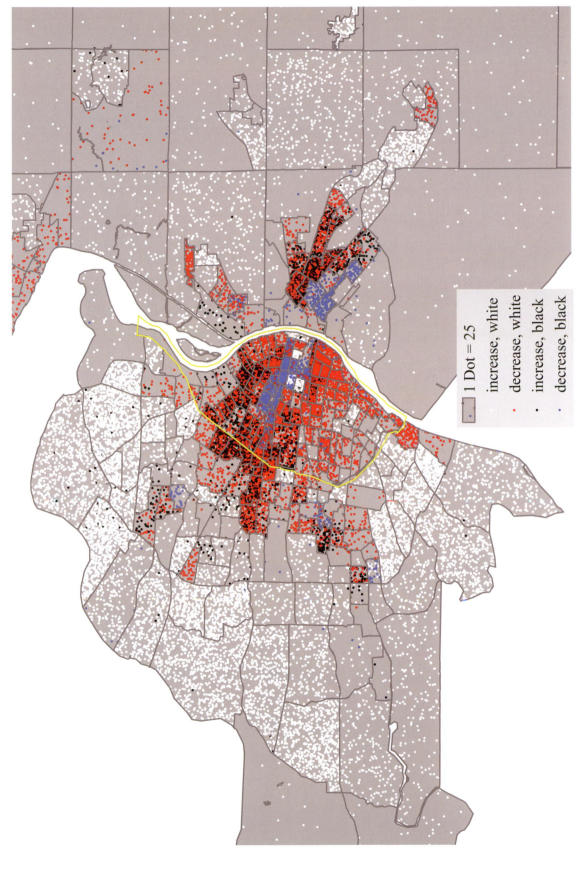

	1 Dot = 25
	increase, white
	decrease, white
	increase, black
	decrease, black

Map I.9. White flight, 1960–1970. Census Bureau (Bogue Files), synthesis of 1960 and 1970 tract boundaries.

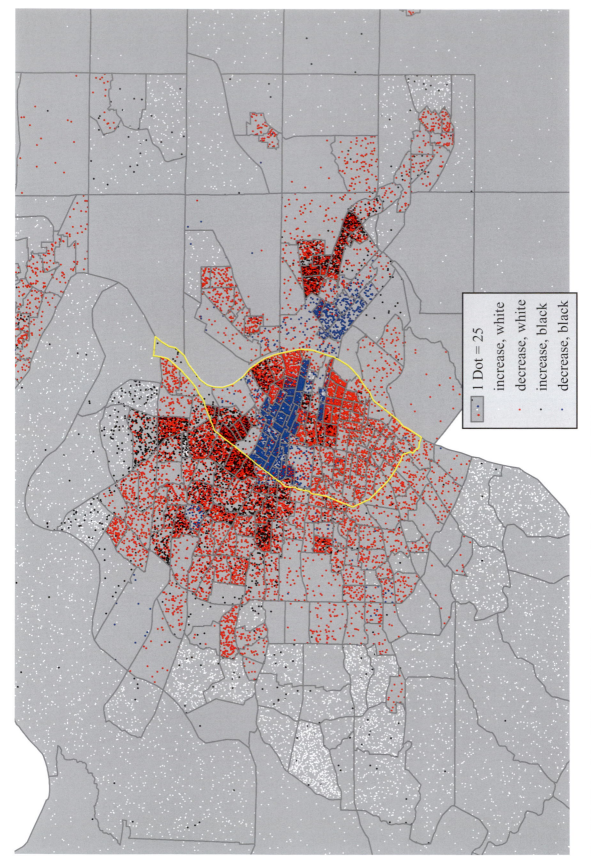

1 Dot = 25	
increase, white	
decrease, white	
increase, black	
decrease, black	

Map I.10. White flight, 1970–1980. NHGIS boundary files; Geolytics Census CD (1980).

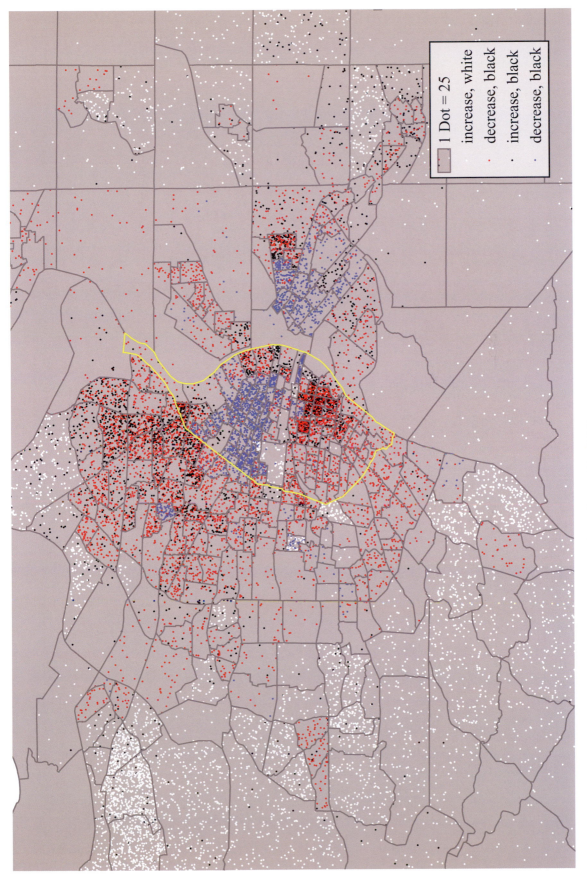

Map I.11. White flight, 1980–1990. NHGIS boundary files; Geolytics Census CD (1980).

Legend:

1 Dot = 25

increase, white
decrease, black
increase, black
decrease, black

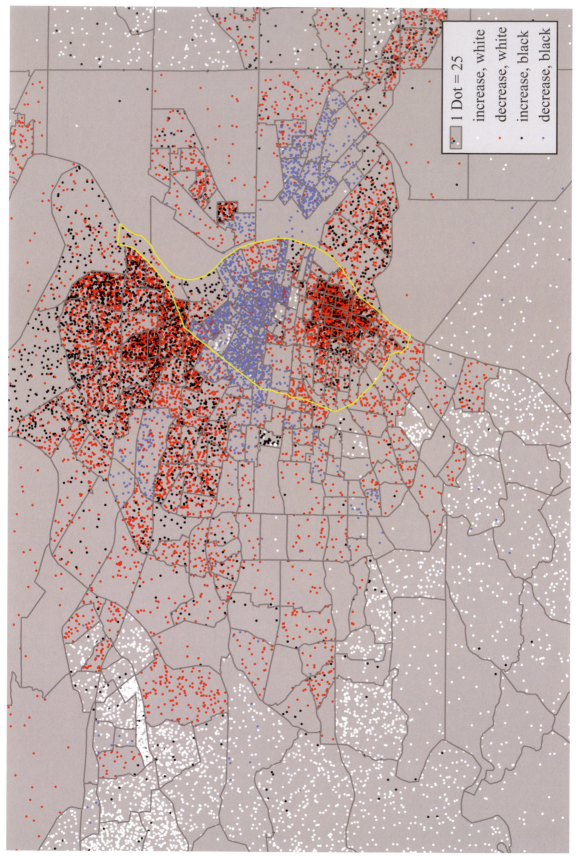

Map I.12. White flight, 1990–2000. 1990 and 2000 Census.

	1 Dot = 25
	increase, white
	decrease, white
	increase, black
	decrease, black

west along the northern edge of Mill Creek Valley toward Forest Park, and scattered (mostly live-in domestics) through the City's southern and western neighborhoods.[65] The only significant pockets of blacks outside the City's near northside were across the river in East St. Louis and in the old "free black" enclave of Kinloch in St. Louis County.

As the African American population increased, so too did its segregation into a few inner City wards—a peculiarly counterhistorical trend alongside the emergence of the modern civil rights movement in American politics and law. Demographers measure such segregation in a variety of ways. Most common is the measure of *evenness* (or the "dissimilarity index"), which gauges the distribution of racial groups across a metropolitan area or the difference between patterns of settlement citywide and those in local settings (usually census tracts). The result is a citywide score, reflecting the percentage of the population that would have to move in order to achieve racial balance. In St. Louis, the segregation index jumped from about 50 percent to over 80 percent between 1910 and 1930 and then settled in: the 1980 index (83.8 percent) was essentially the same as it had been in 1940 (84.6 percent). Through most of this era, segregation indexes hovering in the mid- to high- 80s placed St. Louis among the nation's most segregated urban areas (St. Louis ranked eighteenth of 237 MSAs in 1960, fourteenth of 237 in 1970, and tenth of 318 in 1980).[66] Taking into account other measures—including *exposure* (the likelihood of contact between majority and minority groups), *concentration* (the actual space inhabited by minority groups), *centralization* (concentration in the central city), and *clustering* (the proximity of minority tracts to each other)—St. Louis in 1980 ranked as one of a handful of "hypersegregated" metro areas.[67]

A crude sense of these patterns is suggested by tract-level data. In 1940 (see Map I.13), the African American population was concentrated around the Ville and in pockets on both sides of the river. The vast majority of metropolitan tracts were essentially all white: 135 of 239 tracts had black populations of less than 1 percent; 199 of 239 tracts had black populations of less than 10 percent. In only 33 tracts did blacks make up less than 90 percent and more than 10 percent of the population. By 1970 (see Map I.14), about 30 predominantly (over 90 percent) African American tracts swallowed most of the near northside, running west to the City border. Again, most of the metro tracts were overwhelmingly white: more than half (231 of 416) of all tracts had a black population of less than 1 percent, and almost three-quarters (306 of 416) had a black population of less than 10 percent. Nearly 70 percent of whites lived in "all white" (over 99 percent) tracts; nearly 90 percent lived in predominantly white (over 90 percent) tracts.

By 2000 (see Map I.15), predominantly African American tracts now ran north to the City border, west into the inner-ring suburbs, and across much of the old working-class and industrial suburbs on the Illinois side. This diffusion eroded the metrowide segregation index (now about 74 percent), and fully one-fifth (20.5 percent) of the white population and over half (58.5 percent) of the black population lived in "mixed" tracts in which neither race comprised more than 90 percent or less than 10 percent of the population. Still, more than half of the MSA's tracts (271 of 525),

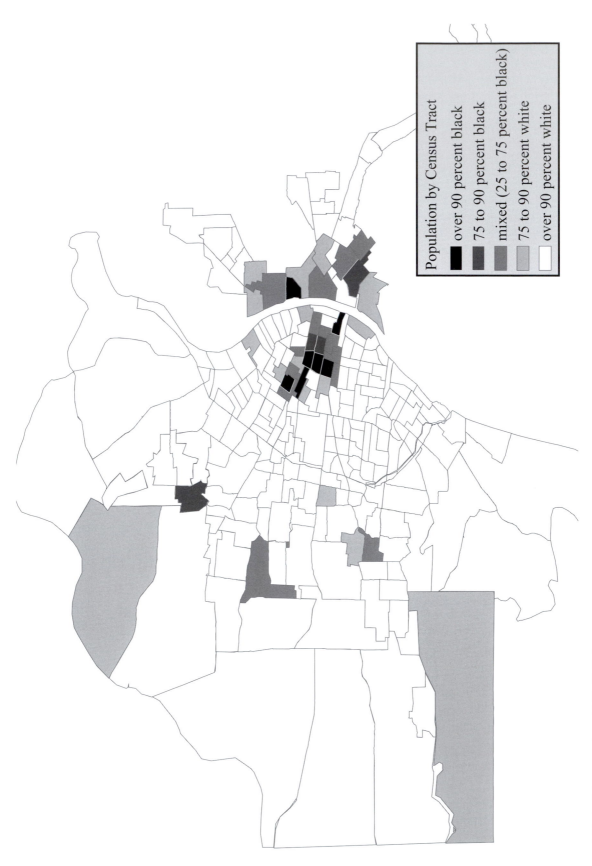

Population by Census Tract

over 90 percent black

75 to 90 percent black

mixed (25 to 75 percent black)

75 to 90 percent white

over 90 percent white

Map I.13. Racial segregation, 1940. 1940 Census.

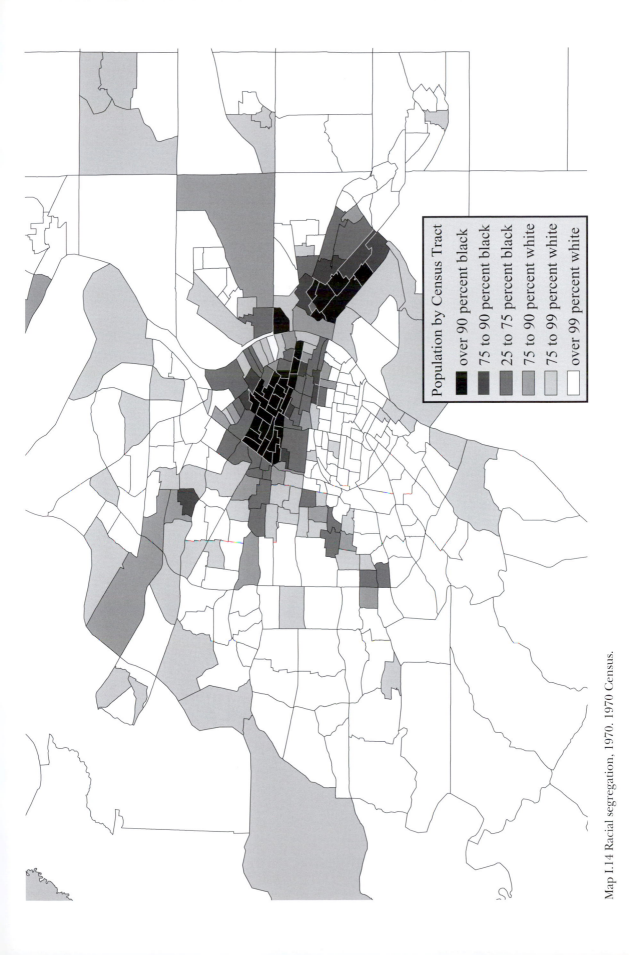

Population by Census Tract

- over 90 percent black
- 75 to 90 percent black
- 25 to 75 percent black
- 75 to 90 percent white
- 75 to 99 percent white
- over 99 percent white

Map I.14 Racial segregation, 1970. 1970 Census.

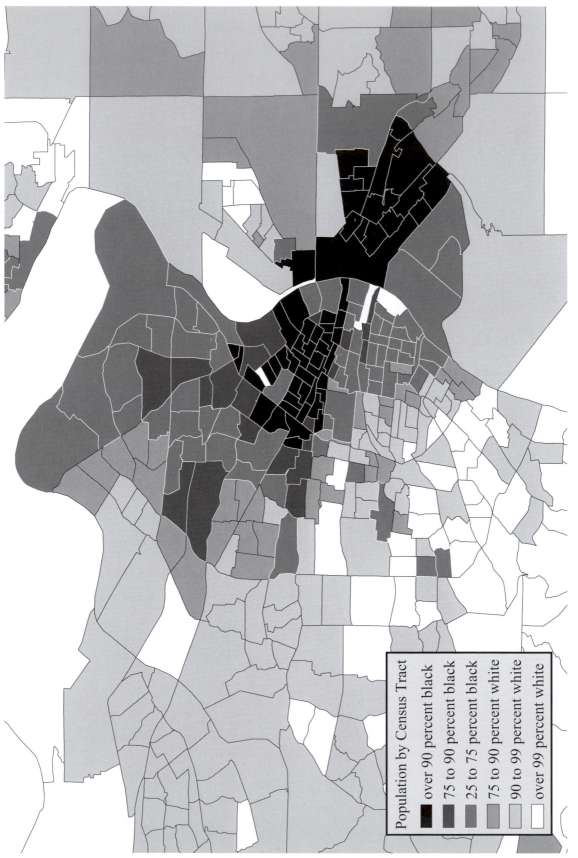

Map I.15: Racial segregation, 2000. 2000 Census.

Population by Census Tract
over 90 percent black
75 to 90 percent black
25 to 75 percent black
75 to 90 percent white
90 to 99 percent white
over 99 percent white

encompassing fully 70 percent of the white population, were at least 95 percent white.[68]

Suburban flight was about people, but it was also about money. Moving out was an economic opportunity, enjoyed disproportionately by those able to clear two hurdles: the racial restrictions embedded in private and public realty and the cost of homeownership. Those who left the City were overwhelmingly young white adults and their families; those left behind were African Americans of all ages and the elderly. The result, peculiar to American urban settings, was a concentration of poverty at the urban core. In most of the world's cities (think Rio or Paris), the affluent live in the city center while the poor settle on the urban fringe. In the United States—in part as a consequence of racial politics, in part as a consequence of exclusive zoning in the suburbs—the reverse has been true.[69]

Mapping the distribution of incomes across greater St. Louis summarizes these patterns. In 1950 (Map 1.16) the poor (those living in census tracts with a median income of less than half the citywide median) were clustered in five northside tracts, an area surrounded by a broader swath of near-poor (50 to 75 percent of the median income) tracts encompassing the rest of the City's northside and the industrial suburbs across the river. Pockets of poverty in St. Louis County included Kinloch in the northwest, the inner suburb of Shrewsbury to the southeast, and a small slice of largely rental residences on unincorporated County land between University City and Clayton (near Washington University). By 1990 (Map I.17), poverty had swallowed the entire northside (running into the adjacent inner-ring suburbs) and most of the urbanized tracts on the Illinois side. Indeed, only 8 of the City's 114 tracts claimed incomes higher than the metrowide median. Over the same span, the "wealthy" tracts (those with median incomes more than double the metro median) drifted farther out into the suburbs. Wealth was increasingly concentrated in a string of suburban enclaves (Frontenac, Ladue, Huntleigh Woods, Des Peres, Creve Coeur, Olivette, Clayton, Sunset Hills, Glendale) running west from Clayton through central St. Louis County.[70]

Suburbanization meant the flight of not only people, but their personal incomes, expenditures, and tax payments as well. Missouri municipalities rely on a mixture of property taxes (on both real estate and personal assets like cars) and sales taxes, and the largest cities (St. Louis and Kansas City) levy a local income tax. For the City (and increasingly its inner suburbs), the spatial distribution of poverty and wealth meant a combination of declining revenues and persistent expenses (including police and fire, schooling, and needs-based programs such as subsidized school lunches), and no choice but to push up property assessments in order to close the gap. The early and outer suburbs, by contrast, routinely met expenses without pushing the state's assessment thresholds, juggled zoning and economic development policies in order to maximize revenues, and provided much of the political energy for the tax revolts of the 1970s and 1980s.

This is a story that can be retold, with local twists and variations, for virtually any American metropolis in the modern era. Local, state, and national policies encouraged economic and demographic flight from increasingly poor, and black, central cities. Sprawl and political fragmentation made those cities—and the larger urban

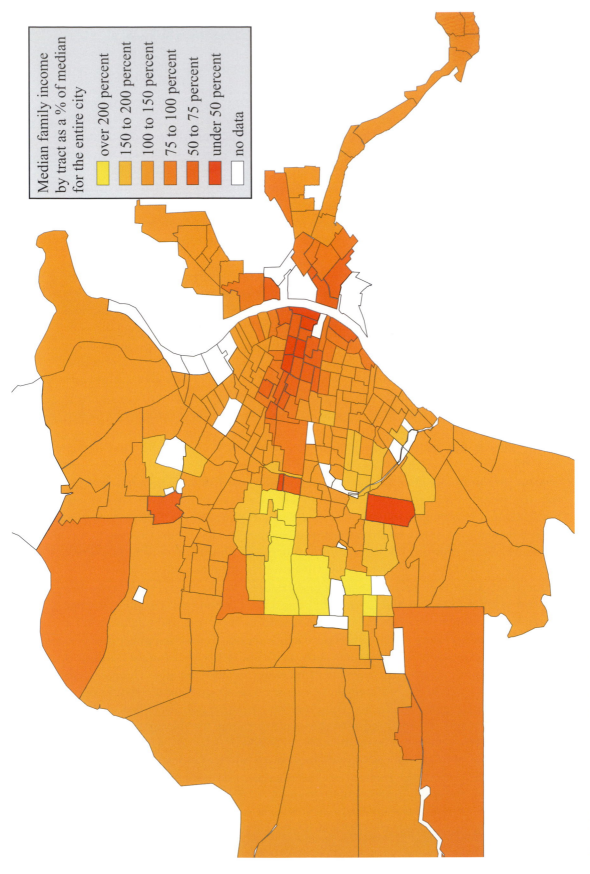

Median family income
by tract as a % of median
for the entire city

over 200 percent
150 to 200 percent
100 to 150 percent
75 to 100 percent
50 to 75 percent
under 50 percent
no data

Map I.16. Family incomes, 1950. 1950 Census.

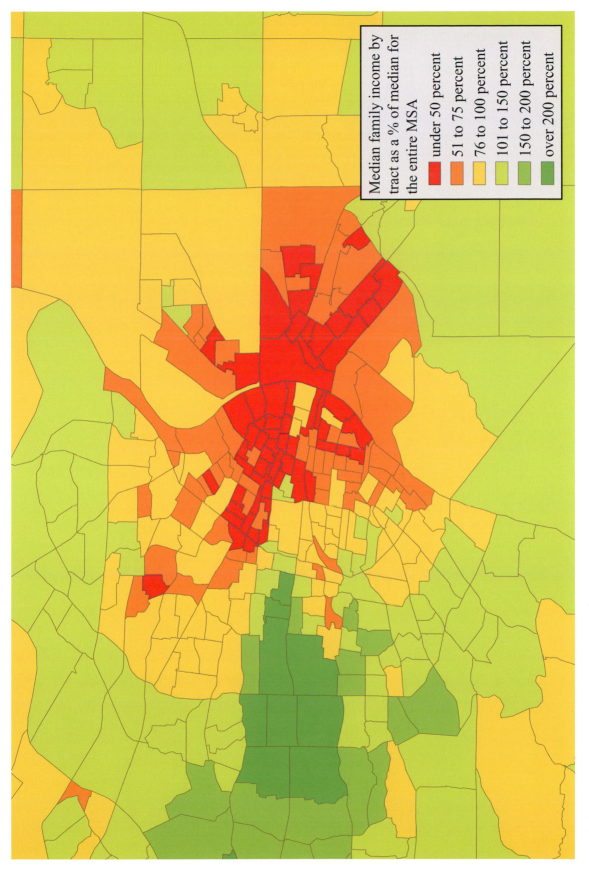

Median family income by
tract as a % of median for
the entire MSA

■ under 50 percent
■ 51 to 75 percent
■ 76 to 100 percent
■ 101 to 150 percent
■ 150 to 200 percent
■ over 200 percent

Map I.17. Family incomes, 1990. 1990 Census (STF-3).

areas they anchored—increasingly difficult to govern or finance. The modern urban crisis was a direct consequence of public policy, not an unfortunate social ill that persisted despite public policy.[71] And the consequence was not simply that cities like St. Louis were neglected but also that the immense political, economic, and cultural resources of those cities were squandered. This tangled failure of public policy lies at the root of our most pressing political challenges—including economic equity, race relations, and the environment. In one respect, 4635 North Market Street is simply an abandoned property in a long-neglected neighborhood in a city long past its prime. In another respect, it is a lasting (if ghostly) reminder of what we have done to our cities; it is a house in which we all live.

Chapter 1
Local Politics, Local Power

Governing Greater St. Louis, 1940–2000

The politics of property and race rest not just on the motives of local interests but also on the discriminatory opportunities opened by fragmented local governance. State and local law regarding incorporation, annexation, and consolidation vary wildly—but in most settings have made it easy to incorporate new localities on the City's fringes.[1] Beginning in the late nineteenth century, new municipalities, widely celebrated as a harbinger of economic growth and political self-determination, not only bounded "the city" but also began competing with it (and each other) for investment in real estate and commercial development. "By the early twentieth century suburbanites had begun carving up the metropolis," urban historian Jon Teaford concludes, "and the states had handed them the knife."[2]

These changes had enormous implications for residential patterns, taxation, and public goods in the nation's growing cities. Metropolitan areas like St. Louis were relatively coherent economic, social, and ecological units. Labor markets, consumer markets, housing markets, and patterns of economic development spanned the urbanized region from the outer suburbs to the central city,[3] but political regulation of those markets stopped and started again at each municipal boundary. Noting the proliferation of governmental units in suburban St. Louis County alone, one 1970 observer concluded that "Nearly all, by separate policies in zoning, subdivision regulation, and more subtle private action—maintain the white noose around the city."[4]

Home Rules: Municipal Fragmentation in Greater St. Louis

The growth of American cities posed a practical and legal riddle. The Constitution vested original sovereignty in the states and remained silent on the political status of cities. By law and practice, the city was a quasi-public corporation, subject to regulation by the state but without "state" powers itself. "Localities could hardly call their souls their own," one observer noted, "so tight were the fetters that bound them." As of the mid-nineteenth century, cities could not levy taxes, go into debt, pursue local improvements, change the structure of local government, or (in many cases) even hire and pay their own staff without passing "special legislation" toward each end in the statehouse. As cities grew, this arrangement proved a headache for both local politicians (who deeply resented the meddling of state legislators) and state legislatures (which spent nearly half their time acting as "spasmodic city councils").[5]

The solution, for local and state politicians alike, was "home rule"—a delegation of state powers to local governments. At their most basic, home rule provisions gave a state's largest cities freedom from special legislation and control over the structure and administration of local government. At their most expansive, home rule provisions gave local governments (first cities meeting varying population thresholds, later counties) the power to shape their own charters, enter into contracts, tax local residents, go into debt, zone and annex land, and provide a range of local services.[6] In Missouri and elsewhere, the practice of home rule was pursued and won for an idealized city—a sort of Florentine or Roman city-state representing a diverse economic and demographic base, a metropolitan anchor for a larger region, and a "more or less natural unit of government."[7] But cities changed. As home rule ceded greater authority to local governments, it also made it possible for fragments of the metropolis to incorporate their own governments. The result was not just cities with some autonomy from state rule but proliferating suburbs with autonomy from the central city and from each other. Over its modern history, St. Louis has, like most American metropolitan areas, been governed by a patchwork of states, counties, incorporated municipalities, school districts, special districts, and public authorities.

Missouri and St. Louis were precocious innovators on the home rule front. In the wake of the Civil War, urban interests felt increasingly underrepresented (and their interests often ignored) by both the state legislature and St. Louis County itself. State and rural interests, for their part, saw the administration of cities swallowing more and more legislative resources and attention. The result, sealed in the state's 1876 constitutional convention, was twofold. First, the state moved to tidy up its own rules for local governance—setting local debt limits, proscribing the passage of "special laws" in the statehouse, and establishing a classification system for villages, towns, and cities. Second, it gave cities the option of adopting charters of self-government—a provision (limited at the time to cities with populations over 100,000) written expressly for the city of St. Louis.[8] Given this opening, the city adopted its present-day boundaries and opted for formal separation from St. Louis County. Because the city was no longer located in a county, the new charter, in effect, made it its own county—resulting in a hybrid government with both municipal (police power) and county (property assessment, courts) responsibilities.[9]

While Missouri's home rule provision was designed and passed for the city of St. Louis, its restrictive population threshold fell quickly: by 1945 home rule had become an option for any Missouri city with over 5,000 residents and any county with assessed property value exceeding $4,500,000. Indeed, since 1876, the importance of home rule has rested less on the autonomy it granted the city of St. Louis than on the opportunity it has afforded surrounding communities, especially those multiplying west of the City limits, to poach St. Louis of its wealth and resources. Under the 1876 constitution, no city or town could incorporate within two miles of the corporate limits of another city in the same county. But since St. Louis was no longer *in* St. Louis County,

Missouri suburbs could crowd along the City limits. In the late nineteenth and early twentieth centuries, bordering towns thrived on "picture shows, gambling devices, vaudeville performances advertised under suggestive titles, . . . roulette wheels, shell games, and other fraudulent schemes"—all aimed at an urban audience but located beyond the reach of the City's police power.[10] As residential pressures and prospects reached the City edges, so did the vice squad, and the suburbs made quite a different appeal: no longer unregulated outposts of the City, they now offered a haven from it.

Early on, the conventional pattern of urban growth—annexation of outlying, often industrial, suburbs—was blocked in St. Louis, whose western border was sealed in 1876 and whose industrial suburbs were largely on the Illinois side of the river. New municipal incorporation began early in the twentieth century, but was concentrated in the decades after World War II (see Map 1.1). St. Louis County claimed six incorporated municipalities in 1900 and only twelve more by 1930—but that number had more than doubled by 1940 and doubled again by 1950.[11] When St. Louis County officials took note of this "epidemic" of incorporation in 1955, fully half of the County's municipalities were less than 12 years old. The driving force behind this, of course, was the rapid residential development of St. Louis County, which added over 225,000 single-family homes between 1950 and 2000. Municipal incorporation on the Illinois side, by contrast, was settled much earlier. And many of the cities and towns in the metro area's more remote Missouri counties were older industrial or agricultural centers overtaken by (but predating) metropolitan sprawl.[12]

In St. Louis County, the central inner-ring suburbs were essentially extensions of the City, and reflected the same patterns of land use (mixed-density housing in University City, commercial development in Clayton, industry in Wellston) as those parts of the City they bordered. Elsewhere, the proliferation of new cities and towns was driven by the pace of residential subdivision and development. Much of the County's postwar housing stock was erected in subdivisions in unincorporated areas of the County. The character of these suburbs was determined by the terms and standards of private construction and realty (including house and lot size and deed restrictions). Residents had little interest in attaching themselves to existing municipalities and often pursued small-scale incorporation as a means of sustaining local standards. City planners (most notably Harland Bartholomew and Associates) routinely discouraged their St. Louis County clients from annexing new territory—arguing instead that smaller municipal units (population 8,000–10,000) were sufficient to provide local services and necessary to avoid the threats posed by mixed density or use. The result, noted as early as the late 1920s, was a "considerable number of small communities," each "separate from the metropolitan city and . . . aloof from its neighbor."[13]

New municipal incorporations rested on a variety of motives: University City began as a planned "city of the future" extension of the 1904 World's Fair. Peerless Park (disincorporated in 1999) was, for most of its history, noted for its disinclination to regulate the sale of fireworks. St. Ann was established as a Catholic enclave. The city of Berkeley grew out of a dispute over school district boundaries with neighboring Kinloch (the lone black enclave in the County): when white residents failed to sustain school segregation by dividing the school district, they created a new town in 1937

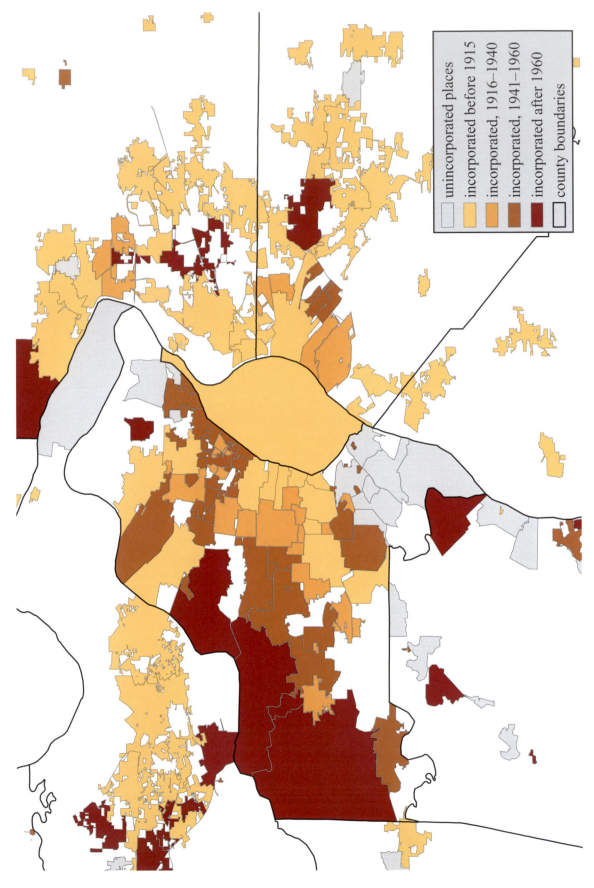

Map 1.1. Municipal incorporation in greater St. Louis, 1915–2000. Illinois and Missouri Secretaries of State (2000 boundaries).

Legend:

unincorporated places
incorporated before 1915
incorporated, 1916–1940
incorporated, 1941–1960
incorporated after 1960
county boundaries

instead. Kinloch itself incorporated in 1948, but its tax base was so meager it moved to disincorporate a year later. Black Jack (as we shall see in Chapter 3) was hastily formed in 1970 to stave off a mixed-income housing project. The sprawling west County municipality of Wildwood (incorporated 1995) was driven largely by fears that St. Louis County was not willing to sustain large-lot single-family residential development.[14] By and large, suburban municipalities existed to sustain local residential standards and patterns: "The prime purpose in forming the village," the founders of Moline Acres underscored, "was to maintain a residential area . . . we were quite anxious to get a zoning ordinance on the books." The provision of local services and police power protections was often an afterthought. Smaller communities contracted with the County or their neighboring towns for most services. Of 86 St. Louis County municipalities surveyed in 1957, only 33 had more than one paid police officer, only 17 had full-time fire personnel, and only 2 (Clayton and University City) had their own health departments.[15]

The pattern (and folly) of patchwork municipal incorporation in St. Louis County was underscored by the tiny village of Champ, incorporated in 1959. Champ's mastermind, Bill Bangert, wanted to build a domed stadium in St. Louis County but needed a municipal sponsor to qualify for industrial revenue bond financing. The County rebuffed the initial incorporation proposal but acceded to a more modest version: At its founding, Champ boasted 7 houses and a church (at the 2000 census it had 4 houses and a population of 12). The stadium plan passed the Missouri legislature but was vetoed by the governor. Undeterred, Bangert pressed to annex 3,000 acres of the Missouri Bottoms for an industrial park—promising to run the expanded city with a board of commissioners elected by commercial tenants on a one-acre per vote basis "to help eliminate municipal harassment of industry." The County dug in against this land grab, challenging not only the annexation plans but the validity of Champ's original incorporation. The case dragged on through the 1960s, the Missouri Supreme Court eventually upholding the original incorporation but quashing the annexation plans.[16]

Most commonly, especially in the decades surrounding World War II, subdivisions incorporated as a means of staving off annexation by their neighbors. Resident of Clayton had considered incorporation off and on in the early twentieth century but only formalized their plans (1913) when University City began exploring annexation. This pattern became even more common after 1929, when established cities began looking to weather the fiscal crisis of the Great Depression by padding their property tax base. Des Peres residents, for example, had long resisted the expectations (and new taxes) of municipal status but quickly circulated an incorporation petition (1934) to stem the plans of Kirkwood to push its boundaries (and those of its school district) north. Members of the Crestwood Subdivision Association, fearing annexation by neighboring Oakland, pressed for the creation of the city of Crestwood (1947). Moline Acres was established in 1949 to stave off annexation by Jennings or Bellefontaine Neighbors.[17]

Much the same pattern held in the latter half of the century, although the constraints and motives shifted. The 1945 Missouri constitution and a subsequent home rule charter gave St. Louis County itself a new standing as a corporate body. In 1951, the St. Louis County Council tried to discourage new incorporations by requiring that detailed budgetary planning accompany any new petition. But the courts left little doubt that the County was required to approve any reasonable petition and expressly "not authorized to deny incorporation . . . merely because it decides that no more municipalities are advisable." In 1953, the state made annexation more difficult by establishing a county-level approval process (administered by a new boundary commission) and pressing annexing governments to demonstrate that annexation was a natural or reasonable extension of their boundaries. Under these new (Sawyer Act) rules, the pace of new incorporations slowed but local interests could forestall annexation just by filing a petition with the county.[18]

These new rules proved especially important in St. Louis County, which waged a monotonous battle with municipalities looking to gobble up "unincorporated" county parcels along their borders. One such skirmish was fought over a roughly 300-acre parcel west of Olivette and north of Creve Coeur. The land was substantially developed for industrial use (including GE and Monsanto) and already serviced by a combination of private and County infrastructure. In 1957 Creve Coeur proposed annexation, conceding at the time that its goal was to create a buffer between existing residential development and commercial development on County land—while at the same time laying claim to a large commercial tax base. The courts summarily rejected the annexation, noting that Creve Coeur (which had no fire department, trash collection, or city hall) offered property owners substantially lesser services than those provided by the County.[19]

No sooner had the dust settled on Creve Coeur's annexation attempt than Olivette made a grab for the same parcel. Again, the County argued that the land in question—fully developed and serviced—hardly fit the definition of "unincorporated land," and that Olivette's annexation proposal was more a tax grab than a natural step in its growth: it was "simply and solely a scheme to inject Olivette into an area within the boundaries of municipally-serviced St. Louis County to acquire the tax base as its own." The trial court reluctantly approved the annexation (noting that the "race for annexations has become somewhat unseemly") but set its ruling aside in order to compel the Missouri Supreme Court to sort out the confusion: On one hand, Missouri law (even after the Sawyer Act) assumed that municipal growth marked a natural and inevitable progression in land use, and that the burden rested on opponents to prove that incorporation or annexation was unwarranted. On the other hand, St. Louis County was not just a rural hinterland and claimed (on the basis of its home rule charter, its mix of land uses, and the services it provided) equal corporate status with cities like Olivette and Creve Coeur. The Missouri Supreme Court (*Olivette v. Graeler*) agreed with the County and put an end to Olivette's annexation plans in 1963.[20]

Although *Graeler* strengthened the County's hand, confrontation between it and its municipalities persisted. As part of a far-reaching charter reform in 1970, the County tried (but failed) to win new authority over zoning and boundary politics. The 1979 County charter established a new countywide sales tax but allowed municipalities to opt out and claim local revenues. This gave these "point of sale" cities powerful incentives to add new retail districts by redevelopment or annexation. It was not until 1987 that the County was able to exempt new annexations from "point of sale" status—and stem a tide of sales-tax-chasing annexation proposals. And (like Olivette in 1963) municipalities continued to eye lucrative commercial and industrial properties. When the County challenged Town and Country's bid to annex an expansive Western Electric facility, the courts (*Town and Country v. St. Louis County*, 1983) pared back the County's standing—largely because state law had been amended in 1978 to allow those living in the targeted area an equal vote in the annexation process. Similar motives led to one of the few new incorporations of the post-1963 era: As Bridgeton, Overland, and Creve Coeur all eyed the commercial tax base along I-270 west of Lambert Field, the area instead incorporated as a new town, Maryland Heights, in 1985.[21]

The end result, routinely noted by local officials, was an almost mind-boggling patchwork of political authority. By 2000, the twelve-county metro area boasted 233 incorporated municipalities, 195 of which were in the core eight-county metro area (excluding Lincoln and Warren counties in Missouri and Clinton and Jersey counties in Illinois); 91 were in St. Louis County alone. Overlapping and bisecting these boundaries were the counties themselves, some 500 school districts, and nearly 100 other special taxing districts or authorities. Residents of Richmond Heights, for example, were governed by (and paid taxes to) the city of Richmond Heights (and a coterminous fire district), St. Louis County, four school districts, the City-County Zoo-Museum District, the Metropolitan Sewer District, and two junior college subdistricts. The grand total for the metro region (as of the 1997 census of governments): 789 distinct political units, an average of 12.5 "general purpose" (excluding school and other special districts) governments for every 100,000 residents, nearly three times the average (4.4 per 100,000) for the nation's 15 largest metro areas. This fragmentation was especially pronounced in the northeast County, where the Normandy school district encompassed all or part of 29 "postage stamp" municipalities.[22]

Only Missouri school districts bucked this trend: State law consolidated local school districts in 1948, cutting the statewide total by more than half and reducing the number in St. Louis County from over 80 to about 30. These districts were independent of the underlying municipal pattern—indeed, nearly half (35 of 74) of St. Louis County municipalities in 1956 fell into more than one school district, and 5 of these fell into at least four school districts. But fragmentation remained a persistent issue. In the long battle over school desegregation in greater St. Louis, for example, the City's embattled Board of Education was the defendant of record and suburban school districts remained largely on the legal sidelines. County school districts and municipalities dug in against an effort to reorganize the metropolitan area into 20 integrated school districts and were able to segregate pockets of African American students (most notably in Kinloch) until in 1975 they were compelled to redraw boundaries by the courts.[23]

This pattern of governance in greater St. Louis was accomplished quite purposefully; it was, in Terrence Jones's apt phrase, "fragmented by design." This fragmentation, in turn, facilitated and invited a prolonged pattern of local piracy as political units sought to maximize local wealth and tax bases while minimizing any claims that might be made on them. This pattern—enshrined in local realty, zoning, taxes, and economic development policies—pitted municipality against municipality and (more generally and starkly) the suburbs against the older central city.

All the Kings' Horses: Regionalism and Reform

It is now conventional wisdom among urban historians and urban scholars that patchwork governance has been disastrous for American cities. Home rule has encouraged local poaching and piracy, hardened local inequalities, and forestalled any functional regional response to serious regional social and economic challenges. This too, not surprisingly, has been the assessment of many interests in and around St. Louis across its modern history. The City itself appreciated early on that it was bearing much of the cost and reaping little of the benefit of suburban sprawl. While unwilling to reconsider its divorce from the City, St. Louis County constantly confronted the costs and confusion of municipal proliferation within its borders. And business groups recognized, fairly early in the twentieth century, that fragmented policy and planning turned growth politics into a local game of musical chairs. For these reasons, the region has monotonously (although never successfully) revisited the structure and logic of local home rule.

The first such effort came in 1924, in the wake of Progressive Era fascination with "business-minded" managerial efficiency in local government. The peculiar political status (and challenge) of the St. Louis area was enshrined in the Missouri constitution: Article VI, Section 30(a) provided for election of an 18-member (9 each from the City and County) board of freeholders, and laid out a range of options for regional consolidation—including a return of St. Louis to St. Louis County, annexation of part of the County by the City, annexation of the entire County by the City, and establishment of "special districts" for certain metropolitan services. The 1924 board quickly deadlocked, with County officials opposing merger in any form—until one of the County freeholders agreed to change his vote in order to put something on the ballot. City residents favored merger by a nearly 8 to 1 margin, but a much heavier turnout in the County defeated the plan.[24] Reformers, led by the Chamber of Commerce, regrouped around a joint Metropolitan Development Committee, which floated a "federal" proposal that would maintain existing municipalities but create a new regional government with responsibility for health, sewers, public utilities, libraries, parks, and city planning. Seeking to dilute County opposition, proponents advocated the "Metropolitan Federation" as an amendment to the state constitution—but lost a statewide vote in 1930.[25]

Into the 1940s, the consequences of fragmentation—at least for the City—only grew worse. St. Louis "suffers like one whose feet are hobbled, whose hands are manacled and whose body is enclosed in a steel corset," pleaded City officials in the run up to the state's 1945 constitutional convention, "which prevents the normal operation of all his vital functions." But attention quickly narrowed to the prospect of creating "special districts" for discrete regional needs. This led to the creation of the Metropolitan Sewer District (encompassing the City and the Missouri suburbs in the Mississippi watershed) in 1954, followed by the establishment of a junior college district in 1962, and the Zoo-Museum District (spreading the costs of the City's cultural attractions to County residents) in 1971. Despite a near consensus that transportation (public and highways) posed the greatest regional planning challenge, the idea of a special transit district stalled—leaving only the Bi-State Development Agency, a combination planning body and bridge/harbor authority, without any taxing power.[26]

These setbacks were enormously frustrating, especially for those invested in local economic development and urban renewal efforts that depended on farsighted regional planning and fiscal policies. The St. Louis Chamber of Commerce continued to promote some form of regional government and helped form a new group, "Civic Progress," in the mid-1950s with the expressed goal of promoting the City and the region. These interests pulled together enough support from business foundations (Ford, McDonnell-Douglas) to underwrite an exhaustive "Metropolitan St. Louis Survey," which suggested a new metropolitan government with responsibility for arterial roads, transit, planning, economic development, sewers, civil defense, police, and property assessment (almost everything but local zoning). The "Survey" plan also challenged the local logic of home rule by hammering away at the inefficiencies of fragmented governance and calling for the disincorporation of municipalities with fewer than 4,000 residents.[27]

By the terms set out in the 1945 state constitution, proposal for city-county cooperation or merger had to be vetted by a board of freeholders made up of nine representatives each from the City and the County, and one at-large member appointed by the governor. As this process ground on, popular support began to wane. The freeholders split fairly predictably along county-city lines and settled on a metropolitan district plan rather than a full-blown merger—a tack that alienated County interests leery of any reform and City interests who feared that token reform would make it harder to do anything more substantive in the future. Raymond Tucker, the City's Democratic mayor, offered no endorsement—at least in part because he identified the whole idea with upstarts (including future mayor A. J. Cervantes) in his own party. County residents again dug in against the threat posed to home rule and neighborhood homogeneity. One of the leading voices in the County, appropriately enough, was a former Republican city alderman who had moved to suburban Webster Groves. And many in the City—including African Americans (who feared losing the moderate clout they now claimed on the Board of Aldermen) and the St. Louis Labor Council (who felt the plan did not go far enough)—voiced doubts. The freeholder's plan was easily defeated in a 1959 special election, losing by a margin of 2-1 in the City and 3-1 in the County.[28]

Having failed again at local reform, regionalists returned to the idea of amending the state constitution, this time around an ambitious 1962 "Borough Plan." Like previous efforts, the Borough Plan proposed a sort of federal solution: an umbrella regional government assuming most core metropolitan responsibilities and 22 local boroughs (collapsing most existing municipal boundaries and carving up the City) providing local representation and a shadow of home rule (see Map 1.2). Proponents, including local business and development groups, reiterated their disdain for the

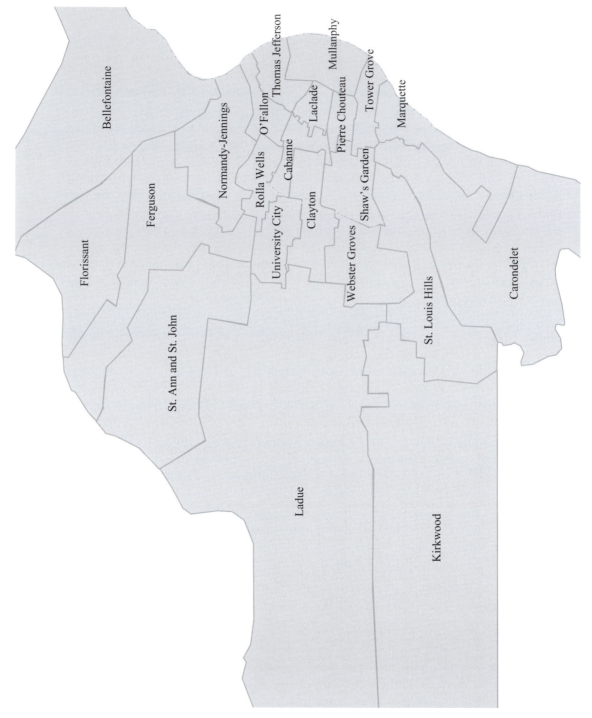

Map 1.2. Borough plan, 1962. Map of Municipal County (1961), Box 1163, League of Women Voters Records, WHMC.

region's "hodge-podge of feeble, self-centered, conflicting governments" and the "crazy-quilt of extravagant burdening and unneeded tax bodies." Critics, especially in the County's suburbs and in the City's African American wards, countered that the Plan was being "forced down the throats of the people of St. Louis and St. Louis County" and that it was all little more than "a clever attempt to delude the people of the area, particularly those in St. Louis County, into believing that their local communities will actually remain in existence." The proposal lost handily, by a near 4-1 margin, in the statewide vote.[29]

After 1962, the "beggar-thy-neighbor" logic of home rule and the urgency of regional solutions persisted, but serious political reforms were rarely broached. Local governments toyed with a regional council (drafted as SLACOG: the St. Louis Council of Governments)—"an umbrella organization with a policy board to which a variety of functional planning and management units could be responsible"—but the idea went nowhere. Local growth interests, most prominently Civic Progress and the City and County Chambers of Commerce (merged and recast as the Regional Commerce and Growth Association in 1973), continued to lament the costs and inefficiencies of local fragmentation. But, as Civic Progress concluded glumly in 1969, the combined opposition of suburban interests and the City's African American wards left "little or no chance of major governmental consolidation." The City did win a minor victory with the creation of the Zoo-Museum District in 1971. For its part, St. Louis County, fearing that municipal incorporation and annexations would leave it with little but substandard housing, farms, and floodplains on its tax rolls, floated a number of proposals for municipal reorganization and new county authority over land use and zoning—but could not overcome the entrenched defense of fragmented home rule.[30]

A more serious regional perspective, which continued to view metropolitan governance as a solution to regional and central city problems, fell to organizations like the East-West Gateway Coordinating Council (now the East-West Gateway Council of Governments). EW Gateway began as a local response to the 1962 Federal Highway Act, which mandated local planning as a condition for federal funds. The organization quickly accumulated a virtual monopoly on local planning expertise, although its financial stability waxed and waned with federal transportation spending (slashed during the 1980s and restored somewhat by the first Intermodal Surface Transportation Efficiency Act (ISTEA) in 1991).[31] Alongside other local "regionalist" interests (including Confluence (now FOCUS) St. Louis, and the Metropolitan Equal Housing Opportunity Council), EW Gateway documented the persistent consequences of political fragmentation, but—as a purely advisory council—could do little to address them. "A large number of local governments may help ensure that government is more accountable and closer to its citizens," allowed its survey of the region in 1999; "However a vast and overlapping array of public sector units may also fragment decision making processes and inhibit cooperative regional initiatives and resource sharing."[32]

The Growth Machine and the Urban Crisis

Political fragmentation allowed local municipalities to prosper at the expense of each other, and of the region. More precisely, it invited suburban municipalities to poach the central city while protecting themselves from its problems. As a result, the motives and strategies of City politics were quite distinct. The City saw itself not as one of many competing regional interests but as the target of that competition, as a lonely advocate of "metropolitan" solutions—as Gulliver to an army of parochial Lilliputians. As suburban municipalities strove to avoid the fiscal and social costs of urban life, the City looked to socialize them. This was a task shaped by both the structure of local government and the peculiar character of "growth politics" in a shrinking city.

The City's response to regional problems, and to its own deepening urban crisis, was constrained by both geography and political structure. Across the twentieth century, St. Louis retained an essentially unreformed, fragmented, weak-mayor form of government. Political power revolved around local ward organizations and their control of patronage appointments, and there was no lasting political machine (akin to the Chicago Democrats) reaching across ward boundaries. Local political authority was innately complex, in part because the City served both municipal and "county" functions. The terms of the 1876 "divorce" split local legislative power between a 28-member house of delegates elected from the wards and a 13-member council elected at large. Business-minded reformers did away with this bicameral structure and ward-based elections in 1914. Members of the new board of aldermen were (in keeping with a state constitutional provision) elected at-large, although each nominally represented one of the City's 28 wards. The 1914 charter included a number of other "Progressive" reforms (including ballot initiative, referendum, and recall) and established three citywide offices—mayor, comptroller, and president of board of aldermen—who shared administrative and budgetary authority. Eight "county" offices (sheriff, clerk of the court, recorder of deeds, etc.) were also elected citywide.[33]

Although stripped of their direct electoral role, the wards remained the locus of political power. Partisan committeemen continued to control employment in city and county offices, the principal spoil of local politics. Charter reform again took aim at "machine rule" in 1941, but the results were mixed. The City adopted new civil service rules—an initiative driven as much by the desire of departing mayors to entrench their supporters as any commitment to merit hiring. But 1941 also saw a return to direct ward-based elections (the state dropped its requirement of at-large elections in 1933). This virtually doomed future reform efforts—including a 1956 proposal to shrink the Board of Aldermen to 14, 7 elected at-large and 7 from wards—as local organizations (including predominantly African American wards) invariably saw reform as a threat to local interests and local power. City politics, before and after 1941, remained a chaos of weak mayoral leadership and aldermanic backrubbing.[34]

St. Louis was a solidly Republican town until the onset of the Great Depression. The emergence of the local Democratic Party rested in part on a national pattern of realignment that saw the New Deal secure the allegiance of organized labor and African Americans (before 1933, as one observer noted, black Democrats in St. Louis were so few and far between "you could count them on your fingers and toes with some left over"). And it rested in part on local factors, including the salience of Prohibition repeal in the shadow of Anheuser-Busch and the importance of federal jobs programs to the City's patronage machine. The Republicans maintained a hold on "county" offices and made modest gains in the 1940s, but, by and large, the GOP followed in the footsteps of the region's affluent white residents—retreating first to the City's southern reaches, then to the suburbs. In 1953, the Democrats claimed 20 of the 28 wards; into the early 1970s they carried a fairly consistent 24-4 edge (26-2 in 1965 and 22-6 in 1967). After 1975, the GOP never claimed more than one or two wards. By the 2001-3 election cycle (half of the board was up for election each odd year), Republicans held one ward and contested only two others.[35]

The Democrats' electoral stranglehold, however, did little to erode the parochial logic of local politics. Electoral competition was now waged within the Democratic Party, a confrontation largely understood as a "banks vs. unions" showdown between working-class wards and civic-minded elites—but complicated by civil rights politics as well. And the success of local Democrats played out against an otherwise Republican backdrop. In this sense, the City's dealings with the state, and with its suburban municipalities and counties, were often overlaid by real and petty partisan differences.[36]

For most of the modern era, the institutional and electoral dimensions of St. Louis politics have been dwarfed by the local politics of growth. As in most urban settings, this "growth machine" was (and is) composed of local business, realty, and development interests—particularly those with a stake in the value and exchange of property. Its goals and strategies are the familiar terrain of civic boosters across the twentieth century: promotion of the local economy, low taxes, protection of private property, and maintenance of a "favorable business climate." But, more starkly in St. Louis than in most urban settings, this growth machine has been fueled less by the prospect of private investment than by its flight; less by local economic growth than by local claims to federal urban renewal dollars.[37]

St. Louis growth politics often played out as a confrontation between parochial ward interests, on one hand, and "respectable" civic leaders—including business groups, local newspapers, downtown interests, and the mayor's office—on the other.[38] This was especially true during the heyday of urban renewal, the mayoral terms of Joseph Darst (1949–53) and his successor Raymond Tucker (1953–65). During these years, urban renewal overshadowed the mundane details of department budgeting and spot zoning, which otherwise dominated city politics. Ward interests on the board of alderman now competed to "blight" parcels in preparation for "slum clearance," but the money (and centralized authority) ran through the mayor's office. "City government went on its merry way dividing the spoils made available by local taxes," Dennis Judd notes, "but urban renewal was now the big game in town."[39] Urban renewal, in effect, privatized a large chunk of the City's politics. Federal dollars and local investment decisions were laundered through an independent urban renewal advisory committee, the City's Land Clearance for Redevelopment Authority (LCRA), and a network of nominally public redevelopment corporations. As importantly, the City's efforts to leverage federal money and new private investment also drew business leadership—via the mayor's office—into new prominence.

The most important venue for business's new political role was "Civic Progress." Mayor Darst first floated the idea for a new business coalition in 1952—looking specifically to replicate the structure and success of Pittsburgh's "Allegheny Conference."

In the eyes of both its members and the mayor's office, Civic Progress was to be a "closely limited fraternity of capable executives" unencumbered by a broad membership, paid staff, or public meetings. Civic Progress held its first formal meeting in 1953—charged with the immediate task of addressing a fiscal crisis brought on by the expiration of the City's earnings tax. The City won an extension from the state legislature on the condition that the issue be put before the voters—a campaign led successfully by Civic Progress. This was followed by leadership of a 1956 bond drive (in which Civic Progress both organized the screening committees for revenue proposals and coordinated the electoral campaign) and the election of freeholders to consider the (ultimately futile) metropolitan reform proposals of the late 1950s. Into the 1960s, Civic Progress accumulated the "responsibility of giving leadership" to the City's entire redevelopment program. Civic Progress was the St. Louis poster child for the "urban growth machine"—it was composed of the CEOs of the large dynastic corporations (Anheuser-Busch, McDonnell Douglas, Ralston Purina) which dominated the City's economy, and other local interests with (as described by *Fortune* in 1956) a "substantial stake in mortgage values, municipal services, and the future of downtown." Its membership included (again quoting *Fortune*) "six manufacturers, five bankers, two department-store executives, two utility presidents, an insurance company president, a real estate manager, a former judge, two chamber of commerce executives and the chancellor of Washington University."[40]

Joining Civic Progress (and sharing many members) was "Downtown, Inc." formed in 1958. Downtown, Inc. began as a sort of "clean-up downtown" campaign and played a prominent public role in promoting redevelopment (especially new parking facilities and the stadium) in the central business district. Pledges in support of Downtown, Inc. came largely from retail and banking interests and ran in the neighborhood of $150,000 per year in its early years—a budget (devoted mostly to staff and promotional campaigns) that grew little over the next three decades.[41]

The St. Louis Chamber of Commerce was also important and—at least as a business organization—dwarfed the membership and resources of either Civic Progress or Downtown, Inc. (the chamber had a dues base of just under $200,000 in 1942, growing to over $300,000 in 1952, almost $450,000 in 1962, and almost $1 million by the early 1970s). But its political clout was uneven. The St. Louis chamber was widely considered a weak and ineffectual body (it "sparked about as much interest as a wet towel and, so far as I could see, accomplished little or nothing" one member recalled)—a perception that in part led to the creation of Civic Progress.[42] Certainly, one mark of the chamber's political uncertainty was its propensity for reinventing itself. Under pressure from the national chamber and many of its members, the St. Louis chamber pursued a working arrangement with its counterpart in St. Louis County. In 1963, the two chambers joined forces and in 1965 spun off two new organizations, the Regional Industrial Development Corporation (RIDC) charged with promoting local economic development, and the Research Council (largely underwritten by Civic Progress firms), charged with identifying local research and development opportunities.[43]

This organizational initiative aside, the city-county chamber was out of the urban renewal loop and left with little to do but promote a local economy in the throes of serious decline. Members complained of the overlapping efforts (and demands) of local economic development or promotional efforts and aside from the most conventional political efforts (taxes, labor law) viewed the chambers' efforts as "a cockeyed waste of time."[44] In 1973, the local chamber brought all of its efforts under the umbrella of a new organization, the Regional Commerce and Growth Association (RCGA).[45]

The creation of the RCGA coincided with a deepening urban crisis and the beginning of the end for federal urban renewal spending. For groups like the RCGA and Civic Progress, this made it harder to overcome the fragmentation of local politics—especially as much of the power of the mayor's office left with the federal dollars.[46] Local business groups (with the exception of Downtown, Inc. and its successors) retreated to a more regional perspective, happy to promote growth in the suburbs even if it came at the expense of the City. In all, the City sustained at best a sputtering growth machine whose clout in local politics depended heavily on federal money, and whose clout in the region paled beside that of the hundreds of little growth machines chugging away in the suburbs.

Paying for It: The Politics of Local Taxes

Local taxation in Missouri is, like the pattern of local governance, fragmented and complex. Municipalities, school districts, counties, and special taxing districts (fire, sewer, transit) all have discrete but overlapping claims on local resources. The ability of local governments to levy taxes is governed by both general enabling state legislation and special laws—some of which apply to only cities of a certain size, some of which identify cities (St. Louis and Kansas City) specifically. Sources of local revenue vary across the state and over time and have included taxes on property, income, sales, and business inventories; fees from local licenses and franchises; and charges for local services (sewer, water, parking). Faced with exceptional burdens, local governments can also resort to debt, usually in the form of project-specific (highways, redevelopment) bonds. This has always been closely regulated by the state, which sets limits on local debt (10 percent of assessed property value in 1968). Local governments have relied increasingly on state and federal aid—especially in areas (like education) in which there were compelling arguments for unshackling services from the uneven ability of local governments to pay for them, or in areas (policing, urban renewal) in which pressing local problems were accompanied by a collapse in local fiscal capacity. And all of this has been shaped by both state and local battles over tax levies and property assessments and by fierce local competition for prospective revenues.[47]

At the core of the local tax structure is the property tax, which in Missouri is levied against both "real" property (land and structures) and tangible personal property (cars, boats). Into the 1940s, municipalities (including St. Louis) counted on property taxes for almost two-thirds of local revenues and for virtually all locally generated revenues. The importance of the property tax slipped in the postwar era, reflecting the increased importance of federal and state transfers, the diversification (sales, income, charges) of local tax bases, and state "tax revolt" restrictions on local taxes. Nationally, the property tax now accounts for between 20 and 30 percent of local revenues and 30 to 50 percent of locally generated revenues. This decline was steeper in Missouri, which turned to both local income (1948) and local sales (1971) taxes, and it was steeper in distressed urban settings like St. Louis with stagnant tax bases. Across this era, however, the property tax remained the most important source of local fiscal autonomy or discretion.[48]

In Missouri, state law establishes the local taxing authority, rules for the classification and assessment of property, and upper limits on local levies for all taxing bodies (including cities and towns, counties, school districts, and special districts).[49] Local governments, in turn, control revenues by setting the local tax rate, by assessing local property, and by (through zoning and economic development) controlling patterns of property use and development. Over much of the postwar era, areas of rapid development (like much of St. Louis County) enjoyed fiscal health at relatively low tax rates. Areas of stagnant growth (like the City), by contrast, struggled to provide local services while pushing local levies to their limits.[50]

By law, property was assessed at its full value, but—especially before the 1970s—local assessors enjoyed wide latitude. Indeed, generally accepted practice was to aim for a 30 percent valuation (the floor set by the state tax commission) as the basis for taxation. This was a system rife with inconsistency and abuse, and a perennial subject of controversy in local and state politics. In the 1950s and 1960s, valuations ranged from 15 to 30 percent in most counties, but pushed as high as 40 percent in those (including the City) facing fiscal pressures. These local variations were driven by both local fiscal demands and local assessment practices. State law required annual assessments but this was the practice only in populous counties (including the City) with professional assessors. In much of the state, values were simply carried forward from previous years (as of 1972, the last full assessment in Jackson County was in 1941), a practice that put much of the local tax burden on property that had changed hands.[51]

Political complaints and legal challenges finally compelled the state to impose a new 33 percent valuation standard in 1975, a mandate that was accompanied by state aid to local assessors and an automatic rollback of local levies when revenue growth from reassessment exceeded 10 percent. But local variation and the inflationary 1970s continued to play havoc with local property taxes, especially as cities were torn between the old politics of local relief through lax assessment and the need to meet ballooning expenditures. In response, local assessors adopted an informal classification system that held commercial and industrial properties at or above the 33 percent threshold while continuing to dampen the values of residential properties.[52] Not surprisingly, commercial landowners complained—citing the core "equal protection" principle that (aside from certain exemptions) property taxes not distinguish among classes of property. This led, in the early 1980s, to another round of state reform that formalized assessment ratios for different properties: public, religious, charitable, and educational properties remained tax exempt; agricultural land was now assessed at 12 percent; residential property at 19 percent; industrial and commercial property at 32 percent; and all personal property at 33.3 percent.[53]

The result, in part, was an uneasy local counter to the trajectory of national tax pol-

icy. While business taxes declined steadily as a share of national revenues, local governments leaned more and more on commercial and industrial assessments.[54] This was
accompanied, however, by increasingly expansive property tax exemptions or rebates
for business investments in redevelopment areas, enterprise zones, or tax increment
financing districts. While commercial assessments bore more of the conventional
property tax burden, the local tax system itself was organized increasingly around an
array of personal taxes—including the earnings tax in St. Louis and the regressive general sales tax. And—in the face of persistent lobbying from various local economic
development interests (including the RCGA)—the state dropped another source of
local business taxation, a "merchants and manufacturers tax" on business inventories,
in 1982 (backfilling some of the lose revenue with a "commercial surcharge" on commercial property taxes).[55]

   The politics of property assessment underscored the larger vulnerability of the
property tax—as a political target and as a source of local revenue (see Figure 1.1).
Across the modern era, state and local pressures carved away at the tax base at both
ends: Proliferating exemptions and credits were crafted both to protect low-income
Missourians from rising property values and to encourage new investment or development. By state law (1955), rising property values automatically lowered tax rates whenever reassessment inflated revenues by more than 10 percent.[56] Exemptions from the

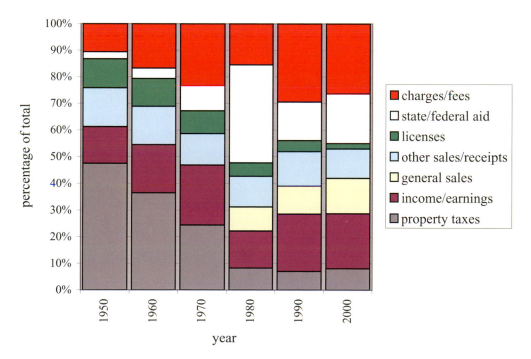

Figure 1.1. St. Louis City revenues, 1950–2000 (general revenues by source). Census Bureau,
City Finances (selected years) through 1990; Census Bureau, *Government Finances* for 2000,
http://ftp2.census.gov/govs/estimate/.

personal property tax grew, including a blanket exemption of all "household goods" in 1972. In 1973, a "circuit breaker" law (Missouri's version of the more conventional "homestead" exemption) reimbursed low-income seniors for property taxes that exceeded 4 percent of income. Exemptions for public and religious properties were broadened to exclude properties in "blighted" redevelopment areas or enterprise zones (as I examine more closely in Chapter 4). Such provisions left such a large chunk of assessed property in the city of St. Louis off the tax rolls that property tax revenues shriveled (as one alderman put it) to an "abused and obsolete" share of City funds.[57]

The final nail in this coffin was the 1980 Hancock Amendment, Missouri's version of the tax and expenditure limits pioneered by California's tax revolt of the early 1970s. Hancock limited growth in state taxes to the rate of growth in family income and prohibited new or increased local taxes without popular approval. This led to a greater reliance on local licenses and fees for service, and to a zero-sum logic that targeted the revenues from any new tax and matched it with relief from another tax—as in a small increase in the state sales tax (1982) whose proceeds were split between state aid to education and a property tax rollback. In effect, Hancock furthered the transformation of the property tax from a source of local revenue to a fiscal tool of the state.[58]

As the proceeds and the potential of local property taxes waned, local governments in Missouri looked for alternatives. The fiscal crisis was especially acute for St. Louis, where the base of assessed property value was stagnant and the cost of local services was growing at an alarming rate. The solution—at least in part—was a local income or earnings tax. City-specific income taxes are not common outside of Pennsylvania and Ohio, and most (especially those installed since 1970) are small local option levies dedicated to schools. For St. Louis, an earnings tax was both a new source of revenue and a way to spread the costs of urban governance to the "daylight citizens" who worked in the City but lived in the suburbs. First established in 1948 (at .25 percent), the City's income tax was immediately struck down by the state supreme court as an unconstitutional extension of home rule. The state used special legislation (applying only to St. Louis and Kansas City) to prop up the local tax until its constitutionality was sealed by popular referendum in 1954. The tax (pushed to 1 percent by 1959) was levied on "salaries, wages, commissions and other compensation earned by [City] residents" *and* "on the salaries, wages, commissions and other compensation earned by nonresidents of the city for work done or services performed or rendered in the city." It was popular with local business and labor interests alike, largely because it reached into the pockets of suburban commuters.[59] By 1960 (see Figure 1.1), the earnings tax accounted for about one-quarter of City revenues; by 1970, it was more important than the property tax; by 1990 it generated more than three times the revenue of the property tax.

While the earnings tax filled much of the gap left by stagnant property values in Missouri's major cities, it could not sustain local budgets ravaged by both declining revenues and rising demands. In the late 1960s, Kansas City and St. Louis leaders pressed for more state aid for both education and general civic needs. As a compromise, the state established a new local sales tax, adding a general sales tax (cities had always taxed discrete sales, such as cigarettes and motor fuels) to the municipal revenue stream. In effect, the City Sales Tax Act (1971) dedicated more of the established state sales tax to local governments; in exchange, local governments ceded a greater share of property tax revenue to schools. This arrangement was juggled again in 1983 with the passage of Proposition C which levied a new 1 percent state sales tax in support of schools and rolled back local tax rates.[60]

In 1979–80, the local sales tax was extended to counties—generating both new revenues and new incentives for suburban municipalities. Under the new St. Louis County Charter (1979), local governments could share in the county sales tax in one of two ways: They could simply claim their share (calculated on a per capita basis) of countywide revenues. Or they could opt out of the countywide pool and claim all the local revenues. The latter, classified as "point of sale" cities, increasingly focused their fiscal futures on sales tax revenues. Many St. Louis County municipalities (16 as of 2002) levied no local property taxes, and instead competed fiercely for the regional sales tax base.[61] This led to another round of annexation fever, stemmed only when the County stepped in (1988) and disqualified all newly-annexed land from "point of sale" status. Another consequence (detailed in Chapter 4) was a competitive flurry of shopping mall development—largely underwritten by tax increment financing (TIF) agreements.[62]

Fragmented Government and Fiscal Crisis

Inescapably, the politics of local taxation and patterns of local fragmentation combined to produce sharp inequities across the metropolitan area and severe fiscal stress—first for the central city, later for its older, inner-ring suburbs. The ability of local governments to provide local services was shaped by their "fiscal capacity"—essentially the relationship (or gap) between available revenues and the cost of necessary services. The general rule of urban fiscal politics, unfortunately, was that declining revenues and increasing expenditures went hand-in-hand. As urban planners and local governments keenly appreciated, a municipality of large-lot single-family homes (with perhaps a new shopping mall thrown in) generated stable revenues and minimal demands. The City and its inner suburbs, by contrast, increasingly struggled to generate property, income, and sales taxes—while facing substantially higher demands for local schooling, police, infrastructure maintenance, and social assistance. This persistent inequity was dampened, but only slightly, by sporadic infusions of state and federal money.

This first arose as an object of concern in school funding. Missouri school districts are independent taxing bodies and in most settings (including St. Louis County) do not coincide with municipal boundaries. While the municipal tax base diversified across the postwar era, schools remained uniquely dependent on local property taxes. In fiscal 1955–56 (see Map 1.3), assessed property value in St. Louis and St. Louis County ranged from over $37,000 per pupil in Clayton to barely $2,200 per pupil in Kinloch. The property tax base in the City was still fairly healthy, and the wealthy central County suburbs (Clayton, Ladue) enjoyed a combination of high property values,

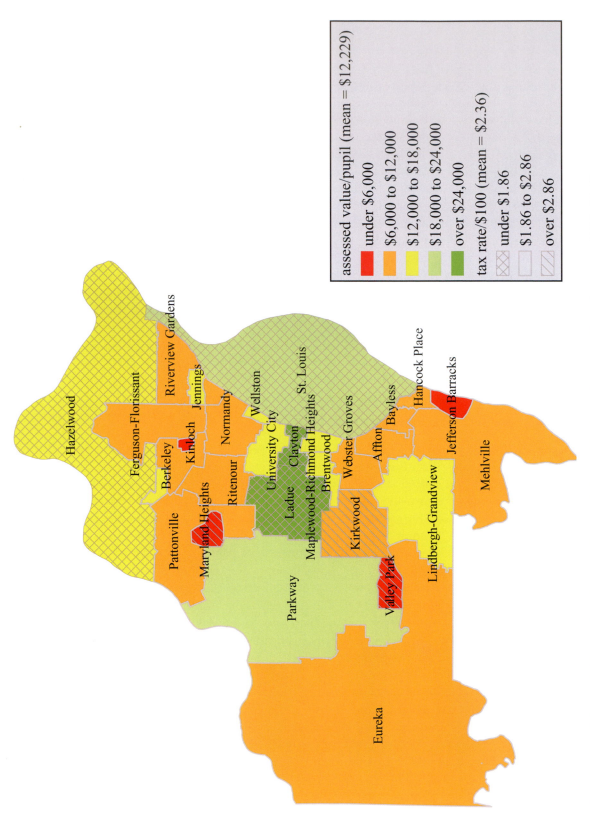

assessed value/pupil (mean = $12,229)

under $6,000
$6,000 to $12,000
$12,000 to $18,000
$18,000 to $24,000
over $24,000

tax rate/$100 (mean = $2.36)

under $1.86
$1.86 to $2.86
over $2.86

Hazelwood

Riverview Gardens

Ferguson-Florissant

Jennings

Kinloch

Berkeley

Normandy

Wellston

St. Louis

University City

Hancock Place

Bayless

Jefferson Barracks

Ritenour

Clayton

Maplewood-Richmond Heights

Webster Groves

Affton

Mehlville

Pattonville

Ladue

Brentwood

Maryland Heights

Kirkwood

Lindbergh-Grandview

Parkway

Valley Park

Eureka

Map 1.3. School funding, 1955–1956. Metropolitan St. Louis Survey, *Background for Action* (University City: The Survey, 1957), 56–67.

small school populations, and low tax rates. Most of the school districts in the north and south County had maintained property values and tax rates near the regional averages. Those districts in fiscal trouble—with low property values and relatively high tax rates—were both poorer and smaller than their peers.[63] A decade later (see Map 1.4) the situation had improved somewhat, largely because two of the four struggling districts had been collapsed into their neighbors. The Clayton, Ladue, and Brentwood districts all boasted assessed values per student of over $22,000 (with Clayton at almost $44,000, or nearly three times the regional mean) and correspondingly low tax rates. Kinloch, the African American outpost surrounded (but also shunned) by the Berkeley School District, persisted on an assessed value of barely $3,000 per student, a circumstance scarcely ameliorated by one of the region's highest tax rates.

By the early 1980s, the wealthy central County districts (Clayton, Ladue, Brentwood) continued to boast a combination to high property values and low tax rates, but the City and inner suburban districts were slipping into deep fiscal crisis (Map 1.5). Indeed, between 1950 and 1980, property tax revenues fall from 56 to 22 percent of total revenue for St. Louis schools—a reflection of plunging property values, rising costs (over 3 times *after* inflation between 1950 and 1984), and increased state and federal aid. The only relief came from declining enrollments in the City. In the 1980–81 school year, average daily attendance (about 63,000) was barely half what it had been a decade earlier. In that year alone, the St. Louis Board of Education shuttered 28 schools.[64] By 2003 (Map 1.6), the situation in the City had stabilized somewhat, but the districts in the inner suburbs of the north County remained in deep crisis.

Missouri, as with most states, was quick to recognize the perils of fragmented school funding but slow to redress it. The state mandated the consolidation of many school districts in 1948, and adjustments in district boundaries reduced the number of districts in St. Louis County (even as new municipalities proliferated) to 23 by 2000. The state also instituted a "foundation" funding formula that assured the poorest districts of state assistance. The formula required local districts to levy a base school tax (at least $1.00 per $100 of assessed value in 1956, increased to $2.75 by 2004). If local taxes did not yield a base revenue ($110 per student in 1956), the state contributed the balance. This was a meager and underfunded threshold: Even Kinloch, whose local taxes raised $112.00 per student in 1956, did not qualify. Over time, the purse strings loosened somewhat, especially as the gap between rich and poor districts persisted and the cost of local schooling swelled. The state share of education funding in Missouri grew from 32 percent in 1960 to 41 percent in 1970, 49 percent in 1980, and 59 percent in 1990. The Proposition C sales tax (1983) bolstered this, but the Outstanding Schools Act (1993) revised the formula—giving more weight to "above average local tax effort" and paring the state share back closer to 50 percent. By 2004, the foundation formula (which ran nearly eight single-spaced pages in the state code) was sufficiently complex "to give motion sickness to a potted plant" but remained chronically underfunded.[65]

These troubles were especially acute in the St. Louis school district, where the state's generic school funding problems (including low tax rates and a heavy reliance on

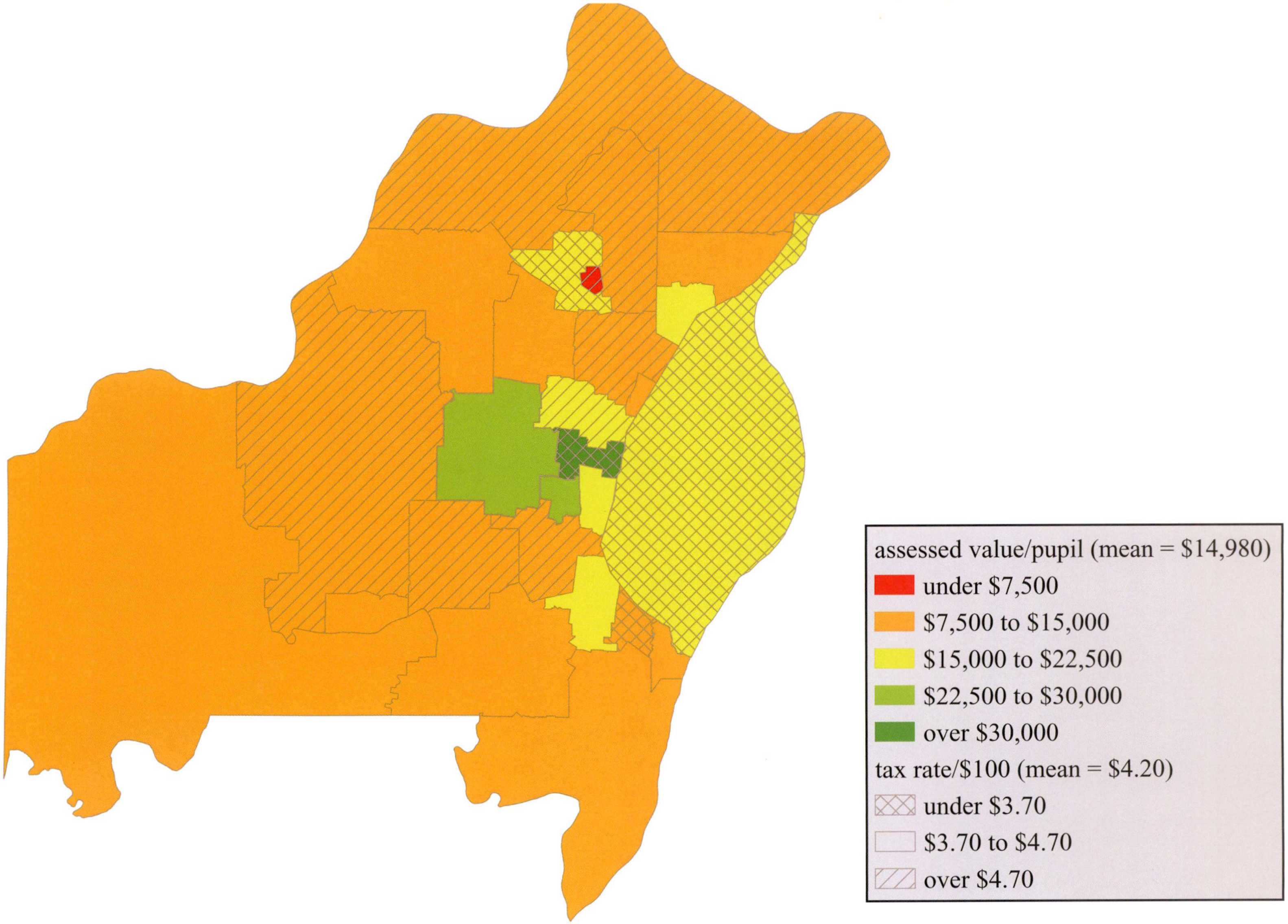

Legend:

assessed value/pupil (mean = $14,980)
- under $7,500
- $7,500 to $15,000
- $15,000 to $22,500
- $22,500 to $30,000
- over $30,000

tax rate/$100 (mean = $4.20)
- under $3.70
- $3.70 to $4.70
- over $4.70

Map 1.4. School funding, 1968–1969. *St. Louis County Fact Book* (St. Louis County: Dept. of Planning, 1969).

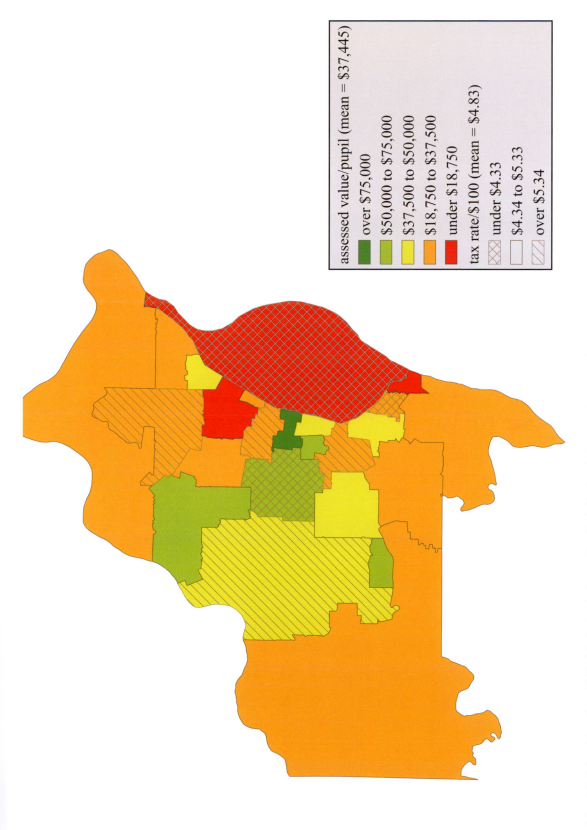

Map 1.5. School funding, 1980–81. *St. Louis County Fact Book* (St. Louis County: Dept. of Planning, 1981); St. Louis Board of Education, General Operating Budget, 1980–81.

assessed value/pupil (mean = $37,445)

over $75,000

$50,000 to $75,000

$37,500 to $50,000

$18,750 to $37,500

under $18,750

tax rate/$100 (mean = $4.83)

under $4.33

$4.34 to $5.33

over $5.34

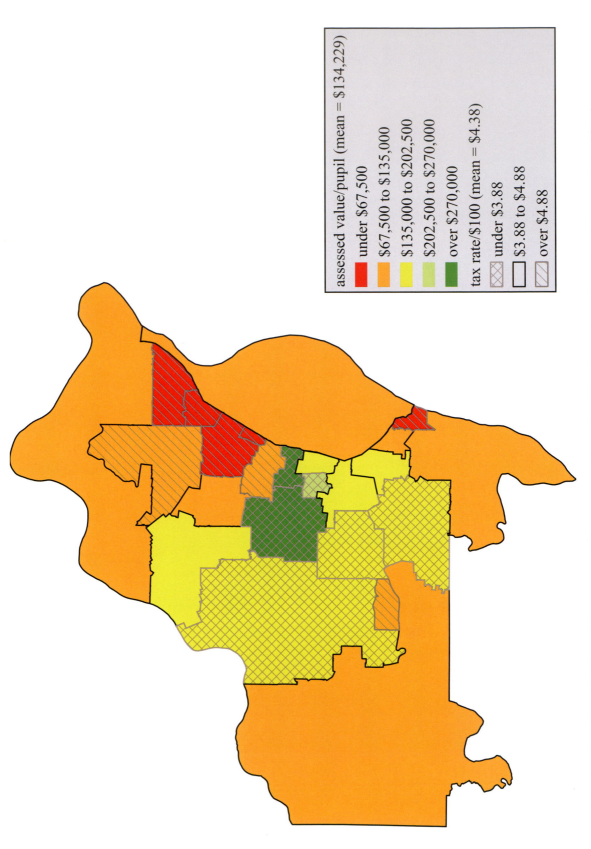

assessed value/pupil (mean = $134,229)

- under $67,500
- $67,500 to $135,000
- $135,000 to $202,500
- $202,500 to $270,000
- over $270,000

tax rate/$100 (mean = $4.38)

- under $3.88
- $3.88 to $4.88
- over $4.88

Map 1.6. School funding, 2001–02. Missouri Department of Elementary and Secondary Education, at http://www.dese.state.mo.us/schooldata/.

local revenues) were exacerbated. Fully developed by the 1930s, the City saw no appreciable increase in its property tax base across the postwar era. Schools, like so much of the City's public infrastructure, were old and expensive to maintain. City schools (reflecting the patterns of residential segregation detailed in Chapter 2) were starkly segregated; indeed, before the *Brown* decision in 1954, most African American students living in St. Louis County were bused *into* the City. While there was little organized resistance to school desegregation after 1954, the region's desegregation plan was unusually protracted and expensive—and swallowed much of the state money earmarked for urban schools. And supplemental funding was scarce, as school bond issues won little biracial support in a city whose remaining white population was elderly and overwhelmingly Catholic (and hence more invested in parochial schools). All in all, St. Louis city schools (whose population, by 2000, was 81 percent African American, and 76 percent eligible for reduced fee school lunches) had much more in common with other central city schools than with other schools in Missouri.[66]

School funding was but one marker of the City's larger fiscal crisis. St. Louis, in this respect, was at the mercy of both the meager local funding options made available by state law and the larger logic of central city finance—in which aging infrastructure, stagnant property values, depopulation, and deindustrialization combined to create a "self-aggravating downward fiscal spiral."[67] The first challenge for the City was the utter collapse of property tax revenues. While the assessed value of St. Louis County grew steadily (increasing more than tenfold between 1920 and 1960), the City's tax base remained flat. Assessed values in the City collapsed during the Great Depression and did not recover to prewar levels until 1951. The real (inflation-adjusted) value of City property peaked in the early 1950s, declined slowly into the middle 1960s, then dropped precipitously into the 1980s. To make things worse, delinquencies and redevelopment schemes were removing large swaths of the City from the tax rolls altogether. The assessed tax base in 1975 was actually smaller than it had been in 1955, a situation that did not improve when statewide property tax reforms mandated new assessments in the late 1970s and early 1980s.[68]

Over time, the City's reliance on the property tax faded—in part because it was an increasingly meager source of revenue, and in part because City officials and St. Louis area legislators pressed the state to open new revenue streams. Through the early postwar era (see Figure 1.1), the City turned first to the new earnings tax. This would become the City's most important source or revenue and, into the late 1960s made up most of the ground lost by the property tax. As property and income tax revenues (taken together) slipped in the early 1970s, the new City sales tax and (more importantly) state and federal aid took up most of the slack. As federal commitments retreated in the 1980s, the City turned increasingly to direct charges. Indeed, by 1984 the City reaped more from the operation of Lambert Field (about $44 million) than it did from either property taxes ($32.5 million) or general sales taxes ($43.7 million).[69] Unlike many of its urban peers, St. Louis was reluctant to make up the gap by borrowing. In the first decade after the war, the City approved only two small general obligation bond issues ($4 million for garbage collection in 1946, $1.5 million for urban renewal in 1953). In 1956, voters approved a sprawling, multipurpose $100 million bond (a large chunk of which was needed to leverage federal highway money).[70] But City borrowing remained modest until the early 1980s, when debt grew quickly—surpassing revenues in 1986 and very nearly doubling revenues by the mid-1990s (see Figure 1.2).

Alongside the declining importance of the property tax, City interests focused their attentions on local disparities in revenue—and particularly the burden of carrying "blighted" properties on the tax rolls. In 1936, the City Plan Commission (with support from the federal Works Progress Administration) calculated the tax revenues and tax burdens for a cross-section of City neighborhoods. Their findings (see Map 1.7) confirmed the longstanding arguments of city planners: that inner-city residential districts cost far more to service than they collected in taxes, and that these "blighted areas" were effectively subsidized by commercial and higher-end residential neighborhoods.[71] "St. Louis has been losing population to the county at such a rapid rate in the last few years," concurred the League of Women Voters in 1941, "that soon it will be left with its slums and too few taxpayers to support them." Early postwar planners reprised these fears, arguing that the City's growing slums were "subsidized directly by the higher value residential districts" and that (as of 1950) substandard housing stock accounted for barely 6 percent of City revenues but fully 45 percent of City spending.[72]

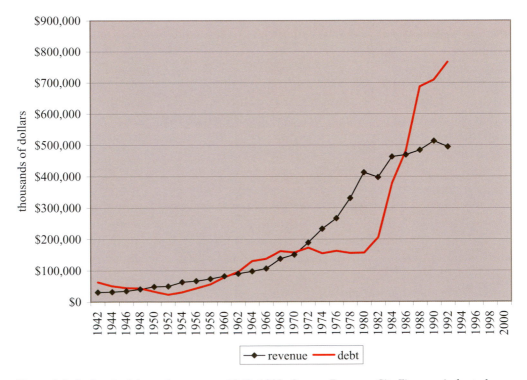

Figure 1.2. St. Louis debt and revenues, 1942–1992. Census Bureau, *City Finances* (selected years) through 1990; Census Bureau, *Government Finances* for 2000, http://ftp2.census.gov/govs/estimate/.

$261.52

$0.08

$50.35

$42.32

($22.95)

($31.96)

$664.33

$64.84

$12.00

($31.79)

$11.46

($18.55)

$10.63

Central Business District

industrial

residential

Map 1.7. Net tax revenue or cost, selected St. Louis districts (based on average annual tax revenues and cost of services, 1930–1935). WPA Project 1443; City Plan Commission, *Urban Land Policy* (St. Louis: City Plan Commission, 1936), table 1.

The prevalence of underutilized, vacant, and delinquent properties animated the politics of postwar urban policy. While the legality of urban renewal rested on "police power" protection of public safety and morals, city planners and private redevelopers routinely cited the uneven incidence and burden of local taxes as their primary concern. The nagging irony of this argument, of course, was that urban renewal eroded the tax base in the name of saving it. We look more closely at urban renewal and its limits in Chapters 4 and 5; the important point, for the moment, is this: As redevelopment reclaimed blighted properties and transformed them into "higher uses" (stadiums, convention centers, public housing), it also exempted them (on varying schedules under different urban renewal programs) from paying property taxes. As of 1978, by the estimate of one alderman, barely half of the City's property base was still on the tax rolls: 30 percent (by value) was tax exempt (churches, schools, city- or state-owned) and nearly 20 percent had been abated under urban renewal programs.[73] "Why must the people be the goat?" one constituent wrote the mayor, ". . . tax exemption and parks will not supply funds to run the city."[74]

The argument contained a touch of hyperbole, as property taxes (by the late 1970s) hovered near 10 percent of all City revenues. But it did capture the dilemma faced by those charged with reclaiming or redeveloping the central city. The urban "growth machine" was essentially a compromise between private interests (banks, realtors, developers), whose prosperity depended on the value and exchange of property, and governments, whose revenue depended on growth in local property values, sales, and incomes. Yet, if the long-term goal of local planners was rebuilding the tax base, their favorite short-term strategy was to dismantle it—the equivalent, in local public policy terms, of burning the village in order to save it.

The economic and demographic crisis of St. Louis—given both the structure of local taxes and the pervasive disadvantages faced by the central city—was also a fiscal crisis. And, over time, the conditions that made local revenues so scarce and local services so expensive spilled over into the inner-ring suburbs—especially in the near north County between the City and Lambert Field. This is captured in Map 1.8, based on work by Myron Orfield's Metropolitan Area Research Corporation (MARC), which sketches the fiscal capacity of the region's incorporated municipalities and counties. The average across the region (MARC examined the metro area's six Missouri counties but did not include the Illinois side) was $1,088 per household. This is a rough measure of the rate at which local governments could raise local revenue, the actual dollar value less important than the benchmark for gauging tax capacity across the metro area. At the time of the survey (1997–98), much of St. Louis County (including its unincorporated portions) fell within a few hundred dollars of this average. Stable, high-capacity municipalities extended west through the central County. The region's low-capacity municipalities—those that MARC judged significantly stressed by a combination of high demands and low revenues—included St. Louis itself and most of the inner-ring suburbs running north from (and including) University City.

This, in St. Louis and elsewhere, was the lasting legacy of fragmented metropolitan governance. Successive rings of suburban development poached the central City—and later the inner-ring suburbs as well—of their population, their wealth, and their tax-

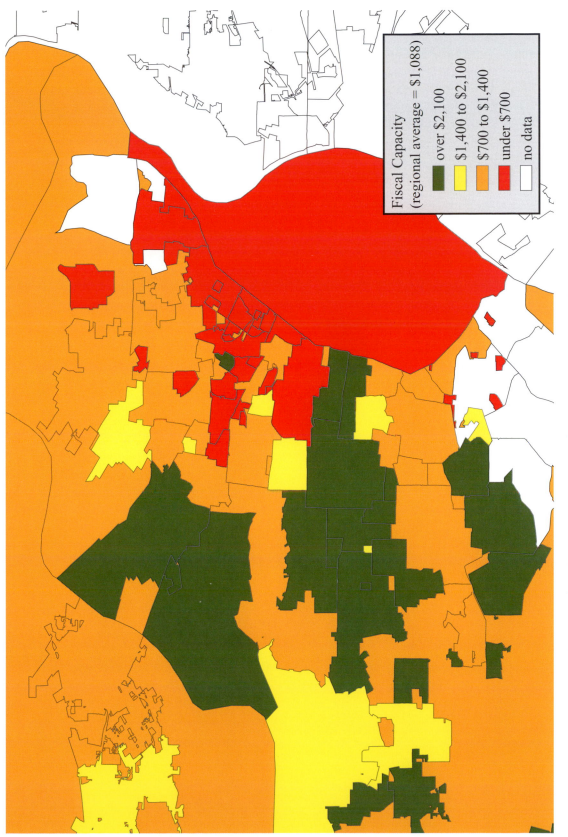

Map 1.8. Fiscal capacity (county and municipality), 1998. Metropolitan Area Research Corporation, *St. Louis Metropolitics* (St. Louis: Metropolitan Area Research Corporation, 1998), appendix A.

Fiscal Capacity
(regional average = $1,088)

- over $2,100
- $1,400 to $2,100
- $700 to $1,400
- under $700
- no data

able value. This was a pattern at once abetted by local public policy (zoning, taxation, and economic development in competing fragments of the metropolis) and only half-heartedly addressed by state (school funding) and federal (urban renewal) palliatives. Local interests left behind had little to offer but this (as Myron Orfield aptly carica-tured the civic boosterism of the City and its inner suburbs): "Please come to our community: Our schools are fast becoming impoverished, we will tax you to death or skimp on services."[75]

Chapter 2
"The Steel Ring"

Race and Realty in Greater St. Louis

The history of 4635 North Market, and of greater St. Louis, is bound up in a tangle of local, state, and federal policies that explicitly and decisively sorted the City's growing population by race. These policies yielded both an intense concentration of African Americans in certain wards or neighborhoods of St. Louis itself and a virtually unbreachable wall between the City and its suburbs. The isolation of African Americans on St. Louis' near northside was accomplished and enforced in a variety of ways; some private and public strategies of exclusion overlapped and reinforced one another, others were cobbled together as legal challenges prohibited some of the more direct tools of segregation. At the center of this story was the local realty industry, which lobbied for explicitly racial zoning in the World War I era; pursued and enforced race-restrictive deed covenants into the middle years of the century; pioneered the practice of residential security rating, which governed both private mortgages and public mortgage guarantees; and—as a central precept of industry practice—actively discouraged desegregation of the private housing market.

Zoning and the "Negro Invasion," 1914–1917

The first such effort was quite blunt. At a time when cities were first exploring the politics and legality of local zoning, St. Louis was one of a handful of cities to propose—as a matter of municipal law and policy—formalizing racial segregation. The logic of "permanent protection from intrusion of business or nuisance of all kinds" was already embedded in local agreements governing land use on the City's private streets. These central city subdivisions (notably Bell Place just north of Forest Park and Vandeventer Place between Forest Park and downtown) were developed in the late nineteenth century as tracts of exclusive "high caste residence property." By design, and by mutual agreement among all property owners, these streets prohibited commercial use and other "nuisances," set a floor (in Bell and Vandeventer Places, $10,000) for the value of single-family homes, and (with an exception for live-in servants) barred occupancy by nonwhites.[1] But the practice and scope of private zoning was quite limited. Such agreements offered no guarantee that private subdivisions would not be eventually surrounded by commercial and racial nuisances, and they offered no protection whatsoever to conventional residential neighborhoods. In St. Louis and elsewhere, these anxieties sparked early interest in citywide rules for land use. And, in St. Louis and elsewhere, the push to clean up the City by regulating the location of tanneries or stockyards or tenements extended logically to the "nuisance" of black occupancy as well.

The fear of "negro invasion" in St. Louis was best expressed, and carefully orchestrated, by local realtors. In 1915, the St. Louis Real Estate Exchange (SLREE) created a new organization—the oddly named "United Welfare Association"—to drum up support for a racial zoning ordinance and to use new initiative and referendum procedures (established by the 1914 City Charter) to place a zoning ordinance on the 1916 ballot. In its campaign, the Exchange (the United Welfare Association shared an address and key officers with the SLREE, and donations to the petition drive were payable to the Exchange) hammered away at the fundamental threat to property values. "Before buying a home in an unrestricted locality, a man usually ascertains very nearly just what his interest, taxes, repairs, etc. are going to cost him," one pamphlet put it, "but there is no present method by which he may determine how much the property will depreciate because of NEGRO invasion." Protection from such an invasion, by this logic, was as reasonable and responsible as fire insurance:

DO YOU REALIZE that at any time you are liable to suffer an irreparable loss, due to the coming of NEGROES into the block in which you live or in which you own property? . . . Perhaps you do not think your neighborhood will be invaded. Neither do you believe you are going to have a fire when you pay your fire insurance. While perhaps you have not yet been affected by this class of people coming into your neighborhood, you surely want protection against this growing danger which is more menacing than fire or the elements. At present you have no remedy in a matter of this kind.

The urgency was starkly evident in those neighborhoods already lost. "LOOK! Look at these homes NOW! An entire block ruined by negro invasion," a photographic postcard of West Belle Place shrilled, "Every house marked 'X' now occupied by negroes. ACTUAL PHOTOGRAPH OF 4300 WEST BELLE PLACE. SAVE YOUR HOME! VOTE FOR SEGREGATION!"[2]

Proponents of racial zoning drew on the principle and practice of school segregation and argued that "mutual restriction" was in the interest of both races. The formal legislative purpose of the ordinance was "to prevent ill feeling, conflict and collisions between the white and colored races in the City of St. Louis," although this logic was often quite tortured: "no self-respecting negro," one pamphlet put it, "wants to live among neighbors who are not congenial to him." The terms of the ordinance itself were fairly straightforward: It barred blacks from purchasing a house or residing on blocks that were more than 75 percent white and vice versa (with an exception for live-in domestics). Where such thresholds challenged existing patterns of occupancy, the law included "reasonable provision whereby gradually such blocks may become in time occupied wholly by either white or colored people." The meaning and implications of the 75 percent rule were clear when applied to existing residential patterns.

The ordinance designated as "Negro blocks" (see Map 2.1) the entire Ville, three blocks of Finney Avenue and West Belle Place running west of Vandeventer, pockets of the central industrial corridor just west of the central business district, two small enclaves near the rail corridor just south of Forest Park, and two small enclaves on the south riverfront.[3]

Despite the efforts of the NAACP and others, the measure won passage by a substantial margin—joining a scattering of such laws, mostly in border cities (Baltimore, Norfolk, Va., Winston-Salem, N.C., Louisville, Ky., Greenville, S.C.). The St. Louis law and others like it were subject to immediate political challenge—both on "equal protection" (Fourteenth Amendment) grounds and as an unwarranted intrusion of the local police power into private property rights. The ordinance sat in legal limbo for about a year until it was effectively struck down when the Supreme Court ruled against a similar Louisville law in *Buchanan v. Warley* (1917). In the wake of *Buchanan*, local property owners and realty interests were torn between their fear of state encroachment on private property rights and their desire to contain and segregate the growing African American population. The solution, in St. Louis and elsewhere, was the restrictive deed covenant.[4]

Hemmed In: Restrictive Deed Covenants

Restrictive covenants attach specific restrictions to the use and resale of property, typically incorporating most of the terms and trappings of conventional property zoning—including rules for building size and placement, density, allowed commercial use, and the like. And covenants served essentially the same purpose as zoning: by setting contractual standards for land use, they freed developers and homeowners from the vagaries of nuisance law and bound future owners to the same standards.[5] Builders and developers routinely attached such covenants to the original title on new properties. In turn, they could be added to deeds after the fact in the form of a restrictive agreement among neighboring property owners willing to "agree with each other and mutually bind themselves" against the intrusion of objectionable use or occupancy.[6] These restrictions, which in most states could not legally run in perpetuity, ran for a term of 20 to 50 years, binding both the original signatories and any successors in ownership. Use of restrictive covenants grew alongside the modern real estate industry and the urban boom of the early twentieth century; indeed, much of the early form and language of such agreements was the work of the National Association of Real Estate Boards.

In settings such as St. Louis, racial occupancy was the focal point of both original deed covenants and restrictive agreements. "It is to the mutual benefit and advantage of all of the parties," the preamble to most of the St. Louis restrictions read, "to preserve the character of said neighborhood as a desirable place of residence for persons of the Caucasian Race and to maintain the values of their respective properties." The St. Louis covenant at issue in *Shelley v. Kraemer* (the 1948 Supreme Court case that prohibited state enforcement of private covenants) bound "the signatories, their heirs, assigns, legal representatives, and successors in title to restrict the property . . .

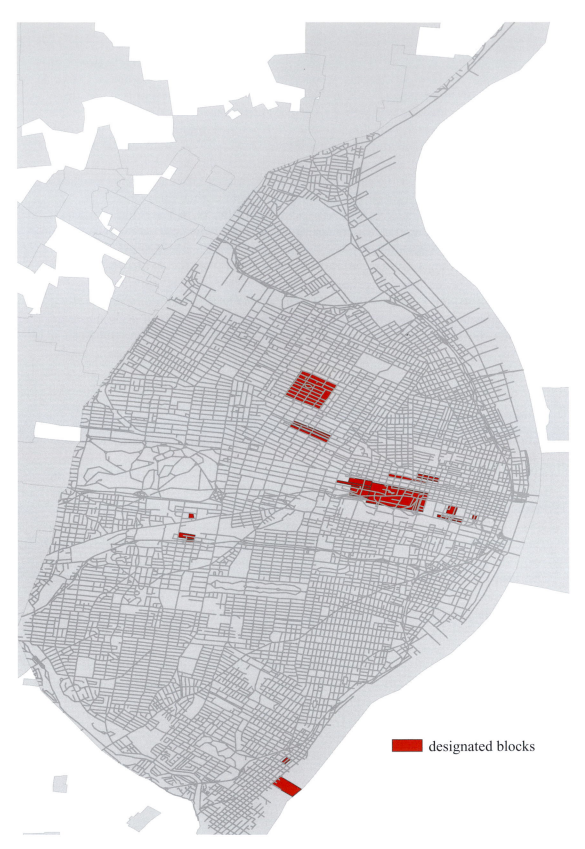

designated blocks

Map 2.1. Designated "Negro" blocks, 1916. "Blocks in Which Negroes May Thereafter Take Up Residence," *St. Louis Post-Dispatch* (2 March 1916), St. Louis Public Library, Clippings Collection.

against sale to or occupancy by people not wholly of the Caucasian race"—specified later in the same document as "people of the Negro or Mongolian Race."[7] The boiler-plate covenant drafted by the St. Louis Real Estate Exchange included "a restriction against selling, conveying, leasing, or renting to a negro or negroes, or the delivery of possession, to or permitting to be occupied by a negro or negroes of said property and properties of the other owners of properties in the said City blocks . . . for a term of such years said attorney may deem proper."[8]

In St. Louis, the earliest covenants (such as those covering the private streets at Van-deventer and Westmoreland Place) did not specify racial restrictions, because black occupancy of such properties was not even a remote possibility.[9] But race-restrictive agreements began to appear as early as 1911. The urgency of race-restrictive covenants heightened in response to the "great migration" spurred by World War I and the accompanying urban turmoil (including race riots in Chicago and East St. Louis). In St. Louis, observers attributed movement of African Americans west from downtown—and the panic of northside homeowners—to both in-migration and the building of a new African American high school at Cottage between Goode and Pendleton.[10] In the wake of *Buchanan* and the war, developers routinely imposed covenants on new subdi-visions, and homeowners associations (often at the prodding of realtors) cobbled them together in established neighborhoods. The view, routinely expressed in the lat-ter, was that such neighborhoods were facing "invasion" and that property values would plummet as soon as blocks were "turned over to them."[11] Such covenants were damaging not only while they were effective but also when they failed: The collapse of a restrictive agreement (which often by its very presence nurtured an "expectation of sudden and rapid racial transition") was like the breaking of a dam. The resulting damage—pent-up demand, rapid property turnover, overcrowding—was swift and severe.[12]

St. Louis covenants typically ran no more than a couple of city blocks (40 to 80 parcels) and often split those blocks—covering the houses facing each other across a street rather than the actual block (circumscribed by four streets). The modest scope of the agreements followed from the strategic and legal importance that all covered properties sign on. In some settings (including Kansas City), the courts viewed restric-tive deed covenants as a contract binding all those who signed; in St. Louis, the courts consistently held that these were "neighborhood schemes" of restriction intended to bind all local property owners—and that incomplete coverage or missing signatures were enough to invalidate agreements.[13] Some restrictions actually specified the cover-age (usually 75 percent of the property frontage) needed to sustain a valid agree-ment.[14] By the 1940s (see Map 2.2), almost 380 separate covenants covered large and strategic swaths of the City's residential property base.

Covenants were common in new developments; indeed, observers estimated that as much as 80 percent of the new suburban housing stock that sprawled west into St. Louis County contained such agreements. "Carefully drawn deed restrictions . . . pro-hibiting commercial and apartment structures, [and] preventing the sale of lots to any person not a member of the Caucasian race," the prospectus for one such develop-ment boasted, "are found in practically all deed restrictions for residential subdivi-

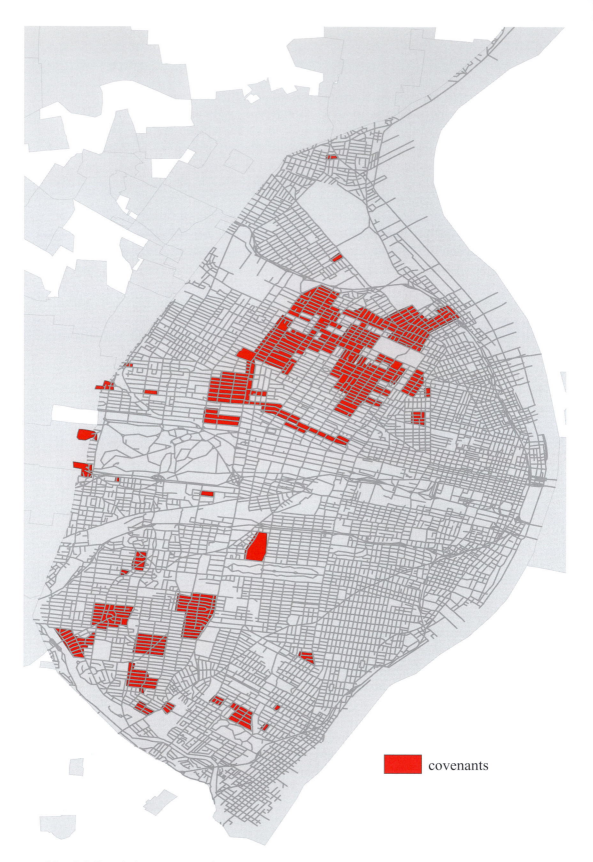

covenants

Map 2.2. Restrictive covenants, St. Louis, 1945. Adapted from Charles Johnson and Herbert Lang, *People vs. Property: Restrictive Race Covenants in Housing* (Nashville: Fisk University Press, 1947), 24, 60.

sion." The covenant accompanying original deeds in the Fox Meadows subdivision (a south County development advertised that "all homesites one acre or more with protective restrictions") specified that "no platted lot or part of any platted lot in said subdivision nor any building or improvement thereon shall ever be sold, leased, conveyed, transferred, willed, devised, or in any way manner given, granted or disposed of to, or occupied by, any person or persons of the Mongolian or Ethiopian races."[15] Suburban restrictions, typically prohibiting "anything which may be or become an annoyance or nuisance to the neighborhood," mimicked—and often stood in place of—municipal zoning well into the 1940s. In one Richmond Hills subdivision, for example, the restrictive agreement included meticulous rules regarding building size and placement, various nuisances (radio broadcasting, fuel storage, cattle, horses, swine, rabbits), and the provision that "no lot or portion of any lot in 'Richmond Hills' or improvements thereon, shall be sold, leased, rented, conveyed, transferred, willed, or occupied by any person or persons not wholly of the Caucasian race." This final provision was set apart, in the agreement, as one for which any violation "shall instantly, per se, operate as a forfeiture of the title to said lot."[16]

The same pattern held for covenants in the City's western or southern reaches. In these more affluent enclaves, covenants offered a largely symbolic or psychological defense and often went hand-in-hand with the development of private streets. Residents in one West End neighborhood went so far as to purchase the street and streetlights from the City in order to impose uniform deed restrictions on the entire property.[17] But more importantly, at least in the St. Louis case, many such agreements were defensive in nature, put together by realtors or ad hoc neighborhood "improvement associations" in response to the tumultuous local history of World War I and the great migration from the rural south that began in the war years. They were the work, as the St. Louis Urban League put it bitterly, of "The Jews, Germans, and Italians in the block, all of whom seem to unite on the common plane of being white to oppose the inroads of colored tenants."[18] Of the 300-odd covenants in place in 1945, about 30 were drafted before 1920, almost half (170) were established between 1920 and 1924, and another third (116) between 1925 and 1929. The creation of new restrictive agreements slowed (as did migration) with the arrival of the Great Depression in 1929, and about 60 new covenants were added during the 1930s.[19] No new covenants were recorded within the City limits during the 1940s, although the pressures of war-era African American migration served, as one observer noted, to "accentuate the already acute housing problem of the colored people within the ring of steel thrown around them by so-called restrictive agreements."[20]

Aside from a few development-specific covenants to the south, St. Louis's covenants formed a ragged quadrangle—bounded by Vandeventer to the east, Kingshighway to the west, Washington Boulevard to the south, and Carter Avenue to the north—at the western boundary of the City's traditionally African American wards.[21] Map 2.3 sketches the reach of these agreements in north St. Louis: the blocks shaded yellow represent the estimate of the local NAACP (as of 1945) as to the general boundaries of restriction; the red parcels identify restricted properties and blocks that I have been able to identify through archival, legal, and deed records; the accompanying

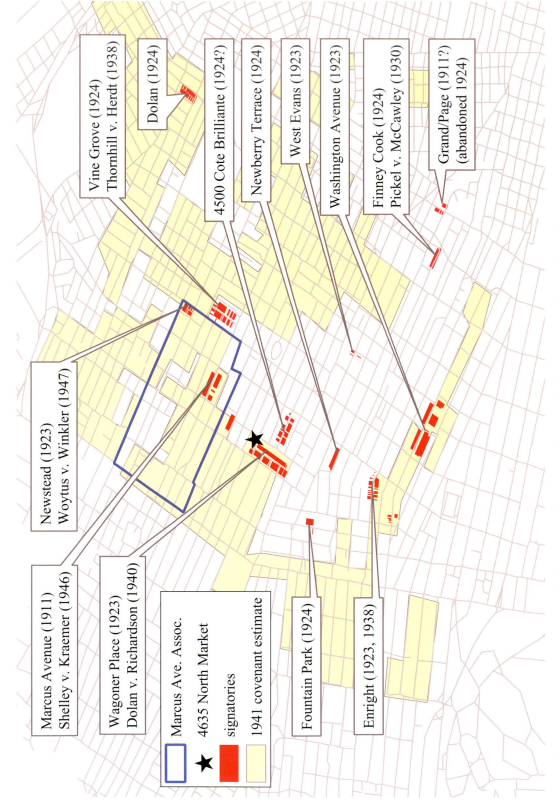

Map 2.3. Restrictive covenants in north St. Louis, 1941. Johnson and Long, *People vs. Property*; Clement Vose, *Caucasians Only: The Supreme Court, the NAACP, and the Restrictive Covenant Cases* (Berkeley: University of California Press, 1959); exhibits and transcripts from *Dolan v. Richardson* (1944); *Kraemer v. Shelley* (1946); *Pickel v. McCauley* (1931); *Meuninghaus v. James* (1930); St. Louis Deed Book 4018:77–81, 4018:339–44, 5896:574–75, SLPL Clippings Collection.

Vine Grove (1924)
Thornhill v. Herdt (1938)

Dolan (1924)

4500 Cote Brilliante (1924?)

Newberry Terrace (1924)

West Evans (1923)

Washington Avenue (1923)

Finney Cook (1924)
Pickel v. McCawley (1930)

Grand/Page (1911?)
(abandoned 1924)

Newstead (1923)
Woytus v. Winkler (1947)

Marcus Avenue (1911)
Shelley v. Kraemer (1946)

Wagoner Place (1923)
Dolan v. Richardson (1940)

Marcus Ave. Assoc.

4635 North Market

signatories

1941 covenant estimate

Fountain Park (1924)

Enright (1923, 1938)

labels identify the agreement, the date it was filed (if known), and any subsequent legal challenge. The parcel-level data provide an incomplete record, but they do offer a sense of the scope of individual agreements—especially where they were most contested.

Across the north side, restrictive agreements were cobbled together like chain letters: Realtors pressed local homeowner associations to canvass for signatures, early signatories went after their neighbors, and the losers were those who committed themselves to an agreement that restricted property but could not stem neighborhood transition.[22] Not surprisingly, given their fragmentary and defensive coverage, these were imperfect instruments. In some cases (as in an agreement on the 4100 block of Page), agreements signed by homeowners were never filed with the City and hence were unenforceable. And, in some cases, African American owners or renters might live on a block for years before local homeowners invoked a longstanding (but little-known) restriction. In 1927, for example, white homeowners dredged up a restrictive agreement covering the 4500 block of Cote Brilliante, an area—at that date—of well-established black occupancy. Suddenly black tenants and owners faced a court order to vacate their homes. As a stopgap measure, some owners sought out white tenants, affording the latter "unusual housing accommodations in property owned by colored people." The St. Louis Urban League weighed in, entering into fruitless negotiations with the Real Estate Exchange. "The Urban League realizes that difficulties attend an expansion of strictly Negro neighborhoods," conceded league president John Clark, "but if we must have them, we think that artificial methods used to control their expansion should operate fairly for all parties concerned." With little prospect of stemming the spread of restrictive agreements, the Urban League argued instead that the Real Estate Exchange should devote some of its attention to rescinding agreements and "opening" some transitional neighborhoods.[23]

This "ring of steel" was breached at points where covenants had never taken hold, had expired, or had simply fallen apart in the face of racial transition. As in other settings, new development not only created new restrictions and exclusions on the suburban fringe but also hastened racial succession and conflict in the blocks and neighborhoods opened up by white flight.[24] In some cases (as at Page and Grand in 1924), property owners voluntarily abandoned a scheme of restriction when the incursion of racial occupancy or commercial development made unencumbered sales more important than neighborhood protection. Indeed, the blocks between the largely unrestricted neighborhoods east of Grand Avenue and the Ville included a number of failed covenants. Here local "protective associations" assembled restrictive agreements in the middle 1920s and were able to evict some black residents, but they could not "hold back the tide."[25]

White homeowners in the 3700 and 3800 blocks of Cook and Finney, for example, were able to garner only a third of the signatures needed to "protect" their neighborhood in the middle 1920s and vainly circulated new (and often competing) covenants covering fewer and fewer parcels. Realtors and officers of a hastily formed Finney and Cook Improvement Association finally broke off their house-to-house canvass and filed two overlapping agreements—one covering properties on Cook Avenue but claiming the signatures of barely a third of the affected property owners and a second (never enforced) covering the south side of Finney. Emma Pickel, a white homeowner, had signed one of the agreements circulated in 1923 (but not the one filed with the City) on the understanding that all her neighbors would sign as well. Instead, "within a very short time the entire neighborhood was densely settled by the colored population of the city" and the "restrictions have been abandoned by all parties concerned." Upholding a lower court's decision to void the restriction, the Missouri Supreme Court concluded (1931) that Pickel and her neighbors were "living under the very conditions and surroundings against which the proposed covenant was to protect them." Or, as Pickel herself put it more bluntly: "If I look out the back window I see negroes, and the front door it is negroes. I am tied up in my own house."[26]

Prior to 1948, such agreements were only successfully challenged in the courts because they had failed. In a few cases, white property owners claimed that the covenant, having failed in its stated purpose, should not prevent them from escaping the neighborhood. Pickel objected not to "colored" occupancy but to the fact that "the restriction covenant on record prevents plaintiffs from disposing of their property." In a similar case on Vinegrove Avenue (near Natural Bridge), landlords in a restricted but transitional neighborhood claimed that their lot was "worthless and without value as rental property unless it could be rented to Negroes." In these settings, agreements were invariably compromised by gaps where white owners refused to sign or black occupancy was already established. In a scattering of other challenges, black homeowners fought eviction on essentially the same grounds: that covenants could not be enforced where black occupancy had already eroded their legitimacy.[27] Only rarely, and not until the 1940s, did any of these challenges raise the constitutionality of private deed restrictions.[28]

Although the reach and legal hold of deed restrictions was uneven, their spatial and political logic was clear. Taken together, the northside covenants were clearly aimed—as both realtors and signatories understood them—at stemming the "contagion" of black residency "spreading westward" or to block the "colonization" of white neighborhoods "at the point of threatened invasion." The drafting of local restrictions was often accompanied by meticulous examination (featuring house-by-house surveys and color-coded plat maps) of the reach and timing of Negro occupancy. The Vinegrove restriction (1924) documented the proximity of "Negro families" and sought to "prevent the further influx of members of that race upon the one particular street." Defenders of one early St. Louis agreement used photographs of nearby neighborhoods to illustrate the danger: "My goodness they are niggers—you can see that." The end result was a frantic, if also fragile, boundary composed of the Mississippi to the east, the commercial core of downtown to the south, and restrictive covenants to the west and north.[29] "Housing is desperately short-handed in St. Louis as it is in most other large cities," the St. Louis Urban League noted in the wake of World War II, "but the lack of housing facilities for Negroes in St. Louis is critical for peculiar reasons. Approximately 97% of the Negro population in St. Louis lives at the geographical heart of the city, surrounded on the east by commerce and business, and on the south, west, and north by neighborhood covenant agreements. There are no outlets to the open county for any kind of expansion. There is a complete circle of restriction.''[30]

In St. Louis, the local real estate industry played an unusually active and formal role in drafting and sustaining restrictive deed covenants. In defense of the industry's core assumption—that African Americans posed a grave threat to property values—the St. Louis Real Estate Exchange maintained a Committee on the Protection of Property whose purpose was "to cooperate with local improvement and protective associations to maintain certain restrictions and shall have the authority to make investigations, to hold hearings, to file charges on violations of restrictions." In most cities, the terms and scope of local covenants varied widely. In St. Louis, fully 85 percent of restrictive agreements used a uniform contract drafted by the Exchange. Realtors launched door-to-door campaigns in threatened neighborhoods, first to organize "neighborhood improvement associations" and then to work through those associations to draft, circulate, and defend restrictive covenants. The Exchange provided local improvement associations with practical and legal assistance, and many of the more active or vigilant associations joined the Exchange as associate members.[31] The most prominent and active of these was the Marcus Avenue Improvement Association, a sprawling organization whose coverage (see Map 2.3) included a number of local restrictions (and nearly 2,000 property owners) south of Natural Bridge and east of Kingshighway—but which assumed responsibility for enforcing the color line across much of north St. Louis.[32]

The Exchange and its officers were also formal parties to most covenants, essentially binding the other signatories (the property owners) to sustain the broader pattern of restriction sought by the realtors:

whereas it is to the mutual benefit and advantage of all parties of the First Part to preserve the character of said neighborhood as a desirable place of residence for persons of the Caucasian Race and to maintain the value of their respective properties . . . [and] whereas the St. Louis Real Estate Exchange . . . is organized to promote the interests of the property owners of the City of St. Louis and is, therefore, in thorough sympathy with such purpose and desires to cooperate in the establishment of said restrictions . . .

Exchange lawyers urged local improvement associations to "impress upon their neighbors the importance of these restriction agreements being in the proper form etc., and that every property owner on every block should sign the restriction agreement without fail." And the Exchange turned to the courts to ensure that local agreements were enforced. Efforts to evade restrictions were more routinely prosecuted as a breach of contract between the property owner and the Exchange than between the property owner and her or his neighbors.[33]

4635 North Market stood in one of the fiercely contested neighborhoods just west of the Ville. In 1922, a few white homeowners formed the Wagoner Place Improvement Association and approached the Real Estate Exchange about putting together a restrictive covenant. Officers of the Exchange went door to door on both sides of Wagoner Place between Easton (now Martin Luther King) Avenue and North Market, soliciting signatures on the 4600 block of North Market as well—including that of

Johanna Schroek, the owner and resident at 4635. The Exchange gathered 73 signatures in the first three months of 1923, crafting a restrictive agreement that captured 79 of 83 parcels. As with most such settings in St. Louis, the local improvement association was more a consequence of the covenant than it was a cause; the boundaries of the neighborhood (see Map 2.3) were determined by the willingness of homeowners to sign the covenant.[34]

The resulting covenant, following the Exchange's now standard boilerplate, imposed two restrictions: the first ensuring that owners did not "erect, maintain, operate or permit to be erected maintained or operated any slaughterhouse, junk shop or rag-picking establishment"; the second ensuring that owners did not "sell, convey, lease, or rent to a negro or negroes, or deliver possession to or permit to be occupied by a negro or negroes (no matter how the right to occupancy or title shall be attempted to be acquired)." From the perspective of any individual signatory, the agreement identified both "other owners of property" and "the President, Treasurer, and Secretary of the St. Louis Real Estate Exchange" as parties to the covenant.[35] In March 1923, the covenant was filed with the City's recorder of deeds, with a "sunset" (expiration date) in 20 years.[36]

Over the next twenty years, 4635 North Market changed hands numerous times. In 1924, Johanna Schroek died and title passed to her brother Jacob. In 1933, the property was sold to Ambrose Altnether, who conveyed it to his brother Joseph in 1937. In July 1941, the property was purchased by Henrietta Good, who sold (in a matter of months) to Victor and Esther Zubenia. At this point, the property was clearly trading hands in preparation for a legal confrontation: The Zubenias immediately sold to an African American couple, Inez and Scovel Richardson. Scovel Richardson, a law professor at Lincoln Law School (the University of Missouri's "separate-but-equal" law school) was interested in both purchasing the property and challenging the legality of the restrictive covenant of which it was a part (a few years later, Richardson would lay out the legal and strategic groundwork for the *Shelley* case). As expected, the Richardsons' right to purchase was immediately challenged by Ray Dolan and John Wehmeyer (officers of the St. Louis Real Estate Exchange), who argued—in this case and in a similar challenge up the street at 4649 Market—that Negro occupancy would "destroy the desirability of the homes of the other lot owners, in said area, and will destroy the value thereof."[37]

Following the lead of successful challenges to neighboring covenants, Richardson argued that demographic change had broken the logic and the legality of the covenant, pointing out that Wagoner Place was by 1941 "surrounded on the South and East by over 70,000 colored persons." Such covenants were especially destructive during the rapid urbanization that marked the early years of World War II: "enforcement on the border of a district wholly or predominantly colored would strike a severe blow to the public health, morals, safety, and general welfare," the defendants maintained, because "it would accentuate the already acute housing problem of the colored people within the ring of steel thrown around them by so-called restrictive agreements." Finally, and most profoundly, Richardson objected to the overarching assumption that equated black occupancy with blight: "I cannot help but have personal feelings about it, and the word 'Negro' to my mind denotes something black and despicable, and if I am to be classified as a Negro according to this agreement, along in the same category with slaughterhouses, junk shops, and rag-picking establishments, it is impertinent and scandalous to me. I have always stated that I am a colored person and an American citizen."[38]

Richardson prevailed at the circuit court level, largely because the original covenant had been so haphazardly assembled. The Exchange and its lawyers found it difficult to establish the accuracy or legitimacy of many of the original signatures. And Richardson's legal team raised serious questions as to whether officers of the Exchange had misrepresented the nature of the covenant and the participation of other property owners while gathering signatures in 1923. The appeal dragged on, delayed by Richardson's employment in the Office of Price Administration and a bout of appendicitis suffered by opposing counsel. The Exchange tried to rally local homeowners in 1943, hoping to use fears about local schooling to renew the covenant—efforts that were pressed by the neighboring Marcus Avenue Improvement Association, which saw its Wagoner Place counterpart as weak and insufficiently vigilant. The Exchange appealed the decision, but the original covenant expired while the case was awaiting trial and the court of appeals declared the issue moot. The Richardsons lived at 4635 North Market for 17 years.[39]

To this point the courts had occasionally vacated agreements that had failed or expired but also routinely held that—like all private contracts—restrictive deed covenants were legal and enforceable. Signatories, and their successors in ownership, were bound by the covenant for its duration and liable for civil or criminal prosecution if they violated its terms. While the Supreme Court had found, in *Buchanan,* that a racially restrictive zoning ordinance deprived private property owners of the right to sell their property, it hesitated to apply the same logic to deed covenants. In *Corrigan v. Buckley* (1926) the highest court upheld the practice, reasoning that the construction of such private agreements did "not involve any constitutional question" and that their enforcement—while a thornier issue—was not a concern because it had not been at issue in the lower courts.[40] The constitutionality of "state action" in support of restrictive covenants resurfaced in the 1940s. The World War II era, in St. Louis and elsewhere, saw a flurry of challenges to restrictive agreements—driven in equal part by the activism of the NAACP and others and by demographic pressures on the boundaries of older covenants. The *Richardson* case was part of this, as was a more famous St. Louis case that would ultimately end up in the Supreme Court: *Shelley v. Kraemer.*

The circumstances in *Shelley* closely resembled that of the covenant surrounding 4635 Market. The Marcus Avenue neighborhood was about six blocks northeast of Wagoner Place, in a similar position on the fringe of the predominantly African American Ville. The Marcus Avenue Improvement Association—which at its peak claimed to represent upward of 2,000 property owners—drew its color line along the northern blocks of Taylor, Cora, Marcus, and Euclid; and along the western blocks of Easton, Cote Brilliante, Leduc, Hammett, Cupples, Northland, and Labadie. The covenant in question (dated to 1911, expired in 50 years and restricted occupancy by any "persons not wholly of the Caucasian race or to persons of the Negro or Mongolian race") claimed more modest dimensions (see Map 2.3): It covered the property fronting Labadie Avenue between Cora Avenue to the west and Taylor Avenue to the east, encompassing 39 owners and 57 parcels of land—of which 30 owners (representing 47 parcels) had signed the restriction.[41]

By the late 1930s, the hold of the covenant was clearly loosening. The Improvement Association convened for the first time in five years in 1937—a meeting marked by anxiety about "Negro" encroachment, the expiration of the original covenant, and (most specifically) "the sale of property at 4610 Labadie Ave. to Negroes." In subsequent years, the association worked to shore up neighborhood boundaries, striving (as in a 1944 meeting) to "secure new restriction agreements when the existing ones lapse, also to secure agreements where none exist." The sale of 4600 Labadie in October 1945 crystallized the fears of the Exchange and its local representatives in the Improvement Association, who immediately challenged its legality. The defendants, J. D. and Ethel Shelley (African Americans) purchased 4600 Labadie through a sympathetic straw party; the immediate past owner was a party to the restrictive agreement by succession (the property had changed hands seven times since 1911) but not one of the original signatories. The plaintiffs, Fern and Louis Kraemer, were parties to the covenant when they took possession of 4532 Labadie in 1927 and were chosen to represent the Improvement Association because Fern Kraemer's mother had been a party to the original agreement.[42]

Of the 14 parcels running west of 4540 on the southside of Labadie, only 7 were included in the original covenant. Of the remaining 7, 5 were already owned by African Americans and had been (with the exception of one recent purchase) for almost 25 years. Indeed, the initial circuit court decision in 1946 found for the defendant (Shelley), not on constitutional grounds but because the agreement in question (as in *Richardson*) was sloppily assembled and "for want of finality and completeness" had failed in its purpose.[43] This decision was reversed on appeal to the Missouri Supreme Court, which rejected the lower court's argument that the covenant's uneven coverage undermined its validity and (invoking *Buckley*) held that enforcement by the courts did not transform a private agreement into "state action."[44]

The Supreme Court disagreed and decided in 1948 that while restrictive covenants were, of themselves, private contracts that "cannot be regarded as a violation of the equal protection clause of the Fourteenth Amendment, judicial enforcement by state courts of such covenants is inhibited by the equal protection clause."[45] In the wake of the decision, private parties were free to draft such agreements but could not turn to the courts for their enforcement. While the pace of restriction slowed, *Shelley* did not end the practice. Existing agreements remained in place, and new agreements continued to be recorded into the early 1960s. Since the decision prohibited state enforcement but not the restrictions themselves, it left open the option for aggrieved homeowners to sue for damages when restrictions were breached. And, for their part, realtors immediately began to explore "various schemes for circumvention . . . without violation"– noting, "some will hike prices 'selectively.' Some will use options to repurchase. Some will organize communities around a social club that is 'exclusive.'"

Homeowner associations, particularly in new developments, could use a right of "first refusal" to control resale.[46]

The Gatekeepers: Private Realty in Greater St. Louis

Realtors and "threatened" neighborhoods redoubled their efforts to corral African American occupancy during the in-migrations that accompanied both world wars. Each era, in turn, was marked by legal challenges to such efforts, resulting in Supreme Court decisions prohibiting racial zoning (*Buchanan*) in 1917 and state enforcement of restrictive deed covenants (*Kraemer*) in 1948. Yet patterns of residential segregation hardened in the decades that followed. Why? The answer lies in a tangle of private practices and public policies that overlapped and outlasted the legal life of the restrictive deed covenant, but pursued and reinforced the same goals.

Restrictive deed covenants formalized the racial policies of local realtors, but these policies existed and persisted in many other forms. Realtors and local real estate boards were dedicated, above all else, to the maintenance of property values. Toward this end, the professional code of the National Association of Real Estate Boards (NAREB), first adopted in 1924, specified that "a Realtor should never be instrumental in introducing into a neighborhood a character of property or occupancy, members of any race or nationality, or any individuals whose presence will clearly be detrimental to property values in that neighborhood." The local Real Estate Exchange incorporated identical language in its own code of ethics (also adopted in the early 1920s) into the late 1940s. Real estate boards, in St. Louis and elsewhere, adhered to the professional conviction that African American occupancy was a public nuisance and a threat to property values. *Fundamentals of Real Estate Practice* put it in 1943:

The prospective buyer might be a bootlegger who would cause considerable annoyance to his neighbors, a madam who had a number of Call Girls on her string, a gangster who wants a screen for his activities by living in a better neighborhood, a colored man of means who was giving his children a college education and thought they were entitled to live among whites. . . . No matter what the motive or character of the would-be purchaser, if the deal would instigate a form of blight, then certainly the well-meaning broker must work against its consummation.[47]

After 1950, both the local and national codes dropped the explicit racial reference and held simply that "a realtor should not be instrumental in introducing into a neighborhood a character of property or use which will clearly be detrimental to property values." But realtors clearly continued to base home values as much on the class or racial homogeneity of the neighborhood as on the physical structure. In 1962, the American Institute of Real Estate Appraisers defined "neighborhood" as an "area exhibiting a fairly high degree of homogeneity as to housing, tenancy, income, and population characteristics."[48]

These guidelines and assumptions shaped the practice of real estate in Greater St. Louis. Beyond its role in creating and enforcing restricted neighborhoods, the Real Estate Exchange also regulated and constrained its members even where no covenants existed. (Like many professions, real estate was segregated well into the 1960s. Black realtors in St. Louis belonged not to the Exchange but to a separate Real Estate Brokers Association).[49] After losing the fight for segregation by zoning in 1916, St. Louis realtors moved to accomplish the same ends by regulating real estate transactions. In 1923, the Exchange adopted, by referendum of its members, three "unrestricted zones"—a proposal that originated in "an executive committee of 17 improvement and property protective associations which have been devising methods to prevent invasion by Negroes." Corresponding roughly to the boundaries of the City's historic black neighborhoods and to the spread of restrictive covenants on their western borders, the unrestricted zones included the entire area east of Grand between Chouteau and Case (the one district, as the local NAACP noted, "in which a so-called 'Protective" or 'Improvement' society does not exist and is therefore 'conceded' by the Real Estate Exchange") and two smaller parcels just to the west (see Map 2.4).[50]

Perhaps better considered a restricted zone covering the *rest* of the City, these unrestricted zones rounded out—as a professional code of conduct—what the legal mechanism of the restrictive covenant could only accomplish by patchwork. "The exchange would recommend that none of its members sell or rent property outside the designated districts to Negroes." Realtors selling to African American buyers outside the restricted zone stood to lose their licenses. Both the City's Real Estate Exchange and the Missouri Real Estate Commission routinely and openly interpreted sales to blacks in white areas as a form of professional misconduct. As of 1930, the City Plan Commission estimated that just over 80 percent of the City's African American population lived within the boundaries of the "Negro" districts established by the Exchange in 1923. In 1941, the 1923 zones were collapsed into a single restricted district whose western and northern boundaries were determined largely by the reach of restrictive deed covenants.[51]

Far from relaxing such restrictions over time, the Exchange underscored them in response to perceived threats, including the in-migration of the war years, the legal challenges culminating in *Shelley v. Kraemer*, and the specter of "blockbusting" in the 1950s and 1960s. Even when a covenant collapsed and realtors acknowledged that a neighborhood had "turned over to colored people," the Exchange refused to adjust its larger sense of the boundaries between white and black.[52] In the wake of *Shelley*, the Exchange quickly "approved a recommendation of the Committee on the Protection of Property that no realtor shall sell to Negroes, or finance any transaction involving the purchase of a Negro of any property north of Easton Avenue and West of Marcus avenue, nor elsewhere outside of the established unrestricted districts." "The method being used here in St. Louis," as Marcus Avenue Improvement Association attorney Gerald Seegers noted, "is to have the Real Estate Exchange zone the City and forbid any member of the exchange under pain of expulsion to sell property in the White zone to a Negro. If the real estate men refused to participate in the sale, the breaches will at least be minimized to those who deal which each other directly or through . . . a nonmember of the exchange who could be easily identified and boycotted."[53]

In the aftermath of 1948, the Exchange did not hesitate to use the threat of professional sanction or boycott. "Our Board of Directors wishes to call to your attention our rule," the Exchange reminded its members in 1955,

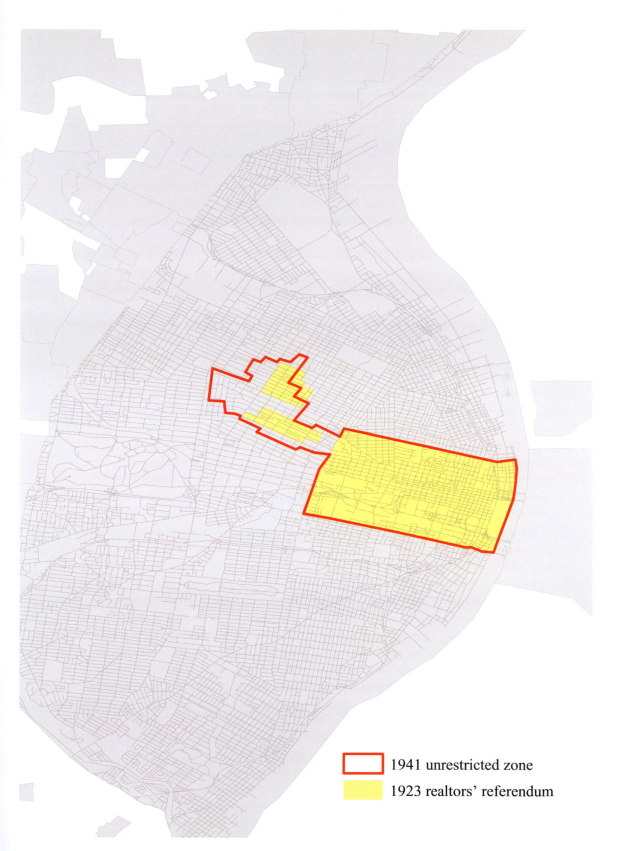

1941 unrestricted zone

1923 realtors' referendum

Map 2.4. Real Estate Exchange restricted zones, 1923 and 1941. Johnson and Long, *People vs. Property*; City Plan Commission, "Distribution of Negro Population" (1930), MHS maps collection; "Plans Advance to Solve Negro Housing Problem," *SLPD* clipping in NAACP Papers, 12C, 16:0191.

that no Member of our Board may, directly or indirectly, sell to Negroes, or be a party to a sale to Negroes, or finance property for sale to or purchase by Negroes, in any block, unless there are three separate and distinct buildings in such block already occupied by Negroes . . . This rule is of long standing, and has our interpretation to be directly associated with Article 34 of the Code of Ethics of the National Association of Real Estate Boards.

In 1958, the Exchange revised its rule to allow one black occupancy per block, essentially "giving up" in much of the City to the inevitability of white flight ("like lava from a volcano") and racial succession. By this point, there was more bluster than bite behind the Exchange's position on City property, as racial transition was often accomplished by intermediary practices—including "contract" sales to black buyers—which bypassed the conventional institutions of residential realty and home finance.[54] The rule of three was still followed in St. Louis County, where racial homogeneity—buttressed by a history of deed covenants and exclusionary zoning—remained a realistic goal. Such warnings also met realtors making even occasional forays into the St. Louis market. "While you are not an active member of the St. Louis Board, you are an active member of the County Board and therefore a REALTOR," the Exchange admonished one suburban broker in the early 1950s; "we would therefore request that you not be party to a transaction involving property in the jurisdiction of the St. Louis Board *which its members are restricted against in the interest of the welfare of the community. . . .* We realize that you may not be familiar with the rules and regulations of our Board in *the matter of where Members may deal in property to Negroes;* therefore this communiqué is sent to you as one of information and not condemnation."[55]

These strategies (and the assumptions behind them) were bolstered by the day-to-day practice of selling and leasing real estate. St. Louis newspapers listed rental and resale properties available to African Americans under a separate "for colored" heading into the late 1950s. Those listed as available for black occupancy were, in turn, crowded into the boundaries of the "Negro Community" bounded by Delmar to the south, Union to the west, Natural Bridge to the north, and Grand to the east.[56] African American realtors tracking these advertisements noted both dramatic fluctuations in overall rental and housing stock and the paucity of options for black renters and buyers. The number of ads for rental property stood at nearly 1,500 in late 1941 (of which fewer than 100 were listed "for colored"). This shrank dramatically as the war boom hit St. Louis: only 300 properties were listed in mid-1942, shrinking to 10 or 20 in the late war and early postwar years—virtually none of which were available to African Americans. As the housing stock recovered, the split market remained intact: of nearly 800 rentals listed in 1956, only 175 were available to blacks. The pattern for property sales was even starker. The ratio of "for colored" options to the larger housing market was 10 of 1,600 in 1940, 80 of 2,200 in 1945, 250 of 3,700 in 1950, and 250 of 4,400 in 1955. Factoring in the uneven availability of federal mortgage insurance, the St. Louis Urban League estimated that, of the roughly 70,000 housing units built in the City and St. Louis County between 1947 and 1952, fewer than 35 were available to African Americans.[57]

This spatial and racial sorting was reinforced in the world of personal contacts and referrals that shaped storefront realty. In St. Louis, discriminatory practices were documented by prospective black homeowners and renters, and by a grassroots "Freedom of Residence" (FOR) committee (which both logged complaints and employed white and black "checkers") established in 1961.[58] Confronted by prospective black clients or FOR checkers, St. Louis realtors routinely denied that apartments or houses were available, often pulling them off the market (or advising the sellers to do so) in response to expression of interest or offers to buy. "We never sell to colored," boasted one realtor in 1969. "When they ask for a specific house, we tell them there is already a contract on that house"—adding that office staff were routinely reminded that "a house is not to be shown to colored."[59]

Realtors also routinely steered clients by race: Regardless of their stated preferences or price range, black clients were only shown houses in transitional neighborhoods in inner-ring suburbs (especially University City) while white clients were warned away from the same neighborhoods. As black employment at McDonnell Douglas (located near St. Louis' suburban airport) expanded in the mid-1960s, prospective homeowners were directed to housing in the City or in Kinloch, the lone African American suburban enclave. In the early 1990s, officials in University City acknowledged that it was "common practice for real estate agents to steer blacks into neighborhoods north of Olive Street Road and west from Sutter Avenue to the Olivette city limits." And even in recent years, prospective buyers and fair housing advocates have routinely charged local realtors with steering African Americans to homes in certain limited geographic areas.[60]

The efforts of FOR and others, alongside the accumulation of local, state, and federal fair housing legislation, eventually curbed the worst of these practices. But the end result (often little more than consent decrees forcing realtors to sign their own Real Estate Board's "Code of Fair Housing Practices")[61] could neither magically integrate neighborhoods nor undo the damage done by decades of explicit discrimination and restriction. In the late 1960s, realtor Jerome Howe assured a client that he could "weed out niggers," while admitting that, as president of the Real Estate Board "sometimes he had to talk out of both sides of his mouth . . . he is more prejudiced than he used to be, and had considered that maybe he should not have accepted the Presidency of the Real Estate Board because of his prejudices, but it has turned out there is no conflict." Most viewed the City's "fair housing" efforts as an understaffed and underenforced sham. Realtors, white homeowners, and others continued to equate black occupancy with blight and collapsing property values.[62]

Even in settings—most notably University City—where local officials tried to make integration work, progress was mixed. In drafting an urban renewal proposal in 1962, University City officials candidly feared that redevelopment might bring with it an influx of "lower class transients and Negroes." Once that transition was under way, the City responded with efforts to stem blockbusting (including a ban on "for sale" signs) with its own fair housing ordinance. But such efforts were trumped by realtors who scoffed at "social do-gooders" and continued to steer white clients away from "changing" neighborhoods. In 1970, the *Post-Dispatch* observed bluntly that University City was "no longer one of the more desirable areas of St. Louis County," citing as its first reason "a great influx of minority groups." In the eyes of local civil rights groups, realtors' "concession" to fair housing amounted to little more than giving up on pockets of the County (especially inner-ring suburbs such as University City) in order to protect the rest.[63]

Subsidizing Segregation: Public Policy and Racial Restrictions

The practices and assumptions of private realtors distorted not only the market for housing but also local and federal public policies that subsidized and regulated that market. The first sustained push for real estate subsidies came during the Depression, which had devastated both the construction and banking industries. Following on the heels of the 1931 Housing Conference, the Hoover administration established the Federal Home Loan Bank (1932) which included the Home Owners Loan Corporation (HOLC). The HOLC was joined, in 1934, by the new Federal Housing Administration (FHA), the New Deal agency that established the basic framework (low down payment, long-term amortization) for modern home ownership by offering federal insurance on qualifying mortgages. Alongside the FHA and HOLC, the New Deal also established federally chartered (and insured) savings and loans and encouraged a wide array of private lenders to plunge into the primary and secondary mortgage markets created by government-backed loans. In the FHA's first five years, it backed the financing of nearly one-quarter of all non-farm home sales. This swelled during the war to nearly one-half of all sales, and then settled in at about 20 percent through the 1950s and early 1960s.[64]

Neither the FHA nor means-tested public housing programs (discussed below) made much of a dent in the persistent urban housing crisis, even as federal housing policy was recast—first around the boundless optimism of the Great Society, later around the fiscal pessimism of the 1970s and 1980s. New initiatives included loan guarantees and below-market rates for developers of low-income housing (1961), rent subsidies for qualifying families living in market housing (1965), federal subsidies (low rates, closing costs) for low-income homebuyers (1968), and federal "Section 8" vouchers for private leases.[65] Over time, the federal strategy drifted from mortgage insurance for middle-income buyers and "big box" public housing for the poor to a variety of programs intended to disperse and privatize federal commitments. The net result, however, was clear and consistent: federal policies abetted white flight and racial restrictions, subsidizing both the market for private real estate and its prevailing commitments to segregation.

All this began, innocently enough, with federal assistance to local planning efforts in the 1930s. Between 1933 and 1940, the St. Louis city assessor completed a massive revaluation of the City's property tax base, made possible by an army of researchers and inspectors (over 700 in all) paid by the New Deal's Civil Works, Federal Emergency Relief, Works Progress, and Work Projects Administrations. Beyond the basic assessment of building size, age, and condition, the revaluation focused on a range of "social and economic influences," foremost of which were the neighborhood density of relief recipients, building vacancy, tenancy, and Negro occupancy. The result (summarized on Map 2.5) was a formula for discounting property values, ranging from 45 percent across much of the central riverfront and downtown to 30 percent through most of the City's African American neighborhoods to 20 percent in the transitional neighborhoods to the west, including the entire strip running west to University City—to 10 percent in the bulk of the City's western residential neighborhoods. The only "full value" property in the City, by this reckoning, lay in the far northwest and southwest corners bordering St. Louis County—the latter largely protected by deed covenants.[66] Such assessments were reflected more broadly in civic politics, as city planners (especially through the 1940s and 1950s) routinely equated black occupancy with "blight" and watched its expansion north and west like the spread of a disease.[67]

These assumptions were replicated and reinforced by the mortgage insurance programs maintained by the FHA. During its heyday from the late 1930s through the late 1950s, the FHA wedded its mortgage guarantee programs to an elaborate system of rating prospective borrowers, properties, and neighborhoods. New suburban developments, by the FHA's reckoning, were vastly preferable to the "crowded neighborhoods" and "older properties" found in central cities. Indeed, the FHA (and the private banks and realtors it nurtured) viewed racially, ethnically, or economically heterogeneous neighborhoods as inherently risky and unattractive. The FHA's policy of deferring to "community standards" underwrote the efforts of white suburbanites to segregate by class and race: Until 1950, FHA regulations held simply that "if a neighborhood is to retain stability, it is necessary that it be occupied by the same racial and social classes." "White flight" suburbanization, in this respect, was the last resort (at least for those who could afford it) of the defensive localism—including bitter protests against the construction of public housing and the anxious profusion of neighborhood and homeowners' associations—that marked American cities during the demographic upheaval of the 1940s and 1950s.[68]

The importance and impact of the FHA/HOLC, as Kenneth Jackson and others have demonstrated, lay both in its transformation of the home mortgage market and in the criteria it used to sort the good risks from the bad. For this, the federal government turned fatefully to the architect of racial zoning and restrictive deed covenants, the real estate industry. The HOLC (which did most of the local "risk rating") followed the lead of private lenders and assumed that neighborhoods "invaded" or "infiltrated" by African Americans had lost all value. The HOLC used a variety of measures—including lot size, setback, owner occupancy, and racial homogeneity—to determine the creditworthiness of individual properties and entire neighborhoods. The FHA, as Robert Weaver (who would serve as secretary of Housing and Urban Development in the late 1960s) noted in 1948, had "turned the agency's operations over to the real estate and home finance boys." Four years later the NAACP scored what it viewed as an "extension of racial discrimination and segregation abetted and furthered by a government agency backed by billions of dollars of insurance secured by taxpayers' money" and concluded bitterly: "We are breaking down the ghetto in old housing only to see federal funds being used to establish impregnable ghettos in new, desirable suburban developments."[69]

The FHA's willingness to sustain and succor segregation was captured in its under-

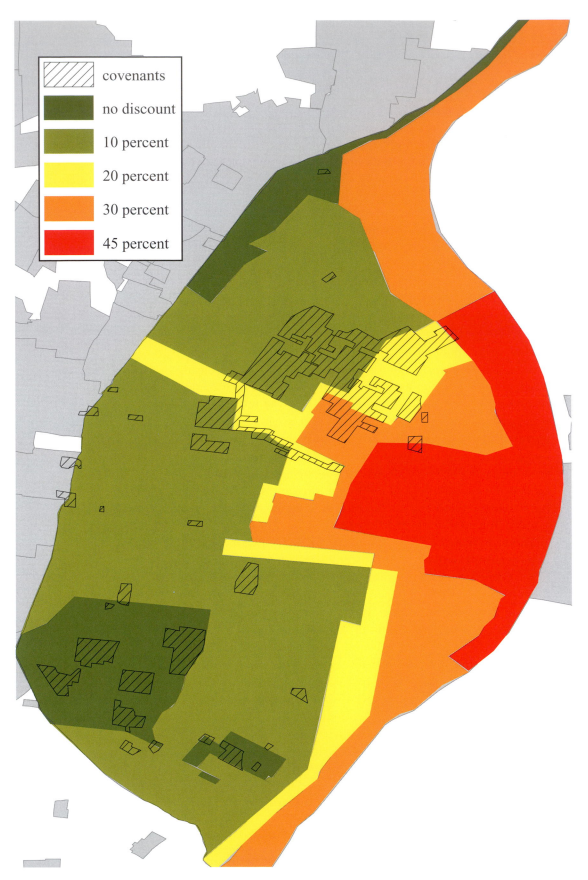

Map 2.5. Residential districts, 1940 (assessed value discounts based on location). City of St. Louis Assessment Division, Real Property Valuation Survey (1933–1940), plate 22.

writing manuals, which echoed the language of similar guides maintained by real estate boards and lenders. Early on, this included explicit support of restrictive deed agreements. "Restrictive covenants should strengthen and supplement zoning ordinances," the 1938 underwriting manual put it; "restrictions should be recorded with the plat, or imposed as a blanket encumbrance against all lots in the subdivision, and should run for a period of at least twenty-five to thirty years." Foremost among its "risk rating instructions" for appraisers, the manual noted that

Deed restrictions are apt to prove more effective than a zoning ordinance in providing protection from adverse influences. Where the same deed restrictions apply over a broad area and where these restrictions relate to types of structures, use to which improvements may be put, and racial occupancy, a favorable condition is apt to exist. Where adjacent lots or blocks possess altogether different restrictions, especially for type and use of structure and racial occupancy, the effect of such restrictions is minimized and adequate protection cannot be considered to be present . . . it must be realized that deed restrictions, to be effective, must be enforced.

Among the recommended restrictions, parroting the same juxtaposition of "nuisances" found in many St. Louis covenants, was the prohibition of "undesirable buildings such as stables, pig pens, temporary dwellings, and high fences" and "*prohibition of the occupancy of properties except by the race for which they are intended*" (italics added). Such sentiments appeared again and again, including the warning that "schools should be appropriate to the needs of the new community and they should not be attended in large numbers by inharmonious racial groups."[70] During the housing crisis of the 1940s and after, civil rights groups routinely identified FHA policies as a source of segregation and housing shortage—even as other federal programs (such as public housing) promised to address some of the damage.[71]

In the demographic and legal tumult of the late 1940s, FHA policies changed little. Its 1947 Underwriting Manual removed most direct racial references but still recommended restrictive deed covenants as the best way of "meeting the needs of a particular development and in promoting maximum possible protection." The FHA's blessing was blunted by the *Shelley* decision, whose prohibition of "state action" in support of restrictions called into question not only enforcement through the courts but encouragement through public zoning and underwriting. Yet, while the FHA officially agreed to drop its support of race-restrictive covenants, it privately assured lenders and developers that there would be no real change in policy and raised no objections to the welter of "gentlemen's agreements" (club memberships, repurchase options) that accomplished the same ends. The Supreme Court decision "will in no way affect the program of this agency," one FHA official maintained, reasoning that it was "our longstanding policy not to suggest, require, or prohibit such restrictions [but to leave] such matters solely to the discretion of property owners."[72]

In late 1949, the FHA finally announced that it would prohibit insurance on properties covered by *new* restrictive deed covenants. But this policy did not apply to those covenants already drafted and in place, and (by every indication) the agency backpedaled in practice and rarely let the existence of deed restrictions sink a deal. Into the 1950s, the FHA's manuals continued—in language drawn directly from commercial realty standards—to champion the homogeneity of "user groups." Even as explicit racial references disappeared from FHA manuals, it remained clear—as the NAACP observed—"that 'race' is still one of the basic considerations of the whole FHA procedure no matter what the language used."[73]

In local settings such as St. Louis, the FHA's guidelines were enshrined on a series of "residential security maps" (crafted by the HOLC) that documented the insidious "spread" of the black population and carved the City into risk-rated neighborhoods. Major metropolitan areas were surveyed annually, and each map was accompanied by textual descriptions justifying each (running into the hundreds for a city the size of St. Louis) of the neighborhood ratings. Taken together, the HOLC concluded, these "map and area descriptions . . . embody all the salient neighborhood information required for the intelligent operation of mortgage lending activities."[74]

In its early maps, the HOLC settled on a four-color code: A areas (colored green) were designated "best," B (blue) areas were "still desirable," C (yellow) areas were "definitely declining," and D (red) areas were simply "hazardous."[75] Over the next decade, the HOLC gradually refined and clarified its security ratings. The 1937 area descriptions for St. Louis, for example, described A areas as residential "hot spots" characterized by both good houses and room for further development; they were "new and well-planned . . . synonymous with the areas good mortgage lenders with available funds are willing to make their maximum loans." B areas shared many of the same characteristics but, because they were fully built, showed less promise: "like a 1935 automobile," the HOLC suggested, "—still good, but not what the people are buying today who can afford a new one." C areas were neighborhoods in the throes of blight, characterized by "age, obsolescence, and change of style." D areas were simply those neighborhoods in which "the things now taking place in the C neighborhoods have already happened."[76]

While city surveys and area descriptions took due note of zoning issues and the age of housing stock, their primary concern—and the key to the rating system—was racial occupancy. The standard local area survey form prefaced its narrative description with required entries for local population, the "class and occupation" of residents, the percentage of foreign born and Negro residents, and the degree of "shifting or infiltration." The most commonly noted unfavorable factors in C areas were "*expiring restrictions* [deed covenants] or lack of them" (italics added) and "infiltration of a lower grade population." D areas were almost invariably marked by "infiltration" or the presence of a "colored settlement" or "Negro colony"—and the summary judgment that "the only hope is for the demolition of these buildings and transition of the area into a business district."[77] African Americans did not, in the logic of the HOLC, live in residential areas; they invaded them and compromised them. Remarkably, even on the eve of World War II, the HOLC cited the first "favorable factor" in St. Louis as the "high ratio of families of the German race," who carried with them the "Germanic traits of thrift, industry, and personal integrity." The City's greatest liability, by the same token, was the "continued rapid growth of the already heavy Negro population."[78]

In St. Louis, residential security rating closely followed the contours of both the black community and the "steel ring" (the Real Estate Exchange's "unrestricted zone" and the patchwork of restrictive covenants) that surrounded it. Under the 1937 survey (see Map 2.6) a swath of A ratings extended out into St. Louis County, but cropped up only intermittently in the City: in the West End running adjacent to and north of Forest Park, in a few small northside neighborhoods, and on the City's far southside—all in neighborhoods long covered by restrictive covenants.

When they resurveyed the City three years later, HOLC assessors largely gave up on neighborhoods east of the County line (see Map 2.7). Yellow C zones, especially on the northside, swallowed most of the properties rated B in 1937. This (following the HOLC's criteria) reflected both further "infiltration" by African Americans and the imminent expiration of many restrictive deed covenants (most of which were 20-year agreements drafted in the early 1920s). City neighborhoods rated A in 1937 were almost all downgraded to B. Indeed, the 1940 resurvey designated only two "first grade" areas within the City limits: a few blocks on the County border west of Forest Park and a horseshoe of homes surrounding Francis Park in the City's still lightly and recently developed (the Francis Park area was subdivided in 1929, but the area immediately to the west was not subdivided until the middle 1940s)[79] southwest corner— both of which enjoyed the protection of restrictive deed covenants far removed from the contested neighborhoods of north St. Louis. As a rule, the 1940 A rated zones featured a high rate of owner occupancy and (see Map 2.7) encompassed almost all the 1940 census tracts in which median house value exceed $7,500. D zones, by contrast, were marked by tenancy and lower home values—and included all the City's predominantly black (over 75 percent) tracts.

In 1937, 4635 Market lay near the western boundary of an expansive D zone that swallowed much of the City's predominantly African American wards, extending westward from Grand Avenue into the neighborhoods north of Lindell Avenue and filling in much of the hole in the defensive ring of northside covenants (see Map 2.6). In much of this area, as the accompanying narrative description noted, "Two-story brick, single-family houses predominate, with many two-family buildings and some row buildings." What set this zone apart from comparable B or C districts was partly its age ("The district is about 45 years old, well-built up, rapidly deteriorating"), but what clearly relegated it to D status was the simple (and, for the HOLC unfortunate) fact that "this area is predominantly occupied by Negroes."[80] The same logic was echoed a year later, when the HOLC duly noted the existence of many "large brick and better appearing homes along Enright and Taylor to Sarah Avenue," with the proviso that they were "occupied by colored people."[81] A large C zone ran west from 4635 Market (starting roughly at the boundaries of the Wagoner Place covenant), along the path of African American settlement, out into the County—covering the northern reaches of University City as well as the unincorporated land on its border. For its part, the local FHA office admitted to following these ratings—including the blanket rule that "below Grand Avenue meant no insurance"—at least until 1962. As late as 1968, the "Valuation Instructions for Appraisers" used in the St. Louis FHA office warned against "change in occupancy" or in the "income or social characteristics of the occupants other than those well established in the neighborhood."[82]

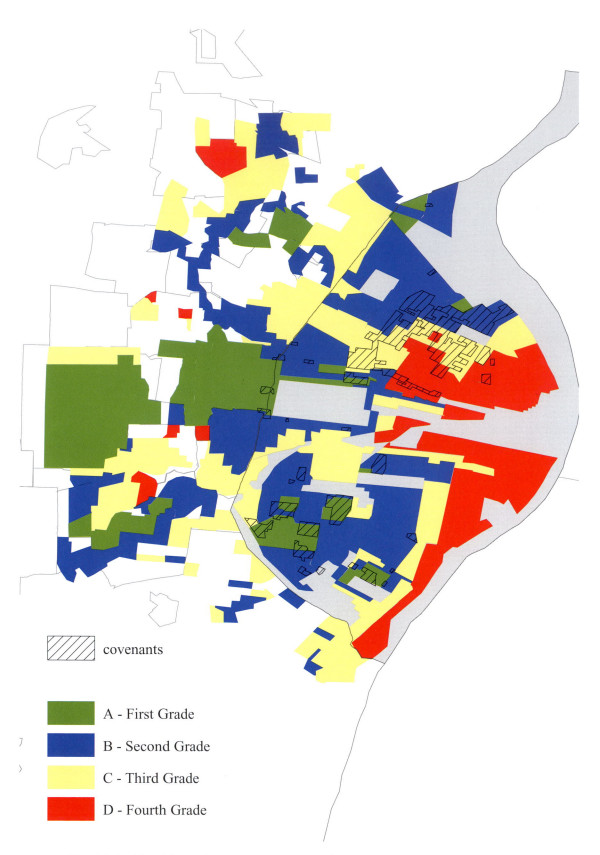

covenants

A - First Grade

B - Second Grade

C - Third Grade

D - Fourth Grade

Map 2.6. Residential security ratings (HOLC), 1937. Charles Hoelscher, "Map of Greater St. Louis," 1937, box 109, City Survey Files, Records of the Home Owners' Loan Corporation, RG 195, National Archives.

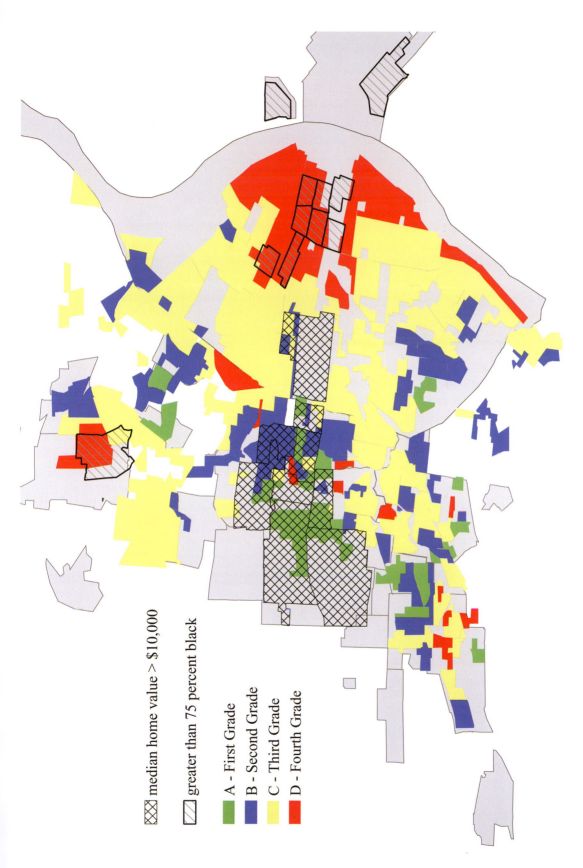

median home value > $10,000

greater than 75 percent black

A - First Grade

B - Second Grade

C - Third Grade

D - Fourth Grade

Map 2.7. Residential security ratings, median house value, and racial occupancy, 1940. Elbring Survey Associates, "Map of Greater St. Louis" (1940), box 2, City Survey Files, Records of the HOLC; 1940 Census (Bogue Files).

It is difficult to assess the precise impact of the FHA rating system on subsequent patterns of private lending and homeownership. The FHA was not a redistributional program but merely promised to make home ownership more widely accessible by securing risks taken by private lenders. Conventional criteria (income, job tenure) still shaped the decisions of banks and mortgage brokers. In turn, the age and density of the City's housing stock, in contrast to the sprawl of new suburban development westward into St. Louis County and beyond, would always draw the attention of the FHA and private lenders alike to the edges of the metropolitan region.[83]

For these reasons alone, the FHA clearly contributed to the white flight and suburban sprawl that left the City—and its African American residents—behind. As Kenneth Jackson has shown, the early FHA was, by design and impact, a largely suburban program. As of 1940, the HOLC estimated that its subsidies were enjoyed by about one of every six residential properties (16 percent) in St. Louis County but fewer than one of every ten (9 percent) in the City. "As matters now stand," one observer noted in 1942, "the FHA practically refuses to insure any mortgage loans throughout the City of St. Louis, while insuring a steady stream of speculative building development in suburban areas." Between 1934 and 1960, the FHA insured 62,772 mortgages in St. Louis County (valued at just under $560 million) and just 12,166 in the City (just under $95 million). In the course of the *Shelley* litigation, federal officials readily conceded that the local pattern of FHA assistance had been decisively shaped by the deference of appraisers and lenders to the reach of restrictive covenants. A survey of just over 400,000 FHA mortgages in greater St. Louis between 1962 and 1967 found that only 3.3 percent went to African Americans—a number that dropped to less than 1 percent (only 56 units) in St. Louis County. "A separate and unequal housing market exists," the Commission on Civil Rights concluded in 1970, adding sadly that federal programs "have had the effect of perpetuating and promoting it."[84]

The FHA also shaped the pace and character of suburban development. For developers of new subdivisions, the highest priority was ensuring that their homes met FHA standards and preferences for single-family, racially homogeneous residential tracts.[85] This was accomplished both by concentrating development efforts in the FHA "green" and "blue" zones that spread west of the City, and by incorporating the same standards in local zoning ordinances. Such ordinances (as I explore in the following chapter) often came at the behest of developers and with the intention of accomplishing a consistent pattern of exclusion. When developers in St. Louis County, for example, wanted the city of Berkeley to adopt a residential zoning ordinance in 1942, they put up $499 of the $500 (the city paid a token $1) it cost to draft the plan—reasoning that "if a zoning law was passed, the FHA would accept the zoning law in lieu of a deed of restriction which they demanded."[86]

But it is a mistake to simply trace the origins of redlining to the FHA and its rating system. There is no systematic locational record of either private mortgages or FHA-insured mortgages in the St. Louis area for the period before the mid-1970s (when federal disclosure rules began collecting such data). A series of FHA maps (circa 1935–40) of new single-family developments in St. Louis County show that most buyers were drawn from adjacent neighborhoods in the City. But such snapshot surveys simply record the market reach of specific suburban developments; it does not necessarily follow that such developments commanded all of the FHA's attention. Federal assessors recognized the failures of the private market—specifically the fact that "areas where mortgage financing may be said to be inadequate embrace most of the East St. Louis portion of the area as well as the older sections of St. Louis . . . and those areas experiencing Negro infiltration"[87]—and made some efforts at redress. Despite its own rating system, the federal government made a modestly substantial investment in central St. Louis—indeed, the highest density of HOLC loans in the region (1935–1939) fell in the northside district bounded by Chouteau to the south, Skinker (the City limits) to the west, St. Louis Avenue to the north, and Grand Avenue to the east.[88] It seems, as Amy Hillier has demonstrated for Philadelphia, that the FHA/HOLC ratings served less to disqualify entire neighborhoods than they did to shape the terms of private mortgages in those areas deemed "declining" or "hazardous."[89]

In effect, the FHA/HOLC ratings acknowledged—and rendered in technicolor—a well-established pattern of residential segregation. In this long and sordid history, the original sin was not the federal rating system but the patchwork of restrictive deed covenants that it embraced. The HOLC echoed the racial anxieties of private realty interests and observed that "local realtors are convinced that solution of the problem can best be obtained by a 'gentleman's agreement' type of arrangement whereby brokers will not undertake to sell property in white areas to persons of the Negro race." But they also recognized that this strategy was failing.[90] The key to the "stability" and "homogeneity" so prized by commercial realtors and federal assessors alike was the deed restriction—a fact conceded by federal officials and clearly reflected in both the descriptive criteria for C and D zones and the precipitous collapse of security ratings on the northside as many of the local covenants ticked toward expiration. For its part, the NAACP deeply resented the ways in which FHA/HOLC appraisals served to "crystallize and extend through federal influence segregation of residence by race," but reserved most of its anger for the federal government's acceptance and promotion of (and later indifference to) deed restrictions.[91]

Taken together, restrictive deed covenants, the practice of realty, and the FHA's "security ratings" reflected and reinforced popular assumptions and prejudices concerning good neighborhoods and bad. Certainly residents and prospective residents of St. Louis understood—without recourse to realtors or FHA maps—which neighborhoods welcomed African Americans and which did not, just as they understood which neighborhoods were "in decline" or "at risk." A 1947 promotional pamphlet, to cite but one example, offered maps of infant mortality, Boy Scout troops per capita, and the density of Negro, foreign-born, and "Russian-born" (Jewish) populations as an index to neighborhood health—all with the tag line "looking for a place to locate? These maps may help you."[92]

And when formal or informal racial boundaries were crossed, the results were often violent. In June 1940, the first black family to move into the 1800 block of Cass Avenue had their car destroyed. When an African American couple, Edith and Vaughn Payne, moved into an unrestricted property at 4645 North Market in September of 1941 they were met with stench bombs and other forms of harassment. This settled into a pattern of intimidation which ran alongside the Real Estate Exchange's formal efforts to evict black residents in the neighborhood covered by the Wagoner Place covenant and elsewhere. The Paynes were busy installing steel gratings and bulletproof glass when the Richardsons moved into 4635 (three doors east) in October—an event that was meet with another round of stench bombs, aimed (over the next few weeks) not only at the Paynes and Richardsons, but also at Jewel Bryant at 4641 Market, Benjamin Harrison at 4649 Market, Emma James at 4570 Market, and Floyd James and John Perkins at 4611 Kennerly.[93]

Segregation and "Slum Clearance": Race, Space, and Public Housing

Federal support for public housing, like the FHA, was a creature of the Great Depression. The Housing Act of 1937, recast in 1949 and 1954, established substantial federal assistance for low-income housing. This flow of federal money (and the local attention and planning it encouraged) held out the promise of counteracting or ameliorating the deeply discriminatory patterns of private realty in settings like St. Louis. Yet federal housing policy had very nearly the opposite result. At the outset, congressional southerners stripped federal housing law of any antidiscrimination provisions. In 1949, public housing was married to the "slum clearance" goals of urban renewal—resulting in both the formal requirement that each newly constructed unit be accompanied by the destruction of a "substandard" unit and the implicit assumption that a primary purpose of public housing was to warehouse those displaced by renewal projects. For political and practical reasons, planning and administration was left in the hands of local housing authorities, who were invariably reluctant to challenge local patterns of racial occupancy. And, because federal programs shouldered the capital costs and local authorities had to cover basic operating expenses, the latter leaned toward bare-bones high-rise projects with few amenities.[94]

For all these reasons, federal housing policy did little to address the paucity of safe low-income housing in Greater St. Louis and actually *deepened* patterns of residential segregation. This was immediately apparent in the regional divergence of local housing policies. Given its unfolding urban crisis and aged housing stock, the City had little choice but to cobble together a housing authority and get in line for federal funds. By contrast, suburban communities ignored the new federal program and declined to even create housing authorities. As late as 1970, isolated (and irretrievably segregated) Kinloch was the only County municipality to claim either a local housing authority or any concentration (150 units) of public housing. As federal housing policy drifted toward private rent and construction subsidies in the late 1960s and early 1970s, local governments (as we shall see in Chapter 3) used preemptive zoning to disqualify proposed developments that carried even a whiff of public assistance. In the later 1970s, both the County and its municipalities risked losing federal community block grants over their stubborn refusal even to consider public housing.[95]

On balance, the impact of federal housing policy was clear: FHA mortgage insurance flowed primarily to the suburbs, subsidizing white flight. Federal public housing assistance flowed primarily to the inner city, cementing the region's spatial organization of race and poverty. Indeed, when the federal government—in the context of protracted litigation over school desegregation—set out to prove that the St. Louis Board of Education was defying the mandate of the 1954 *Brown* decision, both local officials and expert witnesses identified federal housing policies as the prime culprit. "The segregated black community was left to fester," as a City official observed, "while developers aided by the federal government rushed out to build new white enclaves on the city's edge."[96]

The first public housing projects in St. Louis were launched under the terms of the 1937 Housing Act. Clinton-Peabody Terrace and Carr Square Village (both completed in 1942) each consisted of 50-odd low-rise row houses totaling just over 650 units. Clinton-Peabody, south of downtown, was slated for white occupancy; Carr Square, north of downtown, for black occupancy. The war, along with uncertainty over the Missouri tax status of federal housing projects, slowed further construction, and it was more than ten years before the next projects opened: Cochran Gardens (1953) and the Pruitt-Igoe complex (1955–56). These too were planned and built on a segregated basis (with the Igoe homes designated for whites) but all opened as essentially "black" projects. The Supreme Court quashed formal segregation of federal projects in 1955. And, more importantly, relocation pressures from the massive Mill Creek renewal project (which displaced over 16,000—nearly all African Americans) effectively segregated the surrounding neighborhoods. "Igoe was planned and built as housing for white families," Housing Authority officials conceded in 1955. "However, the white families of the neighborhood moved away when the area was cleared. When it became apparent that they had no intention of moving back into what had become almost entirely a Negro neighborhood, Igoe was designated as being primarily for Negroes."[97]

Both local and federal housing officials conceded that the location of major housing projects reflected largely racial considerations—including both neighborhood patterns and existing real estate restrictions. Often this was accomplished by building means-tested projects in black neighborhoods and public housing for seniors in white neighborhoods. Because it was impossible to house "racial minorities outside of the areas to which they are restricted," the FHA's Raymond Foley reasoned in the late 1940s, housing projects were necessarily erected "within these inordinately crowded areas." This practice was especially destructive, as new units lagged well behind those swallowed up by "slum clearance" and local officials turned increasingly to large-scale projects (the basic unit an 11-story high-rise)—including Pruitt-Igoe in the middle 1950s and a series of similar projects (Joseph Darst in 1956, George Vaughn in 1957, and A. M. Webbe in 1961) completed in the next six years.[98]

The racial logic of public housing—within the City and within the region—was especially apparent in its close relationship with urban renewal projects (which I look at more closely in Chapters 4 and 5). Early on, local planners hoped that public housing in the central city would slow the spread of black occupancy or, as Harland Bartholomew put it, "reduce their migration [to] other portions of the city that would not welcome them." As major land clearance projects actually reduced the supply of low-income units, public housing was expected to warehouse those in the bulldozer's path. Federal policy deferred relocation policies to local officials, who routinely steered displaced families by race. For its part, the St. Louis Housing Authority maintained separate relocation offices for white and black residents. The result was twofold: Because the slums and substandard homes targeted for renewal were overwhelmingly occupied by African Americans, so too was the accompanying public housing—widely considered a "dumping ground for families left behind by 'slum clearance'." And because local relocation efforts were so haphazard and halfhearted (of the nearly 6,000 families displaced in Mill Creek, barely a quarter received formal assistance), the African American population moved west and north, creating both new segregated neighborhoods and new demands, in the West End and beyond, for slum clearance.[99] When the City turned to Washington for more help under the Model Cities program in 1967, it all but acknowledged that its past efforts at fair housing and relocation had been inadequate and insincere.[100]

The net result (across the region and across the postwar era) was a pattern of public housing that effectively tightened the noose woven by restrictive covenants, private realty, and the FHA. As Map 2.8 underscores, public housing—and especially the larger projects—was concentrated in the City. Within the City, most of these were built in two clusters, one southwest and one northwest of the central business district. There was little pretense of weaving public housing into the City's existing residential fabric: as one observer noted, "even when they were new, the projects were surrounded by decaying and even abandoned residential and commercial property"—a pattern that continued into the 1970s, often in defiance of HUD's own site standards.[101] Even as federal and local housing assistance moved away from high-rise projects (looking instead to subsidize renters and owners on the private market), public housing and public subsidies remained crowded into the City's black and transitional neighborhoods. Of the nearly 8,000 units made available under various programs between 1950 and 1980, 94 percent were in predominantly (over 75 percent) African American tracts—including *all* of the public housing units and 88 percent of the units subsidized under post-1973 (Section 8) programs.[102]

Even as some of these units cropped up farther west in the City, and out into the County, they were largely in inner suburbs undergoing racial transition. "Federally subsidized services have succeeded in moving many poor people from one place to another," one observer noted in 1970, "but they have provided very few with good housing and have had almost no impact on the poverty problem as such."[103] While the City's public housing policies tended to harden patterns of segregation within St. Louis, those of the County municipalities worked to harden the racial divide between the City and its western suburbs. Urban renewal in St. Louis County, as I detail in Chapters 4 and 5, was often designed and pursued as a means of relocating suburban pockets of African American settlement "back" into the City. For their part, federal officials viewed Greater St. Louis as a stubborn outlier for its resistance to subsidizing housing. "This is the only metropolitan area, the only area in the [four-state HUD] region where you cannot carry on an intelligent discussion of the policies and programs," noted one HUD official, adding that "refusing to accept any responsibility for the problems of the disadvantaged . . . has been profitable for St. Louis County and for several of the leaders in the right sections of St. Louis City." The conclusion was

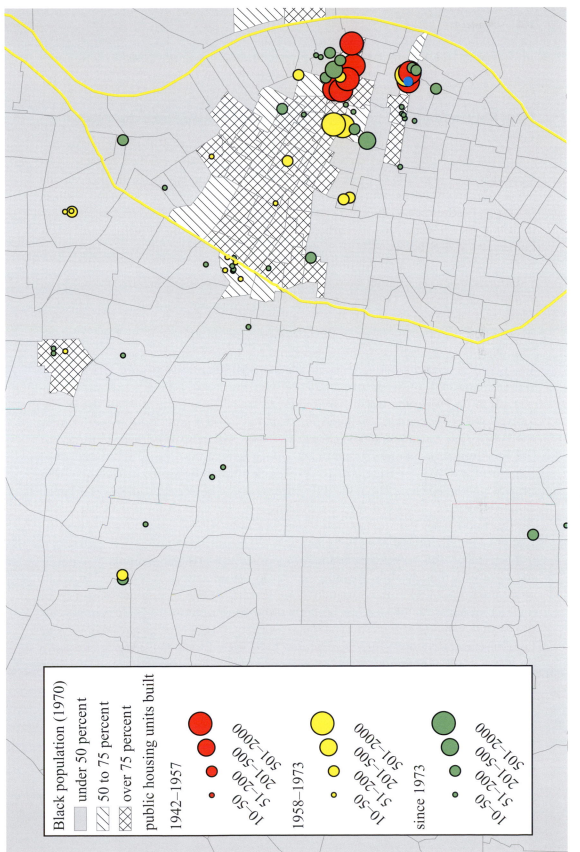

Map 2.8. Public housing and assistance, 1942–2000. 1970 Census (NHGIS); City and County parcel data; various housing reports.

Black population (1970)

under 50 percent

50 to 75 percent

over 75 percent

public housing units built

1942–1957

10–50
51–200
201–500
501–2000

1958–1973

10–50
51–200
201–500
501–2000

since 1973

10–50
51–200
201–500
501–2000

inescapable: "the County is living on borrowed time . . . you are going to solve these problems or the entire metropolitan area will be overrun by them."[104]

Steel Ring to Red Line: Civil Rights and Disinvestment Since the 1960s

Most explicitly racial strategies of exclusion were finally erased in the flurry of civil rights law and legislation of the middle 1960s. City civil rights leaders made at least eight attempts after 1954 to pass a basic public accommodations ordinance, finally succeeding in 1961: The bill erased most of the vestiges of Jim Crow in public settings, but specifically excluded private contracts including "landlord-tenant relationships."[105] Fair housing provisions began to crop up in various Housing and Urban Development (HUD, established in 1965, absorbed the FHA) programs. The city of St. Louis passed its own open housing law in 1966.

In turn—twenty years after the resolution of *Shelley*—another challenge to the exclusionary practices of St. Louis realtors and developers pressed the Supreme Court to outlaw the last vestiges of private deed restriction. In mid-1965, Joseph Lee Jones tried to buy a home in Paddock Woods, an unincorporated subdivision in St. Louis County. The developer, the Alfred Mayer Company, turned Jones away because he was black. Jones filed a complaint in district court but was rebuffed on the grounds that Mayer's refusal amounted to private discrimination and not "state action"—a position supported on appeal to the circuit court. The Supreme Court—on the last day of the Warren Court—disagreed. Ducking the challenge of defining "state action" under the Fourteenth Amendment, the Court's decision in *Jones v. Mayer* instead turned to the Thirteenth Amendment's guarantee: "All citizens of the United States shall have the same right, in every State and Territory, as is enjoyed by white citizens thereof to inherit, purchase, lease, sell, hold, and convey real and personal property." This decision echoed and reinforced the Fair Housing Act (Title VII of the 1968 Civil Rights Act) passed earlier that year, which broadly prohibited discriminatory practices by realtors, developers, and lenders.[106]

The NAREB and its St. Louis branch responded with grudging compliance, pledging to respect the law while advising realtors to manipulate the timing of listings to avoid the point of potential discrimination outright. Realtors opposed "any attempt by force of law to withdraw from property owners the right to freely determine with whom they will deal with respect to their property, irrespective of the reason" and "any measures or efforts which have, or may have, the effect of censoring or abridging the right of a broker to fully advise his client."[107] That advice, logged by the Freedom of Residence Committee and others before and after 1968, maintained the deeply racial assumptions of decades of formal restriction.

Restrictive real estate practices persisted both as a continuation of the pattern set in the middle years of the century and as a response to the disinvestment and physical decay that followed in its wake. Over the course of the twentieth century, the law increasingly prohibited forms of direct discrimination—racial zoning in 1917, state enforcement of restrictive deed covenants in 1948, and discrimination in private sales in 1968. And, especially after 1968, courts and legislators turned their attention to patterns of discrimination or segregation—arguing, in the spirit of the civil rights jurisprudence of the late 1960s, that outcomes could be as important as explicit or observable acts. Title VII of the 1968 Civil Rights Act set the baseline, extending equal protection for prospective buyers and renters to advertising, brokerage services, listings, and lending. The *Jones* decision underscored Title VII and, for African Americans, extended its protections to cover rooming houses and sale-by-owner transactions. Later in 1968, the Missouri Real Estate Commission adopted a fair housing code—adding penalties for blockbusting in 1970. And in 1972 Missouri passed its own open housing law. The result in just a few years, as the Missouri Bar concluded, was a "complete and fundamental change in the law of open occupancy."[108]

All of this was accompanied, however, by an equally fundamental recasting of federal housing policy. In the early 1970s, most federal urban spending was rolled into the new Community Development Block Grant (CDBG) program, and housing assistance turned from bricks-and-mortar spending to direct subsidies to renters (Section 8) or homeowners (Section 235). Just as federal civil rights law reached all corners of the housing market, in other words, federal policy relinquished effective control over housing policy to local and private interests—"yet another chapter," as Gary Orfield noted during his work on the City's protracted school desegregation case, "in the long epic of federally-funded, locally-administered residential segregation and resegregation." Title VII and *Jones v. Mayer* seemed distant promises in a setting and decade marked by the razing of Pruitt-Igoe, the Black Jack zoning controversy (see Chapter 3), and pitched battles between HUD and St. Louis County over the latter's persistent reluctance to accommodate low-income housing.[109] In settings such as St. Louis, quite simply, the damage was done. New fair housing or mortgage disclosure laws made it easier to assess that damage but could do little to reverse it. And efforts to loosen federal housing program standards often proved counterproductive.

Consider the halting efforts of the FHA to retreat from its historic reliance on spatial (and racial) security ratings. Since the late 1930s, FHA underwriting had rated the property, the purchaser, and the neighborhood. In 1966 (in the wake of the urban turmoil of the mid-1960s) the FHA dropped the appraisal of "entire communities or neighborhoods" from this equation—essentially erasing the "redlines" embedded in its longstanding residential security ratings (although the new policy advised appraisers that the new guidelines were not meant to displace longstanding "location eligibility criteria"). Whatever their intent, the new guidelines boomeranged. New FHA loans helped to tip transitional neighborhoods by encouraging high-risk (often predatory) lending, and by making it easier for remaining white property owners to flee.[110]

These patterns were starkly evident after 1968, when the FHA followed up its rating reforms with a new (Section 235) program aimed at low-income homeowners. Section 235 was, in many respects, a bold departure. It signaled the federal government's larger commitment to subsidizing low-income families and individuals, rather than the projects in which they might live. And, within fairly broad eligibility limits, it focused federal policy on prospective homeownership rather than rental assistance. On paper, such programs had the potential to scatter the recipients of housing assistance; in practice, they simply laundered federal subsidies through the deeply discriminatory institutions of private realty: "money and helpless buyers," Orfield concludes, "were simply fed into a segregated market."[111]

The first problem, in this respect, was the continued "steering" of white and black clients. Section 235 was accompanied by counseling programs for low-income buyers, but these were unfunded until the early 1970s—leaving applicants at the mercy of private lenders and realtors. As a rule, black 235 buyers were shown (and purchased) homes in segregated northside or inner-ring neighborhoods (Pagedale, Normandy, north University City) in which they already lived; white buyers—often fleeing transitional neighborhoods—were steered to white suburban neighborhoods (see Map 2.9). Section 235, one black realtor noted, seemed little more than a shell game moving people "from one substandard home to another" so that realtors could collect a commission. Section 235 clients were, a Civil Rights Commission investigation found, sorted by race and "frequently shown one house on a take-it-or-leave-it" basis—a practice readily conceded by local realtors, public housing officials, and the local FHA office. Indeed, HUD was compelled to suspend Section 235 sales in the transitional Skinker-deBaliviere neighborhood when local residents complained that federal subsidies were tipping the local housing market by making mortgages available (in the words of one resident) "to some gal out of Pruitt-Igoe."[112]

This pattern of resegregation was compounded by the dubious practice of locking marginal homeowners into mortgages on substandard housing. Of roughly 1,000 Section 235 mortgages in greater St. Louis, three-quarters were for the purchase of existing houses. Many of these, as one local mortgage company confided at the time, "should have seen their last owner." Section 235, in turn, virtually required that buyers exhaust their household budgets, leaving little for maintenance, let alone renovation. Increased FHA activity, under these circumstances, heightened the instability of transitional neighborhoods—facilitating flight, flipping substandard properties, and (see Map 2.10) yielding a spike in FHA repossessions and foreclosures. The program's performance in St. Louis was so dismal and destructive that HUD suspended all Section 235 subsidies for existing housing in 1971 although subsidies for new construction—overwhelmingly claimed by whites—continued.[113]

Early FHA and public housing policies relied upon or deferred to the expertise and prejudices of local housing authorities and private real estate interests. While federal law clearly repudiated such discriminatory practices after the late 1960s, federal subsidies flowed increasingly through private channels. This focused renewed attention on forms of private discrimination, or redlining. New public commitments to open occupancy left such practices exposed and, by the early 1970s, community groups, including the St. Louis FOR and the local Association of Communities Organized for Reform Now (ACORN) chapter, were pursuing the promise of Title VII in City Hall, in the state capitol, and in Washington.

Redlining took many forms and encompassed not only the willingness of lenders to do business with black clients or in black neighborhoods, but a welter of related concerns—including the availability of homeowner's insurance, the ability to sell mortgages on secondary markets (including federal lenders like Fannie Mae and Freddie Mac), the terms on which credit or insurance were offered, and the ways in which

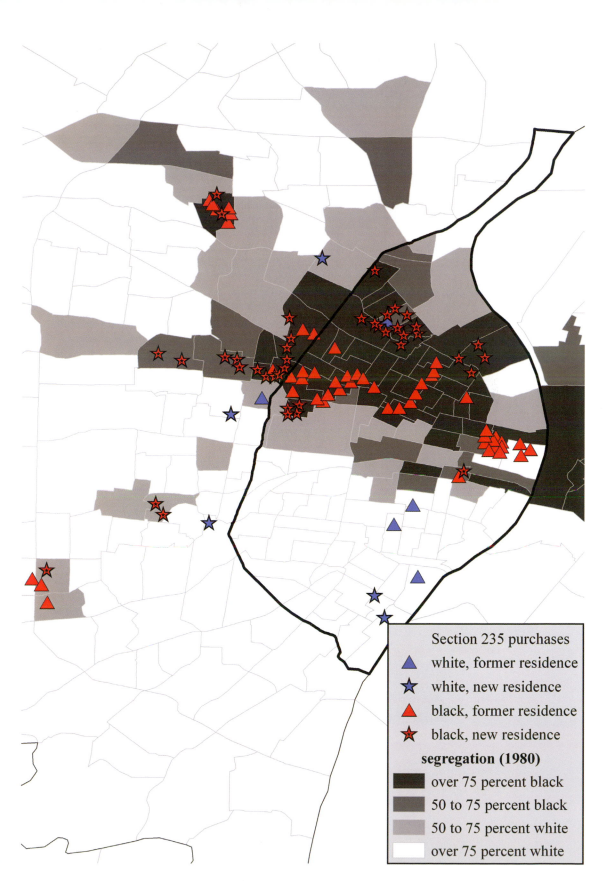

Section 235 purchases

▲ white, former residence

★ white, new residence

▲ black, former residence

★ black, new residence

segregation (1980)

over 75 percent black

50 to 75 percent black

50 to 75 percent white

over 75 percent white

Map 2.9. Section 235 buyers, 1968–1970. USCCR, ''Home Ownership for Low-Income Families'' (June 1971), 22–23; 1980 Census data mapped onto 1970 census tracts (NHGIS).

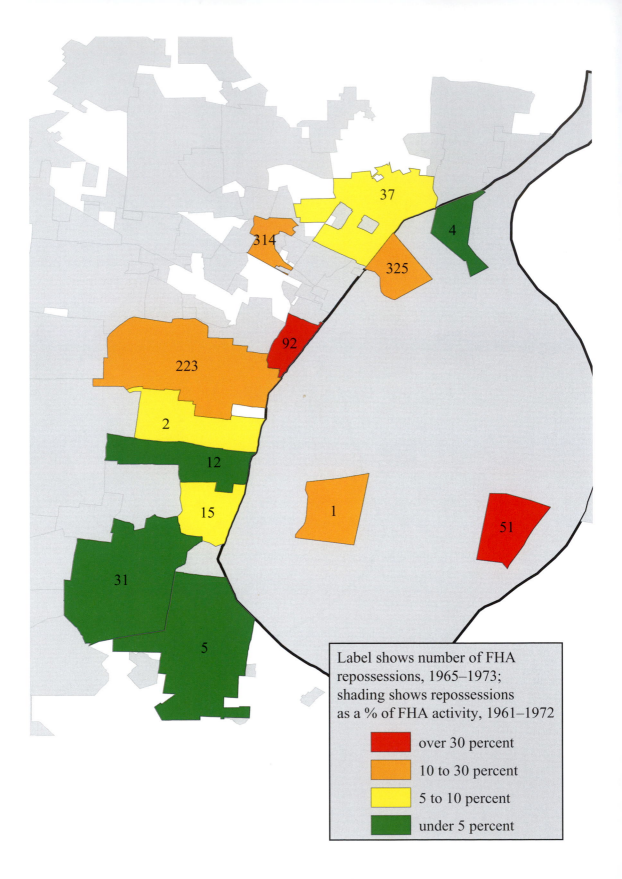

Label shows number of FHA repossessions, 1965–1973; shading shows repossessions as a % of FHA activity, 1961–1972

- over 30 percent
- 10 to 30 percent
- 5 to 10 percent
- under 5 percent

Map 2.10. FHA repossessions, selected areas, 1965–1973. Charles L. Leven et al., *Neighborhood Change: Lessons in the Dynamics of Urban Decay* (New York: Praeger, 1976), 180, table 9.2.

both were marketed (or not marketed) in predominantly black neighborhoods. Discrimination, in turn, was often hard to disentangle from other elements of a loan or an insurance application (including credit history and income) and the costs of doing business in long-neglected central cities. Insurers, for their part, routinely met charges of redlining with the claim that they were responding to "actuarially sound risks such as crime and fire hazard" rather than the race of an applicant or racial profile of a neighborhood. "The higher the risk, the higher the cost of covering that risk," one industry trade group countered in the early 1990s, "There is nothing devious or discriminatory about it."[114]

Before the middle 1970s, fair housing advocates in St. Louis offered scattered and often anecdotal evidence of discrimination by insurers, realtors, and lenders. For their part, lenders and insurers acknowledged (at least privately) the practice of redlining: During early postwar discussions with insurance companies over the prospect of investing in St. Louis, one City official recalled that "the [Equitable] company is thoroughly acquainted with St. Louis and exhibited a map with areas shaded in various colors, which the company uses in considering loans on houses in various areas." Private appraisers did not hesitate to discount properties based on demographic patterns and trends: University City was "no longer one of the more desirable residential areas of St. Louis County," in one such report, because "there has been a great influx of minority groups into the area."[115]

Racial or spatial discrepancies in access to insurance or credit were widely acknowledged but difficult to measure. The Shelleys' purchase of 4600 Labadie (1945) was engineered through a straw party in part because their realtor recognized that "White [people] can secure larger loans, better loans." Mortgages and homeowner's insurance were much harder to get in the City, and the terms or interest rates were much less favorable (as early as the 1940s, surveys found a nearly 2 percent differential in the mortgage rates charged to black and white homeowners in St. Louis). This made it both harder to stem disinvestment and more likely that City properties would churn through foreclosure. A survey of 1972 lending showed little activity in the City and concluded that much of that reflected a few savings and loans rolling over federal repossessions. In 1975, on the eve of the first federal mortgage disclosure law, FOR and ACORN estimated that St. Louis County claimed just over twice as many standard housing units as the City itself, but garnered nearly eight times the access to credit. An investigation by the Phoenix Fund (see Map 2.11) found a precipitous decline in lending (1960–75) by savings and loans across the City, with the most dramatic collapse downtown and across the northside. In the City, they lent one dollar for every 109 dollars on deposit; in the County, the ratio of loans to savings was barely 1:9. The same disparity extended to homeowner's insurance (a prerequisite for most mortgages). Big insurers "are all trying to cut out city business," as one agent admitted, "[but] will carry just a few policies within the city limits to cover themselves."[116]

These patterns emerged more clearly in the wake of the first federal Home Mortgage Disclosure Act (HMDA) in 1976 and the Community Reinvestment Act (CRA) in 1977 (the former required lenders to report data on mortgage applications, including census tract, race and income of applicant, and disposition; the latter imposed

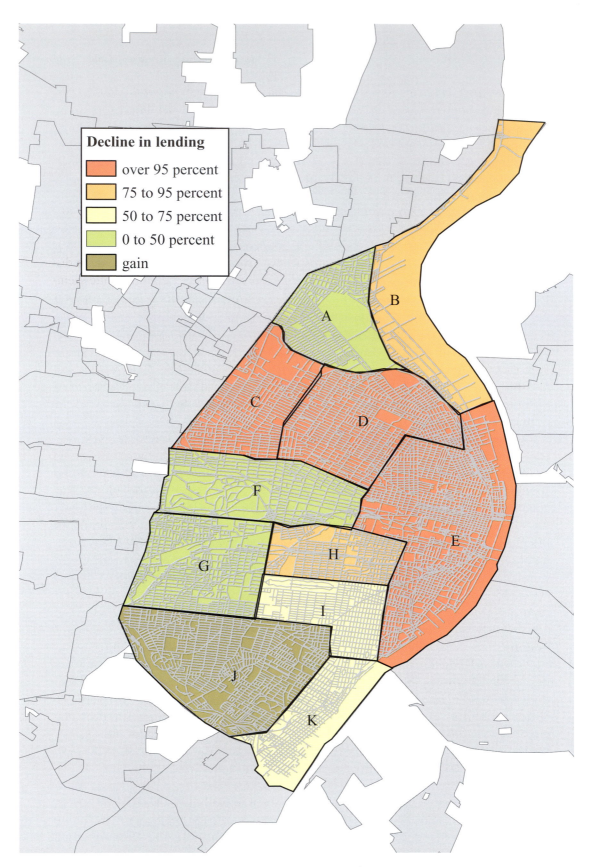

Map 2.11. Decline in lending (saving and loans), 1960–1975. Savings and Loans Lending Activity in the City of St. Louis: A Phoenix Fund Update for 1975 (1976), Imprints Collection, Missouri Historical Society.

broader requirements that banks meet the credit and deposit needs of the entire community they were chartered to serve). The first HDMA survey confirmed what fair housing advocates in St. Louis had long suspected: the City claimed less than 6 percent of all new loans in the metropolitan area, almost all of which were in the southern reaches.[117]

Taken together, the HMDA and CRA provide a wealth of data on lending patterns in greater St. Louis after the late 1970s. Yet, because these laws generated both new rules and new reporting requirements, they offer a skewed portrait: We know the most about financial and actuarial discrimination just at the point when it became harder to get away with. Because lenders simultaneously considered the race and income of the applicant and the location of the prospective property, it is not always easy to distinguish between the spatial and racial logics of housing discrimination. While seemingly the simplest measure, denial rates (by race of applicant or location of property) are not entirely reliable: More aggressive marketing might flood the files with marginal applicants, creating high denial rates for lenders who are otherwise trying to reach out to underserved communities. Conversely, low denial rates might indicate a pattern of predatory lending in transitional neighborhoods rather than a commitment to equal opportunity. And, over the long haul, it is difficult to separate patterns of redlining from larger secular trends in financial services and their regulation.

In turn, and given the multifarious history of residential discrimination in St. Louis, it is important not to overstate the causal implications of spatial lending or insurance patterns in recent decades. An annual HDMA snapshot (see Map 2.12), in this sense, clearly maps the different ways in which lenders assess both applicants and neighborhoods. But, to a large degree, it is also a "paint by numbers" confirmation of past discrimination. Even as both application and origination rates for St. Louis improved in the early 1990s, the underlying pattern—continued sprawl west into the metro area's Missouri counties, and continued disinvestments in north and central St. Louis itself—remained largely unchallenged.[118]

Alongside this general trend, the HMDA data suggest the ways in which older patterns of discrimination persisted in the new regulatory environment. As we have seen, private and federal property assessments both steered investment away from the City and shaped the terms of urban and suburban mortgages—invariably demanding higher rates and shorter amortization in "risky" neighborhoods.[119] Such practices were even starker in the home insurance market. Gathering insurance quotes in the early 1990s (in much the same way that FOR "checkers" had plumbed realty markets a generation earlier), ACORN found that queries from low-income zip codes in the City were far less likely to yield a quote over the phone, and were met with rates that were three to four times as costly (per $1,000 of coverage) as those offered to applicants from the suburbs or elsewhere in the City.[120] Urban policyholders, in turn, relied much more heavily on "limited" plans (despite comparable claim and loss records) and often faced abrupt cancellation after any claim was made.[121]

The HMDA, which allowed federal regulators and local fair housing advocates to assess the ratio between applications and loans or between local deposits and local loans, also made it much easier to identify patterns of institutional discrimination. As

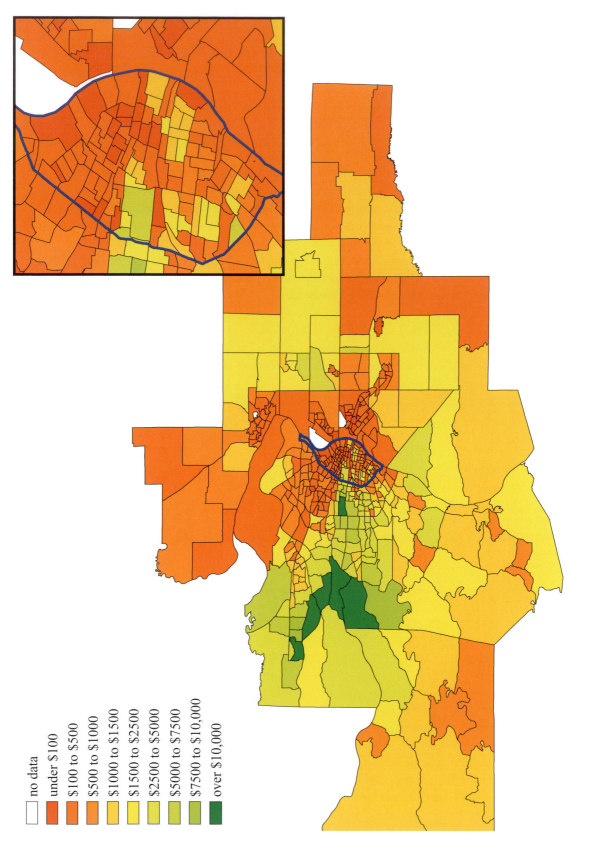

no data

under $100

$100 to $500

$500 to $1000

$1000 to $1500

$1500 to $2500

$2500 to $5000

$5000 to $7500

$7500 to $10,000

over $10,000

Map 2.12. Per capita mortgage lending in greater St. Louis, 2000. 2000 HMDA data; 1990 Census.

Amy Hillier's research on Philadelphia between 1940 and 1960 suggests, loans were made in the central city, but only by some lenders (larger institutional investors, in particular, tended to avoid the central city), at higher interest rates, and at higher risk of foreclosure.[122] Post-HMDA data in St. Louis suggest a similar pattern. Of the nearly $500 million lent by S&Ls in Greater St. Louis in 1977, for example, less than 6 percent (just over 25 million) went to properties in the City—and half of this fell in two zip codes at the City's southern edge.[123] Annual mining of the HMDA data routinely identified individual lenders who systematically avoided doing business in low-income, urban, or minority neighborhoods. On the secondary mortgage market, St. Louis S&Ls reinvested almost nothing, looking outside the MSA entirely for fully 92 percent of their secondary loans.[124] This pattern extended even to the quasi-public secondary lenders, Fannie Mae and Freddie Mac. In 2003, for example, fewer than one in five mortgage applications in predominantly black (over 75 percent) tracts resulted in government-backed loans—a performance that ranked St. Louis next to last (besting only Pittsburgh) among the 32 metro areas with more than 50,000 loan originations. "Local lenders won't make loans in black neighborhoods," one observer noted, "because they can't sell the loan in the secondary market."[125]

Again, the pattern in home insurance was much starker. Residents of predominantly black neighborhoods, as we have seen, found it harder to get insurance, paid more for it when they did find a policy, and often lost coverage the moment they lodged a claim. In a practice evocative of the realtors' agreements of the 1920s or the FHA ratings of the 1940s, some insurers instructed their agents to redline the entire city. In a 1994 investigation, the Missouri Insurance Department unearthed a map of St. Louis in the office of the defendant (Farm Bureau Town & Country Insurance Co.): "The map had the inner city marked with a circle and the words 'ineligible property' were written on it."[126]

Chapter 3
Patchwork Metropolis

Municipal Zoning in Greater St. Louis

The folly of fragmented governance and home rule is most evident in local control over zoning. Local governments interested in maintaining property values and in funding local services by taxing those properties have every incentive to exclude the poor and compete for the rich—to sort the population by race and class in such a way as to maximize tax returns and minimize other demands on the public purse. "At the edge of metropolitan regions," Myron Orfield concludes, "developing communities engage in as restrictive and as low-density a pattern of land-use as their economic circumstances will bear." Zoning, in other words, was a means of controlling access to both housing and the public goods (education, police, etc.) sustained by certain classes of housing or residential development.[1]

Zoning meant very different things to a city and to its suburbs.[2] In suburbia, the dominant practice (emerging in the middle years of the twentieth century) was "exclusionary zoning": land-use controls that ensured a pattern of predominantly low-density single-family settlement through a combination of outright prohibitions (heavy industry, manufactured housing), effective prohibitions (no land zoned for multifamily housing), and area or density standards (minimums for lot size, setbacks, and building size).[3] Older cities, by contrast, did not have the power to zone until long after local land use had been decided by private restrictions and market forces. Zoning laws in such settings were typically marked by widespread nonconformance (people living in industrial zones, for example) and pervasive "spot zoning" (allowances made for commercial lots in residential zones, for example). Unable to compete with the suburbs for high-end residential development, central cities often ran in the other direction—designating large areas for commercial or industrial use (and often "clearing" low-return residential tracts as part of the bargain).

From a metropolitan perspective, the results have not been pretty. Exclusive and fragmented zoning in the suburbs erased any semblance of residential diversity, sorting the white middle class into income-specific single-family enclaves on the periphery and leaving African Americans, the elderly, and the poor to filter into older and higher-density housing stock (much of it unprotected by local zoning) in the central city.[4] Over time, exclusionary zoning also fueled sprawl as those anxious to leave the city, but priced out of established suburban housing markets, leapfrogged to new sub-divisions in unincorporated areas.[5] And, over time, exclusionary zoning created a stark spatial mismatch between the availability of jobs and the availability of affordable housing. Suburbs were not simply bedroom communities from which the middle class commuted to the central city. Workers increasingly criss-crossed the metropolis—from the suburbs to the city, from the city to the suburbs, from one suburb to another.

The Law and Politics of Zoning

From its earliest incarnations, local zoning posed a stark tension between the rights of individual property owners and the goal of sustaining property values by restraining the rights of neighboring property owners. The first local zoning regulations grew out of the same Progressive Era discovery of the urban ills that inspired Lincoln Steffens, Jacob Riis, and others. Efforts to "clean up" the early twentieth-century city included building height restrictions in Boston and Baltimore, prohibition of Chinese laundries (as "nuisance" industries) in residential areas of Los Angeles, and a 1916 ordinance in New York City designed to protect tonier residential neighborhoods from the sprawling garment district. All of these efforts rested on municipal "police power" protection of public health, safety, and morals—indeed, Progressive Era courts consistently held that zoning could not be used to simply sustain property values or the qualities of certain neighborhoods.[6]

This was an important threshold. As long as local ordinances bore "a real and substantial relation" to public health and safety, local governments could control land use (and exercise eminent domain) without compensating affected property owners. At the same time, the police power imposed an expectation of due process and equal protection: Local zoning had to protect the interests of the entire community and do so evenly and indiscriminately. In practice, however, the "substantial relation" test invited considerable (and often inventive) local variation and discretion. Municipalities offered increasingly expansive definitions of "nuisance"—a legal designation that came to include not only its original targets (slaughterhouses, glue factories, junkyards) but almost any business that did not "fit" in a given neighborhood, and racial occupancy as well. As of 1918, most jurisdictions had upheld general zoning ordinances but rejected as arbitrary "piecemeal" ordinances that focused on spot zoning or aesthetic considerations. Generally, municipalities pressed for a more expansive definition of nuisance; property owners sought to narrow that definition and the use of the police power to enforce it.[7]

Expansive use of the police power was blessed by the Supreme Court in *Euclid v. Ambler*, a 1926 decision that resolved considerable confusion among state legislatures (whose enabling acts established the criteria for local zoning) and local governments, and laid the legal foundations for the modern practice of municipal zoning. At issue in *Euclid* was the ability of local governments to extend police power regulation of nuisances to patterns of residential housing. The original (Ohio) trial judge struck down the local zoning law in question, arguing that "in the last analysis the result to be accomplished is to classify the population and segregate them according to their income or situation in life." The Supreme Court agreed, but held that zoning fell within the discretion of the local police power—as long as it rested on a comprehensive plan for local land use. It was the right and duty of local government, as one amicus brief put it, to protect residents from the threat posed by a "disorderly, noisy, slovenly, blighted and slum-like district." At the core of *Euclid* lay the emerging legal and political conviction that residential fragments could and should seek protection from industry, commerce, and residential density. "A nuisance may merely be the right thing in the wrong place," the Court reasoned, "like a pig in a parlor instead of the barnyard."[8]

Euclid capped the effort, primarily of the nation's largest cities, to erect a system of land use controls on the foundation of the municipal police power. In practice, zoning proved less important for these cities than it did for the suburbs multiplying on their borders.[9] Protection of the general welfare came to mean perilously little when the police power—and the community it sought to protect—stopped and started again with each new subdivision or incorporation. In many suburban settings, land use controls were effectively set by private developers and realtors long before a pattern of subdivision was formalized by municipal incorporation. Incorporation and inaugural zoning ordinances were often pursued only when new development, the threat of annexation, or the expiration of private deed restrictions threatened property values. Suburbs employed "use regulations for the same purpose as restrictive covenants," one zoning expert concluded in 1936, "to obtain through a zoning ordinance a community exclusively of high-class private residences"—adding, "It is a grave question whether this is a reasonable exercise of the police power."[10]

After the mid-1920s, land-use law was increasingly organized around local autonomy and exclusionary standards. The Hoover-era Department of Commerce encouraged states to pass zoning enabling acts, and most adopted a version of the federal model within a few years of the *Euclid* decision. Municipalities adopted city plans in which zoning was the key to both sustaining property values and shaping future growth. Through the formative years of modern suburbia, the legal and political logic of *Euclid* was unchallenged. Even when local prohibitions on multifamily dwellings or small lots were recognized as parochial and exclusionary, the courts invariably held that affordable housing was available elsewhere in the region. "The police power is not confined to elimination of filth, stench, and unhealthy places," Justice Douglas argued (*Village of Belle Terre v. Boraas*) in 1974; "urban zoning may legitimately embrace a pastoral vision that separates the home from all other activity: It is ample to lay out zones where family values, youth values, and the blessings of quiet seclusion and clean air make the area a sanctuary for people." State-level challenges to this view did arise after the 1970s—most famously in New Jersey's *Mount Laurel* case, which pressed the state to require that local governments take on their "fair share" of affordable housing. But even in those few states where "fair share" laws curbed exclusionary practices, the central tenets of land-use law—local autonomy and density standards—remained intact.[11]

State enabling acts and local zoning laws embraced two basic principles: separation of use and control over density. A typical zoning ordinance broke the municipality into discrete use districts: residential, commercial, industrial. These districts, in turn, were often divided again: commercial zoning designated neighborhood, highway, and central business districts; industrial zones usually distinguished between heavy industry, light industry (often accompanied by long lists of those that fell under either designation), and planned industry (land banked for future development); residential zoning not only established separate single-family, duplex, and multifamily (apartment) districts but further divided each of these by lot and building size. Over time, zoning ordinances became more complex—offering finer distinctions between zones and using a floor-to-area ratio (FAR) instead of simple lot sizes for multistory commercial and residential developments.[12]

A typical midcentury suburban municipality (see Map 3.1) usually had two or three single-family zones of varying density, scattered strips or intersections of commercial frontage, and pockets of multifamily or light industrial development (although it was common to exclude these as well). Such ordinances usually ranked their zones alphabetically and allowed a "higher use" in any zone—meaning that any land use was allowed in the lowest (usually industrial) district, but only large-lot single-family homes were allowed in A districts. Each municipality, in this respect, sought to isolate and protect large single-family districts (where multifamily housing was allowed, it was typically clustered near commercial districts), to exclude those likely to make demands on public goods and public services, and to accomplish a residential density *just* sufficient to ensure basic public services at a reasonable tax rate.[13]

In Missouri, state law allowed St. Louis (in the early century the state's only "home rule" city) to enforce limited restrictions, but the courts remained leery of more expansive powers—striking down an 1898 ordinance that barred commercial use of homes on a given street and a 1911 ordinance that barred manufacturing within 600 feet of Tower Grove Park (on the grounds that the police power "cannot sanction the confiscation of private property for aesthetic purposes").[14] The City's first general zoning ordinance (1918) was premised on a more expansive use of the police power and new charter powers won in 1914. In 1921, Missouri passed two enabling statutes (one for cities over 200,000; one for cities under 50,000), both of which were eclipsed, on the eve of the *Euclid* decision, by a general enabling law for local zoning in 1925. This law, periodically revised and refined, lays out the basic police power authority for local zoning. Cities and towns are

empowered to regulate and restrict the height, number of stories, and size of buildings and other structures, the percentage of lot that may be occupied, the size of yards, courts, and other open spaces, the density of population, the preservation of features of historical significance, and the location and use of buildings, structures and land for trade, industry, residence or other purposes. . . . Such regulations shall be made in accordance with a comprehensive plan and designed to lessen congestion in the streets; to secure safety from fire, panic and other dangers; to promote health and the general welfare; to provide adequate light and air; to prevent the overcrowding of land; to avoid undue concentration of population; to preserve features of historical significance; to facilitate the adequate provision of transportation, water, sewerage, schools, parks, and other public requirements.[15]

Cities and property owners, in St. Louis and elsewhere, traded legal blows over the meaning of the law—a confrontation heightened by Missouri's constitutional provi-

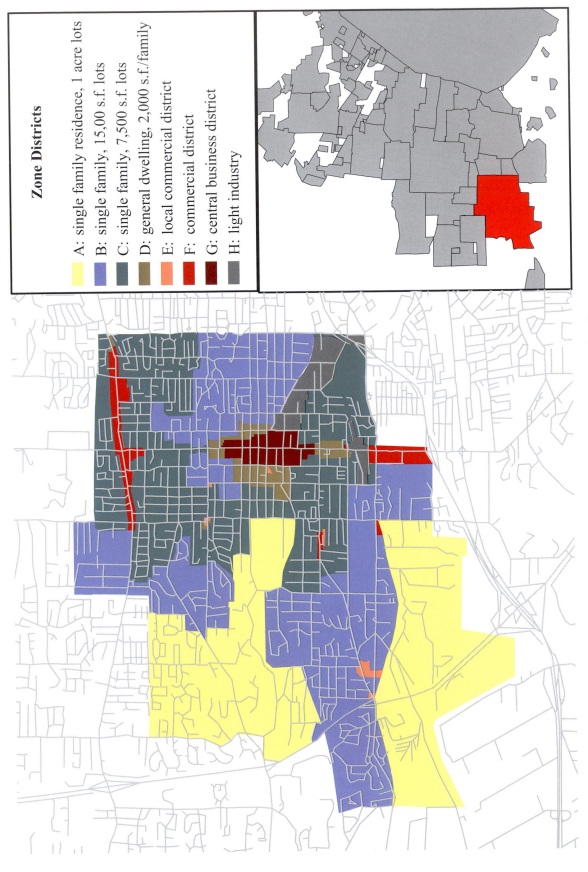

Zone Districts

A: single family residence, 1 acre lots
B: single family, 15,00 s.f. lots
C: single family, 7,500 s.f. lots
D: general dwelling, 2,000 s.f./family
E: local commercial district
F: commercial district
G: central business district
H: light industry

Map 3.1. Zone districts, Kirkwood Missouri, 1959. Harland Bartholomew Papers, Washington University.

sion that "private property shall not be taken *or damaged* for public use without just compensation" (indeed, some City officials felt the only way to salvage the 1918 ordinance was to pass a new one incorporating "compensation for property owners whose rights are restricted").[16] The City's 1918 ordinance stalled against an array of legal challenges and was thrown out by the state supreme court a few years later. In *Penrose v. McKelvey* (1922) and *Evraiff v. St. Louis* (1923), the court found the City's rules on industrial uses unduly restrictive—holding that the regulation of some industries (stables, laundries, dairies) was justified by the fact that these were "trades and occupations prejudicial to the health, morals and good government of the citizens" but that "regulations based on aesthetic considerations [the property at issue was a rag and junk shop] are not in accord with the spirit of our democratic institutions." These decisions sharply curtailed the municipal police power, holding the ordinance "unreasonable and oppressive" because it imposed "restrictions upon the use of private property that have no relation to the health, safety, comfort, or welfare of the inhabitants of the city."[17]

As telling (and in the long run more influential) were the dissents. One justice agreed with the majority, but not with the premise that a zoning ordinance was, by its nature, unconstitutional. The propriety of the law, in this view, rested on a subtler reading of the police power and the question of whether a set of general restrictions amounted to the same "taking" of property as the exercise of eminent domain. Others argued that the ordinance was a perfectly reasonable and defensible use of police powers, and that the effective logic of the decision "instead of protecting the citizens of St. Louis in the enjoyment of their property rights, is to render the city powerless to protect them." This was a view pressed not only by the City but also by suburban municipalities (Webster Groves, Clayton, Richmond Heights) defending or contemplating their own zoning ordinances.[18]

The *Euclid* decision altered the national legal climate in 1926, and soon after the Missouri Supreme Court reversed its 1923 precedent. At issue in *Oliver Cadillac* (1927) was the City's refusal to accommodate a proposed automobile showroom in a mixed-use (but residentially zoned) neighborhood near Lindell and Sarah. The City defended its decision on the grounds that it wanted to maintain (or restore) Lindell as a grand thoroughfare for visiting dignitaries. Echoing the logic of 1923, the plaintiffs argued that no stretch of the police power could transform a storefront showroom for luxury cars into a threat to the general welfare:

Can such a tribute be exacted . . . in order that Queen Marie of Roumania, Prince Gustave of Sweden, the visiting Elks attending their annual conclave, or the convening butter and egg men may recline in fine automobiles as they glide out this "main arterial thoroughfare" to survey a lot of hotels, apartment houses, floats, boarding houses, rooming houses, club and lodge buildings, hospitals, sanitariums and storage garages . . . ? No. Those things, plainly, have nothing to do with the health, morals, security, or general welfare of the inhabitants along Lindell—or anywhere else in St. Louis.[19]

But the court disagreed—and, in aligning itself with *Euclid*, also accepted the basic premises of that decision. In *Oliver* (and in a string of supporting decisions), the Missouri Supreme Court adopted the longstanding tenet of zoning advocates that, while a particular property or use might not pose any threat to public health, safety, or morals, relaxation of broader zoning standards might have that effect. After *Oliver*, it increasingly argued that it was not the judiciary's role to second-guess local legislative authority—even when lower courts found that local zoning laws "do not meet the test of bearing any real or substantial relation to the public good or the general welfare of the community."[20] Once Missouri courts embraced *Euclid*'s expansive interpretation of the police power, local planners were free to control land use without resorting to condemnation and compensation. "To zone a great city like St. Louis through condemnation proceedings would be practically impossible," concluded the *Oliver* decision; "the city as a social unit is a living organic thing; all the while changing, expanding, growing; a zoning by condemnation under eminent domain would tend to fossilize it and thereby defeat one of the essential purposes of zoning. It must be zoned, therefore, under the police power or not at all."[21]

By midcentury, the law and politics of zoning in Missouri were largely settled. State enabling law, sustained by post-*Euclid* legal opinions, gave municipalities broad powers to control and restrict land use. These powers extended as far as two miles beyond a city's boundaries into otherwise unincorporated areas, although by the 1950s counties had also won the right to zone. Missouri cities were empowered to control land use but not required to do so—and many smaller St. Louis suburbs either relied on county ordinances or simply adopted a single (invariably single-family) zone district. Over the course of the twentieth century, the power to zone was used in different ways by different fragments of Greater St. Louis. In the City, zoning tended to describe patterns of land-use rather than to shape them: residential development was relatively dense and substantial areas were set aside for commercial and industrial use (see Map 3.2). By contrast, land use in suburban St. Louis County reflected the preference of midcentury developers for large-lot single-family subdivisions, with only minimal allowance for commercial, industrial, or higher-density residential development.

Too Little, Too Late: Zoning St. Louis

Before World War I, the only land use controls in St. Louis were building permits and piecemeal exclusions in response to the complaints of neighbors. Civic leaders first pressed the idea of citywide zoning as early as 1907, an effort that resulted in the creation of the first City Plan Commission. The commission's inaugural report (1911) recommended, alongside a range of other reforms, a zoning plan that would clearly delineate residential, commercial, and industrial districts. The first stab at a full-blown zoning ordinance, however, came not from professional planners but from the City's anxious and segregationist real estate interests, who (as we saw in Chapter 2) won a racial zoning ordinance by popular referendum in 1916. As this option wound its way through the courts, planners—led by the new engineer of the City Plan Commission, Harland Bartholomew—continued to push for a more conventional zone plan. The City devoted $10,000 in 1916 to a citywide survey of land use, and Bartholomew shepherded a string of major studies including *Problems of St. Louis* (1917), *A Major Street*

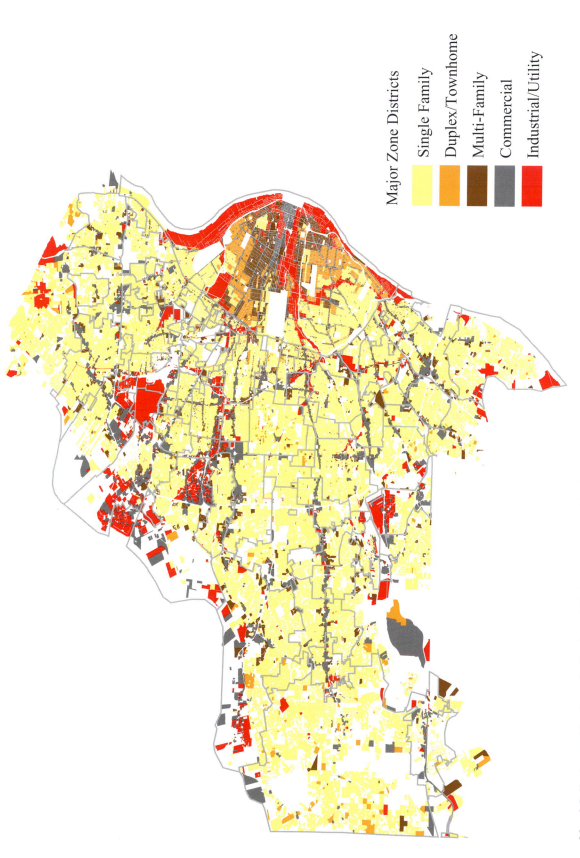

Major Zone Districts

Single Family

Duplex/Townhome

Multi-Family

Commercial

Industrial/Utility

Map 3.2. Zoning and land use, St. Louis and St. Louis County, 2003. Parcel data, St. Louis County, East-West Gateway Coordinating Council.

Plan for St. Louis (1917), *St. Louis After the War* (1918), *Zoning for St. Louis* (1918), and *The Zone Plan* (1919).[22]

This flurry of activity was organized around the conviction that "blight" was caused by the City's inability to protect residential properties from the incursion of industry, commerce, and substandard housing. The resulting zone plan, passed in 1918, was both a lament for the City's "former good residential districts" and an attempt to shore up residential property values. "To enforce a proper districting plan," the authors argued, "is to fix growth and the tendencies of growth so that stability will replace chaos and the destructive element of uncertainty in city expansion will be largely removed."[23] The ordinance identified three overlapping sets of districts. Most important were the five "use" districts: a scattering of still desirable "first residence" districts, a wider swath of "second residence" districts, "commercial" districts running along most major arterial streets, and a combination of "industrial" and "unrestricted" districts covering much of the riverfront, the central city east of Grand Avenue, and the Mill Creek and River Des Peres valleys (see Map 3.3). Overlaying these use districts were five height districts and four area districts—restricting, respectively, the total height of buildings and the percentage of the lot they could occupy (see Table 3.1). The 1918 ordinance sat in legal limbo until 1923, when it was thrown out by the state supreme court.

The distinctions among the use districts were, by contemporary zoning standards, somewhat crude. First residence districts were small pockets of higher-end single-family homes, their scale and location corresponding closely to the City's private streets. These districts merely extended by ordinance a protection already afforded by private ownership and deed restrictions. Second residence districts swallowed the rest of the City's housing stock (everything from single-family homes to tenements), but their restrictions varied according to existing land use: In districts composed entirely of single-family homes, for example, some lesser uses (hotels, hospitals, apartment buildings) were disallowed. Commercial districts encompassed storefront shops and services and professional offices. The only distinction between "industrial" and "unrestricted" districts was that "nuisance" industries (those producing "smoke, noise, gas fumes, or dust") could only locate in the latter.[24]

A revised ordinance passed in 1925 (see Map 3.4) made a few substantive changes. Regulation of building heights was loosened, and the distinction between residential districts was completely revised. The exclusive "first residence" district of 1918 was dropped in favor of a much broader "residential" district. This designation protected single- and two-family homes (although the latter were disallowed when single-family homes claimed over three-quarters of street frontage); it both reflected and reinforced the profusion of restrictive deed covenants in the early 1920s. The rest of the housing stock—primarily the areas immediately north and south of downtown—was now classed as multifamily. And the basic patterns of commercial, industrial, and unrestricted districts remained unchanged.[25]

It is a stretch to dignify the 1918 and 1925 zoning ordinances as "planning." Since the City was already substantially built, zoning was less a blueprint for the future than it was a means of protecting existing investments and managing neighborhood transi-

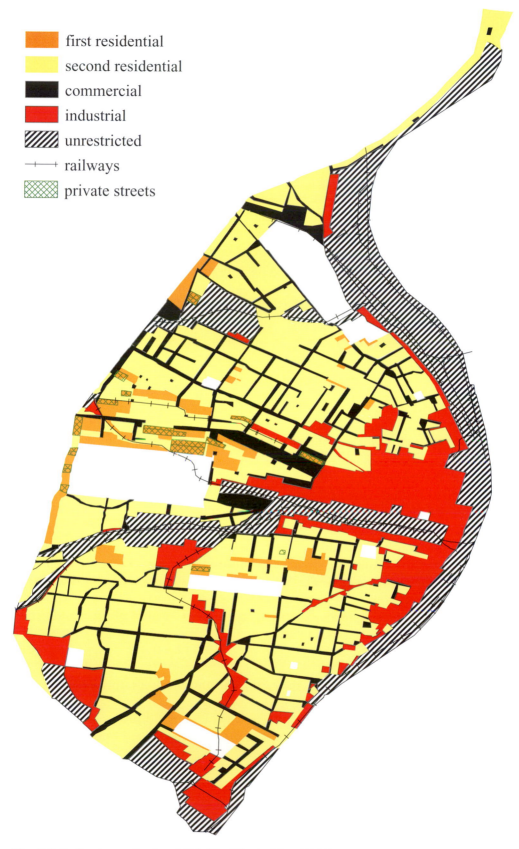

first residential
second residential
commercial
industrial
unrestricted
railways
private streets

Map 3.3. St. Louis use districts, 1918. Use District Map (1918), Exhibit B, *Evraiff v. St. Louis* (1922), RG 600, Supreme Court Judicial Case Files, Missouri State Archives, Jefferson City.

TABLE 3.1. 1918 Zone Districts and Restrictions, St. Louis

Use	Height	Area
first residence	45 feet	50% of lot (60% on corner lots)
second residence	45 feet	60% (75% corners) for apartments, or as above
commercial	60 feet; 150 feet in CBD	as above, except in CBD which is unrestricted
industrial	80 feet	100% first floor; 80% second (90% on corners)
unrestricted	120 feet	as above

Source: City Plan Commission, *The Zone Plan* (St. Louis, 1919), 32–43.

tion. The ordinance was not retroactive, and it imposed no real penalties or pressures on nonconforming uses. The architects of the zone districts readily admitted that they were essentially descriptive and were determined largely by existing patterns of development.[26] At the same time, the City resisted the implication that existing land-use determined zoning—a concession that would have made it impossible to sort out any of the problems the ordinance was designed to address. Much of the subsequent legal turmoil revolved around the City's efforts to go after nonconforming or lesser uses, which undermined the legitimacy of the district plan.[27]

St. Louis realtors (having lost their battle for racial zoning in 1916) generally opposed the City's new zoning authority. While they shared the planners' interest in protecting first residence districts, realtors (represented by the St. Louis Real Estate Exchange) preferred to rely on deed covenants and other private restrictions. Beyond that, zoning threatened the freedom of realtors to make money in transitional neighborhoods. The Exchange, for example, deeply resented residential height restrictions because they prohibited the lucrative development of high-rise apartments and hotels along Lindell and Kingshighway and through much of the West End surrounding Forest Park. Realtors launched the legal challenge (*Penrose v. McKelvey*) that ultimately sank the 1918 ordinance, rushed into the resulting legal vacuum with a frenzy of multistory construction in the West End, and ensured that the new 1926 ordinance retreated on height regulation. The City's industrialists also waded into the debate, worried that protection of residential districts might mean barriers to new commercial development. The result—echoed in every subsequent revision of the zoning code and in the urban renewal efforts of the next generation—was generously drawn industrial and commercial districts that blocked out much of central St. Louis and its river frontage.[28]

The other major undercurrent in the early zoning debate, not surprisingly, was race. The 1918 and 1926 ordinances, as we have seen, used private streets and deed restrictions as a general guide for its most exclusive residential districts—including the neighborhoods bordering Carondelet Park in the southeast, Tower Park in the central southside, O'Fallon Park to the northeast; and Forest Park in the West End. "In practically all cases the first residence districts are areas that now have restrictions in the deeds," Bartholomew admitted—adding that the 1918 districts were "prepared primarily with the view of preserving the more desirable residential neighborhoods" and that the first residence districts were considered little more than insurance "against

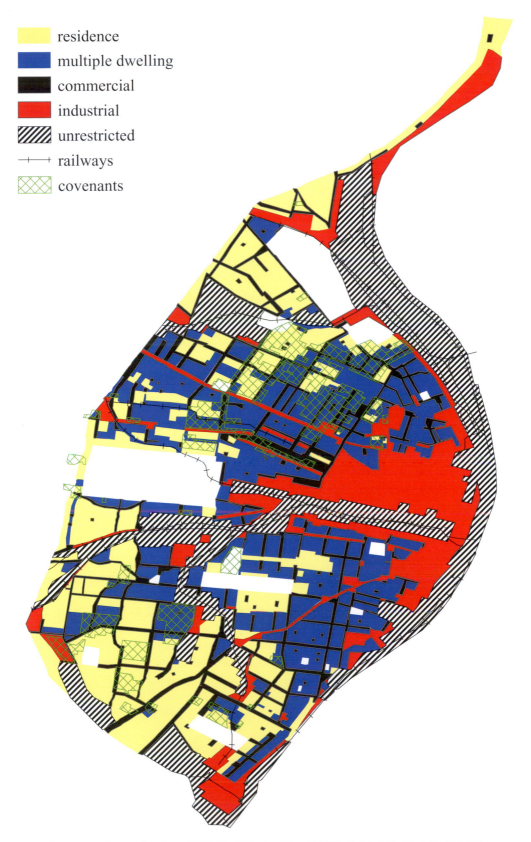

Map 3.4. St. Louis use districts, 1925. Use District Map (1925), Exhibit B, *State Ex Rel. Oliver Cadillac v. Christopher* (1927), 28010, RG 600, Supreme Court Judicial Case Files, Missouri State Archives, Jefferson City.

the day when private restrictions expire." For its part, the Chamberlain Park Improvement Association (representing the first residence district north of Maple Avenue between Union and Goodfellow) viewed the 1918 zoning ordinance as essential to maintaining private agreements—especially as the "building restrictions which formerly protected our property expired about the time the zoning ordinance was passed."[29]

For Bartholomew and his colleagues, the goal was to stem the spread of blight "where values have depreciated, [and] homes are either vacant or occupied by colored people or boarding houses." Failure would put further downward pressure on residential property values, driving "our people" (again quoting Bartholomew) "out into the suburban districts." Residential protections under the 1918 and 1926 ordinances were stronger in south St. Louis, where realtors and homeowners won an essentially suburban deference to single-family neighborhoods. On the northside, commercial and industrial interests had a stronger voice and won expansive districts despite fears (especially in transitional neighborhoods) that commercial zoning would invalidate deed covenants and further invite the westward expansion of the "Negro district."[30]

In these respects, zoning echoed and reinforced the conviction (embedded in private restrictions) that neighborhoods were being "invaded," either by black occupancy or by a pattern of mixed-use that was the precursor to black occupancy. "The natural tendency of an invasion of a quiet, clean district of residences . . . by apartments, hotels, retail stores, or factories, is to bring abut a marked depression of property values in such a district; that the natural tendency of such invasion is to cause an exodus of the home owners of such a district, followed by a condition of landlordism and tenantry resulting generally in a neglected, rundown district with original values practically wiped out." The City's more exclusive districts not only overlay or replaced private restrictions but also tried to contain or channel the expansion of black residency by surrounding black neighborhoods with commercial or industrial areas. In 1927, City planners went so far as to suspend the rule that parks be built in residential zones, "as a means" (as the recreation commissioner argued at the time) "of centering Negro activities in the particular district."[31] Even the location of commercial or industrial districts was often posed as a racial issue. The local Chamber of Commerce distinguished industrial from unrestricted districts on the grounds that the former allowed light industries "which are in no way offensive, which will employ clean and self-respecting men and women, who will, as a rule, live in nearby homes." And commercial interests opposed the abatement of a junk shop at Twentieth and O'Fallon (*Evraiff v. St. Louis*) because "it is a matter of common knowledge that this section of the city is old and dilapidated, populated largely by negroes, and we would term it a 'junk shop' neighborhood."[32]

The racial premises of zoning emerged most clearly in areas of established black occupancy—running from the central business district west to the Ville and the contested neighborhoods surrounding it. The 1918 ordinance defined downtown as an industrial district and placed most of the residential northside under the elastic "second residence" designation. In 1926, the boundaries of the downtown industrial district were widened and almost all the near northside was placed under the new "multiple family" classification. "A decade ago the Zoning Commission left not a single block or neighborhood zoned as residential in the area from Delmar to Labadie and from Grand to Taylor and Cora. Excepting Vandeventer Place," the St. Louis Urban League noted in the late 1930s, "this wide Negro section was zoned as multiple dwelling, commercial, and industrial districts." Barred by private restrictions from settling elsewhere, the black middle class pressed for some protection of single-family residences in north St. Louis. What emerged instead (in the 1926 ordinance and its subsequent revisions) was a pattern of "expulsive zoning," which systematically underzoned African American neighborhoods. In the short term, this pattern denied these neighborhoods protection from commercial or industrial development. In the longer term, it hardened the view that black occupancy was a nonconforming blight on the central city and paved the way for its displacement under urban renewal.[33]

Although its constitutionality was settled by 1926, zoning remained a controversial extension of the police power. There remained a wide gap between actual patterns of land use and the order implied by the zoning districts, and the City could not protect residential districts or attract new industrial development simply by shading areas different colors on a map. As of 1936, fully one-third of all residential property in St. Louis was zoned for a lesser use. Commercial zoning exceeded commercial land use by 94 percent, and industrial land was overzoned by 138 percent.[34] By the mid-1930s, even Bartholomew had come around to the view that zoning (while useful in the suburbs) could have little impact on already-urbanized areas where a clean segregation of land use had already been frustrated. Realtors and homeowners, in turn, embraced zoning when it "protected" neighborhoods but railed against it whenever it constrained the use or sale of private property. This was especially apparent on the northside, where white property owners in transitional neighborhoods besieged the zoning commission with requests for commercial designation of blocks or neighborhoods that were losing residential value. The piecemeal solution, in a city ruled largely by ward politicians, was an endless parade of parcel-by-parcel exceptions, or spot zoning.[35]

Little wonder, a decade after passage of the 1926 ordinance, that the City Plan Commission would find that "the present urban land use policy of St. Louis consists of (1) speculative exploitation, (2) gradual neglect, and (3) eventual abandonment."[36] The Depression put enormous pressure on the City Zone Commission, as hard times brought both systematic violations (particularly residential crowding) and an explosion of spot zoning requests. Federal agencies (rating properties for New Deal programs in the late 1930s) routinely cited the City's "inadequate and poorly conceived zoning ordinances." Revision of the zoning code was encouraged by a city property survey in 1936 (which found widespread discrepancies and nonconformance) and by the 1938 City Plan. But realtors continued to object, and the task of revision was lost in the flurry of mobilization for World War II.[37] The issue arose again immediately after the war, driven in part by the new importance of city planning in the context of federal housing and urban policy.

The 1947 City Plan recycled the catalogue of problems (commercial overzoning, nonconformance, spot zoning) first identified in the 1930s and labeled the City's zone plan "one of the most obsolete ordinances to be found in any of the large cities of the United States."[38] Perhaps the most glaring deficiency, and the one most often implicated in the City's residential crisis, was the mismatch between the planned or "highest use" envisioned by the 1926 ordinance and actual land use (Table 3.2).[39]

Citing the deficiencies of the 1926 ordinance, the expectations of federal agencies like the FHA, the demographic impact of depression and war, and the City's continued decline, the 1947 City Plan returned to the core goal of protecting residential property (although, aside from pockets in the City's far northwest and in a few blocks south of Forest Park, there was no real prospect of *new* residential development):

St. Louis has numerous neighborhoods of homes which are either new and attractive or of middle age but retaining pleasant characteristics, and some that are quite old yet capable of interesting revival. But the good sections cannot be assured of future protection, nor can the poor ones hope for recrudescence, without modern zoning. St. Louis was a pioneer in zoning but we have failed to keep at the head of the parade. The existing zoning code does not even provide for zones limited to one-family units. Manifestly, in a city with a reputation for home-owning, this condition cries out for correction.

Toward this end, the commissioners proposed a revised ordinance that would establish a new single-family district, increase the total area zoned for residential purposes, draw finer distinctions between residential districts based on lot and building size, pare back commercial and industrial zones, distinguish between different kinds of commercial and industrial use, impose new off-street parking standards across all districts, and curtail spot zoning with new provisions for local exceptions.[40]

The new ordinance proceeded slowly, facing a now-familiar array of anxieties from commercial interests and realtors. The first version died in legislative committee in 1949, but a revised version—based substantially on the problems and standards identified in the 1947 City Plan—finally passed in 1950 (see Map 3.5). As promised, the old

TABLE 3.2. Land Use and Zoning in St. Louis, 1945

Purpose	Land Use (1945)		Zoning (1945)		Proposed Zoning	
	Acres	%	Acres	%	Acres	%
single-family dwellings	7,045	28.1	9,814	31.6	10,350	33.4
two-family dwellings	2,576	10.3	—	—	5,720	18.4
multiple dwellings	2,454	9.8	6,246	20.1	4,065	13.1
institutions, City property	6,275	25.1	—	—	—	—
commercial	1,715	6.8	3,438	11.1	3,185	10.3
industrial	1,431	5.7	4,276	13.8	2,510b	8.1b
unrestricted (including railroads)	3,547	14.2	7,242	23.4	5,185	16.7
total net area	25,042	100	31,015	100	31,015	100
streets	8,821	—	8,821	—	8,821	—
vacant	5,973	—	—	—	—	—
total gross area	39,836	—	39,836	—	39,836	—

Source: City Plan Commission, 1947 City Plan, table VII.

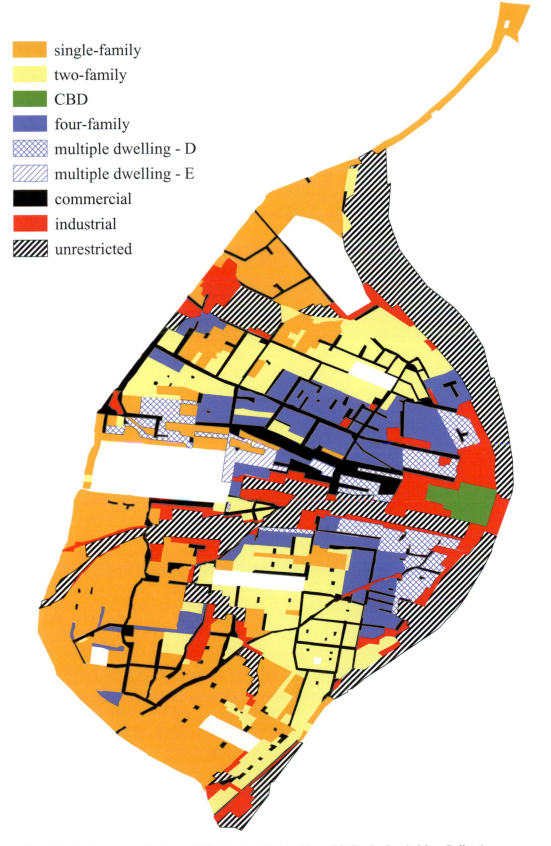

Map 3.5. St. Louis use districts, 1948. Zoning District Map (1948), St. Louis Map Collection,
Missouri Historical Society.

Legend:
- single-family
- two-family
- CBD
- four-family
- multiple dwelling - D
- multiple dwelling - E
- commercial
- industrial
- unrestricted

five districts were subdivided into eleven (see Table 3.3). Residential areas were broken down into a single-family district (lot size minimum 4,000 s.f.), a two-family district
(lot size per family 2,000 s.f.), and three multifamily districts (including a "fourplex"
designation at 1,400 s.f./family, a three-story apartment designation at 1,000 s.f./fam-
ily, and an eight story designation at 350 s.f./family). Four commercial districts,
including a new central business district, were organized around the same residential
standards. The industrial district of 1926 was substantially carried forward, as was the
"unrestricted district" (understood as a "heavy industry" district), in which residential use was prohibited.[41]

After passage of the 1950 ordinance, the City would not revisit its zoning policies in
any serious way until the late 1970s—a surprising indifference, given the scale and
severity of the unfolding urban crisis. Over this period, zoning politics focused largely
on procedural issues (variances, adjustments, appeals). Business interests (including
Downtown, Inc., Civic Progress, and the Regional Commerce and Growth Association)
continued to press for more commercial and industrial land. Realtors continued to
resent the constraints imposed by the Zoning Commission. African American leaders
objected to the systematic underzoning of black residential neighborhoods (a pattern
which both failed to protect residential properties and also rendered them ineligible
for FHA assistance). Despite efforts to control the practice in 1950, spot zoning
remained a civic headache, encouraged by the longstanding practice of "aldermanic
courtesy" (by which ward politicians deferred to each other on local zoning issues).
The spirit of the 1950 ordinance had been so eroded by such amendments that the
League of Women Voters began (in the middle 1950s) to offer "spot zone" tours of
the City. And, by most accounts, spot zoning only furthered white flight by eroding
faith in the stability or permanence of the City's residential districts.[42]

In the debate leading up to a new zoning ordinance in 1980, the City recognized
the need for more low-income housing (focusing, in the wake of the Pruitt-Igoe deba-
cle, on the prospect of medium-density "garden apartments") but also maintained its
longstanding interest in protecting what was left of the first residence districts.[43] In

TABLE 3.3. Zone Districts, 1950

Zone	Use	Height Restrictions	Residential Density
"A"	single family	n/a	4000 s.f. per family
"B"	duplex	n/a	2000 s.f./family
"C"	fourplex	n/a	1400 s.f./family
"D"	multifamily	three stories	1000 s.f. family
"E"	multifamily	eight stories	350 s.f./family
"F"	local business	three stories	same as "B"
"G"	commercial	three stories	same as "D"
"H"	commercial	eight stories	same as "E"
"I"	central business	none	same as "E"
"J"	industrial	eight stories	same as "D"
"K"	unrestricted	none	no residential allowed

Source: City Plan Commission, "Zoning (1949), 17.

turn, the revision debate was shaped by profound changes in urban land-use politics since 1950—especially the fascination with urban renewal, economic development, historic districts, and tourism. Alongside a reconsideration of zone boundaries and definitions, accordingly, the Zoning Commission pressed for a series of procedural reforms such as "incentive zoning" (which would allow developers to exceed height or density limitations in exchange for other concessions such as green space, affordable housing, or cultural amenities).[44] In the end, the 1980 ordinance followed the template set in 1950 very closely. Some adjustments were made in the square footage per family standards for multifamily districts. Floor-to-area allowances were made for high-rise apartments (allowing more than eight stories as long as side yard setbacks increased one foot for every five feet of additional height). And a new ("L") Jefferson Memorial district was added on the central riverfront. With minor changes, this is the zoning ordinance in effect in St. Louis today.[45]

By 1980, the zoning ordinance was increasingly marginal to the politics of planning in St. Louis. In part, this reflected the dramatic depopulation of the City. As Map 3.6 suggests, the neat and formulaic pattern of residential land use suggested by the zoning ordinance largely evaporates when building vacancies and nonresidential uses are taken into account. Residential zones, after all, offered little to neighborhoods in which no one lived anymore. In turn, a tangle of other land-use tools had, by the latter decades of the twentieth century, largely eclipsed the zoning ordinance. Community planners instead invested most of their energies in a profusion of urban renewal tools, including redevelopment corporations, land reclamation authorities, conservation districts, and locational tax incentives (such as tax-increment financing districts). City planners understood that local zoning could and would always be amended to accommodate these efforts. And, after 1986, many of these areas were classed as "planned unit development districts"—a designation that allowed development (given City approval of development plans) to determine zoning rather than vice versa.[46]

Protecting Hearth and Home: Zoning St. Louis County

In St. Louis County, by contrast, zoning proceeded alongside development and was instrumental in shaping patterns of residential land use. Zoning authority rested in the hands of individual municipal governments (numbering 35 in 1940 and 95 by 1960) and the county. Each of these governments had every incentive to maximize tax revenues, stabilize property values, and minimize demands on local government—a combination best accomplished by creating large-lot single-family enclaves. And none of these governments had any incentive to think about broader metropolitan goals or needs regarding commercial development, affordable housing, or regional infrastructure. Fragmented zoning, in this respect, came most directly at the expense of the city of St. Louis, which shouldered many of the costs of urban development even as the suburbs poached its population, retail trade, and employment base. But it also came at the expense of the suburbs themselves. All local governments bore the costs of administrative disarray and unmanaged sprawl. Suburbs engaged in often destructive competition to attract (or avoid) new residential or commercial development. And,

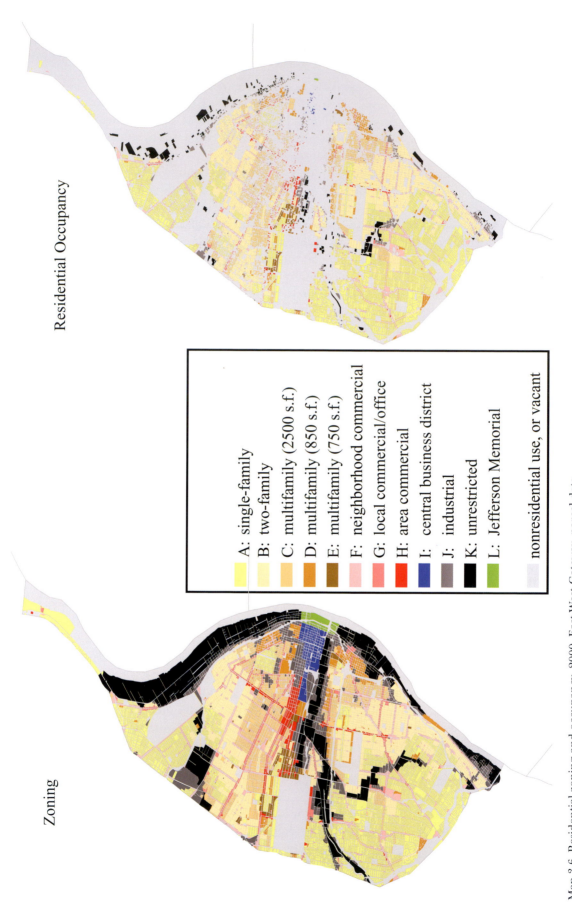

Residential Occupancy

Zoning

A: single-family
B: two-family
C: multifamily (2500 s.f.)
D: multifamily (850 s.f.)
E: multifamily (750 s.f.)
F: neighborhood commercial
G: local commercial/office
H: area commercial
I: central business district
J: industrial
K: unrestricted
L: Jefferson Memorial

nonresidential use, or vacant

Map 3.6. Residential zoning and occupancy, 2000. East-West Gateway, parcel data.

over time, newer subdivisions and incorporations to the west were poaching not just the City but the older inner-ring suburbs as well.

Development of St. Louis County proceeded west from its border with St. Louis in raggedly concentric rings of subdivision, incorporation, and local zoning. Importantly, much of the suburban boom of the middle years of the century was managed by private developers buying and subdividing land, often in unincorporated areas. Through the 1920s and 1930s, such developments included the residential base for the areas later incorporated as Ladue and Huntleigh Woods, and they invariably included private land and deed restrictions designed to "guarantee [the area's] development into a region of high-type homes." County growth and development before 1945 was largely confined to a few well-established municipalities and inner suburbs, and a scattering of estates in the central county. As of 1932, for example, Huntleigh Village (the unincorporated precursor to Huntleigh Woods) consisted of about 30 lots (the smallest 3 acres, the largest 40) traversed by a smatter of private roads.[47]

As the pace of subdivision picked up in the 1940s and 1950s (see Map 3.7), much of the building still preceded incorporation. Between 1946 and 1948, for example, just under half of all building permits (6,868 of 13,803) in St. Louis County were issued for unincorporated areas. Of the County's present-day count of 90-odd municipalities, fully half were incorporated between 1943 and 1954. In only a few settings (Maplewood, Ladue, Webster Groves) did local zoning precede development. As of 1950, barely a third of the metropolitan area's municipalities had a local zoning ordinance on the books.[48] Once developed, these areas often looked to municipal incorporation as a means of maintaining community standards, perpetuating the spirit of private deed restrictions, and forestalling annexation by neighbors.

Suburban zoning ordinances followed a logic of systematic exclusion. These strategies included stark restrictions on multifamily housing (apartments, townhomes, duplexes)—indeed, the rule in the first wave of zoning beyond the inner-ring was to make no allowance for alternatives to detached single-family homes. Residential districts, in turn, were shaped by density controls, including minimum lot sizes and yard or frontage requirements. Between 1930 and 1940, 274 subdivisions (representing just under 12,000 building lots) were platted in St. Louis County: Less than 10 percent of these lots were smaller than 5,000 s.f., just over three-quarters were between 5,000 s.f. and a half-acre (roughly 20,000 s.f.), and the rest ranged from a half-acre to three acres.[49] The city of Ladue, for example, incorporated in 1936 (a consolidation of the suburban villages of Deer Creek, McKnight, and Ladue) and adopted its first zoning ordinance in 1938 (see Map 3.8). The ordinance adopted as its A residential district a lot size of 3 acres, the standard set by the Deer Creek and McKnight subdivisions. Smaller districts were set aside for lots at 1.8 acres (B), 30,000 s.f. (C), 15,000 s.f. (D), and 10,000 s.f. (E)—the latter still more than double the minimum lot size of St. Louis' single-family districts. No land was zoned for multifamily residence.[50]

These proscriptive standards were used both to protect existing properties and to shape (or forestall) new development. Municipalities (and St. Louis County) used large-lot single-family standards to raise the value of undeveloped land and create "holding zones" in which local zoning commissions could approve new construction

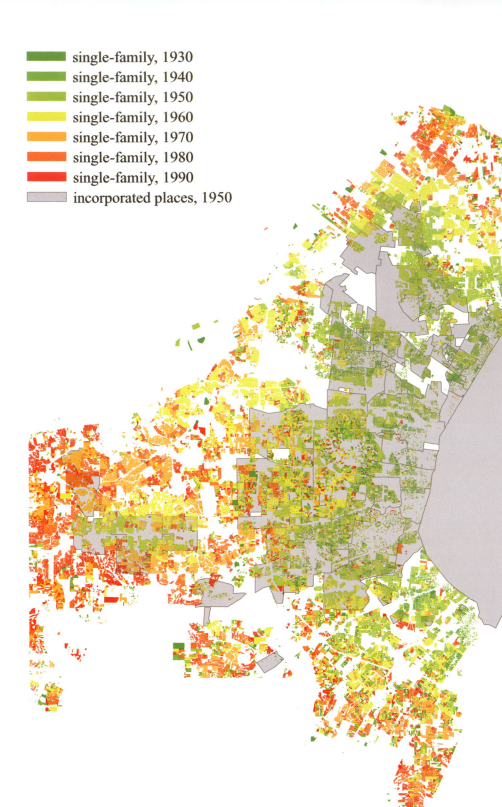

single-family, 1930
single-family, 1940
single-family, 1950
single-family, 1960
single-family, 1970
single-family, 1980
single-family, 1990
incorporated places, 1950

Map 3.7. Single-family home construction in St. Louis County, 1930–1990. St. Louis County Department of Planning, GIS Dataset (2002); Archival maps of municipal boundaries, St. Louis Data Collection, WHMC, University of Missouri-St. Louis.

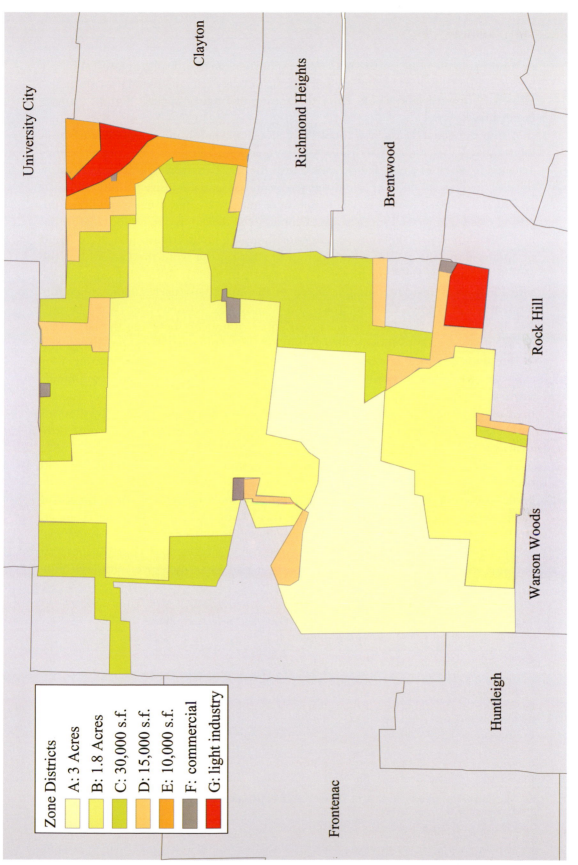

University City

Clayton

Richmond Heights

Brentwood

Rock Hill

Warson Woods

Huntleigh

Frontenac

Zone Districts

A: 3 Acres
B: 1.8 Acres
C: 30,000 s.f.
D: 15,000 s.f.
E: 10,000 s.f.
F: commercial
G: light industry

Map 3.8. Ladue use districts, 1938. Ladue Use District Map, Harland Bartholomew Papers, Washington University.

or subdivision on a case-by-case basis. Many suburban cities and villages (see Table 3.4) incorporated large tracts of undeveloped land, and they often included provisions that all newly annexed land would enter the zoning ordinance at the "highest" single-family use.[51]

Within the general proclivity toward large-lot single-family development, early zoning standards varied widely across the County (see Map 3.9). Generally, municipalities adopted a range of single-family zones, with the most exclusive running between a third of an acre (15,000 s.f.) and three acres and the least exclusive running between 12,000 and 7,500 s.f. Commercial districts were quite spare and usually simply encompassed existing intersections or strips of commercial development, although after the mid-1950s larger packages were set aside for shopping malls. Industrial districts could be found along the rail lines and highways radiating out from the City and in the vicinity of Lambert Field (again, reflecting existing facilities), although many communities had no industrial zoning at all. As of the late 1940s/early 1950s, midcounty municipalities (Ladue, Olivette, Town and County, Creve Coeur, Des Peres) beyond the first suburban ring had the most restrictive ordinances, including the largest lot sizes and the slimmest allowances for multifamily or commercial development. Zoning in the older inner-ring suburbs (Clayton, University City, Maplewood, Jennings), by contrast, more closely resembled that of the City: more mixed use, more multifamily districts, and smaller single-family lot sizes. Others (many quite small) sprinkled across the County presented varying degrees of exclusion, including a number of small towns and villages developed entirely with single-family lots but with no formal zoning ordinances.[52]

Through these years, much of the effective authority for land-use regulation and planning fell to St. Louis County. The County approved new incorporations and its boundary commission sorted out an often competitive scramble for annexation. It had direct responsibility for zoning unincorporated land, including both undeveloped land in the County's western reaches and many subdivisions not yet under municipal control. It had indirect responsibility for land use in smaller towns and villages that had not yet passed a zoning ordinance. And it had some incentive (although little

TABLE 3.4. Land Use (percentage of total), St. Louis and Selected Suburbs, 1955

	SF	MF	Com.	Ind.	RR	Park	Public	Street	Vac.
St. Louis	23.5	6.1	4.4	7.8	4.3	6.8	8.8	22	16
Clayton	35.7	4	2.2	0.3	2.4	3.2	11	18	23
Webster Groves	47.5	0.1	1.3	1.1	2.7	0.4	8.5	13	25
Ferguson	43.5	0	0.5	1.2	1.6	0	8.3	11	34
Richmond Heights	43	2.5	1.1	0.2	1.1	0.3	2.4	17	34
Brentwood	30.3	8	2.1	8.3	0.5	0.8	2.7	13	36
Kirkwood	25.2	0.2	1	0.3	2.4	0.2	6.4	14	51
Olivette	14.3	0	0.7	0.6	1.5	0	7	6.1	70
Berkeley	4	0	0.1	0.4	1.3	0.1	1.7	6	86

Source: Harland Bartholomew, *Land Uses in American Cities* (Cambridge, Mass.: Harvard University Press, 1955), appendix D.

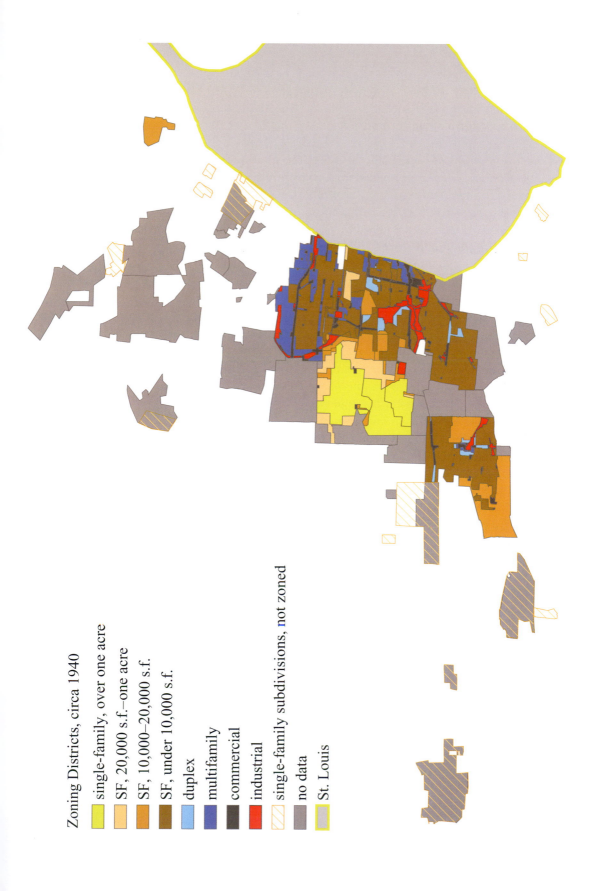

Zoning Districts, circa 1940

- single-family, over one acre
- SF, 20,000 s.f.–one acre
- SF, 10,000–20,000 s.f.
- SF, under 10,000 s.f.
- duplex
- multifamily
- commercial
- industrial
- single-family subdivisions, not zoned
- no data
- St. Louis

Map 3.9. Zoning, St. Louis County municipalities circa 1940. Municipal zoning maps and ordinances, various archival collections.

formal authority) to think regionally, to temper the "spirit of local patriotism" and home rule with the recognition that there were simply too many competing jurisdictions to ensure that each would pursue regionally and fiscally responsible land-use policies.[53]

Early in the postwar era, planners scored the County as a "refuge for uncontrolled subdivision practices" and pressed for a county-wide zoning plan. In 1946, the County adopted a rudimentary zoning order, establishing a range of single-family designations from one acre to 6,000 s.f. as well as more expansive designations for "small farms" and "resorts." Over the next decade, municipal incorporation swallowed most of the smaller-lot residential districts, and the County revised its zoning rules (first in 1961 and then with a full-blown ordinance in 1965). By the early 1960s, the County saw its task as twofold: First, it was to act as a sort of land bank for future residential development. In order to restrain further subdivision of unincorporated land, the 1965 ordinance zoned nearly 90,000 acres (about 70 percent of the County land considered to have residential potential) into "nonurban" three-acre-lot districts. Second, it needed to pick up the slack in commercial and industrial development. As St. Louis County boomed and the City continued its decline, the idea that area residents commuted daily from bedroom suburbs to jobs in the City became increasingly untenable. As its municipalities clung to exclusive single-family zoning, the County often took the lead in zoning to meet suburban employment and retail demands.[54]

Across the County, the most pervasive priority of local zoning was the preservation of large-lot single-family districts. County municipalities already incorporated in the *Euclid* era jumped at the chance to "protect the general welfare" with single-family zoning. As planners readily admitted, single-family zoning not only protected existing homes but also placed "highest use" restrictions on undeveloped land, even if it was unsuitable for residential development. Before 1926, "there was a strong doubt as to the legality of establishing residential districts which excluded two-family and multi-family dwellings," Kirkwood noted upon passage of its first zoning ordinance (1927), but "it is now considered entirely proper not only to set aside areas solely devoted to single-family dwellings but to create several classes of single-family districts in which differentiation is made between permitted lot sizes." When the Kirkwood ordinance was revised in 1941, Harland Bartholomew advised City Officials to establish even larger lot thresholds on the grounds that "the most important function of the zoning ordinance is to give this type of use [single-family] the most protection possible and to encourage its further development in areas now vacant."[55]

This equation of zoning with the protection of existing subdivision patterns and restrictions was most pronounced in the wealthy central county suburbs. Richmond Heights crafted its 1941 ordinance with the expressed "intention of maintaining said subdivision as an exclusive subdivision of single-family residences of substantial value." In Ladue, city planners allowed for single-family districts of less than an acre in 1959, but only with the assurance that property owners could use deed covenants to maintain the one-acre threshold. Defending its exclusive single-family ordinance in 1969, Calverton Park officials cited "a promise made to the original purchasers of land in Calverton Park that there would never be any commercial zoning in this Village."[56]

Legal challenges underscored these motives. In one case, plaintiffs (commercial interests shut out by residence-only zoning in Ladue) argued that the zoning ordinance was adopted "pursuant to a plan to maintain and expand in the city of Ladue a most exclusive 'estate' district available for residences only to the opulent . . . [creating] a section in which citizens in moderate circumstances could not afford to dwell, thereby establishing a special residential area for entrenched wealth." The city of Ladue and its planners offered little dissent, conceding that residential zoning districts had been designed to describe and protect the pattern of private development that had preceded them: "one of the major objectives of our proposed zoning ordinance," as one planner put it, "is to protect and continue the spacious residential character now found within the city."[57] Residents consistently referred to the zoning ordinance as a form of "protection" and testified that they had built in Ladue (rather than in the County) because it offered "definite restrictions on residential property."[58] The logical consequence for the politically fragmented St. Louis suburbs was, as Ladue planners conceded, that "objectionable uses are in somebody else's community." On balance, as the Missouri Supreme Court concluded in the early 1960s, large-lot single-family zoning was "designed entirely to protect values in one subdivision and bears no substantial relationships to public health, safety, morals, or general welfare."[59]

As early ordinances were revised and refined in the 1940s and 1950s, minimum lot sizes swelled—with 10,000 or 7,500 s.f. lots replacing the older 5,000 s.f. threshold in the inner-ring suburbs and minimum lots as large as one or two acres the rule in more exclusive settings. "The properties must be protected against obnoxious uses," Bartholomew reminded his clients, "and lots must be sufficiently large to prevent overcrowding."[60] Large-lot single-family zoning also tempered demands on local schools. But because most suburban school districts encompassed two or more municipalities, more exclusive communities were anxious about neighboring development patterns and zoning plans as well. In the early 1950s, for example, the city of Ladue worried that new residential construction (including smaller lots and multifamily dwellings) in nearby Creve Coeur would "impose an extremely large burden on the school system and would result in very little taxable income because of the cheap character of the homes."[61]

The flip side of all of this, of course, was the paucity of alternatives: duplexes, townhomes, garden apartments, and multistory apartment buildings. As land-use law took shape in St. Louis County, prohibition of multifamily housing reflected both the logic of early twentieth-century campaigns against the tenement and contemporary conflations of race and poverty. "No apartment buildings are now found within the city," reasoned Ferguson city officials during deliberations over a new ordinance in 1932; "this affords an excellent opportunity for controlling this type of housing." Civic leaders in Brentwood, turning down a requested variance for multifamily housing in 1935, echoed this logic—claiming there was "no apparent present or future need . . . the city is now occupied by single-family homes and every effort should be made to preserve this character." By the 1960s, suburban city planners generally considered even a duplex a "nuisance" under the police power, agreeing with single-family homeowners that such uses were "annoying to them, interfered with their proper use and enjoyment of their homes, and tended to depreciate the value of their homes."[62]

Even where scattered multifamily developments existed, local governments did not hesitate to zone them into nonconforming exceptions. "There are very few duplexes or apartments in Kirkwood," observed that city's planners in 1940; "this is a most fortunate condition and every effort should be made to protect the single-family development through the planning program and especially through zoning regulations." Planners in Rock Hill agreed, arguing in 1954 that theirs was "a community of single-family dwellings. There are no duplexes, multiple dwellings or apartment houses . . . This is a healthy situation and the zoning ordinance should be directed towards giving the best protection possible to established single-family areas and to vacant areas potentially suitable for such use." When Ferguson adopted a new ordinance in 1956, it eliminated any allowance for multifamily dwellings in the hope of eliminating a scattering of duplexes that had been allowed during the war-era housing crunch. City officials considering a new ordinance for Webster Groves in 1958 claimed there was no local demand for multifamily dwellings, dropped both duplex and apartment zoning, and left only an allowance for residential apartments in commercial zones. When Bellefontaine Neighbors revised its code in 1959, it not only dropped the smallest (6,000 s.f.) single-family designation but zoned an existing strip of duplexes into nonconformance.[63]

Many municipalities made no provision for multifamily dwelling at all; those that did typically created districts representing a tiny fraction (1 or 2 percent) of zoned land. Where higher-density housing was allowed, it was often spot zoned as a transitional district between single-family zones and less desirable uses—including commercial or industrial properties or lesser zones in neighboring communities. When Ferguson officials contemplated a small multifamily zone in 1932, for example, they did so less to accommodate those with lesser incomes than as a "buffer between the business district and the more quiet residential area."[64] Of the nearly 7,000 residential building permits issued in St. Louis County the first three years after World War II, only 46 (two-thirds of 1 percent) were for duplexes and none were for denser residential development. By 1960, the County had just over 200,000 dwelling units, of which barely 7 percent were in multifamily units (almost all of which were duplexes). Into the 1980s, most of the suburban multifamily housing stock was concentrated in smaller units (unsuitable for families) in the inner-ring suburbs. The same pattern held as the metro area swallowed more counties to the west. On the eve of its inclusion in the MSA in 1970, Franklin County adopted a new county ordinance that increased the land zoned for multifamily dwellings tenfold—to a grand total to 250 acres, or about 4/100 of 1 percent of the developed residential land base.[65]

The result was an unsurprising distribution of multifamily (affordable) housing across the region. There are a couple of ways of looking at this. A composite of local zoning maps (see Map 3.10) shows the meager distribution (circa the mid-1960s) of multifamily zoning in the suburbs—although the sharp distinction in this respect fell not at the County line, but at the western boundaries of the inner-ring suburbs. Zoning in these settings (Clayton, University City, Brentwood, Maplewood, Richmond

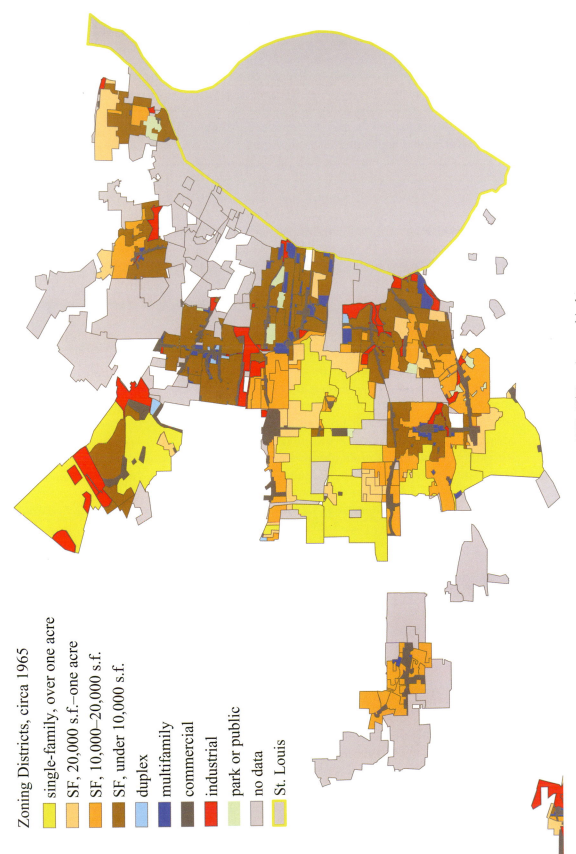

Zoning Districts, circa 1965

- single-family, over one acre
- SF, 20,000 s.f.–one acre
- SF, 10,000–20,000 s.f.
- SF, under 10,000 s.f.
- duplex
- multifamily
- commercial
- industrial
- park or public
- no data
- St. Louis

Map 3.10. Zoning, St. Louis County municipalities, circa 1965. Municipal zone maps, 1958–1974, various archival sources.

Heights, Webster Groves) reflected older patterns of mixed use and mixed density development, earlier pressure on housing and land prices, and distinct postwar motives. By the mid-1950s, for example, Clayton was recasting itself as a new central business district for the Greater St. Louis area. Toward this end, it not only radically revised its commercial zoning (as I discuss below) but also dropped its smallest (5,000 s.f.) single-family designation and adopted a new multifamily district in recognition of the diverse housing demands of its changing workforce. One postwar survey of housing in 19 St. Louis County municipalities found that 10 of the 19 contained no duplexes or multifamily units, and that a high percentage of both (70 percent of duplexes; 98 percent of multifamily units) were in University City and Clayton.[66] These inner-ring suburbs keenly resented the focus on single-family development elsewhere, arguing that, as a result, they bore the burden of flight from the City's northside.[67]

Housing snapshots from census data confirm these patterns: In 1950 (see Map 3.11), less than 5 percent of the housing units in much of the central and south County were anything other than single-family detached homes. Residential density was slightly higher in the north County and in the inner-ring suburbs, but mixed-use and high-density tracts were concentrated overwhelmingly in central St. Louis (the single high-density tract outside the City is Jefferson Barracks, an army base decommissioned just before the 1950 census). It is important to note that while suburban zoning insulated single-family homes from proximity to apartments and duplexes, it did not always prohibit multifamily housing. Under most ordinances, land could always be employed at a "higher use"—meaning that apartments could be built in industrial and commercial zones, often above street-level businesses or stores. By the County's own estimate, the vast majority of available multifamily housing (in incorporated and unincorporated areas alike) was "underzoned" in this way.[68]

Large-lot single-family suburbs were designed and maintained as havens from the City, but they also understood themselves to be part of that City. Residents of Calverton Park or Bellefontaine Neighbors or Country Life Acres lived in "St. Louis," even if the central city was a place they only braved for a baseball game. But planners in the suburban municipalities also saw an inexorable logic to urban growth in which the lots were bigger and the grass greener in each successive ring of suburban development. They appreciated the fact that the metropolitan area needed to offer housing for a range of incomes and life stages. But they invariably argued that such demands could and should be met, not in each corporate fragment, but by different fragments in different ways. Urban renewal projects in the County (as we shall see in the next chapter) proceeded on the assumption that those displaced by the clearance of substandard properties would find public or private housing in the City. By the same logic, multifamily districts belonged in the City or its inner-ring suburbs. "There is more than ample opportunity for apartment house construction to meet the needs of the whole St. Louis region in the City of St. Louis and in certain other suburban communities," argued Ladue city officials in 1939, "without the necessity of introducing it into the city of Ladue, where the overwhelming majority of people own their own homes and where they have come in the hope that they could avoid this class of urban development."[69]

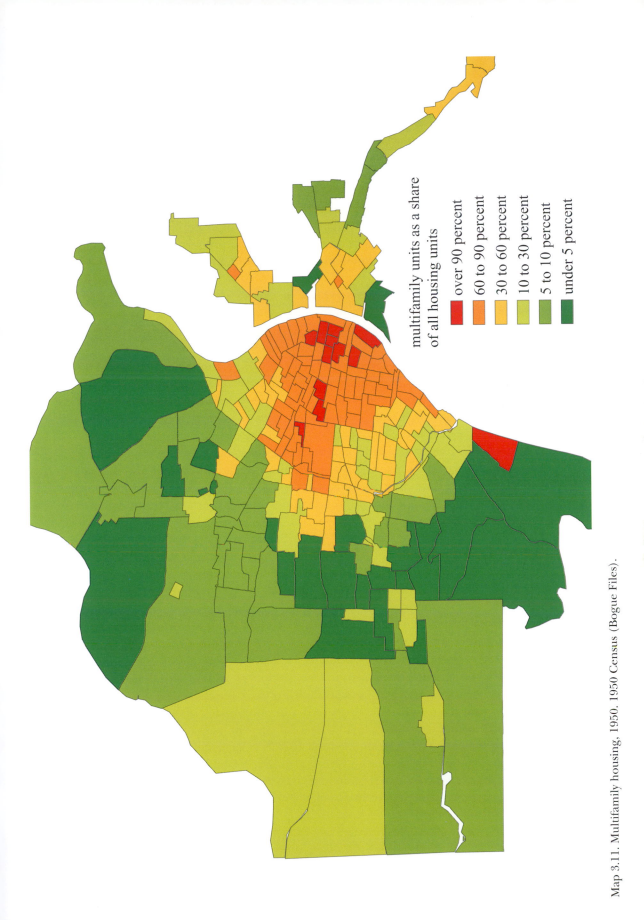

Map 3.11. Multifamily housing, 1950. 1950 Census (Bogue Files).

multifamily units as a share
of all housing units

over 90 percent
60 to 90 percent
30 to 60 percent
10 to 30 percent
5 to 10 percent
under 5 percent

Commercial zoning was a little more complicated. Suburban municipalities were leery of commercial development (as they were of all "lesser uses") because it threatened the value of contiguous single-family tracts and because it could serve as a Trojan horse for "underzoned" multifamily dwellings. At the same time, however, limited commercial development proved increasingly attractive. Suburban residents, less and less oriented toward employment and commerce in the City, wanted goods and services closer to home. Commercial property, in turn, was assessed at much higher rates and made few conventional demands (school funding, for example) on local budgets. This tax advantage was especially pronounced for retail properties; under Missouri's tax structure, "point-of-origin" municipalities were entitled to a share of sales tax revenue.[70]

Different communities responded to these incentives in different ways. Some, echoing the logic behind multifamily prohibitions, simply assumed local residents could be adequately served by commercial (especially retail) development in surrounding communities and in the City. In 1945, Ladue pared back its commercial zones. This is "the one place in St. Louis County that does have fine residences, and I think we ought to keep it that way," argued one resident. "We speak of the distance to and from service industries. It is not that far. Everybody here practically has an automobile. And you can skip in to St. Louis." Business interests challenging local restrictions met the same response from the courts, which typically held that "adequate commercial and business facilities have always existed and are readily available in other areas and other communities."[71] In many suburban settings, commercial land use was established not by a general zoning plan but by spot zoning in response to discrete appeals. In this way, municipalities could pick and choose among proposed commercial projects while maintaining blanket restrictions against commercial use.[72]

Some tried to encourage the "right" kind of commercial development by drawing careful distinctions between commercial districts, often listing in the text of the ordinance which businesses were permitted in "local commercial," "highway commercial," "neighborhood commercial," or "planned commercial" zones. This was an increasingly popular strategy, especially (as I trace in Chapter 4) when local redevelopment plans could manage land acquisition, tax subsidies, and rezoning requests in close cooperation with a particular developer or commercial interest. This was also murkier legal ground, as local governments tried to used "planned" commercial districts to pick and choose among prospective developers—a practice one judge struck down (in a late 1990s case) as "unlawful, arbitrary, capricious and unreasonable" when local officials in Chesterfield rejected a development plan that otherwise met the standards of the zoned area.[73] And, as local governments zoned and rezoned to meet local demand, they also understood this as a beggar-thy-neighbor chase for regional sales tax revenues. As early as 1934, planning consultants cautioned the city of Brentwood not to overreach in its commercial zoning: "While there may be potential purchasing power in the surrounding area, it should be realized that every city has the same objectives as Brentwood."[74]

An outlier in these respects was the city of Clayton. Clayton sat just west of St. Louis at Forest Park, straddling one of the major thoroughfares running from the central city out into the County. Clayton was the County seat before and after the City-County split in 1876 and retained a conventional central business district centered on the County courthouse. Local officials recognized very early the peril and promise of their proximity to St. Louis, and they used zoning to draw commercial (especially professional) interests out from the City. The area surrounding the courthouse was rezoned in 1929 to allow office buildings under 10 stories, but development (in the depths of the Depression) was slow and the height restrictions were gradually lowered again. In the decade after World War II, Clayton attracted a steady stream of professional, business, and retail migrants from the City. In 1959, it decided to compete directly with the City and replaced all height restrictions in its central business district with a floor-to-area formula. The results were impressive: A number of longstanding St. Louis firms moved their corporate headquarters out to Clayton, tax revenues climbed, and investors new to the area saw Clayton as an attractive suburban alternative (newer construction, safer, closer to suburban homes and golf courses) to the downtown. By one 1966 survey, over three-quarters of Clayton's office tenants had relocated or established themselves in the preceding decade, and over half were migrants from the City.[75] By the late 1960s, a number of other suburban municipalities had looked to mimic Clayton's success—although their efforts were usually limited to attracting one or two firms to planned "corporate campuses."[76]

This welter of land-use restrictions—especially the sweeping single-family designations that dominated most suburban zoning ordinances—spurred a number of legal challenges. These usually came from property owners who felt unduly constrained when they wanted to sell, commercial developers looking to tap into the County's lucrative demographics, or residential developers who—after the first wave of subdivision—faced local opposition to further construction. As a rule, the courts were reluctant to second-guess local zoning authority or to suggest any set of uniform standards or expectations. What might seem arbitrary and unreasonable in one setting (drawing on the "pig in a parlor" logic of *Euclid*) might be entirely appropriate in another. In 1952, the courts upheld a Ladue ordinance prohibiting construction of residences on tracts of less than three acres and forbidding institutional use except by special permit. "The police power, as evidenced by the zoning ordinance, is not limited to the mere suppression of offensive uses of property," the decision (*Flora Realty v. Ladue*) reasoned, "but may act constructively for the promotion of the general welfare." Following this logic, it was not necessary to show that three-acre zoning sustained the general health or welfare as long as the City's comprehensive plan served that purpose.[77]

Although the courts occasionally looked askance at local "health and welfare" claims, they only rarely checked the pattern of exclusive zoning. Where local autonomy was questioned, it was usually on the grounds that the ordinance in question was sloppy or imprecise. A 1950 ordinance in Moline Acres, for example, established one single-family residential zone with the same borders as the municipality and barred "use of land within the Village for two-family or multiple dwellings or for business, commercial or industrial purposes." In practice, this was intended primarily to control residential density; commercial parcels were spot zoned on a case-by-case basis. When the City moved to enforce these prohibitions against a property owner renting (as a duplex) to two families, the Missouri Supreme Court struck down the ordinance—not for its exclusive intent (which was hardly unique to Moline Acres) but because it was unaccompanied by any actual planning or survey of land use.[78] When a similar case (involving proposed commercial land use in Calverton Park) showed up on the docket in 1970, the court reversed course, finding nothing arbitrary or unreasonable in single-use zoning:

If one endeavored to formulate a hypothetical village where there would be no need for commercial facilities, and which would be particularly suitable and desirable for one-family dwellings, he could no better than describe Calverton Park. Improvements were constructed on almost 70% of the lots in Calverton Park during the 28 years prior to the adoption of the zoning ordinance. In that period no commercial facility was established in the village and each residence was constructed as "one family." That situation demonstrates that the residents of Calverton Park, in 1953, were substantially unanimous in desiring the type of community the zoning ordinance provided for.[79]

Ironically, the political fragmentation that made exclusive zoning possible also inspired a string of legal challenges as property owners battling restriction in one municipality often pointed to lesser uses in neighboring properties covered by neighboring ordinances. This was a point of particular contention along major central county thoroughfares such as Clayton Road. The County and some inner-ring suburbs were content to let these develop as commercial strips and zoned accordingly. But others, including Richmond Heights and Ladue, wanted to protect residential zones—even if it meant maintaining single-family zoning along streets with limited residential potential and where commercial development proceeded in adjacent blocks or across the road. In such cases, property owners argued that a property's "best use" was that which maximized value to the owner and took regional uses (in neighboring municipalities as well) into account; cities and their planners insisted that the "best use" was that which sustained the comprehensive plan and protected land values across the municipality.[80]

Over time, the logic of large-lot single-family development unraveled somewhat. As the County's population boomed, it became harder to assume that single-family subdivision on the western edge of the metropolis could perpetually satisfy new demand. The city of Florissant, for example, grew more than tenfold (3,737 to 38,266) between 1950 and 1960 and had almost doubled in size again (65,908) by 1970—frantically revising its city plan and zoning ordinances along the way.[81] First in the inner-ring suburbs, and later in much of the urbanized midcounty, municipalities were forced to contemplate more high-density and mixed-use zoning. Developers too became more interested in multifamily housing, especially after 1954 when new federal tax rules (allowing accelerated depreciation of investment properties) made such projects more attractive. For its part, the County adopted an increasingly regional perspective and argued that expansive (and in many cases lightly developed) set-asides for single-family development should be at least partially rezoned for commercial or multifamily use.[82] But, with each new annexation or incorporation, the County's direct authority over land use was shrinking. Even modest efforts at rezoning or infill development, let alone efforts of the County or its larger municipalities to think about metropolitan housing patterns, met substantial (and effective) local opposition.[83]

The only real incentive for individual municipalities to consider more mixed-use and mixed-density zoning was money. Large-lot single-family zoning was sustained not only by federal subsidies and exclusionary zoning but by local property tax policies as well. As the County boomed and property values rose, there was considerable political pressure to dampen the resulting tax burden. The solution (in St. Louis County and elsewhere) was to discount the assessment of residential properties. Until the 1980s, as we have seen, county assessors did this on an ad hoc basis, responding to local and state political pressure by undervaluing residential properties. This uneven, uncertain, and capricious method of assessment lead to widespread resentment (especially from commercial property owners) and to a new statewide formula—setting local assessments (for tax purposes) at 19 percent of market value for residential properties and 33 percent for commercial properties.[84]

As a result, while large-lot single-family homes were considered a sound fiscal base in the early postwar era, this logic gradually evaporated. In their quest to maximize revenues and minimize burdens, local governments increasingly turned to multifamily and commercial development. Before and after the reforms of the 1980s, commercial parcels paid taxes at much higher assessments. Land and building assessments on multifamily parcels were much higher than those developed at lower density, and (although the law was elusive on this point) rental properties containing more than four units paid at the commercial rates. And both provided many of their own services (security and waste management, for example). In 1972, the County estimated that a 13-acre parcel zoned at R-1 (the lowest-density single-family zone) cost it just over $20,000 a year. The same parcel zoned for apartments tipped the balance sheet dramatically, earning net tax revenue of over $16,000. In order to sustain such returns, local planners invariably argued that apartments should be developed for singles, students, young couples, and retirees, and restricted apartment size accordingly—a tack critics recognized as an effort to dampen the school-age population and dubbed "hysterectomy zoning."[85]

American Apartheid: Race and Zoning in Greater St. Louis

All this was designed to sort the metropolis not just by income or family status but by race as well. Just as "tenement" was synonymous with "immigrant housing" in the Progressive Era city, so "apartment" was understood as "black housing" by the planners and residents of suburban St. Louis. This, as we have seen, was the core logic behind the practice of realty in greater St. Louis. And it was the core logic of the zoning ordinances that inherited and perpetuated those practices. Prospectuses for urban subdivisions typically lauded the "protection" afforded by restrictive deed covenants, which (for a time) the FHA not only accommodated but also recommended. Planning consultants like Bartholomew marketed municipal zoning as a means of extending those protections behind a veil of public policy. The deliberations of suburban city planning or zoning commissions, in turn, were invariably haunted by the specter of "the City"—a ghostly reminder of what might happen if residential density and racial occupancy were not controlled.

The African American population of St. Louis County has, until quite recently, been very small. In 1950, the County claimed just over 46 percent of the metropolitan area's total population but only 8 percent of its African American population; St. Louis, with 57 percent of the MSA population, housed over 75 percent of the region's African Americans. By 1970, the County population had more than doubled, claiming just over 40 percent of the population of the (now larger) MSA, while the City's share had shriveled to 27 percent. But most (68 percent) of the region's African Americans still lived in the City, while the County share was 12 percent. In 1990, the City claimed barely 16 percent of the MSA population but was still home to nearly half (44 percent) of the region's blacks—while the County's share of the African American population (32 percent) was now approaching its share (41 percent) of the total MSA. Just as importantly, the distribution of African Americans was confined almost entirely to inner-ring suburbs where the hold of large-lot single-family zoning was the most tenuous. As of 1970, 57 percent of black households (as opposed to 25 percent of white households) in the MSA lived in multifamily housing. Between 1965 and 1969, for example, African American school enrollment in the inner-ring increased dramatically (from 3 to 32 percent in University City, from 47 percent to 90 percent in Wellston). But the nonwhite population of most outer suburbs could still be counted in single or double digits.[86]

The only exception to this pattern, Kinloch in north central St. Louis County, underscored these patterns and the anxieties behind them. Before 1960, fully a third of the County's African American population lived in Kinloch, whose population hovered around 6,000. A historically all-black community, Kinloch claimed few of the advantages enjoyed by its white suburban peers. It remained unincorporated and unzoned, and largely ignored by the County. It was almost surrounded by its neighbors, Berkeley and Ferguson, whose own zoning and planning history were largely animated by the desire to quarantine Kinloch and its residents. Most Berkeley and Ferguson streets dead-ended before they reached Kinloch, and, until 1968, Ferguson barricaded the through streets. Until it was sued by the Justice Department in 1971, Berkeley maintained its own school district, forcing Kinloch to cobble together a meager "separate but equal" alternative. And County planners and realtors treated the Kinloch residential base as part of an entirely separate "nonwhite" housing market otherwise composed of properties in the City. Kinloch was one of the few targets of urban renewal in the County, and, after 1980, its population shrank dramatically—falling to 2,700 in 1990 and under 450 in 2000.[87] Similar pockets of African American settlement, including Elmwood Park, were quarantined by local zoning ordinances, which surrounded such (often unincorporated) parcels with industrial or commercial districts.

Beyond Kinloch and the transitional inner-ring suburbs, patterns of African American settlement were watched closely. Kirkwood planners took worried note of "several scattered Negro developments" in 1940, adding that this posed "certain disadvantages for all citizens and should be corrected in the near future." For Kirkwood and other emerging suburbs, black occupancy simply belonged elsewhere—ideally in the City: It is "much more desirable for all of the colored families to be grouped in one major section where they could be provided with their own school and recreational facilities, churches and stores." A 1955 background study for a prospective shopping center in the central county cited the drift of black occupancy west and south of the City limits as "one of the major threats to the subject area," and while applauding the presence of deed restrictions and large-lot zoning, lamented that there seemed "no legal way in which a southward expansion can be prevented." In 1963, Webster Groves planners underscored the logic of their zoning ordinance on a marked-up city map, identifying commercial and multifamily districts as "100% Negro or very close" and the prospect of a "developing ghetto" across a rail bed (labeled the "Great Divide") near the city's edge.[88]

Given the region's larger demographic patterns, it was hard to miss the underlying racial logic of suburban zoning. When settings like Ladue claimed to be "a section devoted, in large part, to serving Metropolitan St. Louis County and the City of St. Louis area as a better residence section," their implicit benchmark was the declining residential value of the City. Recalling the exceptions in the City's short-lived 1917 racial zoning law, critics of exclusive zoning in the suburbs noted that "the only chance a less fortunate or ordinary thrifty person has to dwell in the 'A' District of Ladue is as part of a ménage, as menials and maids, butlers and chauffeurs, kennel-keepers and stable men." A large-lot single-family zone district—which succeeded (and sustained) private subdivision and private restrictions—was little more than a "restrictive covenant in disguise."[89] When the city of St. Louis applied for Model City funds in the middle 1960s, it concluded simply that "de facto segregation policies are enforced by zoning, building, and subdivision regulations" in St. Louis County.[90]

The politics of race and zoning in Greater St. Louis were underscored in the late 1960s and early 1970s in Black Jack, an unincorporated subdivision scarcely a mile from Paddock Woods (the locus of *Jones v. Mayer*). While unincorporated, the subdivisions of Black Jack and neighboring Spanish Lake worried incessantly about the threats posed by County zoning and the push west and north of the City's population. Residents created the Black Jack and Spanish Lake Improvement Associations in 1950 in order to stave off the annexation designs of their neighbors (Florissant and Ferguson). In the late 1960s, the two groups also dug in their heels against Summerhill, a proposed development of small-lot single-family homes which opponents dubbed "an instant slum." At the meetings called to rally against the Summerhill proposal, residents got wind of an even more insidious threat: a federally subsidized multifamily development.[91]

In late 1969, St. Mark's Methodist Church of Florissant and the United Methodist Ministry in St. Louis decided to cosponsor a federal Section 236 housing development (a provision of the 1968 housing act offering mortgage interest relief for developers of "moderate income" rental housing) and settled on a site adjacent to the Black Jack subdivision (see Map 3.12). The land was undeveloped and zoned R-6 or multifamily by St. Louis County. The plans for the project (Park View Heights) sparked immediate opposition from the Black Jack and Spanish Lake Improvement Associations, which pushed to incorporate the town of Black Jack, annex the Park View Heights site, and impose a single-family zone over everything.[92]

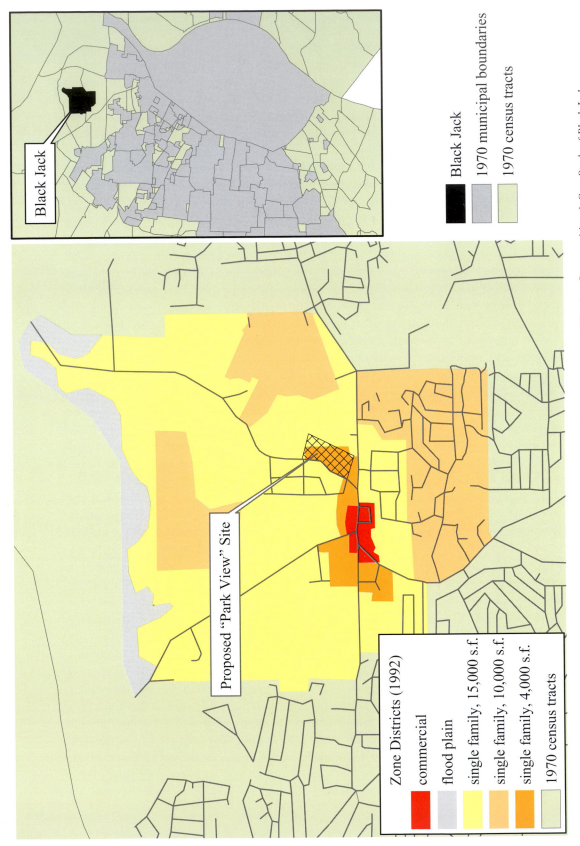

Black Jack

Black Jack

1970 municipal boundaries

1970 census tracts

Proposed "Park View" Site

Zone Districts (1992)

commercial

flood plain

single family, 15,000 s.f.

single family, 10,000 s.f.

single family, 4,000 s.f.

1970 census tracts

Map 3.12. The incorporation of Black Jack, 1970. Ronald Kirby et al., *Residential Zoning and Equal Housing Opportunities: A Case Study of Black Jack, Missouri* (Washington, D.C.: Urban Institute, 1972), figure 4; 1992 Black Jack zone map; 1970 Census.

The racial logic and motivation of this ploy were transparent. As proposed, Black Jack covered parts of two St. Louis County census tracts whose 1970 population (just under 19,000) was 98 percent white and 2 percent black. The new corporate boundaries encompassed 24 census blocks and part of one other, the combined population of which (about 3,250) was 98.8 percent white and .2 percent black. Not surprisingly, opposition to the Park View Heights proposal was "repeatedly expressed in racial terms . . . by leaders of the incorporation movement, by individuals circulating petitions, and by [the] zoning commissioners themselves," an appeals court later observed that "racial criticism of Park View Heights was made and cheered at public meetings." Invoking the unhappy history of large-scale public housing in St. Louis, opponents claimed the development would be "another Pruitt-Igoe." One zoning commissioner tried to deflect charges of local racism by pointing to the existence of a "nigger cemetery" nearby.[93]

In June 1970, the Citizens for the Incorporation of Black Jack presented two petitions with 1,425 signatures requesting incorporation to the St. Louis County Council. Although the St. Louis County Department of Planning "strongly opposed the act of incorporation on fiscal, planning, and legal grounds," it felt bound by state law to approve the petition. The County Council voted to incorporate the city of Black Jack (the County's first new municipality since 1959) in early August. In September, the developers followed through on an option to buy the site. A state court issued a temporary injunction. In October, the new Black Jack government passed a zoning ordinance prohibiting multifamily development. About a quarter of the old County R-6 zone had already been developed as multifamily housing; the new ordinance defined these as nonconforming and effectively banned any new units.[94] In drawing up (and defending) its zoning ordinance, Black Jack leaned heavily on the argument of *Calverton Park,* which justified restrictive zoning on the grounds that land use (commercial, industrial, multifamily) excluded by one municipality would, in a region of patchwork local governance, be allowed by another.[95] By this logic, voiced explicitly in ensuing controversy, the fact that poor people lived in apartments in the City was also an argument against providing similar accommodations in the suburbs.

Park View Heights and the American Civil Liberties Union filed a civil suit in early 1971 and the Justice Department followed in June with an action under the 1968 Fair Housing Act. In 1972, the Eighth District Court dismissed the fair housing case on the grounds that, since the ordinance excluded poor whites as well as blacks, discriminatory intent was impossible to prove. The court of appeals reversed the decision, arguing that the lower court's criteria for "discrimination" ignored not only the clear racial overtones of Black Jack's behavior but also the discriminatory impact of the new ordinance (regardless of intent) and the larger historical context of racial exclusion and anxiety in suburban zoning politics. The Black Jack ordinance, it concluded, was "but one more factor confining blacks to low-income housing in the center city, confirming the inexorable process whereby the St. Louis metropolitan area becomes one that has the racial shape of a donut, with the Negroes in the hole and with mostly Whites occupying the ring." The Supreme Court declined to weigh in, and the zoning ordinance was declared invalid.[96]

The civil suit, and the ultimate fate of the development, took longer to sort out. The district court rebuffed the case, holding that Black Jack's action was zoning rather than rezoning, denying standing to any plaintiffs but Park View Heights (the ACLU had tried to include "potential residents") and finding insufficient evidence of direct discrimination. Again the court of appeals reversed and the parties agreed to wait it out and abide by the final disposition of the Justice Department's case. As the January 1976 trial date approached, Park View Heights and Black Jack reached a settlement: the city paid the developers $450,000, and the "prospective residents" agreed to drop their claim for damages. This did not resolve the fate of the project itself, and the plaintiffs continued to press for a "fair housing" solution in Black Jack. Once again, the district court ruled on Black Jack's behalf—arguing that the city could not be expected to conjure up a new private project out of thin air, and that it did not have the means, authority, or responsibility to provide low-income housing itself. The court of appeals agreed, but directed the lower court to consider intermediate solutions—including an affirmative effort by Black Jack to assemble and zone an appropriate parcel for private development.[97]

Despite the final disposition of the fair housing and civil cases, the prospect for introducing mixed-income multifamily housing to Black Jack had evaporated. The contested site was bought back by the city under the terms of the civil settlement. By the middle 1970s, climbing interest rates made it impossible for Park View Heights to reassemble a realistic financial package. Support from Housing and Urban Development for another run at the project was lukewarm. And the racial climate in Black Jack had, in some respects, been hardened by the intrusion of state and federal courts. "No developer in his or her right mind," observed the lawyers for Park View Heights, "at this point in time would go into the City of Black Jack and attempt to build low and moderate income housing, . . . because the City of Black Jack has indicated its powerful and abiding hostility to such projects."[98]

In the wake of this legal turmoil, Black Jack crafted a new zoning ordinance, again making no allowance for multifamily housing. For a time, this sustained the core logic and goals of the original zoning decision: relatively exclusive house values and little threat to existing patterns of racial occupancy. In 1992, the city's zone plan consisted largely of two single-family designations: an R-2 district (minimum lot size 15,000 s.f.) covering most of the city, interrupted by three R-3 (10,000) districts—the northernmost of which was undeveloped. Higher-density (R-6) single-family development (4,000 s.f.) was allowed in a small district bordering the lone commercial district (see Map 3.12). By 2004, these zones had changed little: a larger R-1 zone (minimum lot one acre) was added, and the least restrictive residential zone (bumped to 4,500 s.f.) now allowed duplexes.[99] But large-lot single-family zoning alone could not stem the longer-term transition of Black Jack and much of the near north County. The African American population of Black Jack grew from 18 percent in 1980, to 44 percent in 1990, to 71 percent in 2000.[100]

As African American occupancy increased in the inner north County suburbs, the logic and pattern of exclusive zoning simply drifted west. As Map 3.13 suggests, multifamily housing in the County remained concentrated in older inner suburbs with rela-

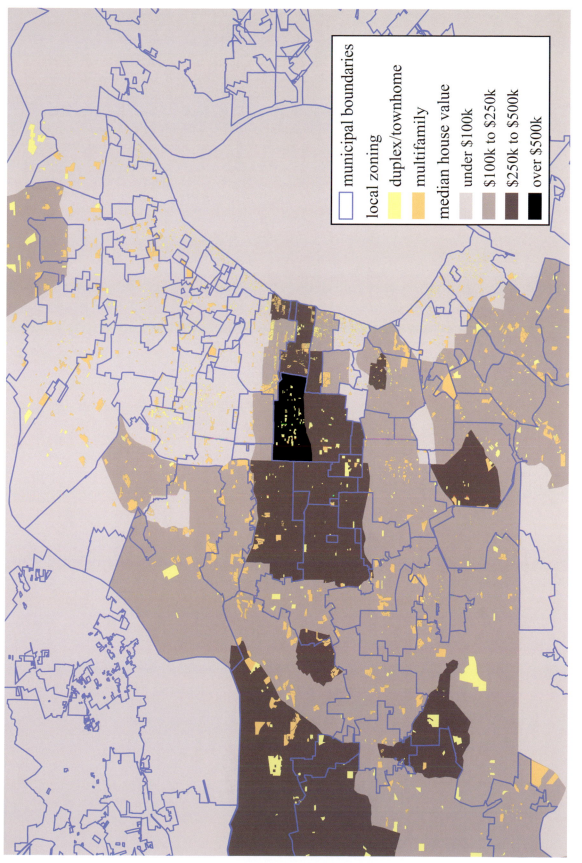

Map 3.13. Median home value and multifamily zoning, St. Louis County, 2000. Census 2000 (SF-3); St. Louis County Assessor.

tively low median home values. Farther west, most of the multifamily housing (much of it duplexes or townhomes) was scattered in planned higher density districts, many of them adjacent to commercial or industrial districts. More broadly, County municipalities maintained their longstanding patterns and strategies—using incorporation and annexation to protect private development patterns, and zoning (or rezoning) to control the class and race of local occupants.[101]

Chapter 4
Fighting Blight

Urban Renewal Policies and Programs, 1945–2000

The net effect of political fragmentation, real estate restrictions, and exclusionary zoning was the virtual devastation of north and central St. Louis. City planners began taking stock of these conditions (substandard housing, abandoned commercial property, aging infrastructure) as early as World War I, but all that really changed over the following decades were the terms—obsolescence, decadence, blight, ghettoization, decay—used to label them. While midcentury urban interests disagreed over the causes of "blight," they had little trouble reaching a consensus that a cure was beyond the reach of either private investors or the municipal police power.

The prescription, in St. Louis and elsewhere, was urban renewal—a tangled combination of federal money, state enabling laws, local initiative, quasi-public redevelopment corporations, and private investment. Indeed, the task of saving St. Louis was marked by often widely divergent understandings of the core problem, a seemingly endless array of policy innovations, and often dramatically dysfunctional consequences in the City and its suburbs. This chapter offers an inventory of the major urban renewal programs at play in greater St. Louis since 1950 and maps the pattern of their use over time and across the metropolitan area. Chapter 5 assesses the underlying premise of these programs (What is blight?), their costs and benefits, and their consequences.

Consider, as an introduction to the process and politics of urban renewal in St. Louis, the postwar history of downtown's two Marriott hotels: the Pavilion at 1 South Broadway and the Renaissance at 800 Washington (see Map 4.1). The South Broadway property lay near the northeast corner of the Civic Center/Stadium Redevelopment Area, declared "blighted" in 1960 under both Missouri's Chapter 353 urban redevelopment law and the state's Chapter 99 land clearance law. Taken together (I look at this process in more detail below) these laws gave the City, working through a tangle of quasi-public redevelopment corporations, the authority to acquire and clear land for redevelopment—in this case, the construction of Busch Stadium (completed in 1966).

The parcel at 1 South Broadway remained undeveloped until 1968, when then-mayor Alfonso Cervantes purchased the Spanish Pavilion from the site of the 1964

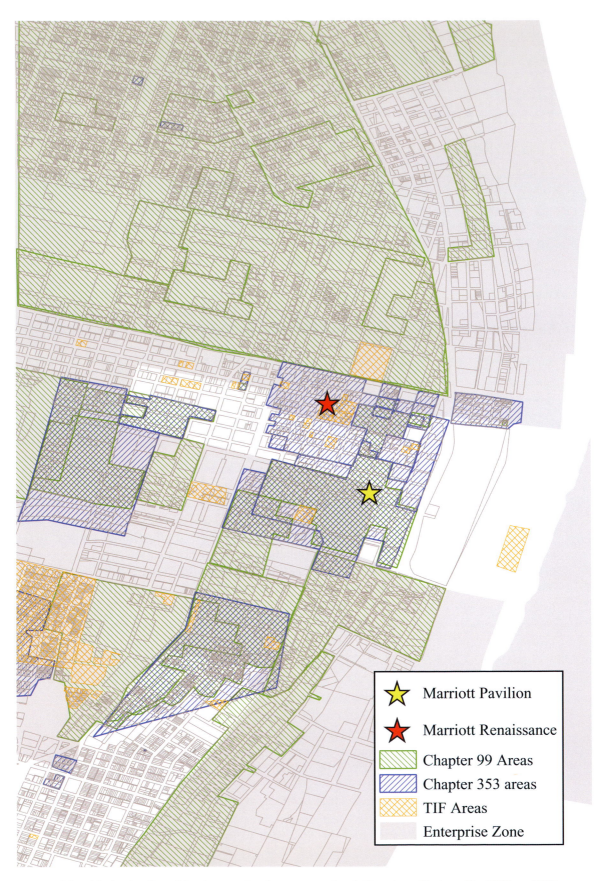

Map 4.1. A tale of two Marriotts: redevelopment on South Broadway. Various City URD and TIF Reports.

Legend:

- ★ (yellow) Marriott Pavilion
- ★ (red) Marriott Renaissance
- Chapter 99 Areas
- Chapter 353 areas
- TIF Areas
- Enterprise Zone

World's Fair in New York and rebuilt it—"with no real sense of purpose," as one observer noted—in the shadow of the stadium. The $6 million bill for buying and reassembling the pavilion was covered by a $3.5 million public subscription and a $2.5 million bank loan. "The business community went along with him," one observer recalled, "in spite of their almost unanimous feeling that the project was ridiculous."[1] This was a novel initiative (soon followed by the purchase, also from the 1964 fair, of a floating replica of the *Santa Maria*). But it sprang from a common determination of struggling cities to recapture downtown prosperity with tourist attractions—museums, sports facilities, convention centers, and boutique shopping.

The pavilion was a magnificent flop: Less than a quarter of a projected 2.5 million visitors materialized in its first year; all three of its resident restaurants lost money; and the whole enterprise closed its doors less than a year after opening. Plans for reinventing the pavilion (now in the reluctant hands of the bank) abounded—including unsuccessful pitches for federal money to turn it into an aquarium or a "Midwest Cultural Center." Amid local speculation as to the property's fate, one of the more popular suggestions was that Mayor Cervantes "should have to live in it and pay all the bills out of his own pocket." To add insult to injury, the *Santa Maria* lasted two months before breaking loose from its moorings during a storm and running aground amid the rusting relics of river-based industry on the Illinois side. It was, the *Post-Dispatch* editorialized at the time, all "cheap, honky-tonk, carnivalized, claptrap." St. Louis-based Breckenridge Hotels purchased the pavilion in 1974, punched a tower through one of its domed roofs and opened a new downtown hotel in 1977. Leery of investing in expansion two years later, Breckenridge sold the property to Marriott.[2]

The Marriott at 800 Washington has a similar, if more complicated history. The property lies at the southern edge of the DeSoto-Carr redevelopment area ("blighted" under Chapter 99 in 1959) and at the northern edge of the sprawling downtown redevelopment area (blighted under Chapter 353 in 1971). The blocks just to the north were redeveloped around the 240,000-square-foot Cervantes Convention Center, which opened in 1977. This complex, "noteworthy for its poor design and rapid descent into near obsolescence within five years of its opening," did little to resurrect downtown. In 1984, the immediate area (now the Washington Avenue Redevelopment Area) was blighted again under Chapters 99 and 353, with the hope of galvanizing redevelopment of two old (and now decrepit) hotel properties: the Lennox (built in 1920) and the Gateway (1928). The Gateway remained unoccupied and undeveloped, falling into such a state of disrepair that the City considered it a serious environmental risk, citing the presence of asbestos, lead paint, PCB, and "a significant amount of pigeon waste." The Lennox, using redevelopment tax abatements, was converted to apartments but struggled to attract tenants and reverted to the City as a tax-delinquent property in 1993.[3]

As is often the case, the abject failure of past redevelopment schemes became an argument for sweeping new plans—including expansion and renovation of the struggling Cervantes Center (completed with $128 million in public subsidies in 1993), a new domed football stadium (completed with $258 million in public subsidies in 1995), and the prospect of a new hotel to pull it all together. In 1999, the City blighted yet another redevelopment area—this time under the auspices of Missouri's tax increment financing (TIF) law—matching the multiblock footprint of a proposed "Convention Headquarters" hotel that would include renovations of the Gateway and the Lennox. The $250 million project drew on between $115 and $135 million in tax-exempt enterprise zone bonds, $50 to $75 million in TIF-based assistance from the City, and $15 or $20 million in state and federal historical renovation tax credits, as well as lesser contributions from federal block grant and brownfield programs. Private investment amounted to less than 10 percent of the project cost: "the hotel doesn't look like a profitable place for private investors to sink their cash," the *Post-Dispatch* concluded simply, "so taxpayers are taking the hit."[4]

Local boosters would point to these (and other) projects as important victories in the battle to reclaim central St. Louis. But the full history suggests a more ambiguous verdict. While private developers and City officials clung to the notion that public policy had simply cleared the way for new private investment, such projects depended on massive public subsidies, including federal money for land clearance, state tax credits, and a tangle of local tax abatements. The properties in question were blighted over and over again in order to qualify for subsidies or tax breaks available under various land reclamation, urban renewal, tax increment financing, and enterprise zone laws (see Map 4.1). Much of this blight was actually the failure or consequence of older redevelopment schemes—including both ill-conceived white elephants (the Spanish Pavilion, the Cervantes Center) and the effect of "slum clearance" on other City neighborhoods. And these properties underscored the retreat of urban renewal from its earliest aspirations to pull local housing and commercial development back into the central city, to a much narrower focus on marquee tourism—hotels, convention centers, stadiums, casinos, shopping malls—whose benefits flowed to a few (often out-of-town) interests.

Policy and Programs

The basic logic of urban renewal is this: In troubled urban settings, the risk of private investment is simply too great to rely on "the market" to turn things around. Investors need some assurance that their efforts will be accompanied by both the development of neighboring parcels and the maintenance of basic public safety and infrastructure. The only way to accomplish this is to assemble relatively large parcels of land, clear them of substandard structures or inappropriate uses, and redevelop them as part of a sweeping renewal plan. Through the middle years of the twentieth century, this raised a series of thorny legal and political questions. The power of eminent domain gave local governments the right to claim private property for public use (roads or bridges), but municipalities, their political and taxing power closely controlled by state governments, simply didn't have the money to acquire and assemble blighted properties. As in the public housing debate, such a large-scale public effort raised the specter of "socializing the city" at the expense of private interests. And it was a stretch, by any conventional legal understanding of "public use," to include transfers from one private owner to another.

For these reasons, urban renewal has always rested on a complex tangle of laws and programs and procedures. Typically, a project might have relied on an infusion of federal money to clear and assemble land, a state law enabling local authorities to delineate and blight a redevelopment area, and the creation of a private redevelopment corporation that effectively borrowed the power of eminent domain. But the initiative usually ran in the opposite direction: a private developer identified a prospective property, the local government responded by blighting the area, and state and federal money followed.[5] In turn, state and local efforts yielded a welter of discrete yet overlapping programs, any number of which might come into play for even a single redevelopment proposal. Over the course of the postwar era, redevelopment interests in St. Louis could avail themselves of the urban redevelopment law (1945), the land clearance law (1951), an Industrial Development Authority with the power to issue tax-exempt revenue bonds (1967), the City's Land Reutilization Act (1969), a Planned Industrial Expansion Authority (PIEA) (1969), a Local Development Company, which packaged local, state, and federal business loans (1978), the state's tax increment financing program (1980), state (1983) and federal (1994) enterprise zones, and a wide array of local, state, and federal programs targeting specific business interests.[6] The major programs are summarized in Table 4.1.

Taken together, these programs suggested a range of overlapping and sometimes

TABLE 4.1. Major Urban Renewal Programs in St. Louis, 1945–2000

Enacted Revised	Program	Law	Eminent Domain	Tax Abatement	Bonding Authority	Pop. Threshold
1943	Urban Redevelopment Corp. Law	MO 353	y			700,000
1945	*lower pop.threshold, tax abatement*		y	25 year (a)		350,000
1969	*lower pop. threshold*		y			20,000
1976	*lower pop. threshold*		y			4,000
1951	Land Clearance for Redevelopment	MO 99	y	10 year (b)	y	none
1967	Planned Industrial Expansion	MO 100	y	(c)	y	400,000
1971	Land Reutilization Authority	MO 92				SL & KC
1982	Tax Increment Financing	MO 99	y	(d)		none
1982	Missouri Enterprise Zone[e]	MO 135		25 year (f)		(g)

Source: Missouri Code, various years.
[a] Under 353, abatements run 10 years on added value, and 5 more on half the added value
[b] LCRA projects qualify for 10-year abatements, but can also be redeveloped under 353
[c] Chapter 100 allows recipients to make payments in lieu of taxes (PILOTS) to retire bonds or pay for improvements; PIE offers no abatements although does allow projects to apply for 353
[d] TIF does not abate property taxes, but collects PILOTS on improved value and dedicates them to a "special allocation fund" until redevelopment costs have been paid off. TIF districts also capture one-half of any increase revenue from sales and income taxes within the district
[e] MO law automatically confers "MO EZ" status on any federal enterprise zone
[f] In addition to tax credits, EZ law abates one/half the property tax on improvements for at least 10 years and no more than 25; and one-half the income tax for new business facilities
[g] Chapter 135 includes a number of place-specific population thresholds

contradictory strategies. The core goals, suggested by the first round of Chapter 353 and Chapter 99 plans, were to make the central business district more attractive for upper-middle-class residents and to make much of the rest of downtown accessible for new industrial or commercial development. Over time, these goals and strategies shifted. Residential projects were increasingly displaced by commercial and industrial projects. As the City's manufacturing base continued to evaporate, attention shifted to investment in research and development (particularly surrounding a few established industries and university-based hospital complexes) and to the tourism dollars promised by the development of retail, sports, and convention centers.[7]

One consequence of this profusion of programs, and its underlying logic, was that urban renewal tended to steer clear of the City's most troubled neighborhoods. Major renewal efforts under Chapters 99 and 353 pushed development west through the central city, linking the central business district with the suburbs but bypassing much of the old urban core. While the "slum" is historically a residential problem, solutions were largely aimed at commercial or industrial development. Indeed, what is remarkable as I trace urban renewal programs across time and across the region is how little attention falls on inescapably blighted residential neighborhoods like those surrounding 4635 North Market. Slum clearance, urban renewal, and the Model Cities program of the 1960s spent billions of dollars but, as one 1978 study concluded, have "had little fundamental effect on the basic economy of the city." Assessments of urban decay in St. Louis have changed little in the last century: the scope of blight mapped in the City plans of 1919 or 1963 or 1947 is essentially the same as that circumscribed by development or enterprise zone programs today.[8]

On-Ramp for Renewal: Urban Highways in Greater St. Louis

While not technically urban renewal projects, major road construction in postwar St. Louis was closely entwined with the politics of blight and slum clearance. Urban highway planning embraced the basic logic of the postwar city: It was designed both to liberate commercial traffic in and around central St. Louis and to make it easier for suburban commuters to get in and out of the City. The locations of urban expressways echoed the larger politics of urban renewal: planners targeted blighted neighborhoods in the hopes of servicing "high-class residences" in the County without disturbing them. The fiscal underpinnings for urban renewal and road construction were essentially similar: local projects relied largely on federal money (fully 90 percent of state urban highway spending was used in Greater St. Louis).[9] And road construction rested on a similar (but stronger) legal premise: while urban renewal projects (as we shall see in the Conclusion) relied on increasingly inventive expansions of the municipal police power, the "public purpose" of road improvements was well established.

Demand for a new urban highway system was generated by surging automobile ownership and the new suburban housing patterns. Between 1911 and 1946, automobile registration in the metropolitan area jumped from 7,700 to 326,000. "Sometime around 1915," the St. Louis Chamber of Commerce noted in the early 1930s, "the class patronage of our street railways commenced to desert it, [and] began using their own automobiles for transit daily from their homes to their places of business in the downtown section."[10] Automobility, in turn, liberated residential development from proximity to public transit and made the sprawl of single-family subdivisions possible. New demands on existing roads, highways, and parking stock (in St. Louis and else-where) generated new interest in the logistics of commuting—understood at the time to be a problem of getting into the city in the morning, finding a place to park, and getting out again at five o'clock. As a *Fortune* feature captured it: "How fast can you get out of town?" Federal money was slow to follow, but the 1956 Federal Highway Act (which famously recast road construction as a cold war urgency) finally opened the spigot for local planners.[11]

Local planning reflected the twin concerns for more parking downtown and more efficient movement of traffic from the central city to the suburbs. "A vast amount of parking space for the accommodation of individual automobile traffic is imperative," the 1947 City Plan underscored, "Provision of this parking space, if not undertaken by private enterprise, may be forced upon the city as a public function. It is the mod-ern substitute for subway construction." Planning for downtown (culminating in a landmark 1953 report) cited "inadequate thoroughfares [and] lack of off-street park-ing" alongside "blight and obsolescence" as the City's most compelling problems and called for a "comprehensive system of multi-story and sub-grade garages on the imme-diate fringes of the central core." The urgency, as most planners saw it, was for a one-time adjustment to the infrastructure demands posed by the automobile. "The curve of parking demand will have reached its climax by [1970]," the 1953 report assured, and "efficient systems of public mass transportation (such as buses, railroad subway, heli-cabs) will provide rapid and adequate service."[12]

Planning for urban expressways proved more complicated, in large part because there was little agreement as to the goal or impact of moving more traffic more quickly and efficiently through and from the central city. Downtown business interests (Civic Progress, the Chamber) hoped that an end to traffic congestion would slow the exo-dus to the suburbs and stabilize downtown by bringing in more cars while diverting those just passing through. Others worried about the implications of building "a 'speedway' through our city" and argued that limited access roads also meant limited benefits for those living in the City. Early plans reflecting these contradictory impulses included various limited-access routes through the City—including a 1928 proposal to double-deck Third Street, with local traffic below and through traffic on an elevated thoroughfare.[13]

The metro area's first expressway, built with federal funds in the 1930s, ran east from the City limits along the southern border of Forest Park and opened in stages—reaching Kingshighway in 1936, Vandeventer in 1937, and downtown (Chouteau) in 1938 (see Map 4.2). It was dubbed the Red Feather Expressway in 1948—although one aldermanic cold warrior bristled at the "red" and lobbied to have the name changed to Easter Bunny Lane. The same road, running west from the City limits, was known as the Daniel Boone Expressway (or U.S. Route 40 Traffic Relief), reaching Lindbergh Avenue in 1938 and Brentwood in the late 1940s. When federal funds for urban highways were first made available in 1944, planners looked to upgrading Route

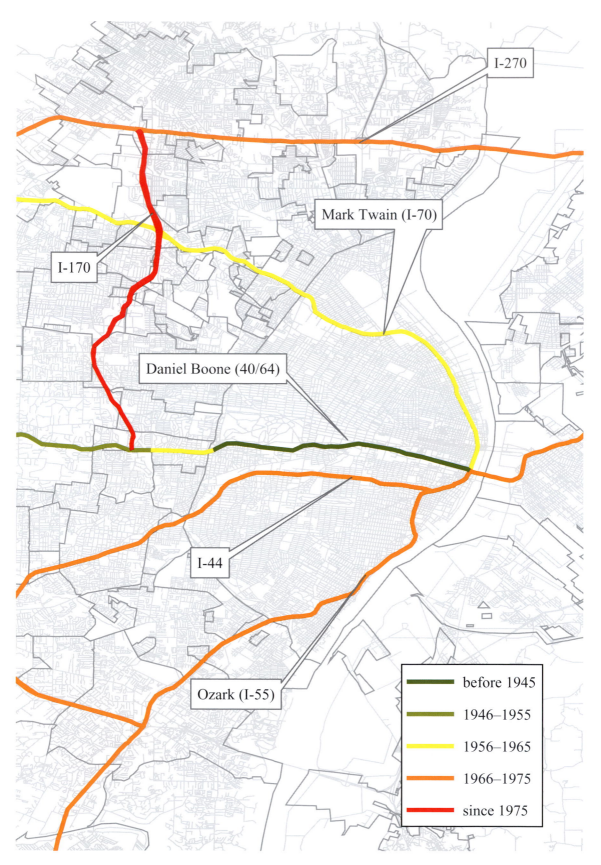

I-270

Mark Twain (I-70)

I-170

Daniel Boone (40/64)

I-44

Ozark (I-55)

▬▬▬	before 1945
▬▬▬	1946–1955
▬▬▬	1956–1965
▬▬▬	1966–1975
▬▬▬	since 1975

Map 4.2. Major highway construction. Elliot Report (September 1951), "Review of Expressway Progress Since 1934" (n.d.), box 1:12, Raymond Tucker Papers; *SLPD*.

40 as a limited access expressway all the way from Brentwood to downtown. But attention soon turned to two new routes—the Ozark Expressway, running out from downtown to the southwest, and the Mark Twain, running northwest from downtown. The emerging plan, for a trio of expressways (Ozark, Daniel Boone, and Mark Twain) radiating from downtown and a loop around the central business district, was elaborated in the 1947 City Plan and (with slightly different routes) in the comprehensive St. Louis Urban Expressway [Elliot] Report of 1952.[14]

The City and County portions of Route 40 (now I-64) were joined in the late 1950s. The Ozark and Mark Twain routes, both of which cut diagonally across the existing street grid, were more expensive and created more contention: And it was not until 1955 that the City passed a bond issue sufficient to start land acquisition. Construction of the Mark Twain (now I-70) began in August 1956, an event that also marked the first ground broken under the new federal Interstate Highway Program. The first 20 mile stretch—running from the Jefferson Memorial site, along the north river front, and then west from O'Fallon Park to Lambert Field—opened in 1961. Land acquisition for the Ozark (now I-55) route began in 1960, and the expressway opened in 1967. Land clearance for urban renewal through the central city opened up another southern route and I-44, an east-west expressway parallel to the Daniel Boone, opened in 1972.[15]

As local planners and federal funds transformed the City's transportation infrastructure, they also called attention to the deteriorating neighborhoods found at each off-ramp and bisected by the new expressways. "17,000 vehicles a day traverse these streets through this blighted area, transporting the public from the residential district to the downtown," the City's Anti-Slum Commission noted in 1948, adding that "this experience has a devastating effect upon the morale of the citizens."[16] This, of course, underscored the much larger (but often equally confused) debate about the fate of downtown. How might the commercial, industrial, and residential life of the City be renewed? And who would it be renewed for?

Urban Renewal and Land Clearance: Chapters 353 and 99

In St. Louis, the first stab at urban renewal came with the City Plan of 1911, which identified a swath of blight along the riverfront and suggested that the entire area be razed and replaced with a great parkway. Such musings, however, included no plans for relocating displaced property owners and no funding for the acquisition of land. The plan failed by municipal referendum in 1915. For the next decade, in St. Louis and elsewhere, sweeping redevelopment proposals were displaced by more modest beautification campaigns, often including building code enforcement, zoning, and smoke abatement. City plans through the 1920s continued to toy with dramatic redevelopment of the central riverfront but invariably ran up against the opposition of local property owners and the paucity of local revenues. All of this changed in the early 1930s, when the federal government began acquiring land for the Jefferson National Expansion Memorial. This project foreshadowed the future of urban renewal in a number of ways. Only the combination of local police powers and federal dollars made radical redevelopment possible. The project displaced longstanding residential and industrial enclaves for the promise of tourism downtown. And enthusiasm for clearing the land ran well ahead of plans to rebuild—in this case, more than a decade passed between the demolitions of the middle 1930s and groundbreaking for the Memorial in 1947.[17]

Work on the statutory and fiscal underpinnings for a broader urban renewal program began in the 1930s. Through the New Deal, urban renewal was inextricably entangled with the debate over public housing, in large part because most saw renewal as an essentially residential program: "slum clearance" would be accompanied by a combination of new high-end housing to lure the well-to-do back to the City and public housing projects to warehouse those displaced. Federal legislators juggled a number of ideas (including placing cleared land under public stewardship and leasing cleared land to developers) while trying to navigate the contradictions—and political pitfalls—of a policy designed to sustain private enterprise while spending billions of federal dollars.[18]

If federal money was the first precondition for urban renewal, the second was the recasting of state and local law. In Missouri and elsewhere, this usually involved two issues: extending and clarifying the local power of eminent domain and establishing some form of tax relief for property owners in development areas. New York and New Jersey pioneered this approach, both passing laws in the late 1920s that "lent" the power of eminent domain to private developers in exchange for rent controls and other conditions on redevelopment. In the wake of World War II, the lure of federal dollars spurred many other states to follow suit, most with laws that carved out a new legal status for private redevelopment corporations. These corporations assumed the power of eminent domain in exchange for a state-imposed limit on their profits.[19]

In Missouri, urban renewal relied on two state laws: the Chapter 353 Urban Redevelopment Act (passed in 1945) and the Chapter 99 Land Clearance Act (passed in 1951). St. Louis planners had long recognized the need for new resources and incentives for large-scale redevelopment. Business and realty interests began meeting with Harland Bartholomew in 1940, their mutual agenda including downtown parking, downtown housing, and downtown redevelopment. The state's urban redevelopment law, first passed in 1943, was essentially a St. Louis bill—limiting participation to cities with populations larger than 700,000 (this threshold was lowered in 1945 to 350,000 in order to accommodate Kansas City, and collapsed to 20,000 in 1969 and 4,000 in 1976).[20] Few were happy with the 1943 bill (which did little but specify the form and function of redevelopment corporations), and St. Louis developers immediately began lobbying for its revision, winning two important changes with the passage of Chapter 353 in 1945: a schedule of tax abatements for property owners in renewal areas and an allowance for out-of-state investment (especially by insurance companies) in redevelopment corporations. "The language of the law," Mayor Kaufman conceded, "was practically written in [the] offices of New York insurance companies."[21]

Local officials saw immense promise in the new law, and the 1947 City Plan included elaborate plans for rebuilding the blighted central city: with Chapter 353, the City could "transform an obsolete area into a fine residential neighborhood with a good standard of housing, enlarged open areas, greatly improved environment, small concentrated shop centers, and much needed park and recreation space."[22] Yet, while Chapter 353 would become the "top gun in the St. Louis redevelopment arsenal," its passage in 1945 did little to galvanize redevelopment—in large part because it offered the legal authority but not the resources to clear and assemble land. These resources began to flow with the National Housing Act of 1949. Under this law, the federal government would advance money to local redevelopment agencies for surveying and planning. If the federal agency approved local plans, federal funds could be used to acquire and clear land—subject to a token match of local dollars and partial repayment when the land was finally sold to private developers. Local participation again required state action, and Missouri responded with the 1951 Land Clearance and Redevelopment Act (Chapter 99) in 1951.[23]

While City planners plowed ahead with a few public housing projects, urban renewal remained stalled. In part, the problem was purely administrative: the City did not pass an ordinance spelling out the local blighting process until 1959.[24] More importantly, the City was struggling to match its increasingly grandiose plans for reclaiming downtown to the federal standards (and funding) set by the 1949 Housing Act. The 1954 Housing Act loosened these constraints, both by appropriating more money for cities and by retreating from the "predominantly residential" focus of the 1937 and 1949 laws. Beginning in 1954, Congress allowed up to 10 percent (increased to 35 percent in 1965) of federal housing funds to be used for non-residential projects.[25] The first run of St. Louis projects (Plaza Square, Mansion House, Mill Creek Valley, Kosciusko) followed in the mid- to late 1950s.

Taken together, Chapters 353 and 99 worked like this: Under the authority of either statute, the Board of Aldermen declared an area "blighted" and in need of redevelopment. Chapter 353 was commonly used for single projects or buildings; Chapter 99 was invoked when federal dollars were needed to clear or acquire land. In many instances, both were used—Chapter 99 to tap federal funds, Chapter 353 to facilitate redevelopment. The blighting process, as we shall see, was less a scientific assessment of local conditions than it was a response to a private development proposal: Having identified a parcel for redevelopment, private interests worked with the City to both blight the area and authorize an Urban Redevelopment Corporation (URC) to undertake redevelopment. Any URC, in other words, could submit a plan for a blighted area, but there was usually one in the wings pushing for the blighting in the first place. Chapter 353 URCs, in turn, borrowed the city's power of eminent domain to clear or acquire property—a task essentially contracted out to the Chapter 99 Land Clearance for Redevelopment Authority (LCRA) when federal funds were needed. Chapter 353 URCs could also buy, sell, hold, or lease property—in exchange for all of which they agreed to limit profits to 8 percent of project costs.[26]

The other benefit of defining private land acquisition and development as a "public purpose" was tax abatement. Chapters 99 and 353 provided two sorts of tax breaks. Land acquired under Chapter 99 became city property and came off the tax rolls. The LCRA not only cleared the land for redevelopment but often completed significant improvements before turning title over to a private developer or URC. In some cases (as in the first downtown stadium project), the St. Louis LCRA perpetuated this "public purpose" tax break by maintaining title and leasing the property to private tenants.[27] More importantly, Chapter 353 granted URCs a sliding 25-year property tax abatement on redeveloped parcels within an urban renewal area: for the first 10 years, property was assessed and taxed at its pre-353 "blighted" value; for the next 15 years, it was assessed and taxed at only half of its "improved" value. These were the maximum abatements allowed under the law, and technically each redevelopment negotiated an appropriate abatement schedule—but no St. Louis projects included anything less than the full 25-year abatement.[28]

Patterns of Redevelopment: Chapters 99 and 353 in Practice

Chapters 99 and 353 underwrote a series of major redevelopment projects in greater St. Louis. Although Chapter 353 was in place in 1945 and Chapter 99 in 1951, the timing and location of major renewal projects rested on a tangle of local political, fiscal, and strategic calculations. Mapping these projects across the region, and over time, presents a series of challenges. While blighting under either 353 or 99 designated broad areas for redevelopment, the grant of tax abatements (and the organization of urban redevelopment corporations) was specific to properties or projects within those areas. Some "umbrella" areas encompassed numerous projects, and development often lagged significantly (years, decades) behind the original blighting—indeed, local ordinances in the 1980s and 1990s often reaffirmed or reconfigured 353 or 99 areas blighted years earlier. In other cases, and especially in recent decades, "spot-blighting" designated individual parcels or addresses. Chapter 353 and 99 areas, in turn, overlapped considerably, although not always and not always precisely. Many areas blighted under Chapter 99 were redeveloped, in whole or in part, by a Chapter 353 URC.[29]

Into the early 1970s, urban renewal—accomplished under Chapter 353, Chapter 99, or a combination—was largely confined to the central business district, and the industrial corridors running south and west from downtown. Between 1954 and 2000, the city of St. Louis blighted just over 100 separate urban renewal areas under Chapter 353. Three-quarters of these were single-address projects; the rest were larger areas encompassing multiple projects. As of the last comprehensive survey of Chapter 353 activity (1989), just over half of the project areas included some residential development, although the emphasis was clearly on commercial and industrial development. As of 1989, an investment of just under $2 billion had yielded 28 million square feet of commercial development and fewer than 7,000 residential units.[30] Map 4.3 summarizes the major project areas, showing the year in which the area was first blighted. Chapter 99 areas, summarized on Map 4.4, betray a similar pattern. While overlapping with Chapter 353 areas in the central business district and West End, Chapter 99 focused more on redevelopment of major industrial areas—including the Mill Creek Valley, the north and south riverfront, and the inner suburbs such as Wellston. Chapter 99 also reached into the County, creating redevelopment areas in Wellston, Univer-

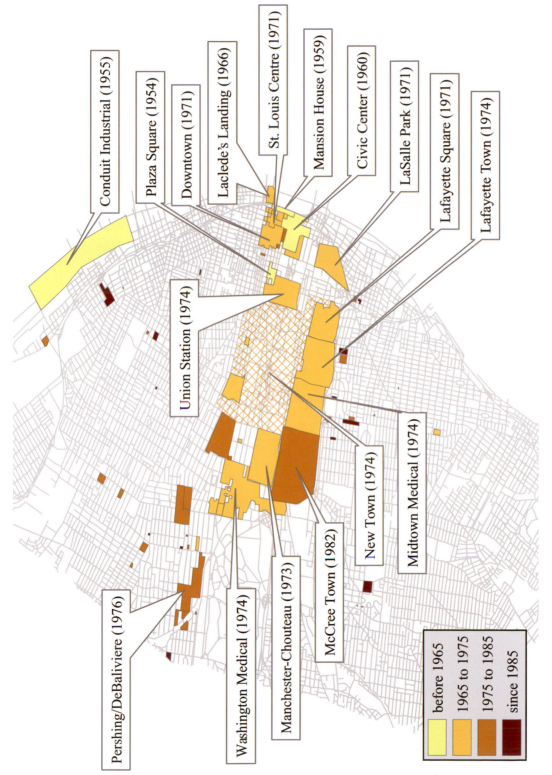

Conduit Industrial (1955)

Plaza Square (1954)

Downtown (1971)

Laclede's Landing (1966)

St. Louis Centre (1971)

Mansion House (1959)

Civic Center (1960)

LaSalle Park (1971)

Lafayette Square (1971)

Lafayette Town (1974)

Union Station (1974)

New Town (1974)

Midtown Medical (1974)

Pershing/DeBaliviere (1976)

Washington Medical (1974)

Manchester-Chouteau (1973)

McCree Town (1982)

before 1965
1965 to 1975
1975 to 1985
since 1985

Map 4.3. Major Chapter 353 areas, 1954–2000. Various LCRA, CDA reports; Margaret R. Collins, *Missouri Urban Redevelopment Corporations Law, Chapter 353: A Policy Study for Existing and Future Application Downtown St. Louis* (St. Louis: Community Development Agency, 1978); Rachelle L. Levitt, *Cities Reborn* (Washington, D.C.: Urban Land Institute, 1987); City ordinances and parcel data; UR map (1981) in Mercantile Library, UMSL.

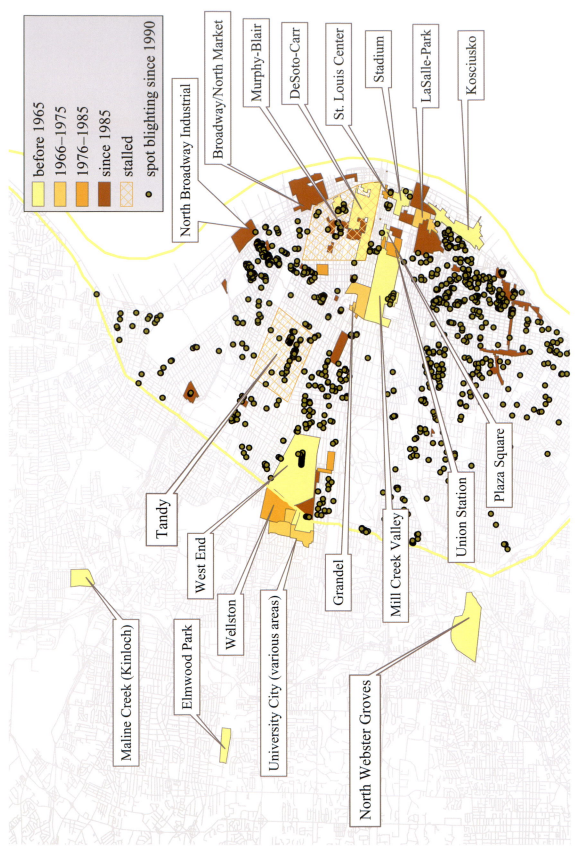

Legend:
- before 1965
- 1966–1975
- 1976–1985
- since 1985
- stalled
- spot blighting since 1990

Labels:
North Broadway Industrial
Broadway/North Market
Murphy-Blair
DeSoto-Carr
St. Louis Center
Stadium
LaSalle-Park
Kosciusko
Tandy
West End
Wellston
University City (various areas)
Grandel
Mill Creek Valley
Union Station
Plaza Square
Maline Creek (Kinloch)
Elmwood Park
North Webster Groves

Map 4.4. Major Chapter 99 areas, 1954–2000. Various LCRA reports, archival maps.

sity City, Kinloch, Webster Groves, and Elmwood Park. As of 2000, about 50 major redevelopment areas had been blighted under Chapter 99.

Into the 1970s, both programs reflected the core logic of urban renewal, under which expansive redevelopment plans were the best way of tapping both local powers of eminent domain and the federal treasury. With the shift in federal attention (and money) from urban renewal to community block grants, local interest in Chapter 99 largely evaporated. Development relied increasingly on the URCs enabled by Chapter 353, especially those with major corporate backing—the Washington University Medical Center, LaSalle Park (Ralston-Purina), and the Midtown Medical Center (St. Louis University). For a time, the City encouraged new redevelopment plans to blight under all available options (Chapters 353, 99, and 100)—an approach that, as one former CDA official conceded, "created a lot of work, and didn't make a lot of sense." In the 1990s, attention swung back to Chapter 99, now seen as a faster and less complicated route to tax abatement or eminent domain.[31] Over the last 15 years, Chapter 99 has been increasingly used to spot-blight individual parcels—an exercise that swallowed nearly 900 properties (and accounted for fully a third of *all* ordinances passed in the City) between 1990 and 2000.

The first (if short-lived) focus of urban renewal in St. Louis was the prospect of attracting high-income residents back downtown and eradicating the City's "worst slum" surrounding City Hall. It included, on and off, plans for a Gateway Mall running west from the Arch between Chestnut and Market to Union Station, but the plans gradually retreated to the Plaza Square area (Fourteenth to Eighteenth Streets between Market and Olive). Planning for Plaza Square preceded the passage of Chapter 99 but immediately took advantage of the new law, blighting the area in 1951 and creating the Urban Redevelopment Corporation of St. Louis under Chapter 353. An initial bond issue to cover the local share of land acquisition failed in 1953 but won approval a year later. Federal grants of just under $2 million covered about two-thirds of the cost of clearing and preparing the site. The project, featuring apartments and a new Blue Cross building, was completed in 1962.[32] The Mansion House area (a stretch between Third and Fourth at the eastern edge of the central business district) was blighted under Chapter 353 in 1959, and a trio of 28-story apartment complexes was completed in 1966. All these residential projects were plagued by high vacancy; within a few years, one Plaza Square building was converted to a senior housing co-op and one Mansion House tower to a hotel. These were the last major efforts at residential redevelopment downtown for quite some time.[33]

The second major focus of urban renewal fell on the City's blighted industrial districts: Mill Creek Valley (about 450 acres running along the Daniel Boone Expressway between downtown and Grand Avenue) and Kosciusko (just over 200 acres running along Broadway south of downtown). Planning for both areas began in the late 1940s, but did not make any headway until federal urban renewal law was amended to include commercial and industrial projects (1954) and a local bond issue (1955) made it possible to begin clearing and assembling land. Both areas were blighted in 1958, and their boundaries were expanded and refined a number of times over the years.[34] In Mill Creek, initial redevelopment plans identified "100 blocks of hopeless

rat-infested, residential slums" and noted that "thousands of outdoor privies per-
fumed the air, and rats as large as spaniels were not exceptional." About a quarter of
the Mill Creek land was set aside for expressway development, another quarter for
industrial redevelopment, and the remainder for residential, public, and commercial
use. In Kosciusko, the focus was more on rehabilitating existing commercial and
industrial areas while clearing out "misplaced" residential pockets in the hopes that
the area's established industries (chemical manufacturing, breweries, foundries)
would expand. While both redevelopment plans paid lip service to the goal of new
employment, the primary concern was clearly the fiscal solvency of blighted areas,
which consumed City services and paid few City taxes.[35]

While Plaza Square and Mansion House aimed to lure the well-heeled downtown,
Mill Creek and Kosciusko had to relocate many of the City's poorest residents—
although both plans made minimal allowances for those displaced. At Mill Creek,
money for new development lagged well behind money for land clearance—earning
the leveled slums the moniker "Hiroshima Flats." A small fraction of the nearly 20,000
displaced by the Mill Creek and Kosciusko redevelopments ended up in public housing, while the majority moved into neighborhoods to the west and north, settling in
already blighted areas and creating new pressures on the housing stock and new
demands for renewal. A scathing federal audit of local relocation efforts (1964) found
that more than half the area's residents received no meaningful relocation assistance
and that the vast majority of those whom redevelopment officials claimed to have
helped simply ended up in substandard housing elsewhere in the City.[36]

The third, and most enduring, focus of the City's early renewal efforts was urban
tourism, beginning with the development of a new baseball stadium. The Civic Cen-
ter/Stadium Redevelopment Area, just under 90 acres on the eastern fringe of the
downtown (just inland from the Jefferson Memorial), was blighted in 1960 under
Chapter 353 and then reblighted under Chapter 99. Redevelopment was shepherded
by the Civic Center Redevelopment Corporation (a Chapter 353 corporation largely
subscribed by Civic Progress firms), which in turn spun off three subsidiary URCs to
develop the stadium (completed in 1966), the stadium parking garages, a Stouffer
Hotel, a string of corporate buildings (Pet Milk, Equitable Life, First National, General
American Life), and the notorious Spanish Pavilion. Tax abatement in the area rested
on a novel tripartite agreement between the City, the St. Louis LCRA, and the Civic
Center URC: the LCRA (a tax-exempt public body) retained title and leased the land
to developers and tenants who, in turn, made payments in lieu of taxes on the pre-
1960 value of the property.[37]

Once built, the stadium served only to underscore the poor condition of the surrounding area, and City officials felt pressed to broaden the scope of downtown redevelopment. Pockets of downtown were blighted, block by block, in the late 1960s,
enabling the development and redevelopment of a string of office towers north of the
stadium (toward what would later become St. Louis Place). Local civic and development officials tired of the building-by-building approach and in 1971 declared all of
downtown—from the river west to Twelfth Street, from Chouteau on the south to Cole
on the north—blighted under Chapter 353.[38] Attention also turned to a derelict ware-

house district at Laclede's Landing, immediately north of the Jefferson Memorial. The area was blighted in 1966. The first URC charged with redevelopment failed to raise any money, and the City terminated its contract and turned to a new Laclede's Landing URC in 1975. Redevelopment—a hodgepodge of restaurants, casinos, and offices—was slow and sporadic, and many of the initial tenants were gone by the early 1980s. The area remains an underdeveloped pipedream, surrounded by blight and disconnected from both the stadium and the riverfront.[39]

The final, and certainly most half-hearted, focus of these early renewal efforts was the blighted residential districts running through the City's core—including the Murphy neighborhood (north of Delmar between Jefferson and the Mark Twain), Tandy (east of Kingshighway between Natural Bridge and Easton), DeSoto-Carr (the southern half of the Murphy), and the sprawling West End (north of Forest Park). Planning for rehabilitation of the West End began in the middle 1950s and was made more urgent by the in-migration of those displaced from Mill Creek and Kosciusko. The area (almost 700 acres in all) was blighted under Chapter 99 in 1963 and received a federal planning grant ($700,000) the same year. West End developers began spending federal money on housing rehabilitation in 1965, but progress was slow and demolition of substandard stock outpaced the construction of anything new. The Department of Housing and Urban Development suspended federal funding in 1971, citing poor progress, fiscal irresponsibility, and the continued deterioration of the project area.[40]

The Tandy and Murphy neighborhoods did not fare much better. Both were blighted under Chapter 99 in 1961—and, although this made them eligible for federal funds, there was little follow-up. A bond campaign in 1966 sought $12 million ($10 million for Murphy, $2 million for Tandy) to jump-start redevelopment but failed at the polls. As of 1974, no federal money had been approved for plans that were now over a decade old, and local efforts amounted to little more than spot rehabilitation and building code enforcement.[41] Planning for DeSoto-Carr (blighted in 1959) followed a similar trajectory, and interest in the project was revived in the late 1960s only because it surrounded the site of the proposed convention center. In the early 1970s, just as the federal Department of Housing and Urban Development (HUD) was pulling the plug on the West End, the City retreated to a few modest renewal areas in the Waterman-DeBaliviere area just north of Forest Park.[42]

In the late 1960s and early 1970s, the target of redevelopment shifted. While plans for redeveloping and reinventing downtown would persist, the City's attention turned to residential and economic development in the area running west of downtown. There were a number of reasons for this. Despite Mill Creek and Kosciusko, the City continued to hemorrhage manufacturing jobs, and many began to view preservation of the old St. Louis economy as a losing battle. Chapter 99 would continue to be used in tandem with other economic development programs, but urban renewal resources and attention drifted to the pursuit of "new economy" jobs promised by a few regional firms (McDonnell-Douglas, Monsanto) and the medical arms of area universities.[43] The retreat of federal funding (from urban renewal to community block grants) in the early 1970s forced city planners and redevelopment interests to think smaller. And the blight targeted by the first generation of urban renewal had itself moved west—in part a reflection of the larger urban crisis gripping St. Louis; in part a direct consequence of slum clearance (without real thought to relocation) downtown.

At the core of the new strategy was the idea of building a New Town-In Town in the area west of downtown and north of Highway 44—a sweeping revitalization plan that overlay the old Mill Creek Valley plan and connected the central business district to the anchors of university-based development surrounding Forest Park. While the New Town area itself was not formally pursued, it was reflected in a series of ambitious redevelopment plans adopted in the early 1970s. The first of these was LaSalle Park, a commercial/residential district surrounding the Ralston-Purina complex on the downtown southside—blighted under Chapter 99 in 1971 and redeveloped by a Chapter 353 URC that was a wholly owned subsidiary of Ralston-Purina. This was followed in short order (moving east to west) by Lafayette Town (1971), Lafayette Square (1974), Midtown Medical (1974), Manchester-Chouteau (1973), and Washington University Medical (1974); and then a decade later by McCree Town (1982).[44]

Once much of the New Town area had been blighted under Chapters 99 and 353, attention turned again to downtown tourism—a drift in renewal strategy that reflected both longstanding dreams of "saving" downtown and a profusion of new local, state, and federal redevelopment policies (enterprise zones, federal urban development action grants, tax-increment financing, historical tax credits). The old Union Station, at the west end of the central business district, had been targeted by a number of schemes over the years (including, at one point, a downtown air terminal), but nothing clicked until it won historic landmark status and eligibility for the accompanying tax credits. In 1976, the City approved a Chapter 353 redevelopment plan for a hotel and retail complex but could scare up no local investors. Plans were redrafted in 1979 and underwritten by a $20 million urban development action grant (UDAG). The resulting redevelopment helped to anchor the area, although it struggled to retain retail tenants. St. Louis Center, at the eastern reach of the central business district, had a similar history: redevelopment was slowed by the paucity of local investment, galvanized by a combination of federal grants and local tax abatements, and marked by chronic vacancies and turnover.[45]

These years also witnessed a continued effort to patch together the fabric of downtown tourism. Plans for a new Convention Plaza in the DeSoto-Carr area culminated in the Cervantes Center (1977)—a complex that was widely criticized and underutilized. The Cervantes Center was spare and disconnected from the rest of downtown, and was seen by many as less a solution to near northside blight than a barrier between that blight and the "tourist" downtown. The City immediately launched plans to reinvent the Cervantes Center (now America's Center) by tying it to a new convention center hotel (the Marriott Renaissance) and a new domed stadium. Plans for the new stadium "smacked of desperation" but marked a rare instance of regional cooperation: the Regional Convention and Sports Complex Authority, which issued nearly $260 million in bonds. Appropriately, at least in the broader context of the City's history, the new TWA Dome was rechristened The Dome at America's Center after TWA's bankruptcy in 2001 (it is now the Edward A. Jones Dome). The new hockey arena (now the Savvits Center), built on the site of the abandoned Kiel Auditorium at Clark and Fourteenth, captured the tangle of public policy and private investment typical of such plans: The City owned the land and leased it to the LCRA; the LCRA, in turn, leased it to the Kiel Center Redevelopment Corporation (a Chapter 353 subsidiary of Kiel Partners); Kiel Partners then sublet the property from its own URC.[46]

As this sketch (and the accompanying maps) suggest, almost all Chapter 353 and 99 activity in greater St. Louis occurred in the City itself. This reflected both the population thresholds attached to the early versions of state law and the reluctance of suburban settings to accept the strings (such as the creation of public housing authorities) that came with federal money. As a result, urban renewal was confined to two areas in St. Louis County: the inner suburbs bordering the City's West End, and pockets of African American population. A cluster of Chapter 99 areas covered much of Wellston and University City. Both (Wellston a largely abandoned industrial area, University City a transitional residential area) were—in terms of demography, economy, and history—less a part of suburban St. Louis County than they were extensions of the kind of development (and redevelopment challenges) found in the City itself.[47] The logic of the outlying urban renewal districts—Maline Creek in Kinloch (1959), North Webster Groves (1960), and Elmwood Park near Olivette (1960)—was quite different. These were the three most prominent and established African American communities in St. Louis County. Each was blighted in the name of urban renewal, and largely eradicated as a result.[48]

Planned Industrial Expansion: Revenue Bonds and Industrial Parks

Against the uneven record of Chapters 353 and 99, attention also turned to other means of leveraging or jump-starting private investment. One such effort was the industrial revenue bond. Unlike general obligation bonds, which were backed by the "full faith and credit" of local governments and counted against local debt limits, revenue bonds were backed by the income of private firms (and not counted against debt limits). Although their rate of return was often modest, local revenue bonds offered investors the tax exemption accompanying all municipal bonds. Local officials shared a general leeriness of the practice ("each law that has been adopted has been more liberal than the previous ones," one noted; "consequently, each state in this competition inevitably digs a deeper tax hole for its communities"). Nevertheless, they were embraced as the only solution to the City's land shortage.[49]

Municipal revenue bonds were pioneered by smokestack-chasing southern states (led by Mississippi) in the 1930s and 1940s. In Missouri, industrial revenue bonds were first authorized by Missouri Chapter 100 (passed in 1960), which allowed state municipalities (but not Kansas City or St. Louis) to float either revenue or general obligation bonds. The Planned Industrial Expansion law, extending this strategy to the state's largest cities, was appended to Chapter 100 in 1967. A city's Planned Industrial Expansion (PIE) Authority had both the power to issue revenue bonds and (as under Chapters 99 and 353) the eminent domain power to blight and clear land. In 1977, Chapter 100 (PIE) revenue bonds were joined by a broader industrial development program

(Chapter 349), which allowed any Missouri city or county to issue revenue bonds through a local Industrial Development Authority, although these authorities did not have the power of eminent domain.[50]

The PIE program got off to a slow start, as opponents immediately challenged the "public purpose" of using municipal bonds to finance private industry. The courts eventually upheld the law in 1975, and the St. Louis Authority issued its first bonds in 1976. Local opponents still questioned PIE's "public purpose"—especially when blighting threatened to displace property owners or local businesses. The state responded in 1977 with a sweeping reform of Chapter 100, eliminating the requirement of both a public vote and a blighting analysis and allowing local governments to authorize PIE projects by simple ordinance. Local PIEs have conventional blighting and eminent domain powers—although Chapter 100 broadened this reach to include not only "blighted" and "unsanitary" areas but "undeveloped" parcels as well.[51]

Map 4.5 summarizes the range and timing of the areas blighted under the St. Louis PIE (usually in consort with Chapter 99, Chapter 353, or both). The first major project areas were the Manchester-Chouteau area (in the industrial area just east of Forest Park) and the Hereford Street area (southwest of Manchester-Chouteau along the same railbed)—the proposals that sparked the 1974–75 litigation over the law. These were followed, after the court test, by a few smaller projects designed to facilitate expansion of existing industrial plants—including US Paint ($2 million) in the downtown industrial corridor at Twenty-First and Papin, and Fin-Clair ($1.3 million), a plating company west of Vandeventer at Gratiot, inside the original Manchester-Chouteau area. These expansion/retention projects were accompanied by the creation of Franklin Industrial Park (27 acres inside the DeSoto-Carr urban renewal area), a land acquisition and clearance project financed by PIE bonds and Community Development Block Grants.[52] In the years that followed, PIEA picked off many of the same parcels already blighted by Chapters 99 or 353, including areas through the downtown and the industrial corridor to the west, along the north riverfront, and in pockets of older industrial development on the north and southsides. By 2000, about 120 project areas had been qualified for bond-financed industrial redevelopment under PIEA, although plant expansion or new development across these areas was very uneven.[53]

However combined, Chapters 353, 99, and 100 could not overcome the City's most serious economic disadvantage: a shortage of land for new commercial or industrial development. While St. Louis County and some of its municipalities advertised a "good supply of land," City planners monotonously documented the underzoning of industrial and commercial land, the paucity of "on-track" industrial sites, and the high price of land—concluding as recently as 2005 that "lack of assembled commercial and industrial land for business expansion creates a competitive disadvantage for the City of St. Louis." An early 1960s survey counted just over 100 prospective industrial sites in the metro area, about a quarter of which (totaling 500 acres) were in St. Louis, and another quarter (totaling over 7,500 acres) in St. Louis County. Most of remaining prospects were across the river, and redevelopment of the old industrial suburbs in and around East St. Louis held out some promise of pulling investment back toward the central city. But regional development interests were leery of the

Map 4.5. Chapter 100 (PIEA) areas, 1976–2000. various PIEA reports, Urban Renewal map (1981) in Mercantile Library, UM-St. Louis.

"unfair labor climate" or the "labor influence of East St. Louis or Granite City" on the Illinois side.[54]

This pattern was underscored by the development of industrial parks across the region. Industrial parks (a form of development assistance pioneered by the railroads and picked up by municipalities after World War II) offered new investors everything from basic infrastructure (roads, railway sidings, services) to "turnkey" warehouses and factory shells.[55] In greater St. Louis (see Map 4.6), these developments were strung out along major rail and highway access on both sides of the river and clustered around Lambert Field in the northwest County. But the development of industrial parks in the City itself was meager—and almost always involved the burden of clearing the land of derelict industry or housing first. The most important efforts of PIEA, on this front, were in the Franklin Industrial Park downtown and the Hall Street industrial area on the north riverfront. But most of PIEA's attention was taken up with smaller scale reclamation or expansion projects.[56]

For a time, much of the City's quest for new industrial land focused on the Columbia Bottoms floodplain north of the City limits at the intersection of the Missouri and Mississippi Rivers. The City raised the funds to acquire the 4500-acre site in a 1942 bond issue, with plans to develop it as an airport. But, while the City purchased most of the land in the mid to late 1940s, the airport plans were shelved in favor of Lambert Field. In 1957, the St. Louis Industrial Park Corporation raised $300,000 from local firms and took out an option on the site. But various feasibility studies pointed to a combination of high development costs and slipping demand for large, river-bound sites. City planners were particularly incensed by a 1959 Arthur Little prospectus that cited both lack of private interest in the site and "a lack of climate of success" in the region. For its part, the County rezoned the area for industrial use and tried a number of times to pull together the $20 million it estimated was needed to both extend streets and services to the site and establish adequate flood control. By the 1970s, local developers viewed development as a losing proposition and conceded that agriculture, parks, and protected wetlands would remain the site's "highest use."[57]

The City's disadvantages became a major focus of the core urban renewal programs (Chapters 353 and 99), especially as federal law allowed local planners to turn away from residential development. To aid in this effort, St. Louis officials pressed the state to pass the Municipal Land Reutilization Law in 1971. This made it possible for the City to consolidate foreclosure suits and to facilitate the assembly of tax-delinquent property, although most of the land acquired in this way was scattered and zoned as residential.[58] Any serious effort to assemble new industrial sites, as local developers argued, required both the ability to clear and assemble land and the money to either prepare the site for prospective investors or help finance the expansion of existing industry. This spawned a number of initiatives, including (in the middle 1960s) a venture capital fund financed by seed money from local banks and a public stock offering. Although many of the large local firms (Anheuser-Busch, Famous-Barr, Brown Shoe) bought in, subscriptions fell far short of the threshold needed to leverage more investment or credit.[59]

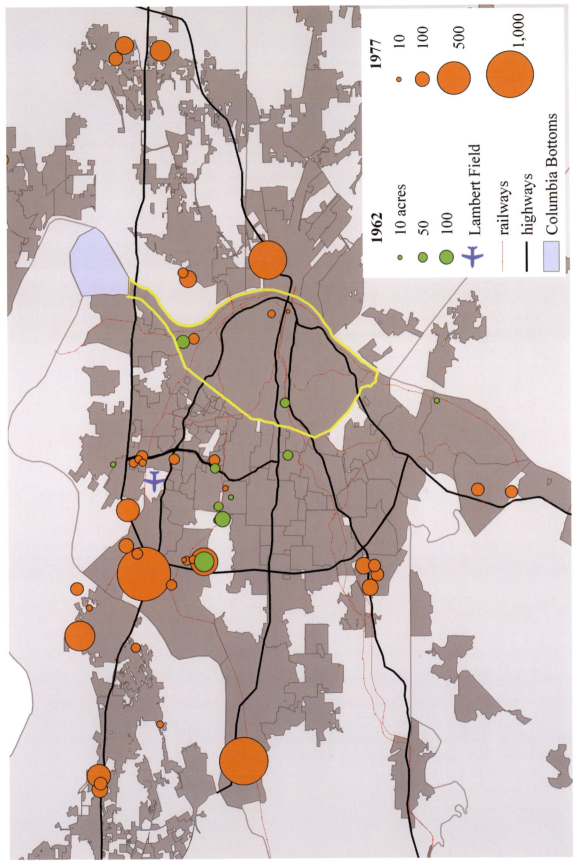

Map 4.6. Industrial parks, 1962 and 1977. City/County parcel data; *St. Louis Commerce* (1977), file 6:16, Roy Wenzlick Papers, WHMC.

1977

10	·
100	●
500	⬤
1,000	⬤

1962

10 acres	·
50	●
100	⬤

✈ Lambert Field

— railways

— highways

Columbia Bottoms

From Model Cities to Community Block Grants

Just as local officials were striving (with PIEA and other initiatives) to focus urban renewal efforts on economic development, the federal government was rethinking the terms of its participation and support. In 1965, Lyndon Johnson's Great Society pulled federal urban programs under the umbrella of a new Department of Housing and Urban Development (HUD) and immediately charged it with the task of streamlining federal spending and ensuring that more of it went to demonstrably needy cities and neighborhoods. The result was the 1966 Demonstration Cities and Metropolitan Development Act establishing the Model Cities program, which was designed to channel federal funds through new local agencies to "demonstration projects" (encompassing housing, employment, health care, recreation, crime prevention, education, and social services) in predominantly residential, poor, and underserved neighborhoods.[60]

In St. Louis, planners viewed Model Cities as just another sluice for federal funds and rushed a proposal to HUD scarcely a month after the act was passed. St. Louis received a $280,000 planning grant in 1967 but was rejected twice by HUD (whose responses cited insufficient civic participation) before receiving programmatic allotments of $9 million (1969–70), $7 million (1971), and $9 million (1972). As its "demonstration project," City officials identified a large chunk of the central city, north of Delmar and south of Grand (see Map 4.7). This area included a number of areas previously blighted and redeveloped under other programs, including the Pruitt-Igoe housing complex, the Grandel Redevelopment Area, and the DeSoto-Carr Redevelopment Area. Population of the area was about 70,000, and rates of unemployment, vacant housing, and reliance on welfare ran at about twice the citywide averages.[61]

The St. Louis Model Cities Plan covered all the bases specified by HUD, including first-year budgets of $2 million each for education and health programs, $1 million each for crime prevention and social services, and about $500,000 each for recreation, employment, and education programs. But local goals and strategies differed little from the old urban renewal model. Despite the "bootstraps" antipoverty/social service model pressed by HUD, St. Louis officials focused on the tired prospect of clearing substandard housing for commercial development. There was no pretense of providing new housing within the project boundaries, and considerable opposition to the hazy idea of dispersing displaced residents across the region. Local efforts to push more federal money into economic development were repeatedly quashed at HUD. And those plans that did fly—including a pedestrian shopping mall on Fourteenth between Warren and St. Louis—were dismal failures.[62]

Model Cities—both as federal policy and as pursued in St. Louis—was hard to distinguish from older renewal efforts. Neither federal money nor local initiatives made a dent in the urban crisis. Critics on the right and left, in St. Louis and Washington, viewed the entire enterprise as yet another opportunity for local development interests to soak up public subsidies under the pretense of fighting blight. By the early 1970s, these familiar complaints were joined by a looming fiscal crisis. As Johnson's Great Society gave way to Richard Nixon's New Federalism, the premises for yet

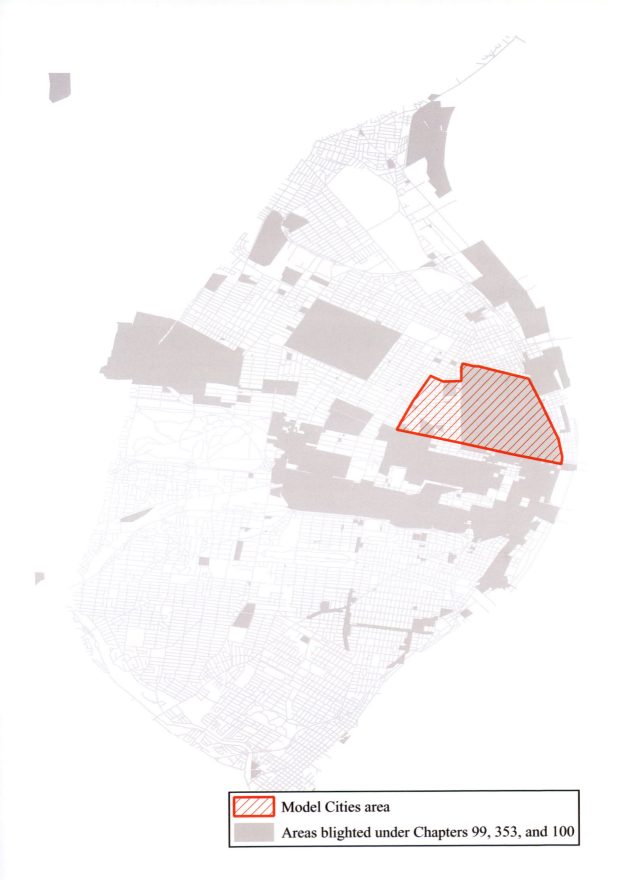

Map 4.7. St. Louis "Model Cities" area, 1967–1972. *St. Louis Model City Program* (December 1968).

Model Cities area

Areas blighted under Chapters 99, 353, and 100

another reinvention of federal urban policy were clear: HUD would continue to put pressure on cities to sort out their priorities, but the flow of categorical (and largely unconditional) grants would end.

Under the Housing and Community Development Act (1974), federal subsidies and categorical grants—including urban renewal, Model Cities, water and sewer, open space, neighborhood development, and facilities programs—were replaced by a new system of Community Development Block Grants (CDBG). Cities would receive an annual CDBG allotment and, under federal guidelines, distribute it to local projects or institutions. At its roots, CDBG had a loose redistributional logic: Cities' share of federal funds was based on a formulaic weighing of population, crowding, and poverty (for the first three years of the program, a "hold-harmless" provision ensured that CBDG allocations would not dip below pre-1974 commitments under older programs). And local spending was required to demonstrate a benefit to low- and moderate-income residents. In practice (and over time), this logic eroded as Congressional pressures broadened the scope of eligible cities and counties, local pressures pushed more resources toward "bricks and mortar" development (HUD added "economic development" criteria in 1977), and the federal government retreated from oversight over local spending. Aside from a brief infusion of categorical spending under the Carter administration's Urban Development Action Grant Program,[63] federal policy tended steadily toward less spending (especially in large MSAs and central cities) and more local discretion.[64]

In St. Louis, federal transfers under CDBG began at around $15 million in 1975—a "hold harmless" level based on federal spending under the programs being replaced. The City's CDBG peaked at $35 million in 1980 and then declined steadily—settling in at around $20 million annually in the early 1990s (see Figure 4.1). Annual grant and spending levels in St. Louis were scrambled by the City's willingness to borrow against future grants—a practice that inflated the federal transfer in some years while committing future CDBG funds to paying off the loan. In real (inflation-adjusted) dollars, recent appropriations (just under $25 million) are the lowest in the history of the program and less than a third of their 1980 levels. As the City (whose own revenue base was collapsing) relied more and more on federal aid, local officials noted "a great zeal to chase whatever particular bag of tricks the Feds have and not question whether those funds ultimately meet the objectives of the City of St. Louis or not." Control over CDBG spending rested largely in the mayor's office, where the practice, as one City official recalled, was to "pay a toll" in local projects to aldermen in exchange for central discretion over the bulk of the grant.[65]

In parceling out CDBGs, the City put supply-side economic development first and steered clear of the most devastated neighborhoods in favor of those (especially downtown) in which private investors were interested. Map 4.8 sketches the pattern of CDBG spending in the City for fiscal 1978, underscoring the preference for most of the same commercial and industrial areas already blighted under older renewal programs. As a general pattern, the City devoted CDBG funds to social services in the poorest wards and to middle-income housing elsewhere. Indeed, the City's four cen-

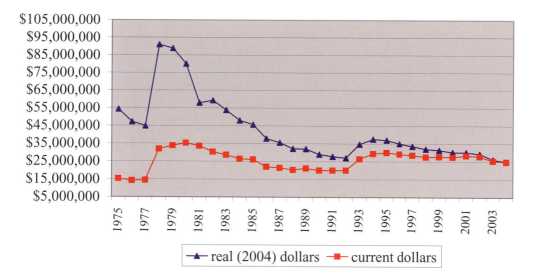

Figure 4.1. CDBG spending in St. Louis, 1975–2004. HUD, *Community Development Block Grant Program: Directory of Allocations for Fiscal Year 1976* (1976); HUD, *Community Development Block Grant Program: Programs: Directory of Allocations for Fiscal Years 1980–1985* (1985); *SLPD*; www.HUD.Gov.

tral wards (running west from the downtown to Forest Park) received as much in "bricks and mortar" CDBG funds in the program's first decade as the twelve wards stretching across the northside. Mayor Vincent Schoemehl (1981–93) defended these choices, arguing that new housing in poor neighborhoods would simply make St. Louis "the region's final repository of all the poor, underemployed and undereducated." The preferred solution, harking back to the urban renewal plans of the 1940s and 1950s, was to "fight blight" by building market-rate housing in stable City neighborhoods. In the late 1980s, the mayor's office went so far as to deny CDBG funding to public housing altogether.[66]

For their part, both federal officials and local social service agencies blasted the City for continuing to pursue commercial development or high-end housing while bypassing its poorest residents and neighborhoods. In CDBG's first four years (through 1978), St. Louis ACORN estimated that just under half of the City's roughly $70 million share was spent on economic development or gentrification. This balance sheet was further skewed by CDBG spending in suburban municipalities, which went largely to basic infrastructure, and by the City's Urban Development Action Grants, which went almost solely to commercial renewal or development. The Community Development Administration (CDA), the City office charged with administering the CDBG program, was almost always in hot water at HUD—for overspending on administration, for underspending on housing, or for squandering federal dollars on ineligible projects (including a million-dollar advertising campaign in 1991 aimed at selling prospective residents on St. Louis).[67]

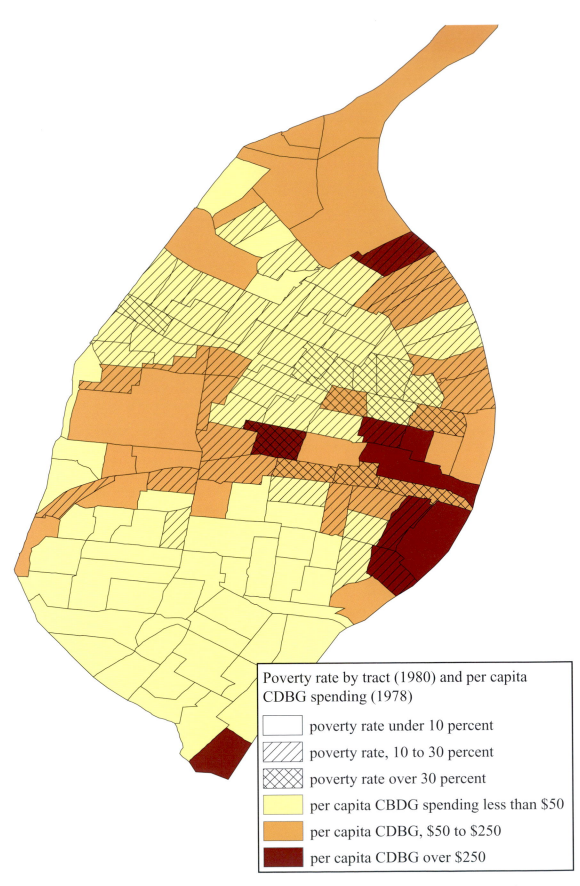

Poverty rate by tract (1980) and per capita CDBG spending (1978)

poverty rate under 10 percent

poverty rate, 10 to 30 percent

poverty rate over 30 percent

per capita CBDG spending less than $50

per capita CDBG, $50 to $250

per capita CDBG over $250

Map 4.8. Community Development Block Grant spending, 1978: City CDBG Reports (1978).

Tax Increment Financing (TIF)

With the onset of the CDBG system, federal funding for large-scale and ongoing renewal projects evaporated. As an alternative, states and localities turned to tax increment financing (TIF). Like conventional land clearance and urban renewal, TIF projects begin with the blighting of a redevelopment area (a statutory threshold often accompanied by a "but for" provision requiring a finding that private development would not occur without public assistance). Assessed land values within the blighted area are effectively frozen: As redevelopment proceeds (and assessed values rise), affected properties pay conventional property taxes on the base value, but all taxes on the increase in value ("the increment") are—for a period of 15 to 25 years—deposited in a dedicated fund. This fund can (with rules varying from state to state) be used to pay off public loans to the developer, to retire bonds used to acquire and clear land, or to finance public infrastructure associated with the development. The idea was pioneered in California in the early 1950s, when the failure of local bond campaigns left Los Angeles unable to raise the local share for federal renewal projects. Six other states had TIF laws before 1970, but most were passed (post-CDBG) in the late 1970s and early 1980s. By 2000, only two states (North Carolina and Delaware) did not have a TIF law on the books.[68]

Missouri's Real Property Tax Increment Allocation Redevelopment Act, a sweeping revision of the old Chapter 99, was passed in 1982. Creation of a TIF district requires a finding of blight, defined (in language pasted in from older renewal statutes) as

an area which, by reason of the predominance of defective or inadequate street layout, unsanitary or unsafe conditions, deterioration of site conditions, improper subdivision or obsolete platting, the existence of conditions which endanger life or property by fire and other causes, or any combination of such factors, retards the provision of housing accommodations or constitutes an economic or social liability or a menace to public health, safety, morals, or welfare in its present condition or use.

Alternatively, a district could qualify as a "conservation" area (defined as "not-yet blighted" but likely to become so based on building age, use, and condition) or an "economic development" area (defined as an area in which redevelopment would discourage business flight, build the tax base, or create jobs). Each of these criteria carried with it a hazy "but for" test: an assessment that the area "has not been subject to growth and development through investment by private enterprise and would not reasonably be anticipated to be developed without the adoption of tax increment financing." The 1982 law froze base values for 23 years and channeled both "payments in lieu of taxes" (PILOTs) on the increased value *and* one-half of the local sales or income taxes generated by redevelopment into a special allocation fund. The allocation fund, in turn, could be used to underwrite studies and plans, professional services, property assembly, rehabilitation or remodeling, construction of public works, and financing costs. In 1998, the state also allowed some TIF districts to claim half of new state revenues (sales and income). Missouri is one of only 10 states to roll sales tax revenues into its TIF legislation—a decision that both shaped the type and location of TIF projects in greater St. Louis and sparked calls for legislative reform.[69] On the

grounds that PILOTs are special assessments (not taxes) representing future revenues, Missouri courts have held that tax increment financing is not counted against
local debt limits.[70]

While older urban renewal areas (Chapters 99, 100, and 353) tended to follow long-
established contours of metropolitan blight, TIF programs in greater St. Louis have
followed a pattern that is very nearly the reverse: TIF districts (especially in the program's early years) were rare in the central city and more prevalent along the path of
suburban sprawl to the west. There are three reasons for this: First, because TIFs can
capture sales tax revenues as well as property tax revenues, they became especially
attractive to big-box retail development on the urban fringe. Second, because TIF is
based on future tax revenues rather than up-front state or federal funds, private developers look to put together deals in areas which—although qualifying as blighted
under the statute—are nevertheless "safe" for investment. Third, because the definition of blight under Missouri law is so elastic (a problem I turn to in the next chapter),
there are few checks on local growth enthusiasts intent on gaming the system.

As of 2000, the state of Missouri had about 125 TIF districts, of which over 70 percent were in the state's major metropolitan areas—50 in the Kansas City MSA, 39 in
the St. Louis MSA. By 2005, the number of districts had swollen to 210, of which over
half (110) were in greater St. Louis—3 in Jefferson County, 11 in St. Charles County,
46 in St. Louis County, and 50 in the City itself. But while the City has stepped up its
TIF efforts in recent years (it had only 9 districts in 2000), many of these projects were
halfhearted efforts to breathe new life into older redevelopment schemes. City TIFs,
as a group, have accounted for a tiny fraction of TIF-based spending or revenues in
Missouri.[71]

Across the St. Louis MSA, as Map 4.9 shows, most of the TIF activity circled the City
on its suburban fringes—including expansive districts in St. Charles and Crestwood
that swallowed much of the municipal tax base. Leading the pack among the suburban
TIFs were a string of retail developments (many of them assembled by TIF-savvy developers, including the Sansonne Group and THF Realty). This kind of development
played out like an elaborate shell game. Federal tax law effectively encouraged retail
developers to abandon older malls and leapfrog new development to the edges of the
metro area. The Missouri sales tax structure encouraged suburban municipalities to
compete with each other for this tax base—to the point that many were "handing out
TIFs like bubblegum" in the hope of attracting new retail tenants or persuading old
ones not to leave. And the TIF law gave developers the incentive and opportunity to
reap vast public subsidies for building and rebuilding shopping centers in some of the
wealthiest tracts in the metropolitan area.[72]

On balance, TIF has underwritten sprawl and worsened the condition—urban
blight—it professes to address. Consider the divergent fates of two major retail developments. In the early 1990s, the City spent $15 million on site improvements to help
private developers transform the old Scullin Steel site (on Manchester south of Forest
Park) into a 500,000-square-foot mall, the St. Louis Marketplace. From the outset, the
development was marred by "bad planning, bad luck, bad access, bad anchor tenants
and lots of litigation." It has struggled to attract or retain its anchor tenants and to

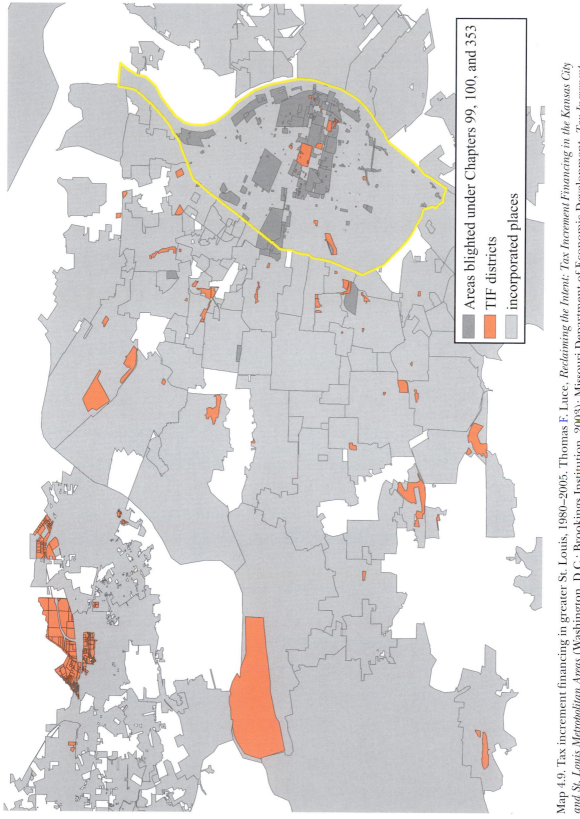

Map 4.9. Tax increment financing in greater St. Louis, 1980–2005. Thomas F. Luce, *Reclaiming the Intent: Tax Increment Financing in the Kansas City and St. Louis Metropolitan Areas* (Washington, D.C.: Brookings Institution, 2003); Missouri Department of Economic Development, *Tax Increment Financing in Missouri, 2004 Annual Report* (February 2005).

cover the annual payments on the original TIF.[73] In the late 1990s, the retail giant Westfield America announced plans to renovate the West County Plaza in suburban Des Peres. Des Peres officials dutifully declared the mall blighted—on the grounds that it lacked an upscale anchor store like Nordstrom's—and assembled nearly $30 million in TIF funds. Despite considerable civic dismay, a court challenge, and a flurry of interest in legislative reform, the deal survived.[74] This enabled the new West County mall, and a string of others like it, to continue poaching retail tenants and sales taxes from elsewhere in the region—especially the city of St. Louis and its inner suburbs.

Enterprise/Empowerment Zones

Like TIFs, "enterprise" or "empowerment" zones began as a state and local response to the end of federal urban renewal spending in the 1970s. Missouri was one of the first states to take the plunge, with an enterprise zone law (Chapter 135) passed in 1982. Unlike TIFs (and other redevelopment programs), enterprise zones rely on quantifiable measures of "pervasive poverty and general distress": In Missouri, at least 65 percent of the zone residents must have incomes below 80 percent of the state median, and the unemployment rate must be more than one and one-half times the state average. In turn, the number of such zones is limited: by law, Kansas City and St. Louis are allowed one primary zone and up to three "satellite" zones; more restrictive formulae govern other cities and counties, and the total number of zones in the state is capped (originally at 25, later at 50).

Under Chapter 135, the Missouri enterprise zone law, local governments propose and define zone boundaries, which are then certified (or rejected) by the state Department of Economic Development. The payoff for employers and investors located in the zone (and reaching basic thresholds for new investment and job creation) is both a raft of state tax credits (including $400 per employee job credit for each new hire or relocation, doubling to $800 if the employee is either a zone resident or a displaced worker, and tripling to $1,200 if the employee is both; a ten-year investment tax credit—10 percent on the first $10,000, 5 percent on the next $90,000, 2 percent on the rest; and a 50 percent exemption on state corporate income tax) and abatement of all local property taxes on improvements. In 2004, an omnibus economic development bill (the Jobs Now Act) absorbed the state enterprise zone law and recast it as a new Enhanced Enterprise Zone Program. Basic qualifications and benefits remained the same, although the new law removed the statewide quota on the number of zones and made business tax credits fully refundable and saleable.[75]

The St. Louis Midtown zone was one of the first formed under Chapter 135. Established in 1983, it covered about 7 square miles west of the central business district between Highways 40 and I-44. In the late 1980s and early 1990s, the zone was steadily expanded until it followed the crooked anchor profile (see Map 4.10) of the City's old industrial corridors—west to east along the Manchester-Chouteau rail corridor, north and south along the riverbank. In 1984, the County won designation of the Wellston enterprise zone just west of the City. And in 1989, just months after the Missouri legislature allowed cities to propose noncontiguous "satellite" zones, St. Louis officials added

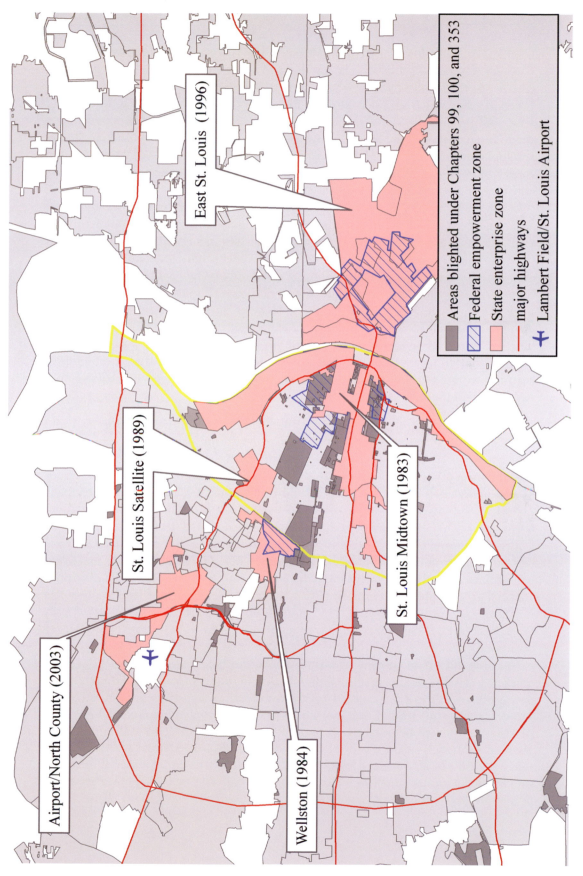

East St. Louis (1996)

St. Louis Satellite (1989)

Airport/North County (2003)

Wellston (1984)

St. Louis Midtown (1983)

Areas blighted under Chapters 99, 100, and 353
Federal empowerment zone
State enterprise zone
major highways
Lambert Field/St. Louis Airport

Map 4.10. Enterprise/empowerment zones in greater St. Louis, 1983–2005. City and federal EZ reports.

another zone near the old General Motors truck and bus plant in north St. Louis. Through the middle 1990s, most of the east side of the river was carved up into Illinois enterprise zones under that state's program. And in 2003, St. Louis County established a second zone, which sprawled through the north County (including most of Hazelwood and portions of Kinloch, Ferguson, Bel-Ridge, and Berkeley) around Lambert Field. The new zone (see Map 5.2 in the next chapter) purported to sustain economic development across the area but was largely designed to retain a Ford plant in Hazelwood. Other areas were gerrymandered into the long, irregular parcel largely to satisfy state requirements (regarding poverty and employment) for the entire zone.[76]

In the early 1990s, the federal government added its own "empowerment zone" program—a reflection both of enthusiasm for supply side solutions under the first Bush Administration and of local complaints that state tax credits alone were insufficient: "We're treading water," conceded the head of the St. Louis zone in 1989, "waiting for the federal enterprise zone legislation to be passed." The federal Empowerment and Enterprise Zone Act (1993) superimposed 11 new zones (and accompanying federal tax credits) on the pastiche of existing state and local zones and made federal seed money available to qualified zones.[77] St. Louis was passed over in the first round of federal empowerment zones (1994) but won federal designation—on the strength of a bistate application—in 1999. The federal zone, which overlay much of East St. Louis, central St. Louis, and Wellston, covered 13.7 square miles and 22 census tracts.[78]

There was little disagreement in the middle years of the twentieth century as to the reach of blight in the City. St. Louis officials, beginning in the 1930s and running through the 1947 City Plan, consistently identified the entire City east of Grand Avenue and most of the residential northside as "blighted," and the residential neighborhoods immediately north and south of the central business district as irredeemably "obsolete" or "decadent." But if we overlay these areas (see Map 4.11) with the cumulative reach of a half-century of urban renewal and economic development programs, a curious pattern emerges. The central industrial corridor and the riverfront are overlaid with a crazy quilt of Chapter 353, Chapter 99, TIF, PIE (Chapter 100), and enterprise zones. And while the areas immediately adjacent to the central business district attract a great deal of attention, the vast swath of residential blight (especially on the northside) is practically ignored. The only real forays into the northside—the Tandy, West End, and DeSoto-Carr urban renewal areas—were notorious (and largely unfunded) failures.

Not only did urban renewal bypass areas like the blocks surrounding 4635 North Market, but slum clearance and economic development projects elsewhere created new problems as those displaced (by downtown highway construction, the Mill Creek project, and so on) moved west and north into already troubled areas. There was a persistent mismatch between the definition of the City's problems and the solutions pursued. Although blight was originally understood as a residential problem, urban renewal efforts in St. Louis skirted the worst residential areas and focused increasingly on large-scale industrial or commercial development. The next chapter takes up the politics of these choices, and some of their consequences.

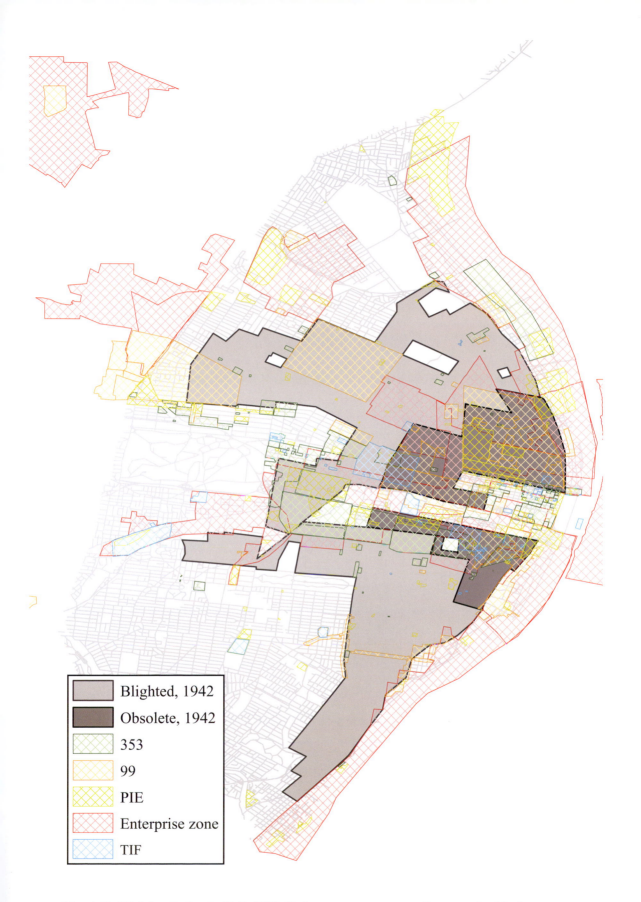

Map 4.11. Blighting St. Louis, 1940–2000. Various sources; see preceding maps in this chapter.

Chapter 5
City of Blight

The Limits of Urban Renewal in Greater St. Louis

A half-century of urban renewal and redevelopment programs, as I traced in the last chapter, not only failed to stem the decline of central St. Louis but pointedly avoided the very neighborhoods in which that decline was most palpable. This was a complex failure—a tangle of good intentions and bad policy, steep challenges and shallow resources. The original postwar concern for substandard living conditions was increasingly distracted by redevelopment schemes that put economic development ahead of residential renewal and the central business district ahead of troubled neighborhoods. In turn, commercial and residential redevelopment projects alike failed to spur the new private investment or new private employment that might have yielded real benefits beyond project boundaries.

In an era in which a few cities (Pittsburgh, Cleveland, Minneapolis) managed to reinvent themselves, St. Louis (and many others) could lay claim to little more than disconnected and halfhearted pockets of urban tourism. Most American cities emerged from the heyday of urban renewal in similar shape—central city decay punctuated by the occasional stadium or convention center; urban problems (segregation, poverty, unemployment, fiscal crisis) spilling into the inner suburbs; employment and the tax base continuing to sprawl into the outer suburbs. The elusiveness of the solution reflected both a set of common conditions (deindustrialization, fragmented governance, limited resources) and the elusiveness of the problem itself. Fighting blight, in St. Louis and elsewhere, was often confounded by the imprecision and elasticity of the concept itself.

What Is Blight?

What is "blight"? Over half a century of federal and state urban renewal policy, and a slightly shorter history of local economic development policies, revolve around this question. These policies, ranging from the first stabs at federally funded urban renewal in the 1940s to the contemporary fascination of local and state governments with tax increment financing, all involve, to some degree, public financing of private economic development or property transactions. In effect, such policies extend the public credit and the public power of eminent domain to private interests—a combination that has often incurred the opposition of both taxpayers and property owners displaced by urban renewal or redevelopment. The legal and political justification for such policies, as a result, leans heavily on an overarching public purpose: the elimination or prevention of blight. But "blight" is rarely defined with any precision in such statutes, and the courts have granted local interests almost carte blanche in the creative search for "blighted" areas eligible for federal funds or local tax breaks.[1]

In practice, blight is less an objective condition than it is a legal pretext for various forms of commercial tax abatement that, in most settings, divert money from schools and county-funded social services. Redevelopment policies originally intended to address unsafe or insufficient urban housing are now more routinely employed to subsidize the building of suburban shopping malls. And such policies (especially state TIF programs) not only ignore the ongoing urban crisis but, by subsidizing sprawl, routinely contribute to blight in the cities under the pretext of fighting it in the suburbs.

The modern statutory definition of blight is rooted in our first urban crisis, the Progressive Era response to urbanization and industrialization in the late nineteenth and early twentieth centuries. Lamentable urban conditions, captured in the investigations of Jacob Riis and others, included the encroachment of commercial or industrial properties on residential neighborhoods, the inadequacy of basic public services, and the threat of moral decay, fire, and disease posed by the tenement housing of urban working families. Cities, in the environmental determinism of urban reformers, had become "nurseries of crime, and of the vices and disorderly courses which lead to crime . . . perpetrated by individuals who have either lost connection with home life, or never had any, or whose homes had ceased to be sufficiently separate, decent, and desirable to afford what are regarded as ordinary wholesome influences of home and family." Tenements, and substandard urban housing more generally, were considered "standing menaces to the family, to morality, to the public health, and to civic integrity."[2]

The political response to such conditions ranged widely and included urban beautification campaigns, the model tenement movement, "managerial" reform of urban governance, early efforts at urban planning and zoning, and Prohibition. But, despite the progress of home rule in many states, municipal powers to regulate or rehabilitate urban blight were quite limited. In part, this reflected political and fiscal constraints. Reformers increasingly understood "blight" as a condition of entire blocks or neighborhoods, but cities lacked the capacity to do much more than fine the occasional landlord or raze the occasional building. In part, this reflected legal constraints on the local regulation of private property. Because the only substantial legal footing for urban reform was the police power, local efforts to address urban conditions leaned heavily on the threats to health or safety or moral order that animated local police powers. While efforts to eradicate blighted conditions were limited, early definitions of blight did begin to crop up in local health and safety codes.[3]

Political attention returned to urban conditions during the Great Depression, accompanied by the efforts of local, state, and federal officials to refine the definition of blight and its relationship to police powers. At a 1930 housing conference, the Hoover administration defined a slum as "a residential area where the houses and conditions of life are of such a squalid and wretched character and which hence has become a social liability to the community." In 1937, the National Association of Housing Officials defined a slum, in language echoed in the second National Housing Act later that year, as "an area in which predominate dwellings that either because of dilapidation, obsolescence, overcrowding, poor arrangement or design, lack of ventilation, light or sanitary facilities, or a combination of these factors, are detrimental to the safety, health, morals, and comfort of the inhabitants thereof." The definition remained imprecise and ambiguous because most viewed "blight" not as synonymous with "slum" but as a set of conditions, often analogized as a disease or a cancer, that resulted in slums: A blighted area was "on the down grade, which has not reached the slum stage" or "a potential slum" or "an insidious malady that attacks urban residential districts . . . first as a barely noticeable deterioration and then progresses gradually through many stages toward a final condition known as the slum." By and large, blight was considered a residential affliction; it was "an area or neighborhood, the buildings in which are used predominantly, though not necessarily exclusively, for habitation and residence" but that posed a moral threat in large part because of the "types of business or industries which have invaded or surround the district."[4]

In turn, local, state, and federal officials linked urban blight to the immediate fiscal crisis of local governments. At the 1930 Hoover conference, a blighted area was defined as an "economic liability" whose demands upon the public purse outstripped its tax revenues. "Structures become shabby and obsolete," one observer wrote in 1938. "The entire district takes on a down-at-the-heel appearance. The exodus of the more prosperous groups is accelerated. Rents fall. Poorer classes move in. The poverty of the tenants contributes further to the general air of shabbiness. The realty owner becomes less and less inclined or able to make repairs." In this view, "slum" remained a residential classification (a synonym for substandard housing), while "blight" was attributed more broadly to any area absorbing more than its share of tax revenues.[5]

In St. Louis and elsewhere, efforts to identify or define blight after 1929 were also a pitch for federal and state political attention. Beginning with *Urban Land Policy* (1936), continuing in *Saint Louis After World War II* (1942), and culminating in the 1947 City Plan, the City Plan Commission identified two broad swaths of blighted property. The first (Map 5.1) was composed of the blocks immediately surrounding the central business district, labeled "decadent" in 1936 and "obsolete" in 1942 and 1947. This was the area targeted by the first urban renewal projects for new middle-income housing downtown. The second area (identified as "blighted" in all these surveys) included much of the remaining central industrial corridor, the eastern third of the residential southside, and virtually all of the residential northside.[6] These designations achieved new importance as the federal government made grants and loans available to local governments under the National Housing Act of 1937 and laid the groundwork (in the housing acts of 1941 and 1949) for more discrete "blighting" under urban redevelopment law.[7]

Federal law deferred the definition and determination of blighted areas to the state governments that enabled the redevelopment corporations and the local governments

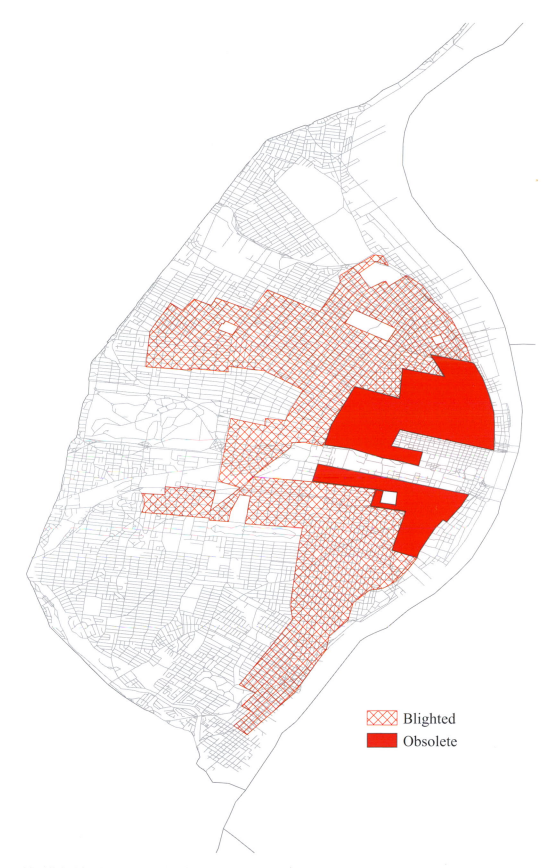

XXXXX Blighted

�\▍ Obsolete

Map 5.1. Obsolete and blighted districts, 1936–1947. City Plan Commission, *Urban Land Policy* (St. Louis: the Commission, 1936); City Plan Commission, *St. Louis After World War II* (St. Louis: Mason Printing, 1942); and 1947 Comprehensive Plan.

that administered them. Most states, in fact, stopped short of defining blight and instead offered a descriptive catalogue of blighted conditions—often pasted verbatim from Progressive Era health or safety statutes. In Missouri, a blighted area was one in which

by reason of the predominance of defective or inadequate street layout, unsanitary or unsafe conditions, deterioration of site improvements, improper subdivision or obsolete platting, the existence of conditions which endanger life or property by fire and other causes, or any combination of such factors, retards the provision of housing accommodations or constitutes an economic or social liability or a menace to the public health, safety, morals, or welfare in its present condition and use.

Even as federal urban renewal was replaced in 1974 with the Community Development Block Grant (CDBG) program, state redevelopment statutes and their Dickensian descriptions of blight persisted. Essentially the same language was imported into new laws, including the profusion of TIF laws in the 1970s and 1980s. TIF statutes echoed and expanded the older statutory definition of blight, typically grafting economic considerations, such as underutilization of land, uneven commercial development, and insufficient tax revenues, onto the older "health and welfare" notion of urban blight. The Missouri enterprise zone law, one of the few statutes to venture an empirical measure of blight, nevertheless opened with an even more expansive definition: "Blight is any condition that impairs growth, halts prosperity and causes decline or decay."[8]

In St. Louis, the meaning of blight remained a practical (and useful) mystery. The City made a few stabs at establishing an index for local blight (in the early 1950s, for example, the City Plan Commission briefly adopted an American Public Health Association measure of block-by-block health, which assigned "penalty points" for crowding and substandard building conditions).[9] But, for the most part, blight was defined on the fly, in response to discrete plans for redevelopment. A consultant hired by St. Louis in 1970 to develop a baseline inventory of blight in the City concluded simply (but vaguely) that blight was "both a noun and a verb, both a condition and a cause." Industrial blight, as the study struggled on, was a measure of facilities that were either "undesirable from a social standpoint or are inefficient from an economic point of view"; residential blight was a "condition of unacceptably low residential quality—a point on the continuum of residential quality." The elasticity of the notion was underscored in recent years, when the City's western suburbs began blighting (under Missouri TIF law) stable retail areas in a bidding war for bigger and better shopping malls. An area does not have to be run down or dilapidated, argued the Des Peres city administrator in 2002; "'blight' could be an aging, 1970s-era mall that is overshadowed by newer and larger shopping centers" – adding apologetically (but accurately) that "the definition of blight in the state statutes is not the same as in the dictionary."[10]

From a legal standpoint, the greatest challenge in all of this lay in reconciling an expansive definition of blight with both the eminent domain powers it enabled and the underlying assumption that redevelopment was in the public interest. For critics of urban renewal, the burden on public authorities was twofold: they had to prove that an area targeted for renewal was really blighted (and not just so designated for the convenience of developers), and they had to prove that the proposed redevelopment served a compelling public purpose. Local businesses routinely challenged findings of blight on the grounds that their very existence (and often prosperity) belied a finding of "unsafe conditions" or "threats to the general welfare."[11] And many (including displaced businesses) questioned whether eminent domain could or should be used to clear land for private development. "The Act is based on the high-sounding purpose of the development of blighted, unsanitary and undeveloped industrial areas," argued a 1974 challenge to blighting under Chapter 100, "[but] the fact remains that the primary beneficiaries are private business and persons." The plaintiffs summarily rejected the notion that "a 'public purpose' can be found in the indirect benefits resulting in a community every time a new business is begun and operated successfully."[12]

The Missouri courts, following a national pattern, rejected these arguments. The core case law—including a pair of 1954 cases challenging the powers of the Kansas City and St. Louis Land Clearance for Reclamation Authorities—held that the acquisition and clearance of land alone was in the public interest; that "the public purpose required by the constitution has been served by a redevelopment project *when the blight has been cleared*." In this reasoning, the final disposition of the property was immaterial. The process of drafting a redevelopment plan and readying the land for its implementation was itself a public purpose—whether the parcel ended up as a stretch of highway, a sports stadium, or a shopping mall. "Any benefits to private individuals are merely incidental to the public purpose." In the St. Louis case (concerning the Civic Plaza project), the court held simply that "the acquisition and clearance of land in said Area for sale to a private developer for redevelopment in conformity with the said final redevelopment plan is the acquisition of such land for a public use and purpose." In 1966 (*Annbar v. West Side Redevelopment*), 1974 (*Parking Systems, Inc. v. Kansas City Downtown Redevelopment Corporation*, and 1977 (*Allright Parking v. Civic Plaza Redevelopment*), the Missouri Supreme Court affirmed this basic assumption: "the fact that special benefits may accrue to some private persons by the exercise of government authority does not deprive the action of its public character . . . if the primary purpose is a public one, the benefits to individuals are incidental."[13]

Such interpretations remained a matter of considerable controversy, especially as the definition of blight and the notion of "public purpose" became harder and harder to pin down. Tellingly, the appeals court judge on one of Missouri's key urban renewal cases (*Allright Parking*, 1975), all but threw up his hands when faced with the task of unraveling the meaning of blight under Missouri law:

COURT: . . . this definition has so many considerations in it, I just wonder who is qualified to pass on such things. Are there such experts? . . . Here are the considerations—here is what the definition of blighted area is, it says it shall mean [reading] "those portions of the City which Council shall determine, that by reason of age, obsolescence, inadequate or outmoded design or physical deterioration, have become economic and social liabilities and that the conditions in such localities are conducive to ill health, transmission of disease, crime, or inability to pay reasonable taxes." The reason I am asking this is that you are asking me to decide who is qualified, and I doubt if it's a question of expertise, that there is anyone expert in all the areas involved.

MR. WARD [attorney for LCRA]: . . . it is a very hard definition to—

COURT: Well, I tell you what, so that we can go on, I think I am going to let anybody express an opinion that wishes to. Do you have any law on this question as to who can express an opinion?

MR. WARD: I think, if he can get into specific features of blight, such as structural analysis of a building, he would have to be qualified as someone who is familiar with such a subject . . .

COURT:—how about whether it is "conducive to ill health," would that take a doctor?

MR. WARD: No, I think that is a finding and not a characteristic of blight . . . in the statute and in the ordinance there is a legislative determination . . . that these characteristics cause those problems.

COURT: That is what I said, how would—they have to find certain things that could be said to involve the opinion of experts, then they have to show that those conditions contribute to certain other things that would not require the opinion of experts.

MR. WARD: I think you will find . . . the enabling act as the legislature of the state of Missouri has found that when these conditions do exist that these other items are the result of it. Because of that, when you find these earlier conditions you have a blighted area, you don't have to find that it causes ill health or whatever they are.

COURT: That isn't what the ordinance says . . . actually the ultimate finding is that it is conducive to ill health, transmission of disease, or crime, or inability to pay reasonable taxes, that is the ultimate finding . . . by reason of certain conditions certain things follow, but you say there has been a decision that says all you have to do is find the first.

MR. WARD: There is a statement in the ordinance, a legislative finding, that when you have these previous conditions . . . these conditions of blight [such as] physical deterioration, they have made a finding [that] when these conditions exist the latter conditions are the result.[14]

The ever-expanding definition of blight, and the confusion surrounding it, remained a central feature of local, state, and national urban policies. The "public use" underlying the eminent domain power was originally conceived as a genuine public use (a road, a hospital, a military base) or at least use by a common carrier or quasi-public entity (a railroad, a public utility, a stadium). But, over time, the test retreated from "public use" to "public purpose"—a far more nebulous and fungible notion. In turn, the courts effectively folded all of the concerns of the police power (safety, health, and morals) into a list of allowable public purposes. As a result, any local policy that claimed to safeguard public safety, health, or morals by eradicating blight could—at the same time—execute the most naked transfer of property from one private interest to another. "The use of eminent domain," the Supreme Court concluded in *Hawaii Housing Authority v. Midkiff* (1984), was justified as long as it was "rationally related to a conceivable public purpose." This latitude was recently affirmed in *Kelo v. New London* (2005): "In certain circumstances and to meet certain exigencies, takings that serve a public purpose also satisfy the Constitution even if the property is destined for subsequent private use."[15]

Who Finds the Blight?

The central thread running through the logic of urban renewal and the state and federal case law on the subject—and the court's confusion in *Allright*—was that local authorities had the responsibility and discretion to define and locate blight in their communities. In Missouri as elsewhere, this latitude drew on the laundry list of health and safety concerns that often served as the only statutory definition: Local officials or developers need only identify one of these problems in a redevelopment area in order to qualify the entire area as blighted. By this logic as well, redevelopment officials did not even have to find that a redevelopment area was demonstrably poorer or in worse condition than surrounding neighborhoods. St. Louis planners made a stab at defining or measuring nonresidential blight in 1957, reasoning that "much of non-residential 'blight' can be related to structural deterioration and general building obsolescence." But they also acknowledged that other factors, including "technological obsolescence," "general desire for newness," and demands for "employee amenities" were often thrown into the mix—"none of which appear readily subject to objective measurement or standardization."[16]

St. Louis did not formalize administrative procedures for blighting property until 1959 and resisted any quantifiable baseline, such as household income, property value, or percentage of vacant buildings, for the determination of blight.[17] A 1969 effort in St. Louis to quantify blight, using an elaborate factor analysis index weighing (1) local, or neighborhood, and regional, or census tract, patterns of land use; (2) crowding; (3) building quality; (4) average rents and assessed values; and (5) school and crime statistics, concluded that such empiricism was eroded by the fact that "virtually all of these . . . original measures were 'opinions' or 'judgments' about what constituted quality." In the early 1970s, the Board of Aldermen adopted a checklist for blight, which considered revenue loss, age of structures, percentage of vacant floor area, land use, deterioration, zoning inventory, and inability to yield reasonable taxes. But, like the state laws they echoed, such standards offered no guidance as to how various factors should be measured or weighed against one another. In practice, blight remained a "loose collection of several conditions" accompanied by the recognition that "different public policies might be needed to 'eliminate' different kinds of blight." When plaintiffs argued, in a 1974 Kansas City case, that the municipality had violated its "customary standard of 'blight'," the trial court found "no reference to any such standards or guidelines" in state or local law. When St. Louis County used "blight" as the centerpiece of a new housing code in 1973, critics pointed out that the law (like the urban renewal legislation it mimicked) "offers no recognizable, working definition of 'blight'."[18]

This local discretion (and inventiveness) sparked legal challenges—especially from commercial interests displaced by redevelopment, forced to compete with new businesses in the redevelopment area or unsuccessful themselves in their bids for redevelopment contracts. But Missouri courts invariably upheld local designations of blight, deferring to local legislative authority in determining both the meaning of blight and the larger public purpose served by redevelopment. In *Dalton v. Land Clearance* (1954), the state supreme court established the basic premise that "a legislative finding under said law that a blighted or insanitary area exists . . . will be accepted by the courts as conclusive evidence that the contemplated use thereof is public." As long as the local decision was not "clearly arbitrary or unreasonable," judges refused to second-guess the many ways local officials might determine that an area could "no longer meet the economic and social needs of modern city life." Even in *Allright*, a case in which the

Kansas City council overruled its own planning commission in declaring an area blighted (an action the trial court found arbitrary and unreasonable), the state supreme court held its nose and refused to second-guess the local legislative determination. This confirmed a sense, among redevelopment authorities and their critics, that local blighting decisions were virtually immune from legal challenge.[19]

For their part, local municipal and redevelopment interests appreciated the ambiguity of the law and the deference of the courts. Blight was in the eye of the beholder, and property was blighted when local officials said it was. Under Chapter 353, as critics noted in the middle 1970s, the Board of Aldermen had the power "to approve any type of project in nearly any location for URC [urban redevelopment corporation] designation." The willingness to blight was exaggerated by the practice of aldermanic courtesy, by which projects in particular wards were rarely challenged by other members of the board. "The definition of a 'blighted area' has been given an extremely broad definition by the Board of Alderman in recent years for purposes of both the PIE and '353' laws," noted one confidant to Mayor Poelker in 1976, "and few, if any development proposals have been thwarted because of the refusal of the Board of Aldermen to designate an area eligible for redevelopment." Ten years later, a review of the effect of tax abatements on school funding in the City concluded that blighting designations were "highly subjective and political" and "almost impossible to deny," given the contours of the law and City politics. Once the TIF law joined Chapters 99 and 353, the blighting door to local tax abatement was wide open. In 1997, the St. Louis Development Corporation assured prospective investors that tax abatement "can be done anywhere in the City by aldermanic ordinance." Or, as a critic of the trend toward TIFing suburban shopping centers put it, "if the legislators wished, they could blight the Taj Mahal."[20]

At least under the 1982 TIF law, blighting for redevelopment in Missouri was constrained by a "but for" provision, intended to ensure that redevelopment, as one observer notes, "produce the desired entrepreneurial response rather than merely subsidize development which would have occurred without it." Chapter 99 required that a prospective TIF zone "has not been subject to growth and development through investment by private enterprise and would not reasonably be anticipated to be developed without the adoption of tax increment financing." But, in practice, this provision was virtually meaningless. Like most states, Missouri did not (and still does not) require that its "but for" test be satisfied by anything approaching an objective or comprehensive feasibility study. As a result, "but for" was just another element of local discretion. There was no consideration of state or regional or metropolitan concerns—including the possibility that development might occur elsewhere without subsidy or that "new" investment was merely being pirated from elsewhere. "Reasonable anticipation" of private development was calculated by the very interests vested in the proposed TIF deal—often in the form of affidavits from private developers attesting to their unwillingness to proceed without public subsidy. And local officials defined "private enterprise" as narrowly as they wished: It was not at all uncommon, for example, for development officials to rebuff unsubsidized private investment in an area because they were holding out for a given investor or tenant—often a big-box chain retailer or an upscale department store.[21]

Finding the Blight That's Right

What makes such local discretion all the more troubling is the fact that the designation of blight often occurred on a proposal-by-proposal basis, at the behest of developers. Blighting, in other words, was driven not by objective urban conditions but by the prospect of private investment. In practice, this meant that investment was actually steered away from the most dismal urban conditions as private interests sought the "blight that's right"—an area with at least some of the conditions needed to make a plausible case for subsidized redevelopment, but not so run-down as to put private investment at risk. As early as 1975, local development corporations in St. Louis understood their "public purpose" as little more than providing "interested developers with the incentive to revitalize the area with new and expanded facilities."[22]

In the scramble to TIF new retail developments in the St. Louis suburbs, for example, the designation of blight was typically sought after local officials had reached a tentative agreement with a new developer or anchor store. In such cases, neither the taxing municipality nor private investors were likely to risk TIFs in areas in which economic growth was not already assured. Indeed, in one such case, the city of Richmond Heights turned to TIF not because the area was in trouble, but because the land was so expensive: "we now have the odd phenomenon," the *Post-Dispatch* observed wryly, "of blight selling for top dollar." This was the political and legal setting that invited suburban interests to blight a shopping mall for no better reason than the assessment (by a potential tenant) that it "was too small and had too few anchor stores," and that constrained the courts from second-guessing even a "fairly debatable" legislative determination. "A tame consulting firm hired by the city of Richmond Heights last week declared that the Galleria neighborhood is 'blighted' too," observed one local critic. "As Yogi Berra said, 'nobody goes there any more, it's too crowded'."[23]

In many cases, the search for the "right blight" encouraged local development officials to raise the specter of "future blight"—to argue for redevelopment of areas not yet blighted but likely to become so. Such notions, in part, rest on the longstanding conviction that blight was not a physical description but a set of circumstances or conditions: Blight was the disease, slums were the result, and redevelopment was the cure. As one federal housing official suggested in the early 1930s, a blighted area was one that was "on the down grade, [but] which has not yet reached the slum stage," or "an insidious malady that attacks urban residential districts. It appears first as a barely noticeable deterioration and then progresses gradually through many stages toward a final condition known as the slum." Federal urban renewal law picked up this reasoning. The 1954 Housing Act expanded its blight definition to include the "conservation and rehabilitation of declining areas." Federal courts held that federal urban renewal law was intended "to eliminate not only slums as narrowly defined . . . but also the blighted areas that tend to produce slums." And local officials proceeded on the assumption that projected blight was sufficient, that blight was "both a condition and a cause."[24]

Redevelopment statutes, in turn, used projected or future blight to justify a wide range of projects. Under Missouri's TIF law, for example, an area can qualify for redevelopment as a "conservation district" if 50 percent of the structures contained by the district are more than 35 years old—regardless of their condition. "Such an area is not yet a blighted area," the statute explains, "but is detrimental to public health, safety, morals or welfare and may become a blighted area."[25] Even when such "conservation" provisions are not explicit in state law, courts have generally supported the idea that redevelopment is as much preventive as it is corrective and that the definition of blight is "broad and encompasses not only those areas containing properties so dilapidated as to justify condemnation as nuisances but also envisions the prevention of deterioration." As with the "but for" test, projections of future growth or decline were left largely to the judgment of those pushing for a given redevelopment project. This meant that even the relative prosperity of an area could be used as an argument for its redevelopment—on the assumption that such prosperity could not last. In the debate over the infamous "Nordstrom's TIF" in suburban St. Louis, all agreed that the mall in question was the region's greatest economic asset. For those pushing the TIF deal, however, this prosperity was inherently fragile, and projection of future competitive losses to newer malls was enough to justify a finding of blight.[26]

Finding More Blight, or the Redevelopment Area That Ate the City

Although local officials had (and still have) considerable discretion in finding blight, they nevertheless needed to make a credible case that a given redevelopment area was deserving of public subsidy or public attention. This was often accomplished as much by stretching the redevelopment area itself as it was by stretching the definition of blight. The larger the urban renewal area or TIF district, as a rule, the easier it is to find blighted conditions inside it and to use the "public interest" to meet the objections of affected property owners. This strategy emerged first in federal housing and urban renewal, which steadily expanded its focus from individual properties in 1934 to housing projects in 1937 and 1949 to neighborhoods in 1956 and then to entire urban areas in 1959. State redevelopment laws and local redevelopment corporations followed suit.[27]

Nowhere was the "bigger is better" strategy pursued more faithfully than in St. Louis. Many of the City's early renewal projects (Civic Plaza, the stadium) were scattered through the central business district. In the late 1960s, redevelopment plans began to spot-blight individual parcels or buildings—a practice clearly incompatible with the pretense of comprehensive planning that underlay the whole enterprise. Since the City's larger goal was to offer abatements to any new investment downtown, the logical solution (first pushed by Mayor Cervantes in 1967 and accomplished by the Board of Aldermen in 1970) was to "pre-blight" the entire central business district. "We are trying to get away from spot blighting," argued one alderman at the time, "and get everything downtown on an even footing for development." Local redevelopment enthusiasts, tellingly, interpreted this not as a declaration that downtown was hopelessly blighted, but it was open for business. "What a wonderful gesture," J. Arthur Baer of Downtown, Inc. thanked Cervantes, "to hand me a completely blighted downtown St. Louis."[28] A similar—if more dramatic and desperate—pattern could be found across the river: By 2001, East St. Louis had been parceled out into 7 TIF zones encompassing the entire city and a patchwork of state and federal enterprise zones that swallowed the city and spilled beyond its boundaries.[29]

The "broad area" approach was especially important in Missouri's TIF districts, because the boundaries of the redevelopment area simultaneously captured increases in property taxes and sales taxes. The larger the TIF district, the easier it was to argue for redevelopment around "one big plan and one big developer." And the larger the TIF district, the more stable the increment claimed to retire project costs. The city of Richmond Heights, for example, turned down numerous private offers to develop properties on the east side of Brentwood Boulevard (across from the Galleria Mall) in favor of a TIF-subsidized plan for the entire area. Existing businesses blasted the tactic as "arbitrary, in bad faith, and a clear abuse of legislative powers . . . no more than a contrived attempt to use the TIF Act to condemn healthy, profitable businesses at artificially low prices." Richmond Heights defended its choice on the grounds that even a thriving commercial strip could be blighted as long as the redevelopment plans promised something bigger and better.[30] This, in turn, was the basic principle upheld by the Supreme Court in *Kelo v. New London* (2005): "there is no allegation that any of these properties is blighted or otherwise in poor condition; rather they were condemned only because they happened to be located in the development area."[31]

Local control over the size and boundaries of redevelopment areas also came to resemble the politics of congressional redistricting; indeed, redevelopment areas were often gerrymandered in such a way as to encompass both commercial parcels targeted for development and enough blighted area to justify the development. *Berman v. Parker*, the Supreme Court case that upheld federal urban renewal policies in 1954, established the rule (followed faithfully by state courts) that blight was a characteristic of a given redevelopment area and not necessarily of individual properties within it. This gave local officials the incentive to draw expansive redevelopment areas, constrained only by the rule that such areas not be composed of noncontiguous parcels.[32] In settings such as St. Louis, this created an ongoing tension between sweeping redevelopment areas (which qualified broad swaths of property for tax abatement) and spot blighting (which targeted abatement at specific parcels). Both ploys, in practice, steered redevelopment away from the City's worst neighborhoods—either by using truly blighted blocks to qualify abatement elsewhere in the redevelopment area or by picking off properties and ignoring their neighbors.

In St. Louis, redevelopment officials often anticipated or responded to objections from owners of "good" properties and tried to massage redevelopment boundaries accordingly. In early 1971, for example, the entire Maryland Plaza was blighted under Chapter 99. Owners of improved properties (21–65 Maryland Plaza) in the area objected, and the City dutifully redrafted the plans to exclude them. Three years later, the City shifted gears once again and passed a bill that blighted the excluded properties and reblighted the rest of the area. The overarching purpose, as owners of some of the blighted parcels noted bitterly, was "not to redevelop an area in fact blighted but is rather to give tax and other improper advantages to a private real estate developer."[33] In turn, redevelopment areas often reached out to find pockets of blight, even if their aim was redevelopment elsewhere. St. Louis County's North County Enterprise Zone (see Map 5.2), for example, was established primarily to retain a Ford plant in Hazelwood. But its boundaries wandered crazily over much of the north County—"plotted," its advocates admitted "to include the proportions of low-income residents, unemployed residents and underused industrial land needed to meet state requirements."[34]

Blight Versus Blight

As blighting and redevelopment drifted more and more into the service of local commercial development, they created an intense (and profoundly counterproductive) pattern of competition for new investment and tax revenues. State and local governments scrambled to make themselves more attractive to prospective investors, a bidding war in which struggling settings (like St. Louis) were generally more desperate and less successful.[35] The argument cutting across many meetings and reports of local economic development groups was not that St. Louis might gain a competitive edge but that it risked falling farther behind if it couldn't come up with the incentives or tax breaks offered in other settings. As promoters of an industrial park at Columbia Bottoms put it in 1963: "St. Louis County is in competition with 16,000 area development organizations throughout the United States in its efforts to retain *present* business and industry and to make the County more attractive to *new* business and industry." Even as national and local evidence (including a Price-Waterhouse survey commissioned by the City in 1975) suggested that tax incentives and abatements played a relatively small role in the location decisions made by firms, local boosters—following a national pattern—cited the importance of such programs as "a clue to the political environment, indicating [a local government's] responsiveness to the demands of business."[36]

What made such competitive anxieties all the more damaging was the way in which they played out on a more local level—in battles between the City and its suburbs, or among those suburbs, for prospective development. This produced (or reproduced) what the East-West Gateway Coordinating Council dubbed the "musical chair effect": By its measure (in 1973), only a small percentage of new investment trumpeted by local governments had not come at the expense of another local government, and the competition between those local governments (bidding down the tax base) then came at the expense of the region. Local enthusiasm for attracting the next hotel or big-box retailer, the *Post-Dispatch* agreed thirty years later, had to be tempered by the recognition that "the results for the entire region are wacky."[37]

In greater St. Louis, this local competition first played out as a confrontation between St. Louis and its suburbs. Despite growing doubts about the efficacy of Chapter 353 abatements, St. Louis officials fiercely defended them on the grounds that they

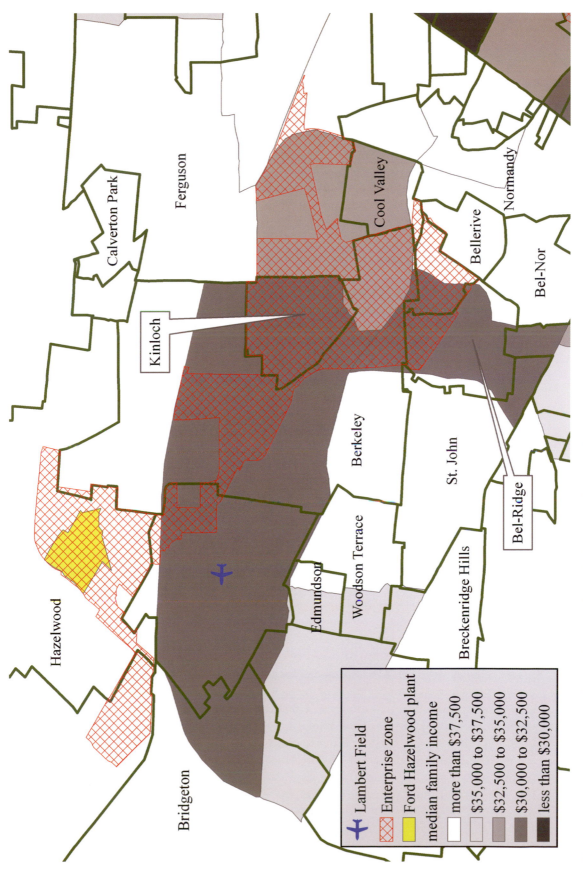

Map 5.2. Airport/North County Enterprise Zone, 2003. St. Louis Development Corporation; 2000 Census.

Calverton Park

Ferguson

Cool Valley

Normandy

Bellerive

Bel-Nor

Kinloch

Berkeley

St. John

Bel-Ridge

Hazelwood

Edmundson

Woodson Terrace

Breckenridge Hills

Bridgeton

Lambert Field
Enterprise zone
Ford Hazelwood plant
median family income
more than $37,500
$35,000 to $37,500
$32,500 to $35,000
$30,000 to $32,500
less than $30,000

gave the City a rare competitive advantage over municipalities in St. Louis County (which, for most of the program's history, could not meet its population thresholds).[38] For St. Louis development officials, the threat or reality of business migration west served as a steady backbeat to a half century of efforts to save downtown, clear slums, and at least retain its core commercial citizens. This often meant pitched battles with St. Louis County and its municipalities. In 1973, for example, Mallinckrodt Chemical floated plans for a new corporate park in St. Louis County. As Mallinckrodt fought a zoning battle over the new site, the City frantically packaged Chapter 353 abatements with any other incentives it could muster: "we'll do anything they want," one alderman concluded hopefully. Ironically, the City's willingness to blight and repackage land for new development actually undermined the business climate for many others: "Some businesses (those that could afford it) moved out to the county," one City business wrote Mayor Poelker in 1973, "where the management knew they would not be bothered every time some promoter got an idea as to how he could make money with the help of the city out of someone else's property."[39]

In state and federal law, and in local practice, urban renewal and economic development policies were rooted in the idea that central cities needed help countering the centripetal force of demographic and commercial suburbanization. Over time, however, the focus on the central city dissipated. Federal urban renewal programs were opened to any municipality willing to make a claim for blight within its borders—a form of municipal entitlement continued under the Community Development Block Grant program. And Missouri lowered (and then largely abandoned) the population thresholds that had confined its core urban renewal programs to St. Louis and Kansas City. What this meant, alongside the evaporation of federal urban spending, was that virtually any local government could use the promise of tax abatement to compete with its neighbors—and that well-heeled suburban municipalities were often in a better position to do so.

In greater St. Louis, competition to blight old investments and tax-abate new ones became largely a competition to build the next big mall in the outer suburbs. This pattern was exaggerated by restrictions on the property tax (a state-level development that begin with California's Proposition 13 in 1973 and included Missouri's Hancock Amendment in 1980). Even in affluent residential suburbs, caps on property taxation encouraged local officials to retreat from long-standing patterns of exclusionary zoning to compete for new retail investment. This pattern hardened after the passage of Missouri's TIF law in 1982. In Missouri (where sales taxes are a relatively important source of local revenue), TIF districts can lay claim to the local increase, or increment, in sales taxes as well. This is true in both "point of origin" cities that get to keep local sales taxes and in other cities that can effectively use TIFs to become point of origin cities. This combination not only created (as we have seen) the ludicrous practice of blighting relatively new malls in order to build newer ones but it also created substantial incentives to buy out middle-income housing and replace it with retail (in effect trading properties that return low revenues and high demands to the local tax base for those promising high revenues and low demands). "Tax incentives and other incentives held promise as a limited tool to lure business into blighted areas," reflected the *Post-Dispatch* in 1998. "But they have become a club with which more prosperous localities can beat up, economically, on less fortunate regions."[40]

Blighting for What?

Perhaps the most important underlying shift in all of this—one that cut across federal, state, and local programs—was the triumph of economic over residential development. Through the first half of the twentieth century, blight was understood as a condition of substandard housing, and "eradicating blight" meant providing decent homes for urban working families. But even amid the worries about a postwar housing crunch that animated state and federal efforts in the 1940s, urban housing policy was already adrift. Urban renewal was compromised by a raft of more generous federal policies, including highway spending, mortgage insurance, and accelerated depreciation for new commercial development, which subsidized and facilitated suburban flight. Federal housing policy, as we have seen, was already committed to improving the housing stock without increasing it. And, under constant pressure from local and real estate interests, Congress opened the door for the use of federal funds for nonresidential development. While the Federal Housing Act of 1949 defined blighted areas as "predominantly residential," it did not require cities or developers to erect affordable housing in redeveloped districts. And Congress gradually amended the "residential threshold," allowing up to 10 percent of federal funds to be spent on commercial development in 1954 and increasing this percentage to 35 in 1965.[41]

Just as importantly, urban redevelopment policy was increasingly distracted by the concerns of realtors, developers, and business leaders representing the central business district (CBD). Between the wars, business interests had been wary of urban policy, especially given the threats to private interests posed by eminent domain and public housing. Increasingly, however, urban business leaders saw redevelopment as a means of loosening the "dirty collar" of substandard housing that encircled most CBDs. These interests, however, had little patience with redevelopment plans that proposed to repopulate cleared slums with working families who neither shopped nor worked downtown. As early as the late 1930s, neighborhood surveys by the FHA typically concluded of D-rated residential slums that "the only hope is for the demolition of these buildings and transition of the area into a business district." As state and local interests poised to spend federal dollars after 1949, the consensus was clear. Low-income and middle-income housing did not match the immense acquisition costs or economic potential of urban redevelopment; slum clearance would pave the way for CBD expansion or higher-end housing. "The main purpose," St. Louis officials concluded in anticipation of the 1949 Housing Act, "is to clear the land for use by private enterprise."[42]

At the intersection of these private and public anxieties, urban redevelopment policies took a decisive turn. Slums were to be cleared, not for better housing, but for a more abstract faith in local economic development and growth. Targeted areas were identified less by demonstrable need than by the willingness of private interests to invest in them. Redevelopment, in turn, rested on an elastic definition of blight that put the health of the CBD—and then simply the health of the overall "business climate"—at the top of the urban agenda. Under state law, the drift from residential to commercial redevelopment was even more pronounced. Most state laws echoed the federal presumption that blight and its rehabilitation were "predominantly residential" concerns, but they also offered other pretexts for redevelopment. As redevelopment plans were challenged, particularly by displaced commercial interests, the courts consistently held that urban redevelopment was "not solely to provide for slum clearance" and that designations of blight were appropriate even if *no portion* of the redevelopment zone could reasonably be considered a slum. All of this was readily apparent in the underlying logic of urban renewal in St. Louis, which cleared swaths of substandard housing around "prominent industries," bisected downtown with urban expressways, and warehoused displaced residents in segregated public housing.[43]

The St. Louis LCRA was always looking for inventive ways of underwriting nonresidential development, but "economic development" definitions of blight, and local discretion in interpreting them, exploded with the urban fiscal crisis and the collapse of federal urban spending in the early 1970s. Local officials in St. Louis admitted as early as 1969 that the deterioration of nonresidential property could not be shoehorned into the old police power definition of blight conditions as those "conducive to ill health, transmission of disease, or crime." But they did not hesitate to expand that definition to include any condition "conducive to the inability to pay reasonable taxes." In 1973, advisers to Mayor Poelker insisted that "we have to emphasize more business and industry for the city and de-emphasize new housing programs."[44]

This drift was formalized by the passage of Missouri's TIF law, which (as in most states) allowed local governments to add slow economic growth or the threat of future economic decline to their working definitions of blight. The 1982 statute recommended the use of TIFs to "discourage commerce, industry or manufacturing from moving their operations to another state," "result in increased employment," or "result in the preservation or enhancement of the tax base of the municipality." Because TIFs use future tax revenues to finance redevelopment, they are actually ill suited to conventional residential urban renewal, which usually involves significant upfront costs for land acquisition and clearance. Instead, TIFs—as we have seen for greater St. Louis—have focused on commercial development at the fringe of the metropolitan area.[45]

Blight and Flight

While "fighting blight" began as an effort to make the City a better place to live, the logic of urban renewal and economic development in greater St. Louis pushed public policy (and its consequences) in very nearly the opposite direction. Local discretion concerning the meaning and the scope of blight, local competition for new investment, and a growing fascination (in federal, state, and local politics) with economic development combined to bury any real commitment to housing people of ordinary means and integrating them into the life and economy of the metropolitan area.

Nowhere was this sorry pattern more evident than in the residential and relocation politics of urban renewal.

As early as 1915, white property owners noted the tendency of expansive redevelopment projects to press displaced residents into other areas of the City. "When work on the Central Parkway [the Jefferson Memorial site] is commenced," worried one pamphlet in the 1916 zoning debate, "some 15,000 Negroes who now live in that district will be forced to find other quarters and some of them may move next door to you." Indeed, as patterns of African American occupancy moved west, so did the City's geography of blight. In 1938, the City Plan Commission declared the predominantly African American Tandy neighborhood blighted and recommended its redevelopment as a commercial and industrial corridor. "Will you kindly give us a definition of what is blighted," responded the local Urban League, "if the majority of property in the area you mentioned is owned by Negro residents?" The disgust was real but rhetorical. The Urban League and others increasingly recognized that, for city planners, "negro occupancy" and "blight" were essentially synonymous.[46]

As early as the middle 1940s, it was unclear whether the City's poor (and largely African American) residents were a target of urban renewal or an obstacle to its success. Captivated by the promise (and federal funding) of large-scale reconstruction, planners envisioned a mix of garden and high-rise apartments in the place of cleared slums. But neither local developers nor the federal government showed any interest in increasing population density (preferring to trade substandard units for middle- and upper-income units). And the fascination with using cleared land for new commercial and industrial development undermined any interest in rehabilitating troubled neighborhoods. Urban renewal, a 1953 report concluded, presented "an opportunity to transform costly slums into economically sound industrial and commercial areas." The St. Louis Chamber of Commerce agreed that the elimination of slums was a prerequisite to new commercial and industrial development downtown— adding that this would merely hasten the "natural" movement of people to the suburbs. A preliminary study for the Mill Creek project understood that its task was to "remove the poorest housing units and their occupants from the market." And planning for rehabilitation of the O'Fallon neighborhood pressed for a "land pattern of relatively small industrial firms while cleaning out the decadent housing in between."[47]

What did it mean, in practice, to "reclaim" the City from its slums and to "remove" the City's poor? Certainly the first solution, pursued alongside the early slum clearance efforts, was to warehouse dislocated residents in high-density public housing. As we have seen, a run of public housing projects—Clinton-Peabody, Carr Square Village, Cochran Gardens, Pruitt-Igoe, Joseph Darst, George Vaughn, Webbe—erected between the late 1940s and the early 1960s accompanied the City's first major renewal projects.[48] More commonly, urban renewal authorities simply expected dislocated residents to fend for themselves and vastly inflated (largely for the consumption of federal officials) their ability to accommodate or assist those losing their homes. The relocation office of the Mill Creek project, for example, claimed it had placed all those displaced by initial land clearance (4,172 families) in decent housing. But a federal audit found that more than half of those eligible for relocation assistance received no help, and that most of the assisted relocations were to substandard dwellings. Little wonder that civil rights leaders equated urban renewal with "negro removal": "It was all legal and proper: Wrecking a Negro's building no longer had to be done by a mob. Here was a way to do it constitutionally."[49]

The overarching irony in all of this was that urban renewal often created, or re-created elsewhere, the very conditions it purported to fight. More than a decade into its urban renewal program, the City concluded glumly that "the gap actually has increased between the quantity of substandard housing that must be replaced (or rehabilitated) and the supply of new or renewed housing." By the late 1960s, the presence of large public housing projects was considered a harbinger of blight, and not a means of fighting it. Urban renewal plans for the DeSoto-Carr neighborhood argued that the "environment is beclouded by the presence of massive public housing totaling nearly 5,000 units." And, as urban renewal attention drifted west, residents and planners alike attributed the decline of these neighborhoods to the migration of those cut loose by the first generation of urban renewal projects surrounding the central business district. The real threat to the public welfare, as many argued, was haphazard and halfhearted redevelopment schemes—and not the "blight" that justified them.[50]

The turmoil of relocation and dislocation first arose around the early postwar work on St. Louis' urban highways. As in many other settings, highway planning (hurried along by federal dollars) was shaped largely by traffic engineering and gave little thought to the local impact of construction. And, as in many other settings, highway planning viewed white residential areas as neighborhoods to be preserved and black residential areas as slums to be cleared.[51] Highway projects displaced those in their path, generating local opposition and reshaping local neighborhoods. "Everyone was for expressways," one City official noted in 1958, "but preferred that they did not go through their property." On the downtown northside—simultaneously targeted for expressway construction and urban renewal—the Mark Twain and Daniel Boone routes eroded much of the residential integrity of the neighborhood.[45] Population in the four downtown census tracts (running west from the river) bisected by the Daniel Boone route collapsed from almost 25,000 in 1950 to fewer than 9,000 in 1960 (see Map 5.3) and fully 75 percent of those displaced were African American.

Opposition from southside residents slowed progress on the Ozark Expressway, and the route was pushed closer to the river before cutting across the City's southern corner to join up with U.S. Route 66 in the County. Residents of "the Hill" (just west of Tower Grove Park) won an extra overpass when I-44 threatened to bisect the neighborhood. And residents of the Lafayette Square area forced the City to scuttle plans for a new "North-South Distributor," which would have offered a downtown expressway between 1–55 and I-70. Nevertheless, the Ozark and I-44 routes resulted in significant displacement (see Map 5.4). Between 1950 and 1970, population of the five tracts running west from the intersection of the Ozark and I-44 fell by half (from 65,000 to 32,000), a collapse dampened only by the *in-migration* of nearly 10,000 African Americans (whose population share of this five-tract area grew from less than one percent to more then 30 percent over this span). In St. Louis County, local interests routinely

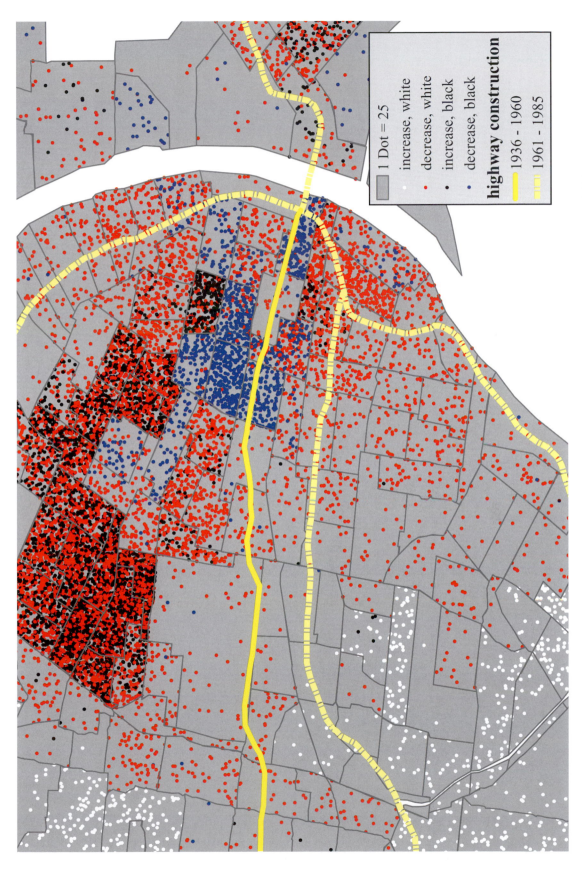

Map 5.3. Highway construction and residential displacement, 1950–1960. Census Bureau (Bogue Files), synthesis of 1950 and 1960 tract boundaries.

1 Dot = 25
increase, white
decrease, white
increase, black
decrease, black
highway construction
1936 - 1960
1961 - 1985

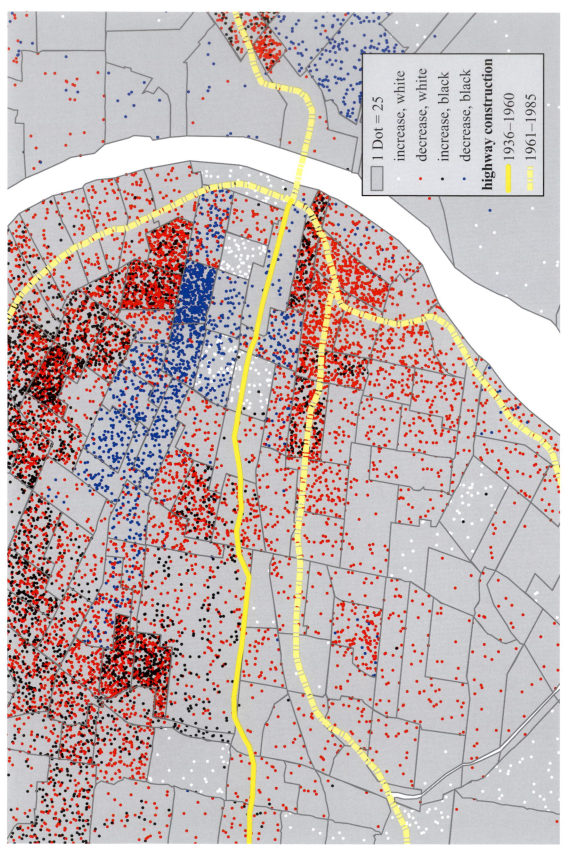

Legend:

1 Dot = 25

- increase, white
- decrease, white
- increase, black
- decrease, black

highway construction
— 1936–1960
— 1961–1985

Map 5.4. Highway construction and residential displacement, 1960–1970. Census Bureau (Bogue Files), synthesis of 1960 and 1970 tract boundaries.

slowed or diverted highway projects—especially as sprawl led to traffic congestion in inner suburbs like Clayton, Richmond Heights, and Webster Groves.[53]

This pattern of renewal—and the relocation it entailed—was multiplied in the City's major early renewal projects: the Civic Center (stadium), Mill Creek Valley, and Kosciusko. Along with the run of "white flight" maps (see Introduction), Map 5.5 neatly captures the haphazard movement of African Americans from cleared tracts—some into local public housing but most into neighborhoods to the west and north. This had the effect of both deepening segregation in many central city neighborhoods and creating demands for clearance in those neighborhoods accommodating the refugees from the latest round of renewal. Local planners eventually acknowledged a "serious problem" with relocations from Mill Creek Valley, the vast majority of which simply drifted north and west into the neighborhoods bounded by Delmar, Hodiamont, Jefferson, and Natural Bridge. Similarly, those displaced by the Kosciusko redevelopment were left with few options and "generally settled in already blighted areas."[54]

The strings attached to federal urban renewal money included requirements that cleared districts be rebuilt (at least in part) in such a way as to accommodate former residents, and that local urban renewal authorities provide permanent or temporary relocation assistance. In practice, these provisions largely evaporated. Since the principal task of urban renewal in St. Louis was to reclaim blighted slums for industrial or commercial use, there was little thought given to the accommodation of former residents—save the piecemeal provision of public housing at the project fringes. Relocation assistance also rested on the willingness of local authorities to contact and advise affected families, a step that federal audits found little evidence of in St. Louis or Kansas City. Indeed, nearly half (3,300 of 7,000) of the families displaced by Mill Creek, Kosciusko, and contemporary projects in Columbia and Kansas City never made an appearance in the workloads of the local relocation offices. Many were understandably reluctant to sit down with those who were kicking them out their homes; many more caustically dismissed the City's LCRA as "Local City Rip-off Artists."[55]

A large part of the relocation problem lay in the pattern of redevelopment: Federal money for clearance was easy to come by, but rebuilding and redevelopment was a much slower proposition. Across St. Louis, the enthusiastic eradication of blight was often followed by years (even decades) in which cleared properties sat vacant—a pattern that earned the Mill Creek Valley the local nickname "Hiroshima Flats." Even admirers of the City's renewal efforts regretted the template (as one observer noted of the LaSalle Park project) of "clearance, mixed land use, some new housing for an ill-defined resident population, and a passing nod to the old residents and institutions that had once given [the neighborhood] its life and character."[56]

Where renewal efforts did entail substantial new or rehabilitated housing, the issue was both relocation and gentrification. This was especially true in the City's West End and in some of the smaller renewal projects it encompassed. As the expansive West End plans foundered, the City proceeded with smaller, targeted plans in the neighborhoods immediately north of Forest Park – including the Pershing-Waterman area, blighted under Chapter 353 in April 1971. The first redevelopment plans could not

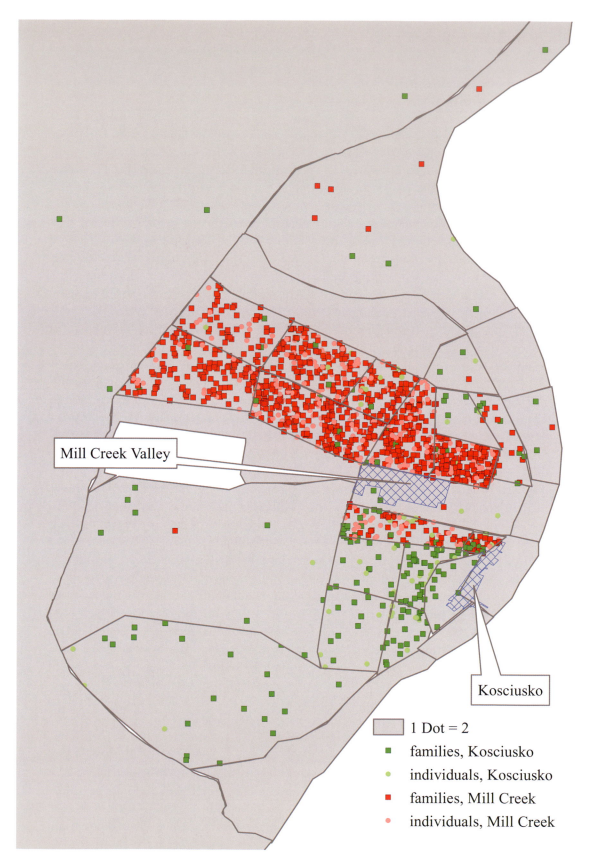

Mill Creek Valley

Kosciusko

1 Dot = 2

■ families, Kosciusko

● individuals, Kosciusko

■ families, Mill Creek

● individuals, Mill Creek

Map 5.5. Relocations from Kosciusko and Mill Creek Valley, 1951–55. St. Louis Development Corporation, *Technical Report: History of Renewal* (St. Louis, 1971).

attract sufficient financing and were recast by the Pantheon Corporation as the "Pershing Redevelopment Corporation" in 1975.[57]

For critics, the Pershing-Waterman project captured the central inequities of the City's experience with urban renewal. The project location underscored a longstanding commitment to downtown and the central corridor, often at the expense of the truly blighted and struggling residential northside. Most agreed that Pershing-Waterman was as much a consequence of urban renewal as it was a target, as the area had become a dumping ground for families displaced by both older urban renewal plans and the razing of Pruitt-Igoe in the early 1970s. While Pantheon was widely admired for its commitment to the City, it had also achieved notoriety in local housing politics for its hardball tactics when it came time to clear tenants from buildings slated for redevelopment. And the displacement of poor rental tenants for well-heeled condominium owners hardened a sense (especially when Mayor Poelker's CDA director left for a job with Pantheon) that redevelopment enriched private interests under the guise of serving a public purpose. Indeed, when displaced residents (500 to 800 families) sued for federal relocation assistance, the courts denied their claim on the grounds that the redevelopment—while justified and enabled under Chapter 353 as a "public purpose"—was a private investment unencumbered by federal relocation guidelines. In a reluctant concurring opinion, one justice remained "saddened by the expediency and callousness exhibited by this rehabilitation scheme toward the original residents of the neighborhood" and concluded that "the dislocation of lower income families as exhibited in this case reveals . . . the shortsightedness in most urban redevelopment planning which, rather than alleviating the inner city ghetto, will merely cause it to geographically shift."[58]

These patterns are also evident if we turn our attention to the (modest) history of urban renewal in suburban St. Louis County. As in the City, urban renewal generally equated black occupancy with blight and targeted pockets of historically (or more recent) African American settlement for clearance and redevelopment: major redevelopment areas included Maline Creek (Kinloch), North Webster Groves, Olivette, pockets of unincorporated County land in Elmwood Park and Meacham Park, and a number of areas in the inner suburb of University City. In these settings, displaced families faced both the stark racial logic of the region's private housing market and the candid determination of redevelopment officials to encourage African Americans to move "back" to the City. Assessing the relocation prospects for former residents of Maline Creek in 1958, realtor Roy Wenzlick counted 155 rental units and 240 sale properties "available to non-whites" in the City, and only 6 sale properties and no rental units in the County. Urban renewal officials in Olivette assumed that displaced families would relocate "across the track in Elmwood Park" (a black neighborhood), but were at a loss when Elmwood Park itself was slated for redevelopment: this "poses quite a relocation problem for St. Louis County," a 1958 HUD memo noted, "since housing available to Negroes is very limited in the County."[59]

A persistent assumption (echoed by local and federal officials) running through urban renewal projects west of the City line was that displaced African Americans could (and should) find private or public housing in the City.[60] In this sense, federal policy subsidized not only white flight but a "black retreat" from scattered residential pockets in the County. The renewal of North Webster Groves called for "the abandonment of any present private and public investment" and its replacement by a "completely new, stable single-family neighborhood"—resting on the implicit assumption that redevelopment and rezoning would effectively bar former residents from moving back to the area. New single-family housing in the Meacham Park redevelopment area (crafted to meet FHA guidelines) was pointedly priced beyond the reach of displaced residents: "for various reasons," local real estate interests reasoned, "these families must be excluded from the market."[61]

Consider the renewal of Elmwood Park, a community of about 170 black families on a small pocket of pointedly unincorporated land near Olivette. Plans for urban renewal began with a St. Louis County resolution in 1956, driven largely by the growing scarcity of land in the central county. The land was blighted under Chapter 99 in 1957, and renewal plans were drafted and refined in the early 1960s. Federal law (and money) required that renewal include a plan for assisting and relocating residents. In its first draft, the renewal plan called for relocation to a public housing complex planned for Jefferson Barracks (a decommissioned military base in the south County), but this was dropped when County voters spurned the housing development. A revised plan called for staging redevelopment so that new homes on Elmwood Park's east side would be available before residents on the west side were faced with relocation.[62] In practice, none of this happened. Relocation efforts became little more, a County Grand Jury concluded in 1966, than "an evasion of responsibility and intent [which] . . . practically wiped out an enclave of Negro property holdings of nearly a century's duration; a community where there was never any question of the right of Negroes to buy, own, and rent property." For displaced residents, urban renewal meant the construction of "dwellings beyond their means, and . . . commercial and industrial improvements completely irrelevant to their well-being." This was not an urban renewal program; it was a "race clearance program."[63]

As the renewal plan progressed, relocation assistance was halfhearted—and in direct violation of both federal regulations requiring the local accommodation of displaced residents and the assurances of the County LCRA that "turnover in existing private housing will be sufficient to permanently or temporarily re-house all of the [current occupants] . . . Almost all relocation will be within the project area." Owners were compensated for their homes, but a welter of private and public restrictions made it difficult to move elsewhere in the County. "I can't get land for that," complained one resident, "at least where they got it for colored people." All residents (owners and renters) were given modest relocation allowances, but these often disappeared as rent on homes claimed and condemned by the renewal authority. In some instances, evicted residents were presented with the same multipage application given to prospective developers as their only "opportunity" to stay in Elmwood Park. In the end, the lag between the condemnation of old Elmwood Park and the availability of new sites ran into years—making it necessary for all residents to find more than short-term options somewhere else.[64]

While the LCRA neglected the task of relocation, it at least tracked the choices made by former residents, which I have summarized in Map 5.6. Of 100 relocations recorded though 1964, 5 had moved out of state and 6 to other counties in Missouri. The remaining 89 relocated across the metro area—the vast majority moving to largely African American tracts on the City's northside, public housing downtown, transitional neighborhoods in the inner suburb of Wellston, or other pockets of African American settlement in the County such as Kinloch and Webster Groves. Of the 170-odd African American households displaced by urban renewal in Elmwood Park, only *one* returned to a new home in the project area. This reflected both the options available and the persistent recommendation of relocation officials that displaced residents look to public housing in the City or "predominantly negro ghettoes" elsewhere in the County. What the map does not show (also faithfully recorded by the LCRA) was that fewer than 1 in 5 displaced residents acknowledged any assistance from the relocation authority in finding new accommodations. Residents were also rebuffed by the courts, which refused them standing to sue once renewal was under way and the property had changed hands—although the trial judge concluded that LCRA officials had as much as "admitted that they had made no relocation plans for all these people."[65]

The prospect of large-scale land clearance and redevelopment evaporated with the end of federal urban renewal programs in the early 1970s, but County municipalities continued both to dig in against the "negro invasion" (underscored in the Black Jack controversy) and to "clean up" older pockets of African American occupancy. In the middle 1970s, for example, the city of Creve Coeur moved to oust black homeowners from Malcolm Terrace, a neighborhood of small (25 by 100 feet) lots platted in the 1890s. Creve Coeur systematically pursued code violations, denied new building permits, and began buying up lots through a straw party. Redevelopment plans were sketchy, but city officials were willing to rezone the entire neighborhood as parkland if it meant "keeping Black Jack from coming in." For his part, the Creve Coeur mayor confided that he "personally did not want any colored in there."[66]

What Does It Cost?

To this point, I have assessed the benefits and the beneficiaries of a half century of site-specific urban renewal and economic development policies. The flip side of this equation, of course, is the cost of those policies. It is virtually impossible—and probably nearly meaningless—to put a dollar value on urban renewal in greater St. Louis over the last half century: the budget lines sprawl across too many years, too many governments (local, state, federal), and too many programs. And much of the spending takes the form of taxes abated, forgiven, or credited—that is, not public dollars spent but public dollars never collected.

In turn, critics and celebrants of local economic development policies viewed such "tax expenditures" from starkly different sets of assumptions. Any simple equation tallying tax revenues gained against the tax revenues forgone is undermined by fundamental disagreement over the trajectory of natural economic growth and the relationship between public policy and new revenues.[67] For local civic officials and developers,

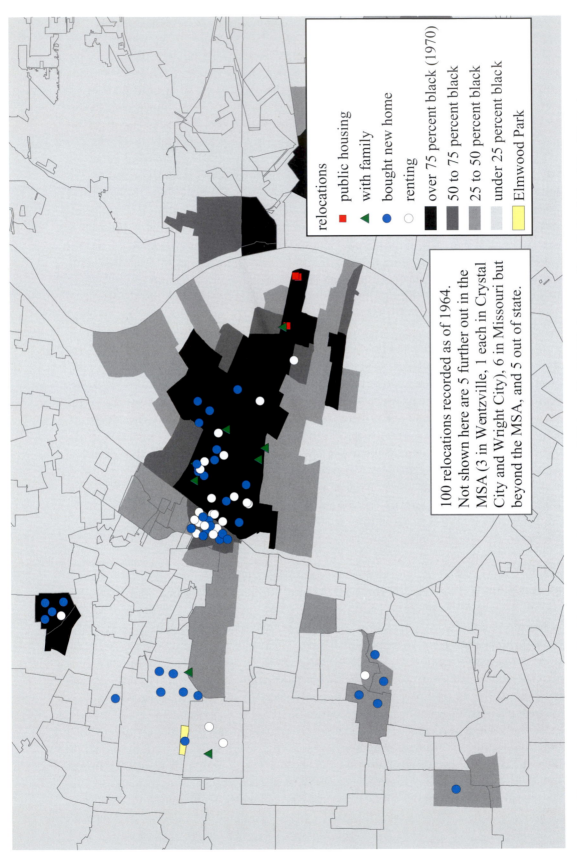

relocations
- ■ public housing
- ▲ with family
- ● bought new home
- ○ renting

- ■ over 75 percent black (1970)
- ■ 50 to 75 percent black
- ■ 25 to 50 percent black
- □ under 25 percent black
- □ Elmwood Park

100 relocations recorded as of 1964.
Not shown here are 5 further out in the
MSA (3 in Wentzville, 1 each in Crystal
City and Wright City), 6 in Missouri but
beyond the MSA, and 5 out of state.

Map 5.6. Elmwood Park relocations, 1958–1964. Relocation Ledger, *Brooks v. LCRA* case file, RG 600, Supreme Court Judicial Case Files, Missouri State Archives.

the basic logic was this: Investment is mobile and fleeing the central city, where property and other local taxes revenues are in free fall as a result. There is a natural and
persistent competition among local governments for new investment, and older urban
areas enter this competition with substantial handicaps. The prevailing assumption, in
the City and its suburbs, is that private investment subsidized by tax abatement is private investment that would not have occurred without tax abatement. Subsidized redevelopment, in this view, arrests decline (especially in the City and its inner suburbs)
or spurs growth—yielding both higher future tax revenues and immediate benefits
(employment, other tax revenues).

For contemporary and academic critics, the logic was very nearly the reverse: Investors are not as footloose as they claim, and local taxes rank well down the list of factors
in investment or expansion decisions. To the degree that local economic development
policies simply move local investment around (from the City to its suburbs, from one
suburb to another), it is worse than a zero-sum game—netting no new investment for
the region but bidding down tax revenues everywhere. The prevailing assumption is
that much of the subsidized investment (and the resulting tax revenues) would have
occurred anyway—maybe in a different manner, maybe on a different timetable. This
is an argument found across the political spectrum—uniting property rights libertari-
ans offended by the use of eminent domain, fiscal conservatives bemoaning the public
costs, good-government liberals resenting the private use of public credit, and social
welfare activists tired of seeing scarce public resources deflected from those in need.[68]

Looking across a half century of redevelopment politics in greater St. Louis, it is
hard to sustain much of an argument with the critics. Despite the seemingly endless
and overlapping abatements proffered by local redevelopment programs (detailed in
the last chapter), the scope of central city blight first sketched in the 1930s and 1940s
remained virtually unchanged. Massive public investment (in the form of real dollars
or tax breaks) has done less to eradicate blight than it has to move it around—as the
City's poor migrate haphazardly from the site of the latest redevelopment venture.
And, in a setting marked by persistent economic troubles and stark political fragmentation, public policy has done less to galvanize new growth than it has to move it
around—inviting prospective investors to play musical chairs with the tax-hungry political fragments of the metropolitan area.

Consider the issue of "attracting" business investment. In 1975, HUD commissioned Price-Waterhouse to assess the effect of property tax incentives in nine local
programs (including St. Louis' Chapter 353 program) on business decisions. The St.
Louis respondents confirmed the study's larger conclusions, ranking the importance
of tax incentives well behind the building code, local consumer demand, the availability of private financing, and neighborhood conditions. A local follow-up survey in 1977
(conducted by Fleischman-Hillard) asked 13 Chapter 353 corporations and 100 tenants to rank the marginal importance of Chapter 353 incentives. While all (not surprisingly) applauded the tax abatement and eminent domain provisions of Chapter 353,
they also all reported that they would have located (or expanded) in the City without
these incentives. Even Chapter 353's champions conceded that its incentives were
important largely in determining location within the metro area (that tax breaks were

considered only after an investor had settled on a particular region)—indeed, fully two-thirds of the tenants in Chapter 353 office developments (as of 1980) moved to abated property from somewhere else in the City. Against this record, advocates leaned increasingly on the argument that tax breaks, if not a decisive locational factor in themselves, were nevertheless an important signal of the larger business climate.[69]

Similar concerns clouded performance of the City's enterprise zones. Although tied explicitly to new employment in targeted areas, enterprise zone tax breaks have a mixed record. St. Louis' initial (1983) enterprise zone covered an area with a population of about 30,000 and an unemployment rate of 13 percent. A state assessment in 1991 counted a paltry 596 new jobs in 8 years—at a cost of $1.5 million in tax credits. Many businesses in the St. Louis zone simply collected retroactive tax credits for jobs created years earlier. The *Post-Dispatch* concluded glumly in 1992 (on the eve of the federal enterprise zone law), that the City's existing zone "has had no major impact on hard-core unemployment or on the ability of public aid recipients to find work," adding that "this tax giveaway, along with the state's poor monitoring of the program, is deplorable." Local governments nevertheless complained that some settings could qualify for zones and others could not, and pressed the state to allow more zones—even if their boundaries had to be gerrymandered in such a way as to lavish out credits while still meeting state thresholds.[70]

Costs also tended to run ahead of demonstrable benefits because the definition of blight proved so elastic. In early 1980s, a consultant's report to the St. Louis Board of Education estimated that tax abatements would accompany *all* new commercial and industrial construction and 90 percent of new residential construction in the City. As the *St. Louis Business Journal* conceded in 1998, investors saw tax abatement as "an entitlement rather than an economic incentive." In the decade between 1988 and 1998 alone, the City extended tax abatements to over 4,500 parcels—fully 11 percent of its property tax base. As of 1998, 25 percent of the City's tax base was blighted for redevelopment, and another 23 percent was (as charitable or public property) tax-exempt. In all, over half of the City paid either discounted property taxes or none at all—a situation even the St. Louis Development Corporation viewed as evidence of a dangerous addiction to tax abatement and a serious threat to the City's finances. "If you have over-abated an area," Michael Jones (chief of staff for Mayor Clarence Harmon) observed in 1998, "you have eliminated the tax base that you need to support the services for the area you are trying to regenerate." By the late 1990s, property tax revenues could be counted on to cover less than 7 percent of the St. Louis City budget. The same plot played out as farce in East St. Louis, where City officials in the early 1990s used TIF revenues (illegally) to pay public employee salaries and cover a massive deficit in the general fund.[71]

As the City sacrificed more and more of its tax base at the altar of economic development, it could not sustain the advantage granted by the first generation of incentive programs. While originally drafted as effectively "special legislation" for St. Louis and Kansas City, Missouri's core urban programs were gradually opened to all comers. This undermined the core premise of local economic development, which was intended to help struggling areas (especially inner cities) counter the disadvantages posed by aging infrastructure and the footprint of the old economy. This raised the cost of these programs where they were needed the most and created new costs (lost revenues) where they were not needed at all. This was especially true of TIFing for retail development in the St. Louis suburbs, and it was a pattern captured by the profusion of local enterprise zones in the state. "I serve eight counties," one Missouri legislator argued, "and if one of them gets something, the rest of them feel like they ought to have it, too." Or, as another state senator concluded in the course of the same debate: "every little community is bidding against each other. If you're going to play ball, you've got to have a bat and a glove."[72]

Expansive definitions of blight and the profusion of programs made it less likely that local abatements could credibly and consistently claim to pose a net fiscal benefit. This was especially ironic, as "inability to pay reasonable taxes" gradually overshadowed the "health and welfare" factors in both state law and local blighting decisions. As early as the 1930s, local development officials were defining blight as an economic liability, an area in which "the taxes do not pay for public services." The Model City Charter adopted by the National Municipal League in 1937 defined blight, in part, as the "stagnation of development and damage and loss to community prosperity and taxable values." Postwar urban renewal programs were largely premised on the costs imposed by blighted neighborhoods. And TIF statutes generally cemented the idea that the prospect of a higher use (even if it was just a bigger shopping mall) was enough to render any lesser use a form of blight. The Missouri TIF statute (1982), for its part, imported its definition of blight from the state's 1945 redevelopment law, but it also declared that redevelopment was in the public interest because it would "result in the preservation or enhancement of the tax base of the municipality."[73]

All of these policies rested on the hopeful but tenuous conviction that new revenues in the future would pay for abated taxes now. Higher property assessments and increases in local sales or employment created new taxable value, but also took much of that value off the tax rolls for decades (25 years for Chapter 353, 23 years for Missouri TIFs). Defenders of Chapter 353 in St. Louis pointed to a few major projects whose direct costs (abated property taxes) were less than projected new revenue from all sources.[74] But such calculations assumed that no new investment, employment, or sales would have occurred without the abatement—and overlooked the fact that most Chapter 353 tenants had moved from elsewhere in the City, from full-value to abated parcels. A 1985 assessment commissioned by the St. Louis Board of Education offered a starker view. Of 13 major 353 projects (see Map 5.7), all but one were reassessed in their eleventh year (the point at which the property tax abatement shifted from all to half of added value) at *less* than their original value. All told, the 13 properties (assessed at just under $80 million at the onset of their redevelopment) amassed over $200 million in project costs and lost over a third of their taxable value. Most outside the St. Louis CDA, including commercial interests that had not managed to qualify under one of the abatement programs, argued that the City was squandering revenues and getting little in return across much of the blighted and reblighted central corridor.[75]

As property tax revenues continued to plummet, development officials increasingly

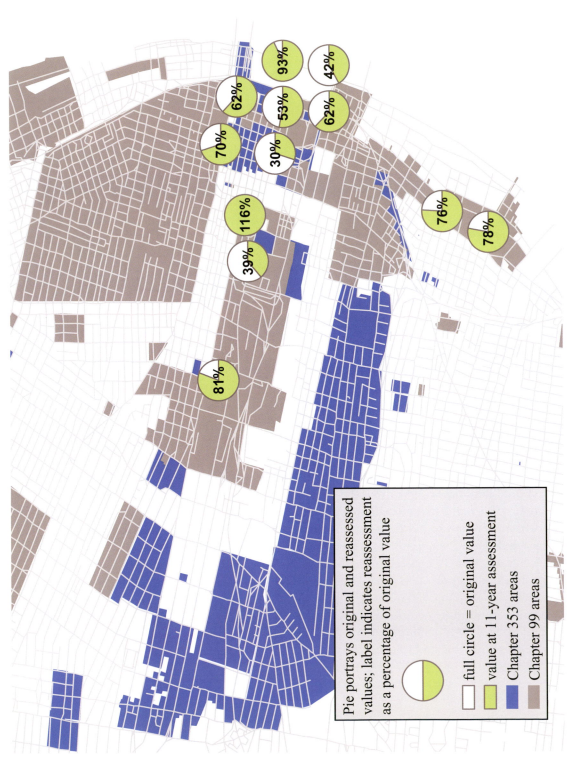

Map 5.7. Eleventh year reassessments, selected 353 properties. Arthur T. Denzau and Charles L. Leven, *Report on Alternative Revenue Sources: Local Revenue Generation* (St. Louis Board of Education Community Advisory Committee, 1985), table V-5.

leaned on the argument that other tax revenues (earnings taxes in the City and sales taxes across the region) would take up the slack. Such logic was difficult to sustain in St. Louis itself, where employment and retail sales showed little growth despite new investment leveraged by various abatement and incentive programs. In the suburbs, economic development programs (and especially TIFs) were employed largely to attract new retail development—following the assumption, as one economic development director put it, that the region's sales taxes would go to the city able to erect "the newest, cleanest centers where there is variety and an excitement in popular stores with the latest shopping amenities."[76] This was, at best, a zero-sum game, as consumers and sales tax revenues followed new retail development around the outer suburbs. And, since TIF districts diverted not only new property tax revenue but also half of all other new revenues (sales, earnings, income), it was often a less-than-zero-sum game: The city building the next big mall was unlikely to see a tangible fiscal benefit before another city, another mall, and another TIF did them one better.

The municipalities blighting and abating property are not the only (or even the primary) claimant on local property tax revenues. In Missouri (as in most states) local property taxes also fund school districts, county services, sewer districts, and zoo or museum districts. And in Missouri (as in most states), these bodies have no substantive voice in the decision to abate local taxes. Not surprisingly, these interests (and especially schools, which get about two-thirds of property tax revenue in Missouri) have proven the most lucid critics of local economic development policies.[77]

The view from the schools was clear: First, local abatements or TIFs robbed schools of their share in any increase in the assessed value of property—a particularly bitter prospect when the blighted property was an old shopping mall and the abated property a newer mall. "Should a municipality be allowed to use tax revenue from the schools," the *Post-Dispatch* opined in the late 1990s, "to pay for street improvements, traffic signals and sewer work for a shopping center?" Second, schools saw no direct benefit from any increase in local sales or earnings taxes. Even if the net new revenue flowing from new investment was in the black, schools still came up short. The impact on school budgets was eased by state programs that backfilled school budgets against the revenue loss of local TIFs and abatements (St. Louis schools, for example, qualified for about $500,000 of such state aid in 1977–78).[78] While such programs spared school budgets the full impact of local economic development policies, they also served as dismal advertisements for their underlying fiscal logic.

The pursuit of new investment or development by local governments betrayed a variety of motives—including the need to compete with other local governments, the intangible benefits of a sunnier business climate, and the (often dim) prospect of future tax revenues. The politics of blight and redevelopment are best understood from a broad historical perspective in which both the original and core problem (the mid-century plight of north and central St. Louis) and the starkly misguided panoply of solutions (stadiums, shopping malls) are clearly visible. Not only did "blight" lose all semblance of practical or legal definition, but the policies designed to eradicate it had the net effect—in political, spatial, and fiscal terms—of making things worse.

Conclusion
Our House Revisited

The Twenty-First Century at 4635 North Market Street

Today, 4635 North Market—vacated, abandoned, razed, and unrenewed—is a poignant monument to the history of the modern American city. At its construction in the 1890s, 4635 North Market was part of a broad swath of middle- and working-class housing that stretched across St. Louis from the western edge of downtown to the eastern edge of St. Louis County. Over the subsequent decades, these neighborhoods were transformed from within and without. Cycles of boom and bust (punctuated by two world wars and the Great Depression) culminated in a drawn-out pattern of deindustrialization, which robbed the near northside of its economic and employment base. At the same time, residential development at the urban fringe—underwritten by an array of local, state, and federal policies—poached the central city of its population, its tax base, its retail and commercial base, and its very civic identity.

More importantly, as both a cause and the consequence of all of this, was the inexorable racial logic of suburban growth and urban decline. White residents of north St. Louis began cobbling together race-restrictive deed covenants after the racial upheaval of World War I; such an agreement first covered 4635 North Market in 1923. In the years that followed, residents, realtors, lenders, and local governments alike understood racial transition (whether it was resisted, managed, or contained) as the core concern of local urban politics. The inchoate anxieties of white residents were, over time, adopted and formalized as an ethical obligation of private realtors, lenders, and insurers, as the organizing principle of both local zoning and federal home ownership policies, and as the key determinant of value whenever property was taxed, blighted, or redeveloped.

While its central thread is private property, this is not a story—at 4635 North Market or across Greater St. Louis—of private markets and private choices. What gives this story its plot, and its sorry ending, are the many ways in which private and public policies shaped or frustrated those choices. Property, after all, was not just bought and sold: It was restricted by private agreement; it was parceled out (subdivided, annexed, incorporated) and zoned for more or less exclusive uses; it was sustained (or not) by local infrastructure and services; it was valued and taxed; it was blighted (or not) and redeveloped (or not) by efforts at urban renewal. On each score, it was the sprawling suburban developments that were rewarded and the older transitional neighborhoods (like those containing and surrounding 4635 North Market) that were penalized or ignored.[1]

What Happened? St. Louis and Its Peers

The St. Louis chapter of this story is exceptional in some respects, unexceptional in others. It followed the general pattern, peculiar to the modern American city, in which wealth sprawled to the urban fringe and the central city suffered stark and sustained decline.[2] In 1950, 69 million Americans lived in 157 urban areas covering 12,715 square miles. In 2000, those same urban areas contained 155 million residents and covered 52,388 square miles—a little more than double the population on a little more than four times as much land.[3] Through all of this, St. Louis and its peers faced a common conspiracy of local, state, and federal policies which—through neglect, indifference, or design—shaped the distribution of resources and people across the metropolis.[4]

There were important regional variations behind these national patterns. St. Louis, in this respect, closely followed the experience of other Midwestern industrial settings (think Detroit, Milwaukee, Chicago, Cleveland, Cincinnati, Buffalo, Pittsburgh), all of which lay at the leading edge of deindustrialization and suffered economic decline and commercial decentralization earlier than most. The pattern, timing, and pace of deindustrialization was shaped by each city's economic profile (steel in Pittsburgh, autos in Detroit) but was especially pronounced in the older river-based economies like those of St. Louis, Cincinnati, or Buffalo.[5] This was a history shared by some other industrial settings (Camden, Newark, Birmingham), but less so by the larger and more diverse economies of the Northeast or by the still-growing economies of the urban West.[6]

St. Louis and its midwestern peers shared not only the region's relative economic decline but also a regionally distinct set of land-use policies and practices that had the effect of compounding that decline and distributing its consequences more unevenly. These metropolitan areas, as a rule, maintained relatively exclusionary land-use practices, weak affordable housing policies, and few restraints on sprawl.[7] Compounding this, in St. Louis and other Rustbelt cities, was a pattern of development and incorporation in which the boundaries of the central city were inelastic and in which economic and demographic growth was hogged by suburban fragments. St. Louis, more dramatically than most, followed a middle-American pattern of concentrated inner-city poverty, intense racial segregation, and dramatic population loss.[8] These cities, and their place in the urban history of the twentieth century, are summarized in Table C.1: The truly troubled settings (led by St. Louis) are those whose population peaked at the 1950 census and whose rank (by population) has plummeted in the decades since.

In each setting, the contours and timing of the urban crisis was shaped by local demographic patterns, by local political geography, and by the catalytic events of the twentieth century. Because its African American population was relatively well estab-

TABLE C.1. Major U.S. Cities, Population Rank at Decennial Census

	1900	1910	1920	1930	1940	1950	1960	1970	1980	1990	2000	2000 Peak
New York	1	1	1	1	1	1	1	1	1	1	1	100%
Chicago	2	2	2	2	2	2	2	2	2	3	3	80%
Philadelphia	3	3	3	3	3	3	4	4	4	5	5	73%
Los Angeles	36	17	10	5	5	4	3	3	3	2	2	100%
Detroit	13	9	4	4	4	5	5	5	6	7	9	51%
Baltimore	6	7	8	9	7	6	6	7	10	12	17	69%
Cleveland	7	6	5	6	6	7	8	10	18	23	33	52%
St. Louis	**4**	**4**	**6**	**7**	**8**	**8**	**10**	**18**	**26**	**34**	**48**	**41%**
Washington, D.C.	15	16	14	14	11	9	9	9	15	19	21	71%
Boston	5	5	7	8	9	10	13	16	20	20	20	74%
San Francisco	9	11	12	11	12	11	12	13	13	14	13	100%
Pittsburgh	11	8	9	10	10	12	16	24	30	40	51	49%
Houston	85	68	45	26	21	14	7	6	5	4	4	100%
Buffalo	8	10	11	13	14	15	20	28	39	50	57	50%
Cincinnati	10	13	16	17	17	18	21	29	32	45	53	66%
Dallas	88	58	42	33	31	22	14	8	7	8	7	100%
San Antonio	71	54	41	38	36	25	17	15	11	10	8	100%
San Diego			93	53	43	31	18	14	8	6	6	100%
Phoenix						99	29	20	9	9	5	100%

Source: Census Bureau.
Note: "Major Cities" are those that show up in the top ten by population in at least one decennial census. The list is ranked at the 1950 census. The final column shows each city's 2000 population as a percentage of its peak population. The gray boxes indicate the year in which each city reached its peak population.

lished early in the century, white St. Louis reacted earlier and more stridently to the "threat" of black occupancy—although most midwestern cities responded in similar ways to the demographic turmoil and aftermath of World War I. Foremost among these responses was the spread of restrictive deed covenants, a common practice whose details (scope, duration) were shaped by local interests and local courts.[9] As Thomas Sugrue and Arnold Hirsch have shown, such restrictive practices were accompanied by an undercurrent of hidden violence—rooted in the white reaction to the first wave of African American migration and in full flower a generation later.[10]

The larger implications and consequences of these practices became apparent in the late 1930s and the 1940s—an era in which dramatic in-migration of African Americans both overwhelmed existing restrictions and formalized them in local and federal policies. In St. Louis, as elsewhere, restrictive agreements and practices designed to contain a small population ended up sorting entire central cities by race. The results, in city after city, were not surprising. As a rapidly growing African American population crowded into hastily but strictly circumscribed blocks or neighborhoods, the immediate consequence was not only extreme stress on the housing stock but also an easy equation of overcrowding, crime, poor sanitation, and poor health with black occupancy itself.[11] This further encouraged local and federal governments to import the basic premises of racial restriction into public policy—ranging from the implicit redlining of federal housing assistance to municipal zoning to public housing and urban renewal. The long-term consequences, remarkable given the parallel progress of civil rights law and policy, was a pattern of residential segregation that hardened with each passing decade.[12]

The ways in which this played out across the metropolitan area varied according to local economies, local geographies, local development patterns, and local politics. In different ways, each city defined a "ghetto" of older inner-city housing (Buffalo's Elli-cott District, Chicago's Southside, Detroit's Paradise Valley) and surrounding neigh-borhoods that were continually redefined by racial transition and redevelopment schemes. In some settings (including Chicago, Buffalo, and Pittsburgh), the existence of old working-class suburbs dampened white flight; in greater St. Louis, these work-ing-class suburbs were crowded on the Illinois side of the river—leaving the City's west-ern boundary open for exclusive and sprawling suburban development. The hollowing out of American cities was well on its way as early as 1940: only Manhattan (a persistent outlier among central cities) maintained average rents close to those of its suburbs. Many troubled cities (Buffalo, Cincinnati) still boasted a few city neighbor-hoods that rivaled their suburbs; St. Louis had the largest disparity, with average rents in suburban Ladue nearly three times those of the City's most wealthiest ward.[13]

Nowhere did local politics offer much resistance to these trends (and ward politics often simply replicated them), although political organization could shape the pace and impact of urban decline. In some settings, the business community invested con-siderable resources in efforts to sustain local economic viability and growth. The single best example of such efforts was Pittsburgh's Allegheny Conference, a peak associa-tion of local firms that spawned many imitators (including St. Louis' Civic Progress) but few successful ones.[14] In some settings, labor unions had a strong presence, although both deindustrialization and the structure of the American labor movement (whose organization focused on industry rather than location) undermined its lasting role in local politics. Where unions did have a lasting presence (the UAW in Detroit, the USWA in Pittsburgh, the UPWA in Kansas City), they were often more important as civil rights organizations than as conventional political actors.[15] The countervailing impact of local civil rights organizations (including the NAACP and the Urban League) also varied widely, although it was generally true that such organizations depended heavily on the same population—middle-class, professional African Ameri-cans—that was most directly threatened by the unfolding urban crisis.[16]

The overarching irony, in St. Louis and elsewhere, is that efforts to save the city from such practices and patterns almost always made things worse. In setting after setting, both the diagnosis (blight) and its prescription (urban renewal) were shaped by—and compromised by—the same assumptions and expectations and prejudices that had created the condition in the first place. The problem, as understood by local and federal planners, was simple enough: Downtown was blighted by a combination of economic obsolescence and substandard housing. The renewal of downtown, accordingly, depended upon attracting new investment by clearing slums, updating infrastructure, and assembling land for redevelopment. In some respects, these efforts were simply counterproductive: a flurry of urban highway building designed to provide better access to the inner city, for example, simply made it easier for traffic (and investment) to bypass it altogether. In some respects, they were easily distracted—by a chase for federal matching funds, by a fascination with "big ticket" fixes (sports stadiums, convention centers), by a nostalgia for a bygone downtown of bustling streets and stores. Grand failures abounded and successes were few and far between. Even the periodic and hopeful celebration of "comeback cities" could boast little more than disconnected pockets of gentrification or tourism—successful only because they were not yet back on the blocks for redevelopment.[17] "You can see failed attempts at urban renewal everywhere," a 2004 assessment of St. Louis' efforts concluded:

The majestic steel trellised Union Station was converted into an uninspired shopping mall in the mid-80s. A new station was supposed to be built but never materialized. Today, visitors arriving by train disembark into an open-air parking lot beneath the Interstate 40 bypass that cuts right through downtown like a blatant afterthought. There is only a small ticket shack, a temporary structure erected 25 years ago, which is filthy, cramped, and stinks of urine. Unless there are taxis waiting, which is rare, you have to walk into downtown, which although not terribly far, requires quite a bit of frustrating navigation through a field of surface lots and across highway interchanges. All this is to say St. Louis does not exactly offer a warm welcome. It is not a city that looks loved.[18]

The causes and consequences of this failure, in St. Louis and elsewhere, were irretrievably racial, a fact captured and acknowledged by the contemporary cynicism that equated urban renewal with "negro removal." In most settings, blight was a near-synonym for black residency. At its worst, urban renewal was an exercise in expulsive zoning, with the intent and effect of razing African American neighborhoods for a higher (often commercial) use.[19] At its best, urban renewal operated under the assumption that slum clearance would be accompanied by relocation and housing policies designed to cement local patterns of segregation and arrest further racial transition.[20] Across this spectrum, the sincerity of these policies often depended on local conditions and local politics. In some settings (Philadelphia, for example), progressive political and religious leadership yielded stronger commitments to integrated and small-scale housing projects. In some settings (Detroit, for example), plans for integrated or scattered-site housing projects were torpedoed by local opposition. In many settings (St. Louis, for example), segregation was a core goal from the outset. On balance, the results were depressingly similar. Even the most progressive efforts destroyed more units than they created and displaced more families of ordinary means than they accommodated. And every city's urban renewal program devoted its attention and resources increasingly to commercial development. Over time, redevelopment trumped rehabilitation, and new housing (public or private) became less a goal of urban renewal than a reluctant and haphazard afterthought.[21]

So What?: Losing St. Louis

Urban policy is now shaped by the pervasive view that cities are politically marginal and economically obsolete. We despair over their current state and pine for a time in which they "worked." There persists a conviction that we *have* tried to save cities but that they threw off the life preserver and sank anyway.[22] The postindustrial information economy, in this view, is both able to flee urban settings and no longer bound to rely on them. There is, as I have tried to make clear, little in the historical record to sustain this assessment as either an account of the urban crisis or a source of pessimism about urban prospects. Cities remain crucial economic and political resources, *despite* decades of willful neglect. And the costs of that neglect (past, present, and future) are immense.

It is difficult to overstate the scale and importance of our urban economies. The ten largest metro areas in the United States (aggregate gross product about $3.5 trillion) make up an economy larger than that of 35 states combined and larger than the economies of Germany, the United Kingdom, and France combined, or Canada, South Korea, and Mexico combined.[23] This, in turn, is not just an artifact of scale (the fact that more people live and work in cities). Cities are demonstrably more productive and more efficient. Urban economies (and particularly some urban sectors) benefit from the "agglomeration effect," the advantage of having suppliers, consumers, skilled workers, and related sectors close at hand. This is especially apparent in areas dominated by a single industry (think Silicon Valley), but it is also more generally true of cities and their leading sectors (think education, research, health care, high-end manufacturing, business services, financial services, law, fashion, media) for whom the benefits of density outweigh the costs (higher rents, higher wages) of urban location.[24]

Beyond the incentives of these firms and sectors, urban economies also promise broad social efficiencies and advantages. The denser the development, the cheaper it is to provide basic public services (schools, fire, police, waste management) and infrastructure (roads, sewers). Local government and local developers choose sprawl not because it is cheaper to push development out into the cornfields but because they are able to avoid its real and substantial costs. And, of course, sprawl leaves a large and lasting environmental footprint. It swallows natural and agricultural land at a rate of nearly 2 million acres a year (more than half of which, in the last decade, has gone to housing lots larger than ten acres). It dramatically exaggerates the impact of development ("heat islands," surface runoff). It consumes more energy and emits more pollutants (on a per capita basis) than denser urban development.[25]

Cities are also, at least potentially, a real boon to the people who live in them. Urban jobs are, by and large, better jobs—in part because cities sustain "high road" sectors, in part because cities sustain more opportunities for advancement and education, and in part because cities sustain other institutions (notably labor unions) able to offer a measure of job protection or security.[26] Cities also sustain a much closer match between employment and residence, avoiding the spatial mismatch that yields longer commutes (an average of 10 miles for workers in the St. Louis metro area), higher housing and transportation costs, and an increasingly unsustainable (or simply obsolete) public transit system.[27] And, despite their horrific historical record of segregation, cities can and do nurture a remarkable demographic and cultural diversity. This is not an insignificant attribute in an economy where cultural industries are increasingly important.[28] And it is a necessary and useful attribute for a population that is older, more diverse, and organized into smaller and later family units.[29] These natural advantages, of course, have been dampened or frustrated by historical patterns of development and segregation (and urban renewal), which have sapped central cities of jobs, wealth, public goods, and private services.[30]

The solutions to all of this are familiar. I make no claims to originality in restating them here, except (I hope) that by employing the history of St. Louis I can underscore their logic and their urgency. The first goal—both the most important reform and the one that makes others possible—is to displace local fragmentation with some form of regional governance. Some citizens and local governments are sure to resent this, and indeed critics are quick to label any move toward regionalism as an antidemocratic putsch by "big government" technocrats. This is silly and shortsighted. One cannot imagine a more overgoverned (and inefficiently so) setting than the modern American city. Regionalism, like federalism, simply proposes to filter political challenges to that level of government at which they can be most directly and efficiently addressed: the government of the metropolis should be conterminous with its economic and demographic boundaries. Put another way, regionalism proposes little more than a social contract in which local governments yield some political autonomy in exchange for equity, efficiency, protection (from the behavior of *other* local governments).[31]

The goal is not just to throw a larger jurisdictional net over metro areas but also to draw that net tighter. Greater density (including controls over indiscriminate fringe development) would be an important and natural priority of regional governments. These governments would have room to grow but no incentive to leave the central city or inner suburbs behind; they would be attentive to the costs created at the leading edge of sprawl and in its wake. This would encourage reconsideration, for example, of land-use regulations (including zoning) and their distribution across the metropolis. And it would encourage a regional approach to local taxation. Even natural patterns of economic growth yield stark variations in property value across a metro area, a pattern exaggerated and entrenched by decades of racial segregation and political fragmentation. Even a modest effort at regional tax sharing (an approach pioneered by Myron Orfield in the Twin Cities) can help to dampen the "poaching" incentives of outer suburbs and to finance public services and public goods where they are needed most.[32]

Regional government also promises to level the economic development playing field, a terrain in which local competition is particularly fierce and fruitless. The larger logic here is clear enough: Public policies or subsidies should reward (and *only* reward) investments that offer tangible and sustainable public benefits (that is, living wage employment, job training, brownfield reclamation). But such high-road policies are notoriously hard to sustain in a setting where local governments (states under federalism, municipalities in metro areas) are at worst throwing tax breaks at any new building or any new job, and at best pirating good investments from their neighbors.[33]

Cities represent perhaps the most fundamental failure of public policy in modern America. In an economy of unparalleled abundance (at least since the end of World War II), central cities and inner suburbs have become progressively and dramatically poorer. In a society of steadily increasing diversity and tolerance (victories claimed by the postwar civil rights movement), central cities and inner suburbs sustain and encourage the most insidious forms of racial segregation. In a polity so fiercely proud of its democratic traditions, central cities and inner suburbs house a population that is largely disconnected and disenfranchised.

We know this, and we rediscover it periodically—in the inchoate rage of the Los Angeles riots, in the flooded lower wards of New Orleans. Yet, as the more thoughtful of these reminders underscore, the problems of American cities have perilously little to do with episodes of police brutality or bad weather.[34] The urban crisis is deeply rooted in our history, in the historical choices made by public and private actors in St. Louis and elsewhere. American cities carry the burden of this history, but also the capacity to draw on its lessons. The future of our cities, and of the plurality of Americans who live and work and raise their families in them, depends upon it.

Notes

Preface

1. Graham Swift, *Waterland* (New York: Vintage, 1983), 106.

Introduction. Our House: The Twentieth Century at 4635 North Market Street

1. The chronological development of subdivisions within the city is plotted on the Wayman Map, original in the collections of the Missouri Historical Society (MHS), online version (Washington University Department of Architecture) at http://library.wustl.edu/vlib/mrdc/index .html; building details are from the Sanborn Company, *Insurance Maps of St. Louis* (1903–50), vol. 7, frame 17.

2. David Beito and Bruce Smith, "The Formation of Urban Infrastructure Through Non-Governmental Planning: The Private Places of St. Louis, 1869–1920," *Journal of Urban History* 16,3 (1990): 263–303; on early St. Louis, see also Eric Sandweiss, *St. Louis: The Evolution of an American Urban Landscape* (Philadelphia: Temple University Press, 2001); neighborhood synopses in 1999 city plan at http://stlouis.missouri.org/5yearstrategy/neighborhoods/index.html

3. *Dolan and Wehmeyer v. Richardson et al.*, Abstract of the Record Before the St. Louis Court of Appeals (1944); 15th Census of Population, 1930, Missouri T626, reel 1239, ED 96–120, frame 36; 1905 Plat Map, St. Louis, Mercantile Library, University of Missouri-St. Louis.

4. 1905 Plat Map, St. Louis, Mercantile Library; Property transfers in St. Louis Assessor Daily Books, numbers 354:86 (1909), 732:77 (1924), 894:18 (1933), 992:94 (1937).

5. Robert Weaver, *The Negro Ghetto* (New York: Russell & Russell, 1948, 1967), 5.

6. Property transfers for 4635 North Market in St. Louis Assessor Daily Books, 894:18 (1933), 992:94 (1937), 1122:74 (July 1941), 1129:96 (Oct. 1941), 149:40 (1958), 1635:72 (1975), 1646:710 (1979), 1633:533 (1985), St. Louis Assessor's Office, City Hall, St. Louis; quotes from Howard Baer, *St. Louis to Me* (St. Louis: Hawthorn, 1978), 261; and 1999 City Plan at http:// stlouis.missouri.org/5yearstrategy/neighborhoods/index.html.

7. Robert Reinhold, "In St. Louis Even the Bricks Are Leaving Town," *New York Times* (*NYT*), 9 July 1978, E5; "Gangs Raze Buildings for Bricks," *NYT*, 25 July 1984, A12.

8. *NYT*, 26 February 1978, in box 1, ser. 3, John Conway Papers, Washington University Archives, Clayton, Missouri.

9. See Daniel Luria and Joel Rogers, *Metro Futures: Economic Solutions for Cities and Their Suburbs* (Boston: Beacon, 1999), 3–4; Myron Orfield, *Metropolitics: A Regional Agenda for Community and Stability* (Washington, D.C.: Brookings Institutition, 1997), 8–9, 27–28.

10. Harland Bartholomew, *The Zone Plan* (St. Louis: City Plan Commission, 1919), 13–14; City Plan Commission, *Urban Land Policy* (St. Louis: City Plan Commission, 1936), 7.

11. The classical version of this argument is Charles Tiebout, "A Pure Theory of Local Public Expenditures," *Journal of Political Economy* 64 (1956): 416–24; a more recent version is Robert Bruegmann, *Sprawl: A Compact History* (Chicago: University of Chicago Press, 2005).

12. David Freund, "Marketing the Free Market: State Intervention and the Politics of Prosperity in Metropolitan America," in *The New Suburban History,* ed. Kevin Kruse and Thomas Sugrue (Chicago: University of Chicago Press, 2006), 11–32. For an incisive critique of "free market" suburbanism, see Thomas Sugrue, "The Geography of Fear," *The Nation* (27 February 2006), at http://www.thenation.com/doc/20060227/sugrue.

13. See Arnold Hirsch, "Less Than *Plessy:* The Inner City, Suburbs, and State-Sanctioned Residential Segregation in the Age of *Brown,*" in Kruse and Sugrue, *The New Suburban History,* 37–40.

14. Katharine Bradbury, Anthony Downs, and Kenneth Small, "Some Dynamics of Central-City Suburban Interactions," *American Economic Review* 70, 2 (1980): 648–55; Peter Dreier, Todd Swanstrom, and John Mollenkopf, *Place Matters: Metropolitics for the Twenty-First Century* (Lawrence: University Press of Kansas, 2001), 40, 42–45.

15. A shift first chronicled in William Schneider, "The Dawn of the Suburban Era in American Politics," *Atlantic* (July 1992), 33–44; and Thomas and Mary Edsall, *Chain Reaction: The Impact of Race, Rights, and Taxes on American Politics* (New York: W.W. Norton, 1992).

16. On "backlash" politics, see Jonathan Rieder, *Canarsie: The Jews and Italians of Brooklyn Against Liberalism* (Cambridge, Mass.: Harvard University Press, 2005); Christopher Lasch, *The True and Only Heaven: Progress and Its Critics* (New York: W.W. Norton, 1991); Heather Thompson, "Rethinking the Politics of White Flight in the Postwar City: Detroit, 1945–1980," *Journal of Urban History* 25 (1999): 165–68. On the roots of suburban conservatism, see Lisa McGirr, *Suburban Warriors: The Origins of the New American Right* (Princeton, N.J.: Princeton University Press, 2001); Kevin Kruse, *White Flight: Atlanta and the Making of Modern Conservatism* (Princeton, N.J.: Princeton University Press, 2005).

17. Lewis Thomas, "Decline of St. Louis as Midwest Metropolis," *Economic Geography* 25, 2 (1949): 118–23; Barry Checkoway and Carl Patton, "The Metropolitan Midwest in Perspective," in *The Metropolitan Midwest: Policy Problems and Prospects for Change,* ed. Barry Checkoway and Carl Patton (Urbana: University of Illinois Press, 1985), 2–5.

18. See, for example, the dismal prospectus compiled in *A Comprehensive City Plan for East St. Louis, Illinois* (1920), vol. 16, ser. 2 (Black), Harland Bartholomew Papers, Washington University Archives.

19. "The Housing Situation in St. Louis" (1953), ser. 1, box 3, St. Louis Data Collection (SLDC) (sl557), Western Historical Manuscript Collection (WHMC), University of Missouri-St. Louis.

20. Reinhold, "In St. Louis Even the Bricks Are Leaving Town"; Bruce Katz, "Six Ways Cities Can Reach Their Economic Potential" (Washington, D.C.: Brookings Institution, Living Cities Policy Overview, 2005), 13.

21. Quoted in Kenneth Jackson, *Crabgrass Frontier: The Suburbanization of the United States* (New York: Oxford University Press, 1985), 141–42; see also William Kottmeyer, "A Tale of Two Cities," St. Louis Board of Education Report (1968), excerpted in Daniel Schlafly, *28 Years on the St. Louis School Board, 1953–1981* (St. Louis: Author, 1995), 170.

22. See E. Terrence Jones, *Fragmented by Design: Why St. Louis Has So Many Governments* (St. Louis: Palmerston and Reed, 2000); Jones, "The Municipal Market in the St. Louis Region," in *St. Louis Metromorphosis: Past Trends and Future Directions,* ed. Brady Baybeck and Jones (St. Louis: Missouri Historical Society Press, 2004), 275–92.

23. Richard Briffault, "Our Localism: Part 1—The Structure of Local Government Law," *Columbia Law Review* 90 (1990): 38–39; Orfield, *Metropolitics,* 5–6; Neil Littlefield, *Metropolitan Area Problems and Municipal Home Rule* (Ann Arbor: Michigan Legal Publications, 1962), passim.

24. Briffault, "Our Localism: Part 2—Localism and Legal Theory," 354–56.

25. See, for example, Arnold Hirsch, *Making the Second Ghetto: Race and Housing in Chicago, 1940–1960* (New York: Cambridge University Press, 1983), 262.

26. "The West End" (n.d.), box 52, ser. 2, Alfonso J. Cervantes Papers, Washington University Archives; Charles L. Leven et al., *Neighborhood Change: Lessons in the Dynamics of Urban Decay*

(New York: Praeger, 1976), quoted at 16; John Farley, "Racial Housing Segregation in the St. Louis Metropolitan Era," *Edwardsville Journal of Sociology* 2 (2002); archived at http://www.siue.edu/SOCIOLOGY/journal/FARLEYV2.HTM.

27. Quoted in Robert Cantwell, "St. Louis Snaps Out of It," *Fortune* (July 1956): 118.

28. See Colin Gordon, "Blighting the Way: Urban Renewal, Economic Development, and the Elusive Definition of 'Blight,' " *Fordham Urban Law Journal* 31,2 (2004): 305–37.

29. Mark Gelfand, *A Nation of Cities: The Federal Government and Urban America, 1933–1965* (New York: Oxford University Press, 1975), 217–18, 228.

30. "What the Downtown Area Needs," *St. Louis Post-Dispatch* (*SLPD*), 16 October 1941, 2C.

31. "Excerpts from Report" (n.d), box 34, ser. 1, Cervantes Papers.

32. See *Saturday Review* clipping in box 16, ser. 1, Cervantes Papers.

33. See also Robert Self, *American Babylon: Race and the Struggle for Postwar Oakland* (Princeton, N.J.: Princeton University Press, 2003), 258–59.

34. For the way this worked across a broader sweep of postwar policies, see Ira Katznelson, *When Affirmative Action Was White: An Untold History of Racial Inequality in Twentieth-Century America* (New York: W.W. Norton, 2005).

35. See Michael Brown, *Race, Money, and the American Welfare State* (Ithaca, N.Y.: Cornell University Press, 1999).

36. This sketch is based on H. L. Purdy, "An Historical Analysis of the Economic Growth of St. Louis" (ICC Finance Docket 15365, 1946), 1–6, 30–36, 44–46, 60–68, 70–85, 91; and Lewis Thomas, *The Localization of Business Activities in Metropolitan St. Louis,* Washington University Studies in Social and Philosophical Sciences 1 (St. Louis: Washington University, 1927), 4–7, 96–98.

37. (Quote) Untitled Chamber of Commerce Study (1931), folder 2, Downtown St. Louis Collection (add), SL 703, WHMC; "Plan for the Central River Front" (1928), folder 1, Downtown St. Louis Collection (add); "Decentralization and the St. Louis Business District" (1940?), reel 11, Bartholomew Papers (Correspondence).

38. Purdy, "An Historical Analysis of the Economic Growth of St. Louis," 91, 99, 106; Gregory Hooks and Leonard E. Bloomquist, "The Legacy of World War II for Regional Growth and Decline: The Cumulative Effects of Wartime Investments on U.S. Manufacturing, 1947–1972," *Social Forces,* 71, 2 (December 1992): 308, 325; Robert Mendelson and Michael Quinn, "Residential Patterns in a Midwestern City: The St. Louis Experience," in Checkoway and Patton, *The Metropolitan Midwest,* 152–53.

39. David Laslo, "The Past, Present, and Future, of the St. Louis Labor Force," in Baybeck and Jones, *St. Louis Metromorphosis,* 72.

40. Scott Cummings, "Racial Inequality and Developmental Disparities in the St. Louis Region," in Baybeck and Jones, *St. Louis Metromorphosis,* 105–7, 112–18.

41. Business and Industrial Development Commission, "Preliminary Proposal" (March 1964), box 8:215, Regional Commerce and Growth Association (RCGA) Records, WHMC; "Economic Development Trip to Cleveland," March 1980, box 55, ser. 2, Conway Papers. The summary of sectoral employment is from *County Business Patterns* (various years), which reports total employment by place of employment—assigning each worksite *in toto* to an appropriate sector. This yields a relatively dramatic measure of deindustrialization, as it counts as "leaving" the manufacturing sector both those who lose their jobs and those who (as a result of outsourcing and reclassification) are counted in a different sector in the next census. The *Census of Manufacturers* offers its own count of "production workers," which shows the manufacturing workforce of St. Louis declining from near 150,000 in the late 1940s to just over 40,000 in 1987.

42. Metropolitan St. Louis Survey, *Path of Progress for Metropolitan St. Louis* (University City, Mo.: The Survey, 1957), 20.

43. RCGA, "Guide to Industrial Parks and Office Parks in the St. Louis Region" (1977), ser. 6, folder 216, Roy Wenzlick Papers, WHMC.

44. Hammler, Siler, George Associates, "Economic Development Strategy Recommenda-

tions for the City of St. Louis" (1978), box 14:179, SLDC (s557), WHMC; Louis, "Urban Decay in St. Louis" (n.d.), box 31:157, St. Louis League of Women Voters Records (sl234), WHMC; Mendelson and Quinn, "Residential Patterns in a Midwestern City," 153.

45. Reid Ross, "Memo for Mayor Poelker" (4 May 1973), folder 491, ser. 4 (roll 21), James Symington Papers, WHMC.

46. "Report upon Wentzville Industrial Center," (1969), vol. 56, ser. 2 (Black-unlabeled), Bartholomew Papers; Renard Memo Re: General Motors Site, box 9, ser. 3, Conway Papers; "GM Goes to Wentzville," *St. Louis Commerce* (September 1980), 42–64.

47. *Business Week* quoted in Hurdy, "An Historical Analysis of the Economic Growth of St. Louis," 116; "Preliminary Report upon Background Studies, Land Use Plan and Zoning, Franklin County, Missouri" (1969), vol. 27, ser. 2 (Black-unlabeled), Bartholomew Papers; "More Construction and Manufacturing Jobs" (7 September 1966), box 11:345, RCGA Records; Thomas Gleason to Cervantes (26 May 1966), box 29, ser. 1, Cervantes Papers.

48. See "Closing Leather Plant," *SLPD*, 3 February 1995, 1C; "Brown Shoe Will Close Plant," *SLPD*, 14 May 1993, 10D; "Writing Was on the Wall for Brown Shoe Plants," *SLPD*, 10 September 1995, 1E.

49. These included, as of 1965, Monsanto, Ralston-Purina, McDonnell-Douglas, Anheuser-Buch, International Shoe, Pet Milk, Brown Shoe, Emerson Electric, Granite City Steel, Falstaff, Wagner Electric, Universal Match, General Steel, Laclede Steel, American Zinc, Hussman Refrigeration, RC Can, Mallinckrodt Chemical, Petrolite, McQuay-Norris, Century Electric, and Huttig Sash. See Industrial Development file, box 29, ser. 1, Cervantes Papers.

50. Peter O. Muller, *The Outer City: Geographical Consequences of the Urbanization of the United States*, Resource Paper 75–2 (Washington, D.C.: Association of American Geographers, 1975), 28–30; Jackson, *Crabgrass Frontier*, 266–69; "St. Louis County Economic Development Report" (1982), box 16:193, SLDC; "Citigroup Joins the Westward Rush to St. Charles County," *SLPD*, 9 January 2002, C1.

51. Charles Leven (Washington University) quoted in "St Louis Tunes Out the Blues," *Planning* 40, 3 (March 1974), in box 15:458, RCGA Records.

52. David Laslo, Claude Louisomme, Don Phares, and Dennis Judd, "Building the Infrastructure of Urban Tourism: The Case of St. Louis," in *The Infrastructure of Play: Building the Tourist City*, ed. Dennis Judd (Armonk, N.Y.: M.E. Sharpe, 2003), 79.

53. Earl Kersten and D. Reid Ross, "Clayton: A New Metropolitan Focus in the St. Louis Area," *Annals of the Association of American Geographers* 58, 4 (1968): 637–45; "Preliminary Report upon Parking Facilities, Central Business District, Clayton, Missouri (1948), 5, vol. 9, ser. 2 (Black), Bartholomew Papers; D. Reid Ross, "Centropolis or Metropolis" (1967), box 7:150, RCGA Records; Gene McNary to David Pansing (21 April 1977), box 15, ser. 2, Conway Papers; "Private Company Profiles," *SLPD*, 19 May 1997, 35; Desiree Hanford, "Mergers Leave St. Louis with Fewer Headquarters" (Dow Jones Newswire, 17 January 2001); Federal Commerce official quoted in Jon Teaford, *The Rough Road to Renaissance: Urban Revitalization in America* (Baltimore: Johns Hopkins University Press, 1990), 212.

54. Kersten and Ross, "Clayton: A New Metropolitan Focus," 642; "Report upon the Master Plan, Clayton, Missouri," (1958), vol. 17, ser. 2 (Red), Bartholomew Papers.

55. "So West County Mall Is Blighted Property?" *SLPD*, 29 July 1998, B7. On federal tax law, see Thomas Haskell, "U.S. Tax Policy and the Shopping Center Boom of the 1950s and 1960s," *American Historical Review* 101, 4 (1996): 1082–1110.

56. Jackson, *Crabgrass Frontier*, 99–100, 112–15, 138–39; Assessment Division, *Real Property Valuation Survey: City of St. Louis* (St. Louis: Civil Works Administration, 1933–40), pl. 9D.

57. FHA official quoted in Kenneth Jackson, "Race, Ethnicity, and Real Estate Appraisal: The Home Owners Loan Corporation and the Federal Housing Administration," *Journal of Urban History* 6,4 (1980): 420; "Re-Survey Report of Metropolitan St. Louis, Missouri, and Illinois" (n.d.; 1940?), 4, box 2, City Survey Files, Records of the Home Owners Loan Corporation, RG 195, National Archives 2, College Park, Md.; Office of the Mayor, "A Plea to the Constitutional

Convention of Missouri for Enlargement of the Boundaries of St. Louis" (1944) in *St. Louis*, ed. Selwyn Troen and Glen Holt (New York: Franklin Watts, 1977), 171; Social Planning Council of St. Louis and St. Louis County, "Graphic Facts" (1947), box 1:8, SLDC; "Introduction," *Comprehensive City Plan, 1947*, archived at http://stlouis.missouri.org/government/docs/1947plan.

58. David Laslo, "The St. Louis Region, 1950–2000: How We Changed," in Baybeck and Jones, *St. Louis Metromorphosis*, 2–3; Barbara R. Williams, *St. Louis: A City and Its Suburbs*, R-1353-NSF (Santa Monica, Calif.: The Rand Corporation, 1973), 4; Peter A. Morrison, "Urban Growth and Decline: San Jose and St. Louis in the 1960s," *Science* 185,4513 (1974): 758–60; Leven, *Neighborhood Change*, 5; Mendelson and Quinn, "Residential Patterns in a Midwestern City," 151–52 (census official quoted at 154); see also Jackson, *Crabgrass Frontier*, 284 (for 1980 rankings); St. Louis County Planning Commission, "Guide for Growth" (1962), box 5:2, St. Louis County Data Collection (SLCDC) (s73); "Population and Housing Characteristics of Wellston" (1963), box 2:41, St. Louis County Municipal Collection (sl74), WHMC; Brady Baybeck, "The Dynamics of Density in the St. Louis Region," in Baybeck and Jones, *St. Louis Metromorphosis*, 25.

59. Williams, *St. Louis: A City and Its Suburbs*, vi.

60. Local, if anecdotal, evidence of flight from the city is offered by "Location and Type of Structure from Which Purchasers Moved to 129 New Single-Family Homes in Normandy, St. Louis County, 1937–1938," and "Location and Type of Structure from which Purchasers Moved to 62 New Single-Family Homes in Affton, St, Louis County, 1937–1938," both in St. Louis Maps, entry 153, Cartographic Records of the Federal Housing Administration, RG 31, National Archives 2.

61. See Leven, *Neighborhood Change*, 62–65.

62. See James Little, Hugh Nourse, and Donald Phares, "The Neighborhood Succession Process: A Summary," working paper HMS 4, Washington University Institute for Urban and Regional Studies, 1975, 10–16; Peter Morrison, "Residential Mobility in the City of St. Louis: An Analysis of the 1967 Home Interview Survey," WN-8114-NSF (Washington, D.C.: National Science Foundation, 1973), 6–20.

63. Paul Fischer, "Racial Patterns in Housing and Schools: A Report on St. Louis" (July 1980); appendix to Gary Orfield, "The Housing Issues in the St. Louis Case," Report to Judge William Hungate, U.S. District Court (St. Louis), *Liddell v. Board of Education* (April 1981), 184.

64. Elwood Street, "Community Organization in Greater St. Louis," *Social Forces* 6, 2 (1927): 249.

65. Weaver, *The Negro Ghetto*, 26, 49; Ralph Carr Fletcher, *Social Statistics of St. Louis by Census Tracts* (School of Business and Public Administration, Washington University, St. Louis, 1935), 20, 24; Lillian Brandt, "The Negroes of St. Louis," *Publications of the American Statistical Association* 8, 61 (1903): 205.

66. William Frey and Alden Speare, *Regional and Metropolitan Growth and Decline in the United States* (New York: Russell Sage, 1988), 264; Farley, "Racial Housing Segregation in the St. Louis Metropolitan Era," table 3; Joe T. Darden, "Black Residential Segregation Since the Shelley v. Kraemer Decision," *Journal of Black Studies* 25,6 (1995): 680–83, 686; Douglas Massey and Nancy Denton, "Hypersegregation in U.S. Metropolitan Areas: Black and Hispanic Segregation Along Five Dimensions," *Demography* 26, 3 (1989): 378–79; Mendelson and Quinn, "Residential Patterns in a Midwestern City," 158–60.

67. Arnold Hirsch, "'Containment' on the Home Front: Race and Federal Housing Policy from the New Deal to the Cold War," *Journal of Urban History* 26, 2 (2000): 158–60; Massey and Denton, "Hypersegregation in U.S. Metropolitan Areas," 378–79. Of 60 MSAs ranked by Massey and Denton, St Louis ranked 9th for "evenness," 6th for "exposure," 2nd for "concentration," and 8th for "centralization." The "clustering" score was much lower, reflecting the discrete pockets of black settlement on the Illinois and Missouri sides of the river.

68. Farley, "Racial Housing Segregation in the St. Louis Metropolitan Era," table 3.

69. Williams, *St. Louis: A City and Its Suburbs*, 19–20, 22–23; Dreier, Swanstrom, and Mollenkopf, *Place Matters*, 36–37.

70. Jones, "The Municipal Market in the St. Louis Region, 1950–2000," 279–81.

71. See especially Thomas Sugrue, *The Origins of the Urban Crisis: Race and Inequality in Postwar Detroit* (Princeton, N.J.: Princeton University Press, 1996); Heather Thompson, *Whose Detroit? Politics, Labor, and Race in a Modern American City* (Ithaca, N.Y.: Cornell University Press, 2001); Hirsch, *Making the Second Ghetto*; Charles Connerly, *"The Most Segregated City in America": City Planning and Civil Rights in Birmingham, 1920–1980* (Charlottesville: University Press of Virginia, 2005); Kevin Fox Gotham, *Race, Real Estate, and Uneven Development: The Kansas City Experience, 1900–2000* (Albany: State University of New York Press, 2002); Jackson, *Crabgrass Frontier*.

Chapter 1. Local Politics, Local Power: Governing Greater St. Louis, 1940–2000

1. This was less true in the nineteenth century, as the political reach of the city (in many American settings) often followed as these early suburbs were annexed or consolidated. See Michael Danielson, *The Politics of Exclusion* (New York: Columbia University Press, 1976), 15–17; Sam Bass Warner, *Streetcar Suburbs: The Process of Growth in Boston, 1870–1900* (Cambridge, Mass.: Harvard University Press, 1978); and Warner, *The Private City: Philadelphia in Three Periods of Its Growth* (Philadelphia: University of Pennsylvania Press, 1968, 1987).

2. Jon Teaford, *City and Suburb: The Political Fragmentation of Metropolitan America, 1850–1970* (Baltimore: Johns Hopkins University Press, 1979), 5–31.

3. Richard Briffault, "Localism and Regionalism," *Buffalo Law Review* 48 (2000): 1–3.

4. Theodore Hesburgh (United States Commission on Civil Rights) in Human Development Corporation, "Social and Economic Poverty" (1971), box 7:81, SLDC (sl75), Western Historical Manuscript Collection (WHMC) University of Missouri, St. Louis.

5. See Cynthia Cumfer, "Original Intent v. Modern Judicial Philosophy: Oregon's Home Rule Case Frames the Dilemma for State Constitutionalism," *Oregon Law Review* 76 (1997): 912–13; Gerald Frug, "The City as a Legal Concept," *Harvard Law Review* 93 (1980): 1098–1115; (quote) Rodney Mott, *Home Rule for America's Cities* (Chicago: American Municipal Association, 1949), 11; William Casella, "A Century of Home Rule," *National Civic Review* 64,9 (1975): 441–42; Richard Briffault, "Our Localism: Part I—The Structure of Local Government Law," *Columbia Law Review* 90 (1990): 8–9; Dale Krane, Platon Rigos, and Melvin Hill, *Home Rule in America: A Fifty-State Handbook* (Washington, D.C.: Congressional Quarterly, 2001), 9–10; Walter Arndt, *Emancipation of the American City* (New York: Duffield, 1917), 240–59; Frank Goodnow, *Municipal Home Rule: A Study in Administration* (New York: Macmillan, 1895), 50–51.

6. See Stephanie Cole, "Illinois Home Rule in Historical Perspective," in *Home Rule in Illinois*, ed. Cole and Samuel Gove (Urbana, Ill.: Institute of Government and Public Affairs, 1973), 11–16; Mott, *Home Rule for America's Cities*, 13–27; Krane, Rigos, and Hill, *Home Rule in America*, 10–16, passim; Goodnow, *Municipal Home Rule*, 56–98; Arndt, *Emancipation of the American City*, 35; Cumfer, "Original Intent v. Modern Judicial Philosophy," 922–25.

7. Howard McBain, *American City Progress and the Law* (New York: Columbia University Press, 1918), 1.

8. E. Terrence Jones, *Fragmented by Design: Why St. Louis Has So Many Governments* (St. Louis: Palmerston and Reed, 2000), 2–3; Truman Port Young, "The Scheme of Separation of City and County Government in St. Louis—Its History and Purposes," *Proceedings of the American Political Science Association* 8 (1911): 100; U.S. Advisory Commission on Intergovernmental Relations, *Local Government Autonomy: Needs for Constitutional, Statutory, and Judicial Clarification* (Washington, D.C.: Advisory Committee, 1993), 41.

9. E. Terrence Jones and Don Phares, "Missouri," in Krane, Rigos, and Hill, *Home Rule in America*, 241–43; "Structure of Government in St. Louis" (1953), box 18:98, St. Louis League of Women Voters Records (sl234), WHMC.

10. Jones, *Fragmented by Design*, 6–7; Land Clearance for Redevelopment Authority of Univer-

sity City, "A New Vision for University City" (1962?), 2; Young, "The Scheme of Separation," 107.

11. In 1900: Bridgeton, Fenton, Ferguson, Florissant, Kirkwood, and Webster Groves; in 1930, these six and Brentwood, Clayton, Glendale, Huntleigh, Maplewood, Oakland, Olivette, Richmond Heights, Rock Hill, Shrewsbury, University City and Valley Park. See E. Terrence Jones, "The Municipal Market in the St. Louis Region, 1950–2000," in *St. Louis Metromorphosis: Past Trends and Future Directions*, ed. Brady Baybeck and Terrence Jones (St. Louis: Missouri Historical Society Press, 2004), 276–77.

12. St. Louis County Planning Commission, "Metropolitan Metamorphosis" (1955), box 3:7, St. Louis County Data Collection (SLCDC) (s73), WHMC; David Laslo, "The St. Louis Region, 1950–2000: How We Changed," in Baybeck and Jones, *St. Louis Metromorphosis*, 20; "Preliminary Report upon Background Studies, Land Use Plan and Zoning, Franklin County, Missouri" (1969), vol. 27, ser. 2 (Black-unlabeled), Harland Bartholomew Papers, Washington University Archives, Clayton, Missouri; Robert Lewis, "The Changing Fortunes of Central City Manufacturing, 1870–1950," *Journal of Urban History* (2002): 574–76.

13. Land Clearance for Redevelopment Authority of University City, "A New Vision for University City" (1962?), 2–4; Jones and Phares, "Missouri," 243; "Problems Involved in Annexation of Unincorporated Area to the North [Webster Groves]" (1950), vol. 64, ser. 2 (Black), Bartholomew Papers; St. Louis County Planning Department, "Kinloch Phase 1: Sketch for Community Development" (October 1970), folder 506, ser. 4 (roll 21), James Symington Papers, WHMC; Elwood Street, "Community Organization in Greater St. Louis," *Social Forces* 6, 2 (1927): 249 (quote).

14. On University City, see Land Clearance for Redevelopment Authority of University City, "A New Vision for University City" (1962?), 2–4; on Berkeley, see "Kinloch" clipping (n.d.); "Kinloch: Yesterday, Today, and Tomorrow" (1983), box 2:23, St. Louis County Municipalities Collection (SLCMC) (sl74), WHMC; on Champ, see Laura Higgins, "The Champ," *Riverfront Times* 14 February 2001, at http://www.riverfronttimes.com/issues/2001-02-14/news/feature .html; other examples from Jones, *Fragmented by Design*, 30–33; and Dennis Judd, "The Role of Government Policies in Promoting Residential Segregation in the St. Louis Metropolitan Area," *Journal of Negro Education* 66, 3 (1997): 235–36.

15. Transcript of the Record, *City of Moline Acres v. Heidbreder* (1963), RG 600, Supreme Court Judicial Case Files (SC Case Files), Missouri State Archives (MSA), Jefferson City; Metropolitan St. Louis Survey, *Path of Progress for Metropolitan St. Louis* (University City: The Survey, 1957), 85–87.

16. *State of Missouri v. Champ* (1965), 49734, RG 600, SC Case Files, MSA; (quote) Brief of the Relator, *State of Missouri v. Champ* (1965), 49734, RG 600, SC Case Files, MSA; *St. Louis County v. Village of Champ* (1968), 53728, RG 600, SC Case Files, MSA; Transcript of Record, 172–73, *St. Louis County v. Village of Champ* (1968), 53728, RG 600, SC Case Files, MSA; Report upon the Development and Administration of the Village of Champ (1962), vol. 15, ser. 2 (Blue), Harland Bartholomew Papers, WU.

17. Jones, *Fragmented by Design*, 29–30; Carl Stolwyk and Florence Stolwyk, *A History of Des Peres, Missouri* (Des Peres: s.n., 1976), 27–28; see also General Planning and Resource Consultants, "A Comprehensive Community Plan, Creve Coeur, Missouri" (June 1969), 6; *Dressel v. Crestwood* (1953), RG 600, SC Case Files, MSA; Transcript of the Record, *City of Moline Acres v. Heidbreder* (1963), RG 600, SC Case Files, MSA.

18. Statement, Brief, and Argument of Respondents, *Olivette v. Graeler* (1959), RG 600, SC Case Files, MSA; St. Louis Metropolitan Survey, *Background for Action* (1957), 34–36; Respondent's Statement, Brief, and Argument, *City of Creve Coeur v. Patterson* (1958), RG 600, SC Case Files, MSA.

19. Transcript on Appeal, 103–5, 127–28, 144–46, *City of Creve Coeur v. Patterson* (1958), RG 600, SC Case Files, MSA; Testimony of Henry Schmandt, Transcript of Record on Appeal, 334–

35, *Olivette v. Graeler* (1959), RG 600, SC Case Files, MSA; *City of Creve Coeur v. Patterson* (1958), RG 600, SC Case Files, MSA.

20. *Olivette v. Graeler*, 30179, Court of Appeals of Missouri, St. Louis District, 329 S.W. 2d 275; 1959 Mo. App. LEXIS 452, 11/17/59; (quote) Statement, Brief, and Argument of Respondents, *Olivette v. Graeler* (1959), RG 600, SC Case Files, MSA; Joint Brief for the City of St. Louis and the St. Louis County Library District as Amici Curiae, *Olivette v. Graeler* (1960), RG 600, SC Case Files, MSA; Jones, *Fragmented by Design*, 32–33; (quote) *Olivette v. Graeler*, 49385, Supreme Court of Missouri, Division 2, 369 S.W. 2d 85; 1963 Mo. LEXIS 739, 06/04/63; Statement, Brief, and Argument of Appellant, *Olivette v. Graeler* (1959), RG 600, SC Case Files, MSA.

21. This paragraph draws on Jones, *Fragmented by Design*, 33, 42–45; see also *Town & Country v. St. Louis County*, 64430, Supreme Court of Missouri, 657 S.W. 2d 598; 1983 Mo. LEXIS 396, 20 September 1983, Motion for Rehearing Overruled 18 October 1983; Transcript of Record on Appeal, *City of Town and Country* (1982), 64430, RG 600, SC Case Files, MSA.

22. Measures of fragmentation are drawn from "The Metropolitan Community," *Comprehensive City Plan, 1947*, http://stlouis.missouri.org/government/docs/1947plan; Robert Cohn and Lawrence Roos, *The History and Growth of St. Louis County, Missouri* (St. Louis County, 1969), 6; Jones, "The Municipal Market in the St. Louis Region, 1950–2000," 276; Jones, *Fragmented by Design*, 95–124; Peter Dreier, Todd Swanstrom, and John Mollenkopf, *Place Matters: Metropolitics for the Twenty-First Century* (Lawrence: University Press of Kansas, 2001), 39.

23. On school districts, see St. Louis Metropolitan Survey, *Background for Action* (1957), 56–57, 67; Missouri Public Expenditure Survey, *Missouri's Patchwork of Local Governments* (Jefferson City, 1958), 4; Gary Orfield, "The Housing Issues in the St. Louis Case," Report to Judge William Hungate, U.S. District Court (St. Louis, Mo.), *Liddell v. Board of Education* (April 1981), 11–14, 65; Daniel Schlafly, *28 Years on the St. Louis School Board, 1953–1981* (St. Louis: Author, 1995), 60.

24. Untitled charter memorandum (n.d.), box 2:29, St. Louis Data Collection (SLDC) (s557), WHMC; Isidore Loeb, "The Proposed Merger of St. Louis City and County," *American Political Science Review* 24,3 (1930): 691; Office of the Mayor, "A Plea to the Constitutional Convention of Missouri for Enlargement of the Boundaries of St. Louis" (1944), in *St. Louis*, ed. Selwyn Troen and Glen Holt (New York: Franklin Watts, 1977), 170–71.

25. Loeb, "The Proposed Merger of St. Louis City and County," 691–92; untitled charter memorandum (n.d.), box 2:29, SLDC; Jones, *Fragmented by Design*, 62–70; Missouri Constitution, Art. VI, Sec. 30 (a), http://www.moga.mo.gov/const/A06030a.htm.

26. Office of the Mayor, "A Plea to the Constitutional Convention of Missouri for Enlargement of the Boundaries of St. Louis" (1944) in Troen and Holt, *St. Louis*, 169; untitled charter memorandum (n.d.), box 2:29, SLDC; "The Bi-State Development Agency" (January 1960), folder 1281, St. Louis League of Women Voters Records (sl530), WHMC; Jones, *Fragmented by Design*, 70; "Study of St. Louis Metropolitan Area" (1955), box 18:98, St. Louis League of Women Voters Records; Robert Salisbury, "The Dynamics of Reform: Charter Politics in St. Louis," *Midwest Journal of Political Science* 5, 3 (1961): 267; Henry J. Schmandt, Paul G. Steinbicker, and George D. Wendel, *Metropolitan Reform in St. Louis* (New York: Holt, Rinehart, 1961), 4.

27. "Study of St. Louis Metropolitan Area" (1955), box 18:98, St. Louis League of Women Voters Records; *St. Louis Commerce* (July 1957), 52; Statement of Aloys Kaufman (October 1959), box 8, ser. 2, Raymond R. Tucker Papers, Washington University Archives; untitled charter memorandum (n.d.), box 2:29, SLDC; "Proposed Plan of the Greater St. Louis City—County District" (St. Louis: Board of Freeholders, 1958); Jones, *Fragmented by Design*, 70–79; Salisbury, "The Dynamics of Reform," 269–70; Cohn and Roos, *The History and Growth of St. Louis County, Missouri*, 6; Metropolitan St. Louis Survey, *Path of Progress for Metropolitan St. Louis* (University City, Mo.: The Survey, 1957), 3, 5, 74.

28. Schmandt, *Metropolitan Reform in St. Louis*, 5–15, 24–25, 37.

29. See Borough Plan materials in folder 1163, St. Louis League of Women Voters Records;

(quote) "For a Single, Effective, Economical Government" (1962), box 6:69, SLDC; untitled charter memorandum (n.d.), box 2:29, SLDC; (quote) Lee Duggan (Richmond Hills Mayor), "A Vote for the Borough Plan Is a Vote Against Local Government" (n.d.), box 6:69, SLDC; (quote) William Human, "Analysis of the Borough Plan" (1961), box 18:100, St. Louis League of Women Voters Records; Jones, *Fragmented by Design*, 79–82; "Some Facts About the Borough Plan" (April 1962), folder 1163, St. Louis League of Women Voters Records.

30. Phoenix Fund, "SLACOG: An Analysis" (1974), folder 1179, St. Louis League of Women Voters Records; (quote) "Draft Proposal" (July 1973), box 7:179, Regional Commerce and Growth Association (RCGA) Records; Civic Progress Minutes (24 February 1969), box 16, ser. 1, Alfonso J. Cervantes Papers, Washington University Archives; Lana Stein, *St. Louis Politics: The Triumph of Tradition* (St. Louis: Missouri Historical Society Press, 2002), 147.

31. "Merger of a Metropolis" (1967), box 7:150, RCGA Records; "East-West Gateway Coordinating Council" (n.d), box 7:180, RCGA Records; Jones, *Fragmented by Design*, 148–50.

32. Jones, *Fragmented by Design*, 50–54, 85–92; FOCUS St. Louis, *Too Many Governments? A Report on Government Structure in St. Louis City and County* (1987, updated 1992); East-West Gateway Coordinating Council, *Where We Stand, 1999* (quote at 25), at http://www.ewgateway.org/library/Archives/ReportsArchives/WWS1999/wws1999 .htm.

33. Jones, *Fragmented by Design*, 12–13, 20–22; Stein, *St. Louis Politics*, 11.

34. Lana Stein, "St. Louis Black-White Elections: Products of Machine Factionalism and Polarization," *Urban Affairs Review* 27, 2 (1991): 42–44, 59–60, 229–30; Salisbury, "The Dynamics of Reform," 267–69; "City-County Matters" (1969), box 1:16, RCGA Records.

35. (Quote) Mary Welek, "Jordan Chambers: Black Politician and Boss," *Journal of Negro History* 57, 4 (October 1972): 354; for electoral patterns, see Charles E. Gilbert and Christopher Clague, "Electoral Competition and Electoral Systems in Large Cities," *Journal of Politics* 24, 2 (May 1962): 322; Stein, *St. Louis Politics*, 13–27, 32, 67–74; Teaford, *Rough Road to Renaissance*, 63–64.

36. Stein, *St. Louis Politics*, 75–84; Gilbert and Clague, "Electoral Competition and Electoral Systems in Large Cities," 324–25; John Kramer, "The Election of Blacks to City Councils: A 1970 Status Report and a Prolegomenon," *Journal of Black Studies*, 1,4 (June 1971): 448, 470; Welek, "Jordan Chambers: Black Politician and Boss," 354–6; East-West Gateway Coordinating Council, Board of Directors (28 February 1973), box 7:180, RCGA Records; Howard Baer, *St. Louis to Me* (St. Louis: Hawthorn, 1978), 269–70.

37. Andrew Jonas and David Wilson, "The City as a Growth Machine," in *The Urban Growth Machine: Critical Perspectives Two Decades Later*, ed. Jonas and Wilson (Albany: State University of New York Press, 1999), 5; Harvey Molotch, "The City as a Growth Machine: Towards a Political Economy of Place," *American Journal of Sociology* 82, 2 (1976): 312–15, 320; Thomas Moore and Gregory Squires, "Public Policy and Private Benefits: The Case of Industrial Revenue Bonds," in *Business Elites and Urban Development*, ed. Scott Cummings (Albany: State University of New York Press, 1988), 97–98.

38. Salisbury, "The Dynamics of Reform," 261–66; Howard Richards, "A Comparison of the Model Cities Programs of St. Louis and Kansas City, Missouri" (Ph.D. dissertation, University of Missouri-Columbia, 1972), 20–33.

39. Dennis Judd, "Strong Leadership," *Urban Studies* 37, 5/6 (May 2000): 952–54.

40. Baer, *St. Louis to Me*, 120–22; Civic Progress clippings, box 1165, St. Louis League of Women Voters Records; Teaford, *Rough Road to Renaissance*, 48; Judd, "Strong Leadership," 952–54; Robert Cantwell, "St. Louis Snaps Out of It," *Fortune* (July 1956), 118; Minutes: Meeting of Civic Progress (15 December 1969), box 24 , ser. 2, Cervantes Papers.

41. See Downtown, Inc. file in box 15, ser. 2, John Conway Papers, Washington University Archives; Teaford, *Rough Road to Renaissance*, 50; "Organizing Committee, Downtown in St. Louis, Inc." (25 March 1958); Minutes of Meeting (3 October 1958); Arthur Wright to Tucker (18 March 1960); and Downtown, Inc., Second Annual Report (1959–60), all in box 11, ser. 2, Raymond R. Tucker Papers, Washington University Archives; Downtown St. Louis, Inc.: State-

ment of Revenue and Expenses (1972), box 27, ser. 2, Cervantes Papers; Summary of Receipts and Disbursements (December 1979), box 15, ser. 2, Conway Papers.

42. "Financial Statements, 1939–70," in box 2:22–24, RCGA Records; Civic Progress Minutes (24 February 1969), box 16, ser. 1, Cervantes Papers; Executive Committee Minutes, box 1:6–8, 15, RCGA Records; (quote) Baer, *St. Louis to Me*, 22.

43. "Chamber of Commerce Proposal" (n.d.), box 8:215; "United Plan for Industrial Development" (13 May 1965) box 8:215; Executive Committee Minutes, box 1:8–9; "Metropolitan Industrial Development Corporation" (1964), box 2:30; "Commitments" (1963), box 4:52, all in RCGA Records.

44. RIDC ExComm Meeting (26 October 1966), box 11:345; "Function of St. Louis Research Council" (1964), box 1:10; William Fogarty to Aloys Kaufman (17 November 1966), box 11:345; "Report of the Political Education Committee" (1965), box 1:10, all in RCGA Records.

45. Minutes: Civic Progress, Inc. (21 January 1974), box 7, John Poelker Papers, Washington University Archives; RCGA, "Report on 1979 and Program and Goals for 1980" and "Memorandum Re: Legislative Implementation" (October 1977), box 55, ser. 2, Conway Papers; Chamber of Commerce, "Achievements, 1972," box 17, ser. 2, Cervantes Papers.

46. Patrick Collins and Ivars Zusevics, "Community Development Politics in St. Louis" (Master's thesis, Washington University, 1975), 118–30.

47. See Paul Merz, "Fiscal Capacities of Counties and Major Municipalities in the St. Louis Metropolitan Area" (East-West Gateway Coordinating Council, 1969), 12–17.

48. See Alvin Sokolow, "The Changing Property Tax in the West: State Centralization of Local Finances," *Public Budgeting and Finance* 20,1 (2000): 85–88; David L. Sjoquist, Sally Wallace, and Barbara Edwards, "What a Tangled Web: Local Property, Income, and Sales Taxes" (2002); at http://frp.aysps.gsu.edu/sjoquist/works/tangled_web.pdf, 22–24; Brian Howes, *Property Tax Law in Missouri* (Eau Claire, Wisc.: NBI, 2001), 3–4.

49. For most of the postwar era, the state cap on municipal taxes has been $1.00 on each $100 of assessed value (with additional levies allowed for recreation, libraries, and health; lower limits for smaller towns and villages; and separate schedules for counties and school districts). See "Background for Action" (1958), box 5, ser. 2, Raymond R. Tucker Papers, Washington University Archives; Missouri Constitution, Art. X; Taxation; Sec. 11(b).

50. Conference on Education, *Missouri: The Property Tax* (St. Louis: The Conference, 1978), 4–5, 9; Merz, "Fiscal Capacities of Counties and Major Municipalities in the St. Louis Metropolitan Area," 9–11, 66; "Study of St. Louis Metropolitan Area" (1955), box 18:98, St. Louis League of Women Voters Records; "How Assessment Works in Missouri," at http://www.dor.state .mo.us/stc/property%20tax%20in%20missouri.htm

51. John Kelley, "The Property Tax: A Study of the Legal, Economic, and Political Barriers to Reform" (LL.M. thesis, University of Missouri-Kansas City, 1972), 40–42, 61–62; Missouri Public Expenditure Survey, *Missouri Property Tax Rates, 1968–1969* (Jefferson City, Mo.: The Survey, 1969), 5–6; "Study of St. Louis Metropolitan Area" (1955), box 18:98, St. Louis League of Women Voters Records.

52. Conference on Education, *Missouri: The Property Tax* (1978), 10, 20–23; Missouri Public Expenditure Survey, "Property Tax Rates of Missouri Local Governments," 14th ed. (Jefferson City, Mo.: The Survey, 1975–76), 1; *Missouri Tax Policy and Education Funding* (State and Regional Fiscal Studies Unit, University of Missouri-Columbia, 2003), at http://econ.missouri.edu/ eparc/TaxRef/Reports/Final.pdf, 11; Missouri Public Expenditure Survey, *Property Tax in Turmoil in Missouri* (Jefferson City, Mo.: The Survey, 1982), 7, 19.

53. *Missouri Tax Policy and Education Funding*, 41; Missouri Public Expenditure Survey, *Property Tax in Turmoil in Missouri*, 1–4; Missouri Constitution of 1945, Superseded § 4, Art. X (Amended 2 November 1922) (Amended 3 August 1982); Taxation, sec. 4(b); Howes, *Property Tax Law in Missouri*, 7–8. The new classification system, in some respects, merely added the question of classification to the longstanding political turmoil surrounding assessment. The law was unclear as to the line between commercial and residential. Section 137.016 used a "rule of four" which

defined rental properties with more than four units in a given structure as "commercial." This prompted many rental units to reinvent themselves as condominiums. And the courts defined "structure" broadly, allowing for more than one structure on a parcel of land *and* more than one structure within the footprint of a given building (determined by the arrangement of load-bearing walls). See Howes, *Property Tax Law in Missouri*, 46–47.

54. In 1950, corporate income taxes accounted for more than a quarter (26.5 percent) of federal revenues; this fell to 17 percent in 1970, 9.1 percent in 1990, and 7.4 percent in 2003. See Office of Management and the Budget, "Historical Documents: Fiscal Year 2006 (Table 2.2) at http://www.whitehouse.gov/omb/budget/fy2006/pdf/hist.pdf.

55. "Report of Municipal Legislation Committee to Board of Directors (December 1961), 1:7, RCGA Records; "Report of Citizens Task Force on Merchants and Manufacturers Tax (1980), box 38, ser. 2, Conway Papers; "Amendment Aimed at Tax on Commercial Property," *SLPD*, 2 August 1992, 1; Mo. Rev. Stat. chap. 139, sec. 139.600; Arthur Denzau and Charles Leven, "Report on Alternative Revenue Sources: Local Revenue Generation" (St. Louis: Board of Education Community Advisory Committee, 1985), 2:13–14.

56. Missouri Public Expenditure Survey, *Property Tax in Turmoil in Missouri*, 8–9.

57. Missouri Public Expenditure Survey, *Property Tax in Turmoil in Missouri*, 2, 8–9, 17; Howes, *Property Tax Law in Missouri*, 4–5; Conference on Education, *Missouri: The Property Tax* (1978), 14; Bruce Somer, "Property Taxes: Abused and Obsolete" (n.d. [1978]), box 1, ser. 3, Conway Papers.

58. *Missouri Tax Policy and Education Funding* (State and Regional Fiscal Studies Unit, University of Missouri-Columbia, 2003), at http://econ.missouri.edu/eparc/TaxRef/Reports/Final.pdf, 7; Elaine Sharp and David Elkins, "The Impact of Fiscal Limitation: A Tale of Seven Cities," *Public Administration Review* (September 1987): 386–87; Jones, *Fragmented by Design*, 107–8; Alvin Sokolow, "The Changing Property Tax in the West: State Centralization of Local Finances," *Public Budgeting and Finance* 20, 1 (2000): 85–86.

59. Sjoquist, Wallace, and Edwards, "What a Tangled Web," 39; "The Housing Situation in St. Louis" (1953), box 1:3, SLDC; "Citizens Committee" memo (13 September 1954), folder 1119, St. Louis League of Women Voters Records; "Report of the Subcommittee on Earnings and Sales Taxes" (1959), box 12, ser. 2, Tucker Papers; Teaford, *Rough Road to Renaissance*, 76–78; "Earnings Tax" files and "The Earnings Tax and Organized Labor" (n.d.), both in box 12, ser. 2, Tucker Papers; "Statement in Support of SB 3" (8 March 1954), Folder 1120, St. Louis League of Women Voters Records; "Earnings Tax" Files, box 23, ser. 1, Tucker Papers.

60. DGH Associates, "An Analysis of the Proposed City Sales Tax" (September 1969), box 80, ser. 2, Cervantes Papers; *Missouri Tax Policy and Education Funding*, 6–7, 10–11.

61. Property taxes in these settings were still levied by the county and by school and special districts.

62. Jones, *Fragmented by Design*, 44; "Opponents See Nothing to Celebrate in New Mall," *SLPD*, 22 September 2002, B1; Bruce Somer, "Property Taxes: Abused and Obsolete" (n.d. [1978]), box 1, ser. 3, Conway Papers.

63. St. Louis Metropolitan Survey, *Background for Action* (1957), 61–63.

64. St. Louis Public Schools, Budget Planning and Development Division, *General Operating Fund Budget for Fiscal Year 1980–81* (1980), 8, 11, 15; Denzau and Leven, "Report on Alternative Revenue Sources: Local Revenue Generation," ES:2.

65. St. Louis Metropolitan Survey, *Background for Action* (1957), 56–57, 67; "Public School Finance and Assessments" (October 1956), folder 1115, St. Louis League of Women Voters Records; *Missouri Tax Policy and Education Funding*, 30–32, 34–35, 37–41; Susan Caba, "A Primer On School Funding: Disparities Must Be Addressed, *St Louis Commerce* (2005); at http://www.stlcommercemagazine.com/archives/march2005/education_2.html; (quote), Dave Drebes, "Grasping School Funding Formula a 'Dizzying' Endeavor," *St Louis Business Journal* (2005), at http://stlouis.bizjournals.com/stlouis/stories/2005/02/21/editorial2.html

66. On the City's school crisis, see John Portz, Lana Stein, and Robin Jones, *City Schools and*

City Politics: Institutions and Leadership in Pittsburgh, Boston, and St. Louis (Lawrence: University Press of Kansas, 1999), 108–10, 113–14; "The Impact of Fiscal Inequity on At-Risk Schoolchildren in St. Louis," (Testimony of Kern Alexander, 12 March 1996), *Journal of Negro Education,* 66,3, Special Issue on The Role of Social Science in School Desegregation Efforts: The St. Louis Example (Summer 1997): 304; Council of the Great City Schools, "Raising Student Achievement in the St. Louis Public Schools," (May 2004), 18–20 at http://www.cgcs.org/pdfs/St%20Louis%20Report.pdf; Denzau and Leven, "Report on Alternative Revenue Sources: Local Revenue Generation," ES: 1–3, 1: 6–8.

67. Anthony Downs, "How American Cities Are Growing," *Brookings Review* (Fall 1998): 10.

68. "City-County Relations" (n.d.), 2:29, RCGA Records; Teaford, *Rough Road to Renaissance,* 74, 218–20; Kenneth Langsdorf, "Recycling of Urban Land and Economic Development Policy in St. Louis" (n.d), box 14, John Poelker Papers, Washington University Archives; "Everybody Benefits" (1956?), box 5, ser. 2, Tucker Papers; "Questions and Answers About St. Louis School Tax Election" (1970), box 24 , ser. 2, Cervantes Papers; Conference on Education, *Missouri: The Property Tax* (1978), 21; Denzau and Leven, "Report on Alternative Revenue Sources: Local Revenue Generation," ES: 3, 2: 4–7.

69. Revenue totals (here and in chart) are from Bureau of the Census series, *City Finances* (selected years) through 1992; and *Government Finances* for 1998 and 2000, at http://ftp2.census.gov/govs/estimate/. See also "Estimate of Revenues" (1970), box 80, ser. 2, Cervantes Papers.

70. On postwar bonds, see "Everybody Benefits" (1956?), and "Summary of Progress in St. Louis in 1960" (1961), both in box 5, ser. 2, Tucker Papers; Teaford, *Rough Road to Renaissance,* 40–44, 67–73; "Confidential Report of the Citizen's Bond Issue Screening Committee" (1956?), box 6, ser. 3, Tucker Papers.

71. See City Plan Commission, *Urban Land Policy* (St. Louis: the Commission, 1936), 13, tables 1, 12.

72. Pauline Lyman to Patrick Walsh (5 February 1941), folder 688, St. Louis League of Women Voters Records; "Missouri-Illinois Metropolitan Guide Plan" (1948), vol. 39, ser. 2 (Black), Bartholomew Papers; "Slum Clearance and Redevelopment Activities" (July 1950), box 24, ser. 1, Tucker Papers.

73. Bruce Somer, "Property Taxes: Abused and Obsolete" (n.d. [1978]), box 1, ser. 3, Conway Papers.

74. Clinton deWimle to Tucker (n.d. 1956), box 13, ser. 1, Tucker Papers.

75. Myron Orfield, *American Metropolitics: The New Suburban Reality* (Washington, D.C.: Brookings Institution Press, 2002), 167.

Chapter 2. "The Steel Ring": Race and Realty in Greater St. Louis

1. Deed of Vandeventer Place (1870), Imprints Collection, Missouri Historical Society (MHS), St. Louis; "Bell Place: Improved and Restricted for Private Residences" (n.d.), Imprints Collection, MHS; "Vandeventer Place Residents Sue" (n.d.), "Discrimination in Housing," St. Louis Public Library (SLPL) Clippings Collection.

2. (Quote) United Welfare Association, "The Negro Question," Race Relations Collection, box 1, MHS; Chilton Anderson, "Observations on the Segregation Ordinance" (1916), Rare Books Collection, SLPL; (quote) "Dear Neighbor" letter (February 1915), Race Relations Collection, box 1, MHS; (quote) Fundraising Postcard (1915), Race Relations Collection, box 1, MHS.

3. (Quote) Anderson, "Observations on the Segregation Ordinance"; Committee on Housing of Negroes, "The Legal Segregation of Negroes in Saint Louis" (1913), National Association for the Advancement of Colored People (NAACP) Papers, pt. 12, Selected branch files, 1913–39, ser. C, The Midwest, reel 16:0006; ordinance cited in "Brief of the United Welfare Associa-

tion of St. Louis" *Buchanan v. Warley,* 245 U.S. 60 (1916); Lana Stein, *St. Louis Politics: The Triumph of Tradition* (St. Louis: Missouri Historical Society Press, 2002), 13–16; "Initiative Petition for Control of Mixed Blocks Occupied by White and Colored People" (1915). box 1, folder 1, Race Relations Collection, MHS.

4. See "Brief of Amici Curiae" *Buchanan v. Warley,* 245 U.S. 60 (1916); Garrett Power, "Apartheid Baltimore Style: The Residential Segregation Ordinances of 1910–1913," *Maryland Law Review* 42, 289 (1983): 312–15; address of Loren Miller (June 1947), NAACP Papers, pt. 1, reel 12: 0167.

5. Patricia Burgess Stach, "Deed Restrictions and Subdivision Development in Columbus Ohio, 1900–1970," *Journal of Urban History* 15, 1 (1988): 46–47, 52; Robert Fogelson, *Bourgeois Nightmares: Suburbia, 1870–1930* (New Haven, Conn.: Yale University Press, 2005), 36–43, 46–52, 59–79, 83–95.

6. Clement Vose, *Caucasians Only: The Supreme Court, the NAACP, and the Restrictive Covenant Cases* (Berkeley: University of California Press, 1967), 7–8; *Porter v. Pryor,* Supreme Court of Missouri, Division 1, 164 S.W. 2d 353, 1942 Mo. LEXIS 544.

7. Carter DeSoto Restrictive Covenant (April 1924), book 4018, 339–44; Finney-Cook Restrictive Covenant (March 1924), book 4018, 77–81; Vine Grove Restriction (July 1924), book 4060, 340–45; Newstead Restrictive Covenant (April 1924), book 5896, 574–76, St. Louis Recorder of Deeds; *Shelley v. Kraemer,* Transcript of the Record Before the St. Louis Court of Appeals (1946).

8. St. Louis Real Estate Exchange Restrictive Agreement and "Dolan" covenant reprinted in *Dolan and Wehmeyer v. Richardson et al.,* Abstract of the Record Before the St. Louis Court of Appeals (1944), Plaintiff's Exhibit A. The covenants themselves are elusive documents. Most of the examples cited here (and plotted on the accompanying maps) were identified through court cases. The agreements themselves are interfiled (by the date of the agreement) among the City's deed records.

9. Deed of Vandeventer Place (1870); "Bell Place: Improved and Restricted for Private Residences" (n.d.), both in Imprints Collection, MHS; see also Fogelson, *Bourgeois Nightmares,* 95–99.

10. Michael Jones-Correa, "The Origins and Diffusion of Racial Restrictive Covenants," *Political Science Quarterly* 115, 4 (2000–2001): 543, 548–51, 557–58; Kevin Fox Gotham, "Urban Space, Restrictive Covenants, and the Origins of Racial Residential Segregation in a U.S. City, 1900–1950," *International Journal of Urban and Regional Research* 24, 3 (2000): 617–19; John Clark, "Historical Sketch of Negro Housing" (1935), box 5, ser. 8, St. Louis Urban League Papers, Washington University.

11. Charles Johnson and Herman Long, *People vs. Property: Race Restrictive Covenants in Housing* (Nashville, Tenn.: Fisk University Press, 1947), 11; *Shelley v. Kraemer,* Transcript of the Record Before the St. Louis Court of Appeals (1946), 67–68; Kevin Fox Gotham, *Race, Real Estate, and Uneven Development: The Kansas City Experience, 1900–2000* (Albany: State University of New York Press, 2002), 39–43.

12. Gary Orfield, "The Housing Issues in the St. Louis Case," Report to Judge William Hungate, U.S. District Court (St. Louis, Mo.), *Liddell v. Board of Education* (April 1981), 30; Robert Weaver, *The Negro Ghetto* (New York: Russell & Russell, 1948 (1967)), 234–35.

13. Testimony of E. D. Ruth (SLREE), in Appellant's Abstract of the Record, 115–17, *Pickel v. McCawley* (1930), RG 600, Supreme Court Judicial Case Files (SC Case Files), Missouri State Archives, Jefferson City; Long and Johnson, *People vs. Property,* 19–20; Appeal from the Circuit Court of Jackson County, *Swain v. Maxwell* (1946), RG 600, SC Case Files, MSA

14. Carter DeSoto Restrictive Covenant (April 1924), book 4018, 339–44; Finney-Cook Restrictive Covenant (March 1924), book 4018, 77–81; Vine Grove Restriction (July 1924), book 4060, 340–45; Newstead Restrictive Covenant (April 1924), book 5896, 574–76, St. Louis Recorder of Deeds.

15. (Quote) "Prospectus for Huntleigh Woods" (1935), and "Report on the Proposed

Development of Huntleigh Woods" (1935), both in vol. 26, ser. 2 (Black), Harland Bartholomew Papers, Washington University Archives, Clayton, Mo.; "Preliminary Subdivision Ordinance, Ladue, Missouri" (1927?), vol. 33, ser. 2 (Black), Bartholomew Papers; Fox Meadows promotional pamphlet (1937?), and "Mutual Agreement of the Property Owners of Fox Meadows" (1937), both in box 2, Federer Realty Records, MHS.

16. "Restrictions: West Kingsbury Hills" (1946), box 4; Clifton Hills: Conditions, Controls, Covenants, Easements, and Restrictions (1953), box 1; Concord Court: Conditions and Restrictions (1957), box 1; "Restrictions: Richmond Hills" (June 1946), box 3, all in Federer Realty Records.

17. "Maryland-Euclid Shopping Center" (1955), vol. 39, ser. 2 (Red), Bartholomew Papers; Long and Johnson, *People vs. Property*, 31.

18. Long and Johnson, *People vs. Property*, 14–15; Weaver, *The Negro Ghetto*, 29–32; (quote) "Housing—Cote Brilliante Ave" (June 1927), ser. 1, box 5, St. Louis Urban League Papers, Washington University.

19. Long and Johnson, *People vs. Property*, 12–13.

20. *Dolan and Wehmeyer v. Richardson et al.*, Abstract of the Record Before the St. Louis Court of Appeals (1944).

21. Long and Johnson, *People vs. Property*, 29–30.

22. Appellant's Abstract of the Record, *Pickel v. McCawley* (1930), RG 600, SC Case Files, MSA.

23. "Home Sale to Negro Arouses Page Blvd" (18 July 1937), "Discrimination in Housing," SLPL Clippings Collection; (quote) "Housing—Cote Brilliante Ave" (June 1927); (quote) John Clark to Real Estate Exchange (November 1927); and "Open Letter to Cote Brilliante Property Owners" (July 1927), all in ser. 1, box 5, St. Louis Urban League Papers.

24. Arnold Hirsch, *Making the Second Ghetto: Race and Housing in Chicago, 1940–1960* (New York: Cambridge University Press, 1983), 27–28.

25. "Release and Waiver of Restrictions" (12 June 1923), book 3841, 539, St. Louis Recorder of Deeds; *St. Louis Argus* clipping (1926), in NAACP Papers, pt. 12, Selected branch files, 1913–39 ser. C, The Midwest, reel 16:0452; *Pickel v. McCawley*, 329, Mo. 166; 44 SW 2d 857; 1931 LEXIS 693.

26. *Pickel v. McCawley* (1931), RG 600, SC Case Files, MSA; Appellant's Abstract of the Record, 50, 64, 90–91; *Pickel v. McCawley* (1930), RG 600, SC Case Files, MSA.

27. *Meuninghaus v. James*, 324 Mo. 767; 24 S.W. 2d 1017; 1930 LEXIS 548; *Pickel v. McCawley* (1931), RG 600, SC Case Files, MSA; *Thornhill v. Herdt* (1939), RG 600, SC Case Files, MSA; *St. Louis Argus* (4 April 1941), 1, (6 June 1941), 1, (11 July 1941), 1. In Chicago, the pattern was similar but came later; see Hirsch, *Making the Second Ghetto*, 29–30.

28. Appeal from the Circuit Court of the City of St. Louis, 3–4, *Kraemer v. Shelley* (December 1946), RG 600, SC Case Files, MSA; Transcript of Record on Appeal, 463–64, *Woytus v. Winkler* (1947), RG 600, SC Case Files, MSA.

29. Social Planning Council of St. Louis and St. Louis County, "Graphic Facts" (1947), box 1:8, St. Louis Data Collection (SLDC) (s557), Western Historical Manuscript Collection (WHMC), UM-St. Louis; Annual Report of the City Plan Commission (1943–44), box 5:63, SLDC; *Shelley v. Kraemer*, Transcript of the Record Before the St. Louis Court of Appeals (1946), 67–68; Long and Johnson, *People vs. Property*, 11, 25–30; Transcript of Record on Appeal, *Woytus v. Winkler* (1947), RG 600, SC Case Files, MSA; *Thornhill v. Herdt* (1939), RG 600, SC Case Files, MSA; Appellant's Abstract of the Record, *Koehler v. Rowland*, Supreme Court of Mo. (1917), RG 600, SC Case Files, MSA; (quote) "To the Congressional Committee Investigating Housing Problems," box 5, ser. 1, Urban League of St. Louis Records.

30. John Clark to Congressional Committee Investigating Housing Problems (24 October 1947), ser. 1, box 5, St. Louis Urban League Papers.

31. (Quote) SLREE, "1927 Diary and Manual," 63, Imprints Collection, MHS; Long and Johnson, *People vs. Property*, 17–20, 68–69; testimony of residents, *Shelley v. Kraemer*, Transcript of

the Record Before the St. Louis Court of Appeals (1946), 66–111; *Dolan and Wehmeyer v. Richardson et al.*, Abstract of the Record Before the St. Louis Court of Appeals (1944); *Pickel v. McCawley*, 329 Mo. 166; 44 SW 2d 857; 1931 LEXIS 693; Vose, *Caucasians Only*, 106–7.

32. Dittmeier to Clarke (1 February 1945), Defendants' Exhibit no. 7, *Woytus v. Winkler* (1947), RG 600, SC Case Files, MSA; Transcript of the Record Before the St. Louis Court of Appeals, *Kraemer v. Shelley* (1946), RG 600, SC Case Files, MSA; Transcript of Record on Appeal, 330–1, *Woytus v. Winkler* (1947), RG 600, SC Case Files, MSA; see also Vose, *Caucasians Only*, 100–108.

33. Carter DeSoto Restrictive Covenant (April 1924), book 4018, 339–44; Finney-Cook Restrictive Covenant (March 1924), book 4018: 77–81; Vine Grove Restriction (July 1924), book 4060, 340–45; Newstead Restrictive Covenant (April 1924), book 5896, 574–76, St. Louis Recorder of Deeds; St. Louis Real Estate Exchange Restrictive Agreement, reprinted in *Dolan and Wehmeyer v. Richardson et al.*, Abstract of the Record Before the St. Louis Court of Appeals (1944), Plaintiff's Exhibit A; *Pickle v. McCawley*, 329 Mo. 166; 44 S.W. 2d 857; 1931 LEXIS 693; Vose, *Caucasians Only*, 105 (quote). For examples of eviction suits pressed by the Real Estate Exchange, see *St. Louis Argus*, 4 April 1941, 1, 6 June 1941, 1, 11 July 1941, 1.

34. *Dolan v. Richardson*, St. Louis Court of Appeals (March 1944), 26502, 21; Plaintiff's Exhibit A, *Dolan v. Richardson*, St. Louis Court of Appeals, 181 S.W. 2d 997.

35. Plaintiff's Exhibit A, *Dolan v. Richardson*, St. Louis Court of Appeals, 181 S.W. 2d 997.

36. *Dolan v. Richardson*, St. Louis Court of Appeals (March 1944), 26502, 1. Covenant filed at book 3841, 386 with the St. Louis Recorder of Deeds.

37. St. Louis Assessor Daily Books, 732:77 (1924), 894:18 (1933), 992:94 (1937), 1122:74 (July 1941), 1129:96 (October 1941), 149:40 (1958); *Dolan v. Richardson*, St. Louis Court of Appeals (March 1944), 26502, 2–3. See Scovel Richardson in *National Bar Journal* (1945); Defendant's Affidavit, *Dolan v. Richardson* (1944), RG 600, SC Case Files, MSA.

38. *Dolan v. Richardson*, St. Louis Court of Appeals (March 1944), 26502, 15; *Dolan and Wehmeyer v. Richardson et al.*, Abstract of the Record Before the St. Louis Court of Appeals (1944), 8–9, 18, 85.

39. Memorandum of the Court (February 1944), *Dolan v. Richardson* (1944), RG 600, SC Case Files, MSA; Respondent's Motion for Continuance (1943); Appellant's Motion for Continuance (1944), *Dolan v. Richardson* (1944), RG 600, SC Case Files, MSA; *Dolan v. Richardson*, St. Louis Court of Appeals, 181 S.W. 2d 997. On the role of the Marcus Avenue Association, see Vose, *Caucasians Only*, 103–4, 107–8; St. Louis Assessor Daily Books, 1129.96 (October 1941), 149:40 (1958).

40. *Corrigan et al. v. Buckley*, no. 104, 271 U.S. 323; 46 S. Ct. 521; 70 L. Ed. 969; 1926 U.S. LEXIS 884; Jones-Correa, "The Origins and Diffusion of Racial Restrictive Covenants," 544.

41. Transcript of Record, *Kraemer v. Shelley*, St. Louis Circuit Court (March 1946), 2–3; *Shelley v. Kraemer* file, box 5, ser. 8, Urban League of St. Louis Records; Vose, *Caucasians Only*, 100, 103–4, 112.

42. Transcript of Record, *Kraemer v. Shelley*, St. Louis Circuit Court (March 1946), 2–3; *Shelley v. Kraemer* file, box 5, ser. 8, Urban League of St. Louis Records; Vose, *Caucasians Only*, 100–4, 112.

43. *Shelley v. Kraemer*, Transcript of the Record Before the St. Louis Court of Appeals (1946); Transcript of Record, *Kraemer v. Shelley*, St. Louis Circuit Court (March 1946), 217.

44. *Kraemer v. Shelley*, no. 39997, Supreme Court of Missouri, 355 Mo. 814; 198 S.W. 2d 679; 1946 Mo. LEXIS 510; Vose, *Caucasians Only*, 114–19.

45. *Shelley v. Kraemer*, no. 72, Supreme Court of the United States, 334 U.S. 1; 68 S. Ct. 836; 92 L. Ed. 1161; 1948 U.S. LEXIS 2764; 3 A.L.R. 2d 441.

46. Gotham, "Urban Space, Restrictive Covenants and the Origins of Racial Residential Segregation," 623–24; (quote) Landres Chilton to Roy Wilkins (12 May 1948), NAACP Papers, pt. 5, reel 22: 0041; Stach, "Deed Restrictions and Subdivision Development in Columbus, Ohio, 1900–1970," 59; Rose Helper, *Racial Policies and Practices of Real Estate Brokers* (Minneapolis: Uni-

versity of Minnesota Press, 1969), 204–5; the Missouri decision allowing suits for damages is *Weiss et al. v. Leaon*, Supreme Court of Missouri, 359 Mo. 1054; 225 S.W. 2d 127; 1949 Mo. LEXIS 706.

47. SLREE, "1927 Diary and Manual," 73; "1931 Diary and Manual," "1931 Diary and Manual"; and "1946 Yearbook," all in Imprints Collection, MHS; *Fundamentals* quoted in Long and Johnson, *People vs. Property*, 58.

48. (Quote) SLREE, "1951 Yearbook," 123; "1958 Yearbook," 141, both in Imprints Collection, MHS; Helper, *Racial Policies and Practices of Real Estate Brokers*, 187–89, 201, 220–21; William H. Brown, Jr., "Access to Housing: The Role of the Real Estate Industry," *Economic Geography* 48,1 (January 1972): 66–78; (quote) "General Neighborhood Renewal Plan, University City" (1962), folder 68, box 3, Roy Wenzlick Papers, WHMC.

49. "Help Us End Restrictions Against Negro Housing" (n.d.), box 1:2, James Bush Papers, WHMC.

50. "Plans Advance to Solve Negro Housing Problem," *SLPD* clipping in NAACP Papers, pt. 12, Selected branch files, 1913–39 ser. C, The Midwest, reel 16:0191; W. P. Argus et al, to St. Louis Real Estate Exchange (2 June 1925), NAACP Papers, pt. 12, Selected branch files, 1913–19 ser. C, The Midwest, reel 16:0199. Boundaries of unrestricted zones based on physical description in "Plans Advance to Solve Negro Housing Problem."

51. W. P. Argus et al to St. Louis Real Estate Exchange (2 June 1925), NAACP Papers, pt. 12, Selected branch files, 1913–39. ser. C, The Midwest, reel 16:0199; "Segregation of Negro Districts Approved by Realtors' Referendum," *Globe-Democrat* clipping (31 August. 1923) in NAACP Papers, pt. 12, Selected branch files, 1913–39. ser. C, The Midwest, reel 16:0190; Long and Johnson, *People vs. Property*, 61, 66–67; Helper, *Racial Policies and Practices of Real Estate Brokers*, 226–28; Real Estate Board of St. Louis, "Segregation of Negro Districts Approved by Realtors' Referendum," *St. Louis Real Estate Bulletin* no. 1 (September 1923); City Plan Commission, "Distribution of the Negro Population" (1930), City Plan Maps, MHS.

52. Appellant's Abstract of the Record, 112–15, *Pickel v. McCawley* (1930), RG 600, SC Case Files, MSA.

53. *St. Louis Star-Times* clipping (2 October 1948) in NAACP Papers, pt. 5, reel 21:0303; Seegers quoted in Vose, *Caucasians Only*, 223.

54. See Hirsch, *Making the Second Ghetto*, 31–32.

55. Justice Exhibits D-15, D-10, folder 7, Black Jack Collection, WHMC; Real Estate Exchange correspondence quoted in Helper, *Racial Policies and Practices of Real Estate Brokers*, 107, 233–34; Vose, *Caucasians Only*, 224 (emphasis original).

56. "Integration and Housing in St. Louis" (1957?), box 12, ser. 2, Urban League of St. Louis Records; "Location of Current Listings for Negro Occupancy" (1956), box 3:78, Wenzlick Papers.

57. "Trends in Classified Ads" (1956), box 3:78, Wenzlick Papers; "Housing for Minorities in St. Louis" (1957), box 12, ser. 2, Urban League of St. Louis Records.

58. Memo for local fair housing groups (1968?), box 7:310, Greater St. Louis Freedom of Residence Committee (FOR) Records (s1509), WHMC; Untitled memorandum, box 3:126, FOR Records.

59. See "Complaints Files," box 3:133–34; Memo on Cornet Ziebeg (July 1969), box 3:148; and "Summary of Material on Discriminatory Practices," box 7:327, all in FOR Records.

60. "Summary of Material on Discriminatory Practices," box 7:327; testimony in USCCR Staff Report, "Housing in St. Louis" (1970), box 3:127; untitled memorandum, box 3:126, all in FOR Records; Elise Glickert (University City) quoted in Charles Oswald, "Real Estate Solicitation Bill Opposed . . . Residents Fear 'Redlining,' Racial Steering by Agents," *SLPD*, 20 June 1991, 1; "St. Louis Company Settles Steering Suit" *SLPD*, 26 April 2001, 1; "Discrimination in Housing," SLPL Clippings Collection.

61. "Fair Housing Agreement" file, box 5:226, FOR Records.

62. "Summary of Material on Discriminatory Practices," box 7:327, FOR Records.

63. Land Clearance for Redevelopment Authority of University City, "A New Vision for University City" (1962?), 35; for the progress of fair housing in University City, see Advisory Committee on Fair Housing, "Report to the Mayor" (October 1967), box 33, ser. 1, Alfonso J. Cervantes Papers, Washington University Archives; "U. City Dispute over Appraisal," *SLPD*, 24 November 1970, cited in Donald Phares, "Racial Transition and Residential Property Values" (Center for Community and Metropolitan Studies, UM-St. Louis, 1971), 3; Report of the University City Human Relations Commission (1966), box 17:799, FOR Records; Orfield, "The Housing Issues in the St. Louis Case," 87–88; Solomon Sutker, "New Settings for Racial Transition," in *Racial Transition in the Inner Suburb: Studies of the St. Louis Area*, ed. Solomon Sutker and Sara Smith Sutker (New York: Praeger, 1974), 10–17.

64. For this history, see Amy Hillier, "Searching for Red Lines: Spatial Analysis of Lending Patterns in Philadelphia, 1940–1960," *Pennsylvania History* 72 (Winter 2005): 25–47; Kenneth Jackson, *Crabgrass Frontier: The Suburbanization of the United States* (New York: Oxford University Press, 1985); Jackson, "Race, Ethnicity, and Real Estate Appraisal: The Home Owners Loan Corporation and the Federal Housing Administration," *Journal of Urban History* 6, 4 (1980): 431–32; Thomas Hanchett, "The Other 'Subsidized Housing': Federal Aid to Suburbanization, 1940s to 1960s," in *From Tenements to the Taylor Homes: In Search of an Urban Housing Policy in Twentieth Century America*, ed. John Bauman, Roger Biles, and Kristin Szylvain (University Park: Pennsylvania State University Press, 2000), 165; M. Carter McFarland, "Major Developments in the Financing of Residential Construction Since World War II," *Journal of Finance* 21, 2 (1966): 388; Charles L. Leven, James T. Little, Hugh O. Narse, and R. B. Read, *Neighborhood Change: Lessons in the Dynamics of Urban Decay* (New York: Praeger, 1976), 152–53.

65. Leven et al., *Neighborhood Change*, 157–58.

66. Assessment Division, *Real Property Valuation Survey: City of St. Louis* (St. Louis: Civil Works Administration, 1933–40), pl. 21 and passim.

67. See, for example, Annual Report of the City Plan Commission (1943–44), box 5:63, SLDC (s557).

68. Jackson, *Crabgrass Frontier*, 203–8, 215–18; Thomas J. Sugrue, "Crabgrass-Roots Politics: Race, Rights, and the Reaction Against Liberalism in the Urban North, 1940–1964," *Journal of American History* 82, 2 (1995): 551–78.

69. Jackson, "Race, Ethnicity, and Real Estate Appraisal," 423–25, 428, 436; Mark Gelfand, *A Nation of Cities: The Federal Government and Urban America, 1933–1965* (New York: Oxford University Press, 1975), 216–17, 219–21; Weaver, *The Negro Ghetto*, 79; Memorandum re: FHA (June 1952), NAACP Papers, pt. 5, reel 6:1051.

70. See Federal Housing Administration, *Underwriting Manual: Underwriting and Valuation Procedure Under Title II of the National Housing Act with Revisions to February 1938* (Washington, D.C.: U.S. G.P.O., 1938), pt. 2, sec. 9; Memorandum re: FHA Underwriting Manual (n.d.), NAACP Papers, pt. 5, reel 4:0945.

71. "Factual Statement and Petition Concerning Housing" (1944), and "Housing" (n.d.), both in box 12, ser. 2, Urban League of St. Louis Records.

72. 1947 Underwriting Manual quoted in Weaver, *The Negro Ghetto*, 153; Arnold Hirsch, "Choosing Segregation: Federal Housing Policy Between *Shelley* and *Brown*," in *From Tenements to the Taylor Homes*, 208–9, 211–13; Gary Orfield, "Federal Policy, Local Power, and Metropolitan Segregation," *Political Science Quarterly* 89, 4 (1974–75): 788–99; FHA officials quoted in Address of Loren Miller (July 1949), NAACP Papers, pt. 1, reel 12: 0742; Franklin Richards (FHA) to Raymond Foley (21 May 1948), NAACP Papers, pt, 5, reel 5:0645.

73. Arnold Hirsch, "'Containment' on the Home Front: Race and Federal Housing Policy from the New Deal to the Cold War," *Journal of Urban History* 26, 2 (2000): 164–65; Helper, *Racial Policies and Practices of Real Estate Brokers*, 203; Minutes of Conference on Strategy in Connection with Federal Housing Administration (5 August 1948), NAACP Papers, pt. 5, reel 5:0664.

74. "Re-Survey Report of Metropolitan St. Louis, Missouri and Illinois" (n.d.; 1940?), 35, box

2, City Survey Files, Records of the Home Owners Loan Corporation (HOLC), RG 195, National Archives 2, College Park, Md.

75. Miscellaneous City Maps, Entry 437, Cartographic Records of the HOLC; Jackson, "Race, Ethnicity, and Real Estate Appraisal," 423–25, 436–37; Gotham, *Race, Real Estate, and Uneven Development*, 53.

76. St. Louis Area Descriptions (1937), box 110, City Survey Files, HOLC Records.

77. See Area Descriptions (1938), box 2, and St. Louis Area Descriptions (1937), box 110, both in City Survey Files, HOLC Records.

78. These quotes from "Re-Survey Report of Metropolitan St. Louis, Missouri and Illinois (n.d.; 1940?), 8, 41; and "Metropolitan St. Louis" (1941), 11, 23, both in box 2, City Survey Files, HOLC Records.

79. For subdivision dates, see Wayman Map, original in the collections of the MHS, online version (Washington University Department of Architecture), http://library.wustl.edu/vlib/mrdc/index.html.

80. St. Louis Area Descriptions (1937), box 110, City Survey Files, HOLC Records.

81. Area Descriptions (1938), box 2, City Survey Files, HOLC Records.

82. FHA official quoted in Pretrial Brief for the United States (1971), folder 11, Black Jack Collection, WHMC; United States Commission on Civil Rights, *Home Ownership for Low Income Families: A Report on the Racial and Ethnic Impact of the Section 235 Program* (Washington, D.C.: U.S. G.P.O., June 1971), 85.

83. As Amy Hiller has shown for Philadelphia, it is also a mistake to assume that private lenders (or the FHA) actually curtailed their lending in the FHA's "high risk" zones. See Amy Hiller, "Redlining in Philadelphia," in *Past Time, Past Place: GIS for History*, ed. Anne Kelly Knowles (Redlands, Calif.: ESRI Press, 2002), 79–92.

84. (Quote) Harland Bartholomew to John Blandford (NHA) (29 May 1942), reel 11, Bartholomew Papers (Correspondence). For the 1934–39 and 1935–60 surveys, see Jackson, "Race, Ethnicity, and Real Estate Appraisal," 440, 442; the 1940 survey is from "Re-Survey Report of Metropolitan St. Louis, Missouri and Illinois (n.d.; 1940?), 83, box 2, City Survey Files, HOLC Records; 1954 and 1955 numbers from "Market Analysis and Reuse Appraisal of Mill Creek Urban Renewal Area" (1956), folder 78, box 3, Roy Wenzlick Papers; 1962–67 numbers from United States Commission on Civil Rights, Staff Report, "Housing in St. Louis" (1970), in United States Commission on Civil Rights, *Hearings: St. Louis* (January 1970), 5516–17, and USCCR Staff Report, "Housing in St. Louis" (1970), both in box 3:127, FOR Records.

85. Hanchett, "The Other 'Subsidized Housing,'"166–67.

86. *Bartholomew v. Leahy*, 1942 (typescript), reel 11, Correspondence Files, Bartholomew Papers.

87. Division of Research and Statistics, "Metropolitan St. Louis" (1941), 19, box 2, City Survey Files, HOLC Records.

88. "Location of Properties Held by the Home Owners Loan Corporation in the St. Louis Area, 1939," St. Louis Maps, Entry 153, Cartographic Records of the Federal Housing Administration, RG 31, National Archives 2, College Park, Md.

89. Amy Hillier, "Searching for Red Lines," 35–40.

90. "Re-Survey Report of Metropolitan St. Louis, Missouri and Illinois (n.d.; 1940?), 41, box 2, City Survey Files, HOLC Records.

91. See "Concerning the Present Discriminatory Policies of the Federal Housing Administration" (October 1944), reel 5:0555, and Memorandum re: FHA (June 1952), reel 6:1051, both in pt. 5, NAACP Papers; Orfield, "The Housing Issues in the St. Louis Case," 28; unsigned letter to Robert Weaver (11 June 1938), in NAACP Papers, pt. 5, reel 4:0917.

92. Social Planning Council of St. Louis and St. Louis County, "Graphic Facts" (1947), box 1:8, SLDC.

93. See *St. Louis Argus*, 28 June 1940, 1; Long and Johnson, *People vs. Property*, 76–78; and *St.*

Louis Argus, 19 Septrmber 1941, 1; 26 September 1941, 1, 24 October 1941, 1; 14 November 1941, 1, 5 December 1941, 1.

94. For this background, see Gail Radford, *Modern Housing for America: Policy Struggles in the New Deal Era* (Chicago: University of Chicago Press, 1996); John Quigley, "A Decent Home: Housing Policy in Perspective," *Brookings-Wharton Papers on Urban Affairs* (2000): 55–58, 73; Jackson, *Crabgrass Frontier*, 223–26; Hirsch, "Choosing Segregation: Federal Housing Policy Between *Shelley* and *Brown*," 214–15; Eugene Meehan, *Public Housing Policy: Convention Versus Reality* (New Brunswick, N.J.: Rutgers University Press, 1974), 14–18.

95. Quigley, "A Decent Home," 56; Jackson, *Crabgrass Frontier*, 225; USCCR Staff Report, "Housing in St. Louis" (1970), box 3:127, FOR Records, also in USCCR, *Hearings: St. Louis* (January 1970), 546–7; Robert Mendelson and Michael Quinn, "Residential Patterns in a Midwestern City: The St. Louis Experience," in *The Metropolitan Midwest: Policy Problems and Prospects for Change*, ed. Barry Checkoway and Carl Patton (Urbana: University of Illinois Press, 1985), 163–64.

96. USCCR Staff Report, "Housing in St. Louis," (1970), box 3:127, FOR Records; Orfield, "The Housing Issues in the St. Louis Case," 1–5, 9–11, 33–35; Daniel Schlafly, *28 Years on the St. Louis School Board, 1953–1981* (Author, 1995), 121–23; (quote) "The West End" (n.d.), box 52, ser. 2, Cervantes Papers.

97. Annual Report of the City Plan Commission (1943–44), box 5:63, SLDC; *SL Globe Democrat* clipping in folder 284, box 8, Roy Wenzlick Papers; Meehan, *Public Housing Policy*, 14, 30–41; Lee Rainwater, *Behind Ghetto Walls: Black Families in a Federal Slum* (Chicago: University of Chicago Press, 1970), 8; Orfield, "The Housing Issues in the St. Louis Case," 35–38 (housing officials quoted at 37–38).

98. Foley quoted in Arnold Hirsch, "'Containment' on the Home Front," 161; Meehan, *Public Housing Policy*, 34–41.

99. Bartholomew to Walter Head (19 March 1946), reel 11, Correspondence Files, Bartholomew Papers; Leven, *Neighborhood Change*, 155–59, 166–68; untitled memo from NAACP Housing Committee (1952), folder 707, St. Louis League of Women Voters Records; Testimony of Karen Kruegger, United States Commission on Civil Rights, *Hearings: St. Louis* (January 1970), 260–61; Tucker to Leo Harvey (LCRA) (23 October 1953), box 13, ser. 1, Tucker Papers; Rainwater, *Behind Ghetto Walls*, 9–10; Orfield, "The Housing Issues in the St. Louis Case," 52–53.

100. "Application to the Department of Housing and Urban Development for a Grant to Plan a Comprehensive City Demonstration Project" (26 April 1967), 203–4.

101. Meehan, *Public Housing Policy*, 8–10, (quote) 33; Orfield, "The Housing Issues in the St. Louis Case," 111.

102. Paul Fischer, "Racial Patterns in Housing and Schools: A Report on St. Louis" (July 1980); Appendix to Orfield, "The Housing Issues in the St. Louis Case," 185–89.

103. Rainwater, *Behind Ghetto Walls*, 408.

104. "Showdown St. Louis" (transcript of interview with HUD officials) (January 1973), folder 491, ser. 4 (roll 21), James Symington Papers, WHMC.

105. Lana Stein, *St. Louis Politics: The Triumph of Tradition* (St. Louis: Missouri Historical Society Press, 2002), 127–29.

106. *Jones v. Alfred H. Mayer Co.*, no. 645, Supreme Court of the United States, 392 U.S. 409; 88 S. Ct. 2186; 20 L. Ed. 2d 1189; 1968 U.S. LEXIS 2980; Samuel Liberman, "The Implications of Jones v. Alfred H. Mayer," *St. Louis Bar Journal* (n.d.).

107. "Open Housing: How to Avoid the Law" (1968), box 8:367; and "NAREB Policy on Minority Housing" (1967), box 13:582, both in FOR Records.

108. Missouri Bar, *Missouri Real Estate Practice*, 2nd ed. (Jefferson City, 1972), 307 (quote), 314, 16 Sup. 1–3.

109. This paragraph draws on Orfield, "The Housing Issues in the St. Louis Case," 61 (quote), 93–95, 101–7.

110. HUD Commissioner Letter, "Prohibition of Arbitrary Exclusions" (July 1967), and

HUD Circular, "Identification of Areas Ineligible for FHA Mortgage Insurance" (December 1970), both reproduced in United States Commission on Civil Rights, *Home Ownership for Low Income Families*, 120–21; James Little et al., "The Contemporary Neighborhood Succession Process: Lessons in the Dynamics of Decay from the St. Louis Experience" (Washington University Institute for Urban and Regional Studies, 1975), 183–85; Orfield, "The Housing Issues in the St. Louis Case," 43–46; Leven, *Neighborhood Change*, 174–81.

111. USCCR, *Home Ownership for Low Income Families*, 6–7; Orfield, "The Housing Issues in the St. Louis Case," 60.

112. Leven, *Neighborhood Change*, 175; USCCR, *Home Ownership for Low Income Families*, 16–17, 52–53, 73–74 (realtor quoted at viii–ix); Orfield, "The Housing Issues in the St. Louis Case," 56–57; *Virgil Wright et al. v. George Romne*, Case 70C291(3), District Court of the U.S. for the Eastern District of Missouri, reprinted in USCCR, *Home Ownership for Low Income Families*, 105–11.

113. USCCR, *Home Ownership for Low Income Families*, viii–ix, 12, 46; Little et al., "The Contemporary Neighborhood Succession Process," 181–82, 185–88.

114. Insurers quoted in Missouri House of Representatives, "Interim Committee Report on Redlining" (1993), 7; Alliance of American Insurers Press Release (1 April 1993), in Missouri House of Representatives, "Interim Committee Report on Redlining" (1993), App. B.

115. "Visits to Eastern Insurance Companies" (December 1945), reel 11, Correspondence Files, Bartholomew Papers; Hallauer and McReynolds, "Appraisal Report for City of University Heights" (October 1970), folder 518, ser. 4, roll 21, James Symington Papers, WHMC.

116. Vose, *Caucasians Only* (quote) 110; statistical snapshots of redlining are drawn from "Savings and Loans Lending Activity for the City of St. Louis: A Phoenix Fund Update for 1974," Imprints Collection, MHS; "Redlining" file, folder 15, and "Redlining" (September 1976), folder 18, both in ACORN (St. Louis) Records, WHMC; Long and Johnson, *People vs. Property*, 63; Murdoch testimony before Board of Aldermen (July 1974), box 15:677, and "Savings and Loans Lending Activity" (1974), box 15:676, both in FOR Records. Insurance agent quoted in "Conversations with Insurance Agents" (n.d.), folder 15, ACORN (St. Louis) Records.

117. See "Redlining" file, folder 15, and "Redlining" (September 1976), folder 18, both in ACORN (St. Louis) Records.

118. Heather MacDonald, "Mortgage Lending and Residential Segregation in a Hyper-Segregated MSA: The Case of St. Louis," *Urban Studies* 35, 11 (1998): 1978–80, 1987–90.

119. Hillier, "Searching for Red Lines," 35–37.

120. Test calls from upper-income white neighborhoods almost always yielded an immediate quote; fewer than half (43 percent) of callers from urban zip codes could get a telephone quote. As of 1993, rates per $1,000 of coverage ranged from $3.50 in the Missouri suburbs, to $4.89 in high-income urban areas to $13.60 in lower-income urban areas. See ACORN, *A Policy of Discrimination? Homeowners Insurance Redlining in 14 Cities* (n.p.: ACORN, 1993), 2, 9, 68.

121. See Missouri House of Representatives, "Interim Committee Report on Redlining" (1993), 4, App. B, 7.

122. Hillier, "Searching for Red Lines," 34–40.

123. Missouri ACORN, "Mortgages in St. Louis: A Study of Mortgage Lending and 'Redlining' by Savings and Loans Associations" (n.p., 1976).

124. Adam Goodman, "Five Lenders Here Accused of Bias," *SLPD*, 13 August 1993, 9D; Missouri ACORN, "Mortgages in St. Louis."

125. Rankings based on GSE data sets hosted by the "GIS for Equitable and Sustainable Communities," at http://63.111.165.45/index.php; see also Jim Gallagher, "Redlining Is Alleged on Mortgages," *SLPD*, 19 June 1990, 8B; *Ring v. First Interstate Mortgage*, no. 92–1019; 984 F. 2d 924; 1993 U.S. App. LEXIS 1251.

126. "Federal Judge Rules That Insurance Redlining Is Covered by the Fair Housing Act in Missouri Case," *National Fair Housing Advocate* (April 1997), at http://www.fairhousing.com

(accessed September 2004); "Company Won't Insure City Homes, State Says," *SLPD*, 13 January 1994, 1A; "Erase The Red Line Around St. Louis," *SLPD*, 24 January 1994, 6B.

Chapter 3. Patchwork Metropolis: Municipal Zoning in Greater St. Louis

1. Richard Briffault, "Our Localism: Part 1—The Structure of Local Government Law," *Columbia Law Review* (January 1990), 57: Myron Orfield, *Metropolitics: A Regional Agenda for Community and Stability* (Washington, D.C.: Brookings Institution, 1997), 5, 66–73.

2. My focus in this chapter is on the Missouri side of the metro area. The relationship between St. Louis and St. Louis County provides the clearest example of the historical confrontation of a city and its suburbs. By and large, land use was much more haphazard in the old industrial suburbs on the Illinois side: communities like Belleville and East St. Louis had a large percentage of substandard housing on irregular lots. And these communities devoted much less attention to planning and zoning. Indeed, East St. Louis was in such fiscal disarray after the 1970s that it endured six years without regular trash collection in the late 1980s, six city managers in five years in the early 1990s, and—for most of the 1990s—did not even have a zoning commission. See "Report upon Land Use and Proposed Zoning, St. Clair County, Illinois" (1956), vol. 48, ser. 2 (Red), Harland Bartholomew Papers, Washington University Archives, Clayton, Mo.; Margaret Gillerman, "East St. Louis to Create Planning Commission," *SLPD*, 13 June 1997, 5D.

3. Briffault, "Our Localism: Part 1," 1–3, 21–22, 42–56, 58; Howard McBain, *American City Progress and the Law* (New York: Columbia University Press, 1918), 98–115; Orfield, *Metropolitics*, 58–63; Kenneth Jackson, *Crabgrass Frontier: The Suburbanization of the United States* (New York: Oxford University Press, 1985), 206–8.

4. Anthony Downs, "Housing the Urban Poor: The Economics of Various Strategies," *American Economic Review* 59, 4 (1969): 649.

5. Richard Briffault, "Localism and Regionalism," *Buffalo Law Review* 48, 1 (2000): 8–9.

6. Edward Bassett, *Zoning: The Laws, Administration, and Court Decisions During the First Twenty Years* (New York: Russell Sage, 1936), 13, 27–28, 48; Keith Revell, "The Road to *Euclid v. Ambler*: City Planning, State Building, and the Changing Scope of the Police Power," *Studies in American Political Development* 13, 1 (1999): 50–51, 56–58, 62–64; Raphael Fischler, "The Metropolitan Dimension of Early Zoning: Revisiting the 1916 New York Zoning Ordinance," *Journal of the American Planning Association* 64 (1998): 170–88.

7. Frank Williams, *The Law of City Planning and Zoning* (New York: Macmillan, 1922), 280–81; Revell, "The Road to *Euclid*," 58–59, 87–89. For examples of such concerns, see Plaintiff's Brief and Argument, *City of St. Louis v. Evraiff* (1922), and Motion for Rehearing, *Penrose v. McKelvey* (1923), both in RG 600, Supreme Court Judicial Case Files (SC Case Files), Missouri State Archives (MSA), Jefferson City.

8. Richard Babcock and Fred Bosselman, *Exclusionary Zoning: Land Use Regulation and Housing in the 1970s* (New York: Praeger, 1973), 26–28; Richard Chused, "Euclid's Historical Imagery," *Case Western Reserve Law Review* 51 (2001): 608–10; Charles Connerly, *"The Most Segregated City in America": City Planning and Civil Rights in Birmingham, 1920–1980* (Charlottesville: University Press of Virginia, 2005), 47–49; Richard Babcock, *The Zoning Game: Municipal Practices and Policies* (Madison: University of Wisconsin Press, 1966), 1–4, 115–25; Revell, "The Road to *Euclid*," 116.

9. Revell, "The Road to *Euclid*, 97–99.

10. Robert Fogelson, *Bourgeois Nightmares: Suburbia, 1870–1930* (New Haven, Conn.: Yale University Press, 2005); Babcock and Bosselman, *Exclusionary Zoning*, 4–5; Patricia Burgess, *Planning for the Private Interests: Land Use Controls and Residential Patterns in Columbus, Ohio, 1900–1970* (Columbus: Ohio State University Press, 1994), 93–95, 160–62; Gerald Korngold, "The Emergence of Private land Use Controls in Large Scale Subdivisions: The Companion Story to Village

of *Euclid v. Ambler Realty,*" *Case Western Law Review* 51 (2001): 640–41; (quote) Bassett, *Zoning,* 68.

11. Richard Briffault, "Smart Growth and American Land Use Law," *St. Louis University Public Law Review* 21 (2003): 253–61 (Justice Douglas quoted at 260); Paul King, "Exclusionary Zoning and Open Housing: A Brief Judicial History," *Geographical Review* 68, 4 (1978): 459–69; see also Revell, "The Road to *Euclid,*" 118–19; Burgess, *Planning for the Private Interests,* 133–35; Babcock and Bosselman, *Exclusionary Zoning,* 30–31; Richard Babcock and Charles Siemon, *The Zoning Game Revisited* (Boston: Lincoln Institute, 1985), 207–15.

12. "Floor Area Ratio Height Requirements" (1966), vol. 56, ser. 2 (Black—unlabeled), Bartholomew Papers.

13. Harland Bartholomew, *Land Uses in American Cities* (Cambridge, Mass.: Harvard University Press, 1955), 14–15; Sheila Mosley, "Zoning Ordinance Revision for the City of St. Louis" (1977), 1: 15; "Preliminary Report upon Past and Probable Future Growth of the City" (1946) vol. 20, ser. 2 (Black), Bartholomew Papers.

14. See Joseph McGoldrick, *Law and Practice of Municipal Home Rule, 1916–1930* (New York: Columbia University Press, 1933), 17–36 (*City of St. Louis v. Dreisoerner* 243 Mo. 217 147 S.W. 998 [1912] cited at 18); *St. Louis, Plaintiff in Error, v. Dorr et al.,* 145 Mo. 466; 46 S.W. 976; 1898 Mo. LEXIS 103; *City of St. Louis v. Evraiff* (1923), RG 600, SC Case Files, MSA.

15. Plaintiff's Statement, Brief and Argument, *City of St. Louis v. Evraiff* (1921), RG 600, SC Case Files, MSA; Carroll J. Donahue and Shulamith Simon, "Zoning and Subdivisions," in *Real Estate Practice: Missouri* (Jefferson City: Missouri Bar Association, 1964), 221–23; Missouri Code 89:020–89:030; E. Terrence Jones and Don Phares, "Missouri," in *Home Rule in America: A Fifty-State Handbook,* ed. Dale Krane, Platon Rigos, and Melvin Hill (Washington, D.C.: Congressional Quarterly, 2001), 243–44; Brief Submitted by the City of Richmond Heights, *City of St. Louis v. Evraiff* (1921), RG 600, SC Case Files, MSA.

16. *State Ex Rel. Oliver Cadillac v. Christopher* (1927), 28010; RG 600, SC Case Files, MSA; George Haid to J. Allen (22 November 1923), *City of St. Louis v. Evraiff* (1921), RG 600, SC Case Files, MSA.

17. *City of St. Louis v. Evraiff* (1923), RG 600, SC Case Files, MSA; *Penrose v. McKelvey* (1922), RG 600, SC Case Files, MSA; Relator's Abstract of Record, *Penrose v. McKelvey* (1922), RG 600, SC Case Files, MSA; On Motion for Rehearing, *Penrose v. McKelvey* (1923), RG 600, SC Case Files, MSA.

18. Separate Concurring Opinion; On Motion for Rehearing; Dissenting Opinion; and Application on Behalf of the Cities of Webster Groves, Clayton, and Richmond Heights, all in *Penrose v. McKelvey* (1923), RG 600, SC Case Files, MSA.

19. Respondent's Statement, Brief, and Argument, *State Ex Rel. Oliver Cadillac v. Christopher* (1927), and *State Ex Rel. Oliver Cadillac v. Christopher* (1927), 28010; RG 600, SC Case Files, MSA.

20. See Appellant's and Intervenor's Joint Abstract of the Record, *Glencoe Lime and Cement v. St. Louis* (1937); Statement, Brief, and Argument of Respondent, *Richmond Heights v. Richmond Heights Memorial Benevolent Association* (1948), 40817; Appellant's Statement, Brief, and Argument, and Respondent's Statement, Brief, and Argument, *St. Louis v. Friedman* (1948); and Transcript of the Record on Appeal, *St. Louis v. Friedman* (1948), all in RG 600, SC Case Files, MSA.

21. *State Ex Rel. Oliver Cadillac v. Christopher* (1927), 28010; RG 600, SC Case Files, MSA.

22. Barbara J. Flint, "Zoning and Residential Segregation: A Social and Physical History, 1910–1940" (Ph.D. dissertation, University of Chicago, 1977), 47, 35–44, 72–73; City Plan Commission, *Zoning for St. Louis* (St. Louis: the Commission, 1918), 17; City Plan Commission, *A Major Street Plan for St. Louis* (St. Louis: the Commission, 1917); City Plan Commission, *St. Louis After the War* (St. Louis: the Commission, 1918), City Plan Commission, *Zoning for St. Louis* (St. Louis: the Commission, 1918); Harland Bartholomew, *The Zone Plan* (St. Louis: City Plan Commission, 1919); Michael Jones-Correa, "The Origins and Diffusion of Racial Restrictive Covenants," *Political Science Quarterly* 115, 4 (2000–2001): 548; Eric Sandweiss, *St. Louis: Evolution of An American Urban Landscape* (Philadelphia: Temple University Press, 2001), 213–17, 273.

23. Bartholomew, *The Zone Plan*, 30; Frank Lawrence, "Zoning Progress in Missouri," (1931), vol. 61, ser. 2 (Black), Bartholomew Papers; City Plan Commission, "Zoning" (St. Louis, 1949), 4; Relator's Abstract of Record, *Penrose v. McKelvey* (1922), RG 600, SC Case Files, MSA.

24. Bartholomew, *The Zone Plan*, 32–43; 1918 Ordinance excerpted in Plaintiff in Error's Abstract of Record, *City of St. Louis v. Evraiff* (1923), RG 600, SC Case Files, MSA; Lawrence, "Zoning Progress in Missouri"; City Plan Commission, "Zoning," 4.

25. Zoning Ordinance of the City of St. Louis, Exhibit B, *State Ex Rel. Oliver Cadillac v. Christopher* (1927), 28010; RG 600, SC Case Files, MSA.

26. Bartholomew, *The Zone Plan*, 26, 34.

27. Argument for Respondents by Glen Arnold, Amicus Curiae, *Penrose v. McKelvey* (1922), RG 600, SC Case Files, MSA.

28. See Flint, "Zoning and Residential Segregation," 137–39, 143, 196–97, 236–38, 268–73.

29. Motion of Chamberlain Park Improvement Association to Intervene as Amicus Curiae, *Penrose v. McKelvey* (1922), RG 600, SC Case Files, MSA; Bartholomew, *The Zone Plan* (quote) 30.

30. Flint, "Zoning and Residential Segregation," 146–48, 214–15, 352–53 (Bartholomew quoted at 93, 103).

31. Argument for Respondents by Glen Arnold, Amicus Curiae, *Penrose v. McKelvey* (1922), RG 600, SC Case Files, MSA; Suggestions for Support of Motion for Rehearing, *Penrose v. McKelvey* (1923), RG 600, SC Case Files, MSA; recreation commissioner quoted in Gary Orfield, "The Housing Issues in the St. Louis Case," Report to Judge William Hungate, U.S. District Court (St. Louis, Mo.), *Liddell v. Board of Education* (April 1981), 32; see also Flint, "Zoning and Residential Segregation," 355–57.

32. (Chamber of Commerce) Brief on Behalf of the City of St. Louis, and Statement, Brief, and Argument, Karl Kimmel Amicus Curiae, both in *City of St. Louis v. Evraiff* (1921), RG 600, SC Case Files, MSA.

33. (Quote) "Recommendations for Changes in Zoning in Negro Residential Area" (1938), and "Proposed Zoning of the Negro Residential Area West of Grand Avenue" (1938), both in ser. 1, box 5, St. Louis Urban League Papers, Washington University; Yale Rabin, "Expulsive Zoning: The Inequitable Legacy of *Euclid*," in *Zoning and the American Dream: Promises Still to Keep*, ed. Charles Haar and Jerold Kayden (Chicago: American Planning Association, 1989), 103–7.

34. City Plan Commission "Urban Land Policy" (1936), box 3:28, St. Louis Data Collection (SLDC) (s557), Western Historical Manuscript Collection (WHMC), UM-St. Louis.

35. Harland Bartholomew, "Population Growth, Land Uses, Zoning" (1935), box 6:89, SLDC; Flint, "Zoning and Residential Segregation," 283–84, 344–45; Transcript of the Record on Appeal, *St. Louis v. Friedman* (1948), RG 600, SC Case Files, MSA.

36. City Plan Commission, *Urban Land Use Policy* (1936) (quote at 21), vol. 53, ser. 2 (Black), Bartholomew Papers.

37. "Re-Survey Report of Metropolitan St. Louis, Missouri and Illinois" (n.d., 1940?), 38, and Division of Research and Statistics, "Metropolitan St. Louis" (1941), 15, 17, both in box 2, City Survey Files, Records of the Home Owners Loan Corporation, RG 195, National Archives 2, College Park, Md.; Flint, "Zoning and Residential Segregation," 361–83; "Meeting with Mr. Harland Bartholomew" (November 1945), folder 1338, St. Louis League of Women Voters Records (sl530), WHMC; City Plan Commission, "Zoning," 9.

38. "A Preliminary Report on Zoning (St. Louis)," (1947), vol. 53, ser. 2 (Black), Bartholomew Papers.

39. Bartholomew, "Population Growth, Land Uses, Zoning"; Annual Reports of the City Plan Commission (1946–), box 5–6, SLDC.

40. "Location of Number of New Dwelling and Demolition Units" (1956), box 3:78, Roy Wenzlick Papers, WHMC; "Land Use and Zoning," *Comprehensive City Plan, 1947*, archived at http://stlouis.missouri.org/government/docs/1947plan (quote in "Introduction").

41. Terms of the 1950 zone plan drawn from City Plan Commission, "Zoning," 17; Annual

Report of the City Plan Commission (1949–50), box 5, SLDC; "Land Use and Zoning," *Comprehensive City Plan, 1947*, archived at http://stlouis.missouri.org/government/docs/1947plan; "A Preliminary Report on Zoning [St. Louis]," (1947) , vol. 53, ser. 2 (Black), Bartholomew Papers.

42. "Recommendation in Changes of Zoning in Negro Residential Area" (n.d.), box 5, ser. 1, Urban League of St. Louis Records; Sheila Mosley, "Zoning Ordinance Revision for the City of St. Louis" (1977), 1:2; Annual Reports of the City Plan Commission (1946–), box 5–6, SLDC; "Zoning, 1954–1955," folder 1355, St. Louis League of Women Voters Records; Orfield, "The Housing Issues in the St. Louis Case," 32; Charles Leven, *Neighborhood Change: Lessons in the Dynamics of Urban Decay* (New York: Praeger, 1976), 165–66.

43. Mosley, "Zoning Ordinance Revision for the City of St. Louis," 2:100–102.

44. Mosley, "Zoning Ordinance Revision for the City of St. Louis," 2:115–21.

45. City of St. Louis Zoning Ordinance (1980); St. Louis Zoning Code (2004); archived at http://www.slpl.lib.mo.us/cco/code/title26.htm.

46. See sect. 80, St. Louis Zoning Code (2004); at http://www.slpl.lib.mo.us/cco/code/title26.htm.

47. Jackson, *Crabgrass Frontier*, 238–42; Korngold, "The Emergence of Private Land Use Controls," 617–21; "How to Buy a Home with Safety" (1929) reprinted in *St. Louis*, ed. Selwyn Troen and Glen Holt (New York: Franklin Watts, 1977) (quote 164–66).

48. For this pattern of incorporation and initial zoning, see Development of the Missouri-Illinois Metropolitan District (1950), vol. 42, ser. 2 (Red), Bartholomew Papers; "Residential Building Permits Survey, St. Louis County" (1949), box 3:1, St. Louis County Data Collection (SLCDC) (s73), WHMC; Huntleigh Village: Present Use and Ownership Map (1932), SL 74, folder 22; St. Louis County Planning Commission, "Metropolitan Metamorphosis" (1955), box 3:7, SLCDC; *Bartholomew v. Leahy*, 1942 (typescript) reel 11, Correspondence Files, Bartholomew Papers; "Report upon Land Use, Zoning, and Subdivision Regulations, Bellefontaine Neighbors" (1950), vol. 5, ser. 2 (Red), Bartholomew Papers; *Huttig v. Richmond Heights*, 372 S.W. 2d 833; 1963 Mo. LEXIS 643; *McDermott v. Village of Calverton Park*, 454 S.W. 2d 577; 1970 Mo. LEXIS 977; Preliminary Zoning Ordinance, Maplewood, Missouri (1928), vol. 38, ser. 2 (Red), Bartholomew Papers.

49. "Preliminary Report upon Land Subdivision, St. Louis County, Missouri" (1940), vol. 53, ser. 2 (Black), Bartholomew Papers.

50. *Deacon v. City of Ladue*, 294 S.W. 2d 616; 1956 Mo. App. LEXIS 165; *Flora Realty v. City Of Ladue*, 362 Mo. 1025; 246 S.W. 2d 771; 1952 Mo. LEXIS 605; Preliminary Zoning Ordinance, City of Deer Creek, Missouri (1934), vol. 13; Report upon the Preliminary Zoning Ordinance, Deer Creek, Missouri (1934), vol. 13; "Preliminary Zoning Ordinance, Ladue, Missouri" (1927?), and "Zoning Ordinance, City of Ladue, Missouri" (1938), both in vol. 33, all in ser. 2 (Black), Bartholomew Papers.

51. Transcript of Record, 135–40, *Richmond Heights v. Richmond Heights Memorial Benevolent Association* (1948), 40817, RG 600, SC Case Files, MSA; "Zoning Ordinance, Kirkwood, Missouri" (1941), vol. 31, ser. 2 (Black), Bartholomew Papers; Defendant's Case (typescript), *Flora Realty v. City of Ladue* (1950), RG 600, SC Case Files, MSA.

52. This sketch and the accompanying map are drawn from local zoning maps and ordinances. The best sources for these are the St. Louis County Municipalities Collection (SL 74), WHMC, UM-St. Louis and the Bartholomew Papers at Washington University. Others were obtained though interlibrary loan from the Library of Congress and by correspondence with city clerks and planning departments throughout the County. See also "Zoning Ordinance, Kirkwood, Missouri" (1941), vol. 31; "Zone Ordinance for University City, Missouri" (1930?), vol. 61; "Preliminary Zoning Ordinance, Maplewood Missouri" (n.d.) vol. 36; City Plan of Brentwood (1934), vol. 4, 8, 20–26; "Preliminary Zone Ordinance for Webster Groves, Missouri" (1930), vol. 64; "Revised Zoning Ordinance, Ferguson, Missouri" (1946), vol. 20, all in ser. 2 (Black), Bartholomew Papers.

53. St. Louis County Planning Commission, "Metropolitan Metamorphosis" (1955), box 3:7, SLCDC.

54. "Zoning Order for the Unincorporated Portions of St. Louis County" (1946), vol. 53, ser. 2 (Black), Bartholomew Papers; Harland Bartholomew and Associates, "A Report upon the Rezoning of the Unincorporated Portion of St. Louis County, Mo." (January 1961), 1–2; United States Commission on Civil Rights (USCCR), Staff Report, "Housing in St. Louis" (1970), in USCCR, *Hearings: St. Louis* (January 1970), 537–38.

55. Testimony of Richard Riley, Transcript of Record, St. Louis Court of Appeals, 2:337–38, *Deacon v. Ladue* (1955), RG 600, SC Case Files, MSA; Transcript of Record, 68–71, *Richmond Heights v. Richmond Heights Memorial Benevolent Association* (1948), 40817, RG 600, SC Case Files, MSA; Preliminary Zoning Ordinance, Maplewood, Missouri (1928), vol. 38, ser. 2 (Red), Bartholomew Papers; "Report on the City Plan of Kirkwood Missouri" (1927); and "Preliminary Report upon the Proposed Revised Zoning Ordinance, Kirkwood, Missouri" (1941), both in vol. 31, ser. 2 (Black), Bartholomew Papers; Bartholomew to Kirkwood City Council (June 1941), reel 11, Bartholomew Papers (Correspondence).

56. (Quote) Transcript on Appeal, vol. 1, 27, *Huttig v. Richmond Heights* (1963), RG 600, SC Case Files, MSA, Mo.; Ladue Zoning Commission to City Council (June 1959), reel 11, Bartholomew Papers (Correspondence); (quote) Transcript on Appeal (1969), 715, in Supreme Court of Missouri, *McDermott v. Calverton Park* (1970), 55224, RG 600, SC Case Files, MSA.

57. (Quote) Plaintiff's Case (typescript), *Flora Realty v. City of Ladue* (1950), RG 600, SC Case Files, MSA; Transcript of Record on Appeal, 222, *Tealin v. Ladue* (1976), 59250, RG 600, SC Case Files, MSA; (quote) Defendant's Case (typescript), *Flora Realty v. City of Ladue* (1950), RG 600, SC Case Files, MSA.

58. (Quote) Transcript of Record, St. Louis Court of Appeals, 2:422–25, *Deacon v. Ladue* (1955), RG 600, SC Case Files, MSA, Mo.; see also Defendant's Case (typescript), *Flora Realty v. City of Ladue* (1950), RG 600, SC Case Files, MSA; Declaratory Judgment, *Huttig v. Richmond Heights* (1963), RG 600, SC Case Files, MSA, Mo.; Richard Waltke (Ladue City Planning Commission) to City Council (15 November 1945), in *Deacon v. Ladue* (1963), RG 600, SC Case Files, MSA; Transcript of Record, St. Louis Court of Appeals, 2:422–81, *Deacon v. Ladue* (1955), RG 600, SC Case Files, MSA; Plaintiff's Case (typescript), *Flora Realty v. City of Ladue* (1950), RG 600, SC Case Files, MSA.

59. (Quote) Transcript of Record on Appeal, 269, *Tealin v. Ladue* (1976), 59250, RG 600, SC Case Files, MSA, Mo.; Declaratory Judgment, *Huttig v. Richmond Heights* (1963), RG 600, SC Case Files, MSA.

60. Zoning Ordinance, Village of Huntleigh (1934), and Zoning Ordinance (1936), both in vol. 26, ser. 2 (Black), Bartholomew Papers; (quote) "Preliminary Report upon Past and Probable Future Growth of the City" (1946) vol. 20, ser. 2 (Black), Bartholomew Papers.

61. "Probable Future Residential Development, Ladue, Mo." (1950), vol. 35, ser. 2 (Red), Bartholomew Papers.

62. See "Preliminary Report upon the Business Area, Des Peres, Missouri" (1970), vol. 13, ser. 2 (Brown); "Preliminary Report on a Comprehensive City Plan for Ferguson, Missouri" (1932), vol. 20, ser. 2 (Black); "Minutes of the Meeting of the Zoning Committee of Brentwood" (1 May 1935), vol. 4, ser. 2 (Black), all in Bartholomew Papers; (quote) Transcript of the Record, *City of Moline Acres v. Heidbreder* (1963), RG 600, SC Case Files, MSA.

63. "Preliminary Report upon Population and Other Urban Problems, Kirkwood, Missouri" (1940), vol. 31, ser. 2 (Black); Bartholomew to Kirkwood City Council (June 1941), reel 11, Bartholomew Papers (Correspondence), WU; "Land Use and Zoning: Rock Hill, Missouri" (1954), vol. 48, ser. 2 (Red), Bartholomew Papers; "A Report upon Land Use and Zoning, Ferguson, Missouri" (1956) vol. 24, ser. 2 (Red); "Final Report upon a City Plan for Webster Groves, Missouri" (1958), vol. 56, ser. 2 (Red); "Report upon Land Use, Zoning, and Subdivision Regulations, Bellefontaine Neighbors" (1950), vol. 5, ser. 2 (Red), all in Bartholomew Papers.

64. "Proposed Zoning District (Webster Groves)" (1966), vol. 58, ser. 2 (Black—unlabeled),

and "Preliminary Report on a Comprehensive City Plan for Ferguson, Missouri" (1932), vol. 20, ser. 2 (Black), both in Bartholomew Papers.

65. "Preliminary Report upon the Revised Comprehensive Plan [Florissant]" (1969), vol. 15, ser. 2 (Brown), Bartholomew Papers; "Residential Building Permits Survey, St. Louis County" (1949), box 3:1, and St. Louis County Planning Commission, "Multifamily Housing in St. Louis County" (1965), box 3:4, both in SLCDC; Orfield, "The Housing Issues in the St. Louis Case," 80; "1959 Land Use Summary, St. Louis County," vol. 17, ser. 2 (Red); and "Preliminary Report upon Background Studies, Land Use Plan, and Zoning, Franklin County, Missouri" (1969), vol. 27, ser. 2 (Black—unlabeled), both in Bartholomew Papers.

66. Bartholomew, *Land Uses in American Cities*, 86; University City Zoning Code (various dates), Washington University Law Library; "Proposed Revised Zoning Ordinance and Report, Brentwood, Missouri" (1952), vol. 11, ser. 2 (Red); "The Land Use Plan [Webster Groves]" (1966), vol. 56, ser. 2 (Black—unlabeled), and "Report upon the Master Plan, Clayton, Missouri" (1958), vol. 17, ser. 2 (Red), all in Bartholomew Papers; "Residential Building Permits Survey, St. Louis County" (1949), box 3:1, SLCDC (s73), WHMC.

67. Land Clearance for Redevelopment Authority of University City, "A New Vision for University City" (1963?), 6.

68. See Harland Bartholomew and Associates, "A Report upon the Rezoning of the Unincorporated Portion of St. Louis County, Mo." (January 1961), 4–5; "Report upon Land Use and Zoning [Florissant]" (1960), vol. 20, ser. 2 (Blue); "Proposed Zoning District [Webster Groves]" (1966), vol. 58, ser. 2 (Black—unlabeled); "Preliminary Report upon Land Use, Zoning, and Subdivision Regulations, Crestwood, Missouri" (1968), vol. 16, ser. 2 (Black—unlabeled), all in Bartholomew Papers.

69. "Preliminary Report upon a City Plan [Ladue]" (1939), vol. 33, ser. 2 (Black), Bartholomew Papers.

70. Bartholomew and Associates, "A Report upon the Rezoning of the Unincorporated Portion of St. Louis County, Mo.," 10–12; Babcock, *The Zoning Game*, 27–37; General Planning and Resource Consultants, "A Comprehensive Community Plan, Creve Coeur, Missouri" (June 1969), 17–20.

71. "Public Hearing on Report of Zoning Commission, Ladue, Missouri" (1945), vol. 33, ser. 2 (Black), Bartholomew Papers; *McDermott v. Village of Calverton Park*, 447 S.W. 2d 837; 1969 Mo. App. LEXIS 736; *Deacon v. Ladue* (1963), RG 600, SC Case Files, MSA; Richard Waltke (Ladue City Planning Commission) to City Council (15 November 1945), in *Deacon v. Ladue* (1963), RG 600, SC Case Files, MSA; Transcript of Record, St. Louis Court of Appeals, 1:157–58, 180–82, 2:333, *Deacon v. Ladue* (1955), RG 600, SC Case Files, MSA.

72. Transcript of the Record, *City of Moline Acres v. Heidbreder* (1963), RG 600, SC Case Files, MSA; Testimony of Richard Riley, Transcript of Record, St. Louis Court of Appeals, 2:330, *Deacon v. Ladue* (1955), RG 600, SC Case Files, MSA.

73. Marianna Riley, "Circuit Court Judge Calls Chesterfield's Zoning Unreasonable," *SLPD*, 29 July 1999, 3.

74. Letter of Transmittal, City Plan of Brentwood (1934), vol. 4, ser. 2 (Black), Bartholomew Papers.

75. "Report upon the Master Plan, Clayton, Missouri" (1958), vol. 17, ser. 2 (Red), Bartholomew Papers; Earl Kersten and D. Reid Ross, "Clayton: A New Metropolitan Focus in the St. Louis Area," *Annals of the Association of American Geographers* 58,4 (1968), 642–45.

76. General Planning and Resource Consultants, "A Comprehensive Community Plan, Creve Coeur, Missouri" (June 1969), xiv.

77. *Flora Realty v. City of Ladue* (1952), RG 600, SC Case Files, MSA; *Flora Realty v. City of Ladue*, 362 Mo. 1025; 246 S.W. 2d 771; 1952 Mo. LEXIS 605.

78. Transcript of the Record, *City of Moline Acres v. Heidbreder* (1963), RG 600, SC Case Files, MSA; Report upon the Proposed Zoning and Subdivision Ordinance, Frontenac, Missouri (1948), vol. 21, ser. 2 (Black), Bartholomew Papers; *City of Moline Acres v. Heidbreder*, 367 SW 2d

568; 1963 Mo. App. LEXIS 792; *City of Moline Acres v. Heidbreder* (1963), RG 600, SC Case Files, MSA; Transcript of the Record, *City of Moline Acres v Heidbreder* (1963), RG 600, SC Case Files, MSA.

79. *McDermott v. Village of Calverton Park*, 447 S.W. 2d 837; 1969 Mo. App. LEXIS 736; *McDermott v. Village of Calverton Park*, 454 S.W. 2d 577; 1970 Mo. LEXIS 977; Appellant's Brief, St. Louis Court of Appeals, *McDermott v. Calverton Park* (1969), RG 600, SC Case Files, MSA, Mo.; Transcript on Appeal (1969), 722–28, in Supreme Court of Missouri, *McDermott v. Calverton Park* (1970), 55224, RG 600, SC Case Files, MSA.

80. Declaratory Judgment, *Huttig v. Richmond Heights* (1963), RG 600, SC Case Files, MSA, Mo.; *Tealin v. Ladue* (1976), 59250, RG 600, SC Case Files, MSA, Mo.; Transcript on Appeal, vol. 1, 20–22, *Huttig v. Richmond Heights* (1963), RG 600, SC Case Files, MSA, Mo.; Statement, Brief, and Argument of Appellant, *Deacon v. Ladue* (1956), RG 600, SC Case Files, MSA, Mo..

81. "Revised Comprehensive Plan [Florissant]" (1974), vol. 15, ser. 2 (Brown), Bartholomew Papers.

82. St. Louis County Planning Commission, "Multifamily Housing in St. Louis County" (1965), box 3:4, SLCDC (s73), WHMC; St. Louis County Planning Commission, "Guide for Growth: The Land-Use Plan, an Element of the St. Louis County Comprehensive Plan" (1961), 33–35; Bartholomew and Associates, "A Report upon the Rezoning of the Unincorporated Portion of St. Louis County, Mo.," 14.

83. See, for example, East-West Gateway Coordinating Council, Board of Directors (9 April 1973), box 8:192, RCGA Records, WHMC; Alex Posorske, "Hazelwood Residents Battle Developer over Use of Land," *SLPD*, 29 March 2001, 3; Janet McNichols, "Kirkwood Approves Rezoning of Meramac Highlands Property," *SLPD*, 11 April 2002, 1.

84. See Missouri Public Expenditure Survey, *Property Tax in Turmoil in Missouri* (1982), 1–4, 8–9.

85. See "A Report upon Land Use and Zoning, Ferguson, Missouri" (1956), vol. 24, ser. 2 (Red), Bartholomew Papers; United States Commission on Civil Rights (USCCR), Staff Report, "Housing in St. Louis" (1970), in USCCR, *Hearings: St. Louis* (January 1970), 538; St. Louis County Planning Commission, "Multifamily Housing in St. Louis County" (1965), and St. Louis County Department of Planning, "Apartments in St. Louis County" (1972), both in box 3:4, SLCDC (s73), WHMC; Peter O. Muller, *The Outer City: Geographical Consequences of the Urbanization of the United States* (Association of American Geographers, Resource Paper 75-2, 1975), 23; General Planning and Resource Consultants, "A Comprehensive Community Plan, Creve Coeur, Missouri" (June 1969), xiv, 15, 38–39, 106.

86. USCCR, Staff Report, "Demographic, Economic, and Social Characteristics of City of St. Louis and St. Louis County" (January 1970), USCCR, *Hearings: St. Louis* (January 1970), 30, 540–41; Ronald F. Kirby, Frank De Leeuw, and William Silverman, *Residential Zoning and Equal Housing Opportunities: A Case Study in Black Jack, Missouri* (Washington, D.C.: Urban Institute, November 1972), 5–10; General Planning and Resource Consultants, "A Comprehensive Community Plan, Creve Coeur, Missouri" (June 1969), 15.

87. On Kinloch, see "Kinloch, The Negro Municipality" (1948), box 13, and "The Negro in St. Louis" (n.d.), box 18, both in ser. 2, Urban League of St. Louis Records; "Market Analysis and Reuse Appraisal of the Maline Creek Urban Renewal Area" (1958), folder 73, box 3, and "Market Analysis and Reuse Appraisal of Meacham Park Urban Renewal Area" (1959), folder 74, box 3, both in Roy Wenzlick Papers; "Proposal for Fair Housing and Racial Reconciliation" (n.d.), box 15:688, and *U.S. v. Missouri Board of Education et al.* (1971), box 11:476, both in Freedom of Residence (FOR), Greater St. Louis Committee Records (sl509), WHMC.

88. "Preliminary Report upon Population and Other Urban Problems, Kirkwood, Missouri" (1940), vol. 31, ser. 2 (Black), and "Maryland-Euclid Shopping Center" (1955), vol. 39, ser. 2 (Red), both in Bartholomew Papers; Webster Groves map, box 12:523, FOR Records.

89. (Quote) Appellant's Brief, *Flora Realty v. City of Ladue* (1952), RG 600, SC Case Files,

MSA; (quote) Appellant's Reply Brief, *Flora Realty v. City of Ladue* (1952), RG 600, SC Case Files, MSA.

90. "Application to the Department of Housing and Urban Development for a Grant to Plan a Comprehensive City Demonstration Project" (St. Louis: Community Development Administration, 26 April 1967), 80.

91. "Answering Brief of Defendant," *Black Jack v. U.S*, 8th Circuit brief 74-1435, 10, 18.

92. Kirby, *Residential Zoning and Equal Housing*, passim.

93. Kirby, *Residential Zoning and Equal Housing*, 27–33; "Brief for the United States in Opposition," *Black Jack v. United States* 74–1293 (1974); *U.S. v. City of Black Jack* (1973), box 17: 810, FOR Records.

94. *United States v. Black Jack*, no. 71 C 372 (1), U.S. District Court for the Eastern District of Missouri, Eastern Division, 372 F. Supp. 319; 1974 U.S. Dist. LEXIS 9426; Kirby, *Residential Zoning and Equal Housing*, 25–26.

95. "Memorandum on Zoning Law," *Black Jack v. U.S.*, 8th Circuit brief 74–1435.

96. J. Mark Powell, "Fair Housing in the United States: A Legal Response to Municipal Intransigence," *University of Illinois Law Review* (1997): 290–91; *U.S. v. City of Black Jack* (1973), box 17:810, FOR Records; "Brief for the United States in Opposition," *Black Jack v. United States* 74–1293 (1974).

97. Appellees' Brief, *Park View Heights v. City of Black Jack* (1972), folder 2, Black Jack Collection, WHMC; *Park View Heights Corp. v. Black Jack*, no. 78–1660, U.S. Court of Appeals, 8th Circuit, 605 F. 2d 1033; 1979 U.S. App. LEXIS 12198.

98. *SLPD* clipping (13 January 1976), folder 12, Black Jack Collection; *Park View Heights Corp. v. Black Jack*, No. 78–1660, U.S. Court of Appeals, 8th Circuit, 605 F. 2d 1033; 1979 U.S. App. LEXIS 12198, 10 January 1979.

99. Terms of current zoning from Municode.com at http://library12.municode.com.

100. See MCDC Demographic Profile 3 Trend Report, 1990–2000 Black Jack City, Mo. 29–06004; at http://mcdc2.missouri.edu; see also E. Terrence Jones, "The Municipal Market in the St. Louis Region, 1950–2000," in *St. Louis Metromorphosis: Past Trends and Future Directions*, ed. Baybeck and Jones (St. Louis: Missouri Historical Society Press, 2004), 289.

101. For examples, see USCCR, Staff Report, "Housing in St. Louis" (1970), in USCCR, *Hearings: St. Louis* (January 1970), 556–57; Orfield, "The Housing Issues in the St. Louis Case," 84–85; Mark Schlinkmann, "Wildwood Joins Ranks of Cities at Noon Today," *SLPD*, 1 September 1995, 1A.

Chapter 4. Fighting Blight: Urban Renewal Policies and Programs, 1945–2000

Earlier versions of portions of this chapter previously appeared as "Blighting the Way: Urban Renewal, Economic Development, and the Elusive Definition of 'Blight,'" *Fordham Urban Law Journal* 31, 2 (January 2004): 305–37; reprinted by permission.

1. (Quote) "Draft Request for Matching Funds" (1971), folder 439, ser. 4 (roll 18), James Symington Papers, Western Historical Manuscript Collection (WHMC), UM-St. Louis; Howard Baer, *St. Louis to Me* (St. Louis: Hawthorn, 1978), 16; "Economic Parameters of Locating the Spanish Pavilion in St. Louis, Missouri" (1966), folder 23, Downtown St. Louis Collection (add), SL 703, WHMC.

2. See Henry Kendall to James Symington (24 November 1971); Eugene Bajnok to James Symington (16 February 1972); and "Draft Request for Matching Funds" (1971), all in folder 439, ser. 4 (roll 18), Symington Papers; "Market Analysis of Proposed Aquacenter" (1972), folder 32, Downtown St. Louis Collection (add); quote in J. Anthony Lukas, "New York World's Fair Hit Turns into St. Louis Fiasco," *New York Times*, 30 June 1970, 18; blighting study accompanying St. Louis City Ordinance 64931; at http://www.slpl.lib.mo.us/cco/ords/data/ord4931

.htm; "Three St. Louis Landmarks Saved by Owners," *New York Times* (*NYT*); 31 July 1974, 34; "Breckenridge Receives Urban Renewal Award," *St. Louis Business Journal*, 14 September 2001.

3. David Laslo, "Policy Communities and Infrastructure of Urban Tourism," *American Behavioral Scientist* 46, 8 (2003): 1074 (quote); Blighting study accompanying St. Louis City Ordinance 64931; at http://www.slpl.lib.mo.us/cco/ords/data/ord4931.htm.

4. St. Louis City Ordinance 64931; at http://www.slpl.lib.mo.us/cco/ords/data/ord4931 .htm; Charlene Prost and Jim Gallagher, "\$243 Million Plan Hinges on an Unusually Large Amount of Public Money," *SLPD*, 27 February 2000, A6; "Projects Funded" and "St. Louis Regional Empowerment Zone 2004 Annual Report to HUD," both at http://www.stlouisezone .org/projects/tax.htm; David Laslo, Claude Louisomme, Don Phares, and Dennis Judd, "Building the Infrastructure of Urban Tourism: The Case of St. Louis," in *The Infrastructure of Play: Building the Tourist City*, ed. Dennis Judd (Armonk, N.Y.: M. E. Sharpe, 2003), 82–85.

5. Robert Fogelson, *Downtown: Its Rise and Fall, 1880–1950* (New Haven, Conn.: Yale University Press, 2001), 364–65.

6. For various laundry lists of business programs, see Kenneth Langsdorf, "Recycling of Urban Land and Economic Development Policy in St. Louis" (n.d), box 14, John Poelker Papers, Washington University Archives, Clayton, Mo.; "Overall Economic Development Program" (1977), box 10:172, St. Louis Data Collection (SLDC), WHMC; E. Terrence Jones, *Fragmented by Design: Why St. Louis Has So Many Governments* (St. Louis: Palmerston and Reed, 2000), 153; CDA Working Paper (14 January 1980), box 7, ser. 3, John Conway Papers, Washington University Archives; Missouri Division of Commerce and Industrial Development, "Missouri Corporate Planner" (n.d.), box 15:452, Regional Commerce and Growth Association (RCGA) Records, WHMC; Financial Incentive Program (30 June 1980) box 7, ser. 3, Conway Papers; "Application to the Department of Housing and Urban Development for a Grant to Plan a Comprehensive City Demonstration Project" (St. Louis: Community Development Administration 1967), 246–50

7. See Joseph Heathcott and Maire Murphy, "Corridors of Flight, Zones of Renewal: Industry, Planning, and Policy in the Making of Metropolitan St. Louis, 1940–1980," *Journal of Urban History* 31, 2 (2005): 154, passim.

8. Heathcott and Murphy, "Corridors of Flight, Zones of Renewal," 153–54; (quote) "Economic Development Strategy Recommendations for the City of St. Louis" (1978), box 14:172, SLDC; Susan Kristine Walker, "The Prevalence of Blight and Brownfield Redevelopment in St. Louis" (Ph.D. dissertation, University of Missouri-St. Louis, 2003), 338–39.

9. "Expressway Plan for the St. Louis Urban Area" (1951), box 2, Milton Kinsey Papers, Washington University Archives; Raymond Mohl, "Planned Destruction: Interstates and Central City Housing," in *From Tenements to the Taylor Homes: In Search of an Urban Housing Policy in Twentieth Century America*, ed. John Bauman, Roger Biles, and Kristin Szylvain (University Park: Pennsylvania State University Press, 2000), 226–45; Gary Orfield, "The Housing Issues in the St. Louis Case," Report to Judge William Hungate, U.S. District Court (St. Louis, Mo.), *Liddell v. Board of Education* (April 1981), 47.

10. Untitled Chamber of Commerce Study (1931), folder 2, Downtown St. Louis Collection (add).

11. See "Missouri-Illinois Metropolitan Guide Plan" (1948), vol. 39, no. 2 ser. 2 (Black), Harland Bartholomew Papers, Washington University Archives; Kenneth Jackson, *Crabgrass Frontier: The Suburbanization of the United States* (New York: Oxford University Press, 1985), 174–89; *Fortune* clipping in folder 1283, St. Louis League of Women Voters Records (sl530), WHMC; "Report on a Comprehensive System of Highways, St. Louis County" (1943), vol. 53, no. 2, ser. 2 (Black), Bartholomew Papers; Mark Gelfand, *A Nation of Cities: The Federal Government and Urban America, 1933–1965* (New York: Oxford University Press, 1975), 224–28; Jon Teaford, *The Rough Road to Renaissance: Urban Revitalization in America* (Baltimore: Johns Hopkins University Press, 1990), 162–65.

12. See "Preliminary Report on Proposed Parking Garages for the St. Louis Central Business

District" (1945), vol. 52, ser. 2 (Black), Bartholomew Papers; "The Central Business District (Adequate Parking Facilities)," *Comprehensive City Plan, 1947*, archived at http://stlouis.missouri .org/government/docs/1947plan; "General Neighborhood Renewal Plan, University City" (1962), folder 68, box 3, Roy Wenzlick Papers, WHMC; Russell, Mullgardt, Schwarz, Van Hoefen, "Study for a Comprehensive Plan for Redevelopment of the Central City Area" (1953), box 8, ser. 1, Raymond R. Tucker Papers, Washington University Archives.

13. "Plan for the Central River Front" (1928) folder 1, Downtown St. Louis Collection (add), SL 703, WHMC; Willis Hadley to Richard Amberg (30 January 1957), box 12, ser. 1; Russell, Mullgardt, Schwarz, Van Hoefen, "Study for a Comprehensive Plan for Redevelopment of the Central City Area" (1953), box 8, ser. 1; Sidney Baer to Tucker (29 January 1954), box 12, ser. 1; and "Staff Recommendations: Daniel Boone Expressway" (1954) box 12, ser. 1, all in Tucker Papers.

14. See Virgil Tipton, "The Way West: Highway 40 Grew in Fits and Starts," *SLPD*, 19 September 1994; City Plan Commission to Frank McDevitt (15 April 1955), box 12, ser. 1; "Review of Expressway Progress in St. Louis City and County Since 1934" (1954), box 13, ser. 1; and Russell, Mullgardt, Schwarz, Van Hoefen, "Study for a Comprehensive Plan for Redevelopment of the Central City Area" (1953), box 8, ser. 1, all in Tucker Papers.

15. Robert Duffe to Robert Sullivan (13 June 1958), box 13, ser. 2, Tucker Papers; Harry Levins, "Interstate Highways," *SLPD*, 13 January 2004; "Summary of Progress in St. Louis in 1960" (1961), box 5, ser. 2, Tucker Papers.

16. James Ford to Walter Head (Anti-Slum Commission) (26 May 1948), reel 11, Correspondence Files, Bartholomew Papers.

17. Barbara J. Flint, "Zoning and Residential Segregation: A Social and Physical History, 1910–1940" (Ph.D. dissertation, University of Chicago, 1977), 43–44; Eric Sandweiss, *St. Louis: The Evolution of an American Urban Landscape* (Philadelphia: Temple University Press, 2001), 208–21, 224–25; Teaford, *Rough Road to Renaissance*, 32–33.

18. For this background, see Philip Funigiello, *The Challenge to Urban Liberalism: Federal-City Relations During World War II* (Knoxville: University of Tennessee Press, 1978), 223–28; Statement on Public Policy for Slum Clearance" (1943), reel 11, Correspondence Files, Bartholomew Papers; David Beatty et al., *Redevelopment in California* (Point Arena, Calif.: Solano Press, 1991), 2; Fogelson, *Downtown: Its Rise and Fall*, 339–40, 358–59.

19. Peter Eisinger, *The Rise of the Entrepreneurial State: State and Local Economic Development Policy in the United States* (Madison: University of Wisconsin Press, 1988), 148–49; Fogelson, *Downtown: Its Rise and Fall*, 337, 341–43; Beatty et al., *Redevelopment in California*, 2–3; Daniel Mandelker, Gary Feder, and Margaret Collins, *Reviving Cities with Tax Abatement* (New Brunswick, N.J.: Rutgers University Center for Urban Policy Research, 1980), 2.

20. Martha Shull, "Chapter 353 Property Tax Abatements" (Jefferson City, Mo.: Missouri Division of Budget and Planning, 1981), 1–2; Mandelker et al., *Reviving Cities with Tax Abatement*, 13; Missouri Municipal Review clippings (1977), box 38, ser. 2, Conway Papers; "Overall Economic Development Program" (1977), box 10:172, SLDC; Margaret Collins, *Chapter 353: A Policy Study for Existing and Future Application* (St. Louis Community Development Administration, 1978), 2; Robert Olson, "Critical Analysis of Missouri's URC Law" (1975), box 16, Poelker Papers.

21. City Plan Commission, "Rebuilding Industry and Commerce in St. Louis," (1960?), box 8, ser. 1, Tucker Papers; Eldridge Lovelace, *Harland Bartholomew: His Contributions to American Urban Planning* (Urbana: Department of Urban and Regional Planning, University of Illinois, 1992), 103–17; Teaford, *Rough Road to Renaissance*, 27; Mandelker, *Reviving Cities with Tax Abatement*, 12; "Visits to Eastern Insurance Companies" (December 1945), reel 11, Correspondence Files, Bartholomew Papers; Eisinger, *Rise of the Entrepreneurial State*, 149; Kaufman quoted in Robert Olson, "Critical Analysis of Missouri's URC Law" (1975), box 16, Poelker Papers.

22. "Housing (Obsolete Areas)," *Comprehensive City Plan, 1947*, archived at http://stlouis .missouri.org/government/docs/1947plan.

23. Rachelle L. Levitt, *Cities Reborn* (Washington, D.C.: Urban Land Institute, 1987), quote 163; Gelfand, *A Nation of Cities*, 143–45, 153; Beatty et al., *Redevelopment in California*, 3–4; Mandelker et al., *Reviving Cities with Tax Abatement*, 2–3; John Quigley, "A Decent Home: Housing Policy in Perspective," *Brookings-Wharton Papers on Urban Affairs* (2000): 74–75; miscellaneous memoranda in box 32, ser. 2; and C. L. Farris to Granville Moore (7 August 1956), box 13, ser. 1, both in Tucker Papers.

24. Mandelker et a., *Reviving Cities with Tax Abatement*, 15–16.

25. Tucker to Stuart Symington (24 April 1953), box 13, ser. 1, Tucker Papers; Gelfand, *A Nation of Cities*, 175, 185–87.

26. Collins, *Chapter 353*, 3; Levitt, *Cities Reborn*, 162; Robert Olson, "Critical Analysis of Missouri's URC Law" (1975), box 16, Poelker Papers; St. Louis Development Program, "Technical Report on History of Renewal" (1971), 51–52; Mandelker et al., *Reviving Cities with Tax Abatement*, 13–14; Mo. Rev. Stat. 353.20 (2) 2001.

27. Shull, "Chapter 353 Property Tax Abatements," 2; Testimony of James Sporleder (1973), in box 16:743, Freedom of Residence (FOR), Greater St. Louis Committee Records, (sl509), WHMC; Collins, *Chapter 353*, 18–19.

28. Collins, *Chapter 353*, 2–3, 8; Mandelker et al., *Reviving Cities with Tax Abatement*, 3–4, 14–15.

29. Collins, *Chapter 353*, 25–26. A full historical inventory of Chapter 353 and Chapter 99 parcels is quite complicated. The City's own record keeping has been sporadic. At any point in time, some areas were undergoing redevelopment, some had been blighted but attracted no redevelopment, some were in the planning stages, and some had designations that had long expired. In many instances projects were merely variations on older projects or fell under programmatic overlap with other redevelopment statutes. The following sketch (and maps) rely upon St. Louis Development Program, "Technical Report on History of Renewal" (1971); St. Louis Urban Renewal Map (1981), St. Louis Maps and Guidebooks (M-153), Mercantile Library, UM-St. Louis; City of St. Louis Community Development Agency, *Chapter 353 Status Report, 1988* (1989); Mandelker et al., *Reviving Cities with Tax Abatement*, 27–29; and Levitt, *Cities Reborn* (1987).

30. Mandelker et al., *Reviving Cities with Tax Abatement*, 27–29; Levitt, *Cities Reborn*, 163–64; City of St. Louis Community Development Agency, *Chapter 353 Status Report, 1988* (1989), 6–8.

31. Daniel J. Monti, *Race, Redevelopment, and the New Company Town* (Albany: SUNY Press, 1990), 25–32; Charles Kindleberger (St. Louis CDA) to author (e-mail, May 2005).

32. "Plan for Redevelopment of Gateway Mall" (1982), folder 59, Downtown St. Louis Collection (add); "Slum Clearance and Redevelopment Activities" (July 1950), box 24, ser. 1; Minutes, LCRA Board of Commissioners (10 June 1954), box 14, ser. 1; "Report of Clifford Gaylord" (1 December 1950), and misc. Urban Redevelopment Corporation files (1950–51), box 24, ser. 1, all in Tucker Papers; Collins, *Chapter 353*, 15–16; "Facts About Urban Renewal in St. Louis" (n.d.), box 15, ser. 3, all in Tucker Papers; Robert Olson, "Critical Analysis of Missouri's URC Law" (1975), box 16, Poelker Papers; St. Louis Development Program, "Technical Report on History of Renewal" (1971), 5–6.

33. Robert Olson, "Critical Analysis of Missouri's URC Law" (1975), box 16, Poelker Papers; Collins, *Chapter 353*, 16–17; Shull, "Chapter 353 Property Tax Abatements," 4; *SLPD*, 14 October 1941, 3A.

34. Mill Creek added the 138-acre Mill Creek North area in 1969; Kosciusko refined its boundaries in 1970, 1973, 1978, 1986, and 1999. See LCRA, "Mill Creek North Urban Renewal Plan (1969); Amended Redevelopment Plan for Kosciusko, LCRA 413, Ordinance 64976 (1999).

35. C. L. Farris to Granville Moore (7 August 1956), box 13, ser. 1, Tucker Papers; St. Louis Development Program, "Technical Report on History of Renewal" (1971), 12–15, 18–20; "Facts About Urban Renewal in St. Louis" (n.d.), box 15, ser. 3; Mill Creek Valley Urban Renewal Plan, Project MO R-1: Mill Creek Valley (15 March 1957), box 13, ser. 1; Kosciusko

Urban Renewal Plan, Project MO R-2, box 16, ser. 2; and Minutes, LCRA Board of Commissioners (7 July 1954), box 14, ser. 1, all in Tucker Papers; Heathcott and Murphy, "Corridors of Flight, Zones of Renewal," 159–63.

36. Bernard Frieden and Lynne Sagalyn, *Downtown Inc.: How American Rebuilds Cities* (Cambridge, Mass.: Harvard University Press, 1989), 43–44; Memo Re: Mill Creek Valley (21 May 1956), box 13, ser. 1, Tucker Papers; St. Louis Development Program, "Technical Report on History of Renewal" (1971), 14, 21; Maire Murphy, "National Policy, Local Initiatives, and Industrial Redevelopment in America's 'Rustbelt': Revitalizing Mill Creek Valley in Post WWII St. Louis" (Paper presented at the Policy History Conference, St. Louis, 2002); Comptroller General of the United States, *Inadequate Relocation Assistance to Families Displaced from Certain Urban Renewal Projects in Kansas and Missouri* (June 1964), 5, 10.

37. Collins, *Chapter 353*, 17–20; Robert Olson, "Critical Analysis of Missouri's URC Law" (1975), box 16, Poelker Papers; Laslo et al., "Building the Infrastructure of Urban Tourism: The Case of St. Louis," 90–91; St. Louis Development Program, "Technical Report on History of Renewal" (1971); LCRA, "Downtown Sports Stadium Project Redevelopment Plan" (1961) and O. O. McCracken to David Hemenway (19 October 1960), both in box 32, ser. 2, Tucker Papers.

38. Levitt, *Cities Reborn*, 188.

39. Robert Olson, "Critical Analysis of Missouri's URC Law" (1975), box 16, Poelker Papers; Collins, *Chapter 353*, 19–22; Laslo et al., "Building the Infrastructure of Urban Tourism: The Case of St. Louis," 90–91.

40. St. Louis Development Program, "Technical Report on History of Renewal" (1971), 34–37; "Facts About Urban Renewal in St. Louis" (n.d.), box 15, ser. 3, Tucker Papers; HUD to Charles Farris (29 September 1971) and HUD, "Report on West End Urban Renewal Project" (December 1971), both in box 52, ser. 2, Alfonso J. Cervantes Papers, Washington University Archives; Monti, *Race, Redevelopment, and the New Company Town*, 30–32; HUD to Cervantes (30 January 1973), box 52A, ser. 2, Cervantes Papers.

41. "Facts About Urban Renewal in St. Louis" (n.d.), box 15, ser. 3, Tucker Papers; "Nov. 8, 1966 Bond Election" (n.d.), box 5, ser. 2, Cervantes Papers; HUD, *Urban Renewal Directory* (June 1974), 132.

42. St. Louis Development Program, "Technical Report on History of Renewal" (1971), 38–39; DeSoto-Carr file; "Economic Development Planning Analysis: DeSoto-Carr Urban Renewal Project Area" (1968), both in box 32, ser. 1, Cervantes Papers; "Kingsbury and Forest Village Redevelopment Corporations" (July 1975), box 16, Poelker Papers; "North Side Redevelopment Opportunities" (1963), folder 16, Downtown St. Louis Collection (add).

43. Heathcott and Murphy, "Corridors of Flight, Zones of Renewal," 165–70.

44. St. Louis City Plan Commission, "A New Town in the City of St. Louis" (1973), box 15:456, RCGA Records; St. Louis Redevelopment Authority, *Annual Report 1974*; Levitt, *Cities Reborn*, 181–82; "New Town In-Town Redevelopment Corporation Proposal" (June 1975), box 16, Poelker Papers.

45. "North Side Redevelopment Opportunities" (1963), folder 16; "Redevelopment Plan: St. Louis Core Retail Area" (1970), folder 29, both in Downtown St. Louis Collection (add); Laslo et al., "Building the Infrastructure of Urban Tourism: The Case of St. Louis," 85–88; "Union Station Historic District," Ordinance 57878 (April 1979).

46. See Laslo et al., "Building the Infrastructure of Urban Tourism: The Case of St. Louis," 82–96.

47. Land Clearance for Redevelopment Authority of University City, "A New Vision for University City" (1963?), 3–4.

48. USCCR Staff Report, "Housing in St. Louis" (1970), box 3:127, FOR Records; Maline Creek Urban Renewal Plan (1958), box 3, Roy Wenzlick Papers, WHMC.

49. Advisory Commission on Intergovernmental Relations, *Industrial Development Bond Financing* (1965), box 12:405, RCGA Records; Eisinger, *The Rise of the Entrepreneurial State*, 158; Reid

Ross to Herbert Sampson (Northern Natural Gas) (31 July 1967), box 10:296, RCGA Records; Thomas Moore and Gregory Squires, "Public Policy and Private Benefits: The Case of Industrial Revenue Bonds," in *Business Elites and Urban Development*, ed. Scott Cummings (Albany: SUNY Press, 1988), 101; (quote) Reid Ross (RIDC) to Stuart Symington (29 June 1966), box 7:163, RCGA Records; "Economic Development Planning Analysis: DeSoto-Carr Urban Renewal Project Area" (1968), box 32, ser. 1, Cervantes Papers.

50. See Mo. Rev. Stat., Chapter 349, Industrial Development Corporations.

51. "Financing for Industry in Missouri" (1979), box 1, Division of Economic Development Records, Missouri State Archives, Jefferson City; Kenneth Langsdorf, "Legal Chronology of the PIE Problem" (7 September 1973), box 16, Poelker Papers; "Overall Economic Development Program" (1977), box 10:172, SLDC; *Missouri Municipal Review* clippings (1977), box 38, ser. 2, Conway Papers; Robert Renard to Poelker (2 June 1976), box 64, Poelker Papers; "Petition Regarding the Blighting Ordinance to the PIEA for the Central Industrial Corridor" (1980), box 11, Lafayette Square Restoration Committee Records, Mercantile Library, UM-St. Louis; "Tax Increment Blighting Analysis and Redevelopment Plan for the Scullin Redevelopment Project Area" (St. Louis: St. Louis Economic Development Corporation, 1990), 28.

52. St. Louis Planned Industrial Expansion Authority, *1977 Annual Report* (1977), 3–5; PIE Authority Annual Report (1976), box 64, Poelker Papers; "Overall Economic Development Program" (1977), box 10:172, SLDC; Levitt, *Cities Reborn*, 162.

53. "Hall Street Industrial Area Development Plan" (1980); "Hall Street Industrial Area-Extension 1 Industrial Development Plan" (1981), "Blighting Study and Plan for the Gravois/Salena Area" (1988), "Blighting Study and Plan for North Broadway/North Market Area" (1990), "Blighting Study and Plan for North Broadway/E. Taylor Area" (1990), all provided by Charles Kindleberger at CDA; PIEA, "The Jefferson-Sidney Commercial/Industrial Area Development Plan" (1988), SLPL; "Hereford Street Industrial Development Plan" (1973), and "Manchester-Chouteau Industrial Development Plan" (1974), both in *Ex Rel Atkinson v. Planned Industrial Expansion Authority of St. Louis*, RG 600, Supreme Court Judicial Case Files, Missouri State Archives, Jefferson City.

54. See "Zoning" in 1947 City Plan at http://stlouis.missouri.org/government/docs/1947plan/landuse.html; City Plan Commission, "Rebuilding Industry and Commerce in St. Louis," (1960?), box 8, ser. 1, Tucker Papers; "St. Louis County Economic Development Report" (1982), box 16:193, SLDC; "Projects Funded" at http://www.stlouisezone.org/projects/commercial.htm; Survey of Potential Industrial Sites" (n.d.), box 2, Milton Kinsey Papers, Washington University Archives; Reid Ross to Eugene Moody (10 November 1973), box 8:191, RCGA Records; Booz, Allen and Hamilton, Inc., *Proposal to Develop and Implement an Industrial Land Inventory System: City of St. Louis* (St. Louis: Community Development Administration, 1979).

55. Peter O. Muller, *The Outer City: Geographical Consequences of the Urbanization of the United States*, Resource Paper 75–2 (Washington, D.C.: Association of American Geographers, 1975), 34.

56. "Overall Economic Development Program" (1977), box 10:172, SLDC.

57. On Columbia Bottoms, see "The St. Louis County Bond Election" (1963), box 1:9, SLDC; Reid Ross, "Columbia Bottoms Industrial Park" (1963), box 14:79, St. Louis League of Women Voters Records; appraisals and reports in "Columbia Bottoms" file, box 10, ser. 2, Tucker Papers; Arthur Little to John Kerr (21 August 1959), box 2, Kinsey Papers; Chamber of Commerce to Tucker (23 May 1956), box 8, ser. 1, Tucker Papers; RIDC Executive Committee Meeting (23 November 1965) box 8:215, RCGA Records; Roy Wenzlick, "Consultation Report" (May 1972), box 26 , ser. 2, Cervantes Papers.

58. "Economic Development Subsystem" (9 January 1966) box 9:272, RCGA Records; Kenneth Langsdorf, "Recycling of Urban Land and Economic Development Policy in St. Louis" (n.d), box 14, Poelker Papers.

59. "St. Louis Venture Capital (Working Copy)" (5 Dec. 1967), box 12:403, RCGA Records.

60. Bernard Frieden and Marshall Kaplan, *The Politics of Neglect: Urban Aid from Model Cities to Revenue Sharing* (Cambridge, Mass.: MIT Press, 1975), 4–6, 14–29; Quigley, "A Decent Home: Housing Policy in Perspective," 76; Howard Richards, "A Comparison of the Model Cities Programs of St. Louis and Kansas City, Missouri (Ph.D. dissertation, University of Missouri-Columbia, 1972), 1–13; Dennis Judd, "Strong Leadership," *Urban Studies* 37, 5/6 (May 2000): 952–54.

61. Lucius Cervantes, "Confidential Memorandum" (13 July 1965), box 9:272, RCGA Records; Richards, "A Comparison of the Model Cities Programs of St. Louis and Kansas City, Missouri," 118–19; "Application to the Department of Housing and Urban Development for a Grant to Plan a Comprehensive City Demonstration Project" (26 April 1967), 1–2, 25, 37–39; Confidential Discussion Paper (n.d.), box 10:275, RCGA Records; HUD, "Opportunities to Improve the Model Cities Program in Kansas City and St. Louis, Missouri, and New Orleans, Louisiana" (Washington, D.C.: GPO, 1973), 12–13.

62. "Application to the Department of Housing and Urban Development for a Grant to Plan a Comprehensive City Demonstration Project," passim; *St. Louis Model City Program* (December 1968), 11–12, 21; *NYT* clipping (5 June 1967), box 10:275, RCGA Records; Confidential Discussion Paper (n.d.), box 10:275, RCGA Records; HUD, "Opportunities to Improve the Model Cities Program in Kansas City and St. Louis, Missouri, and New Orleans, Louisiana," 20; Andrew Hurley, "Draft of Text for Historical Markers on Old North St. Louis History Trail," at http://www.umsl.edu/~ahurley/poi.htm.

63. Between 1978 and 1985, the City received just under $80 million in Action Grants. See Levitt, *Cities Reborn*, 162.

64. Richard Nathan et al., *Block Grants for Community Development* (HUD, 1977), 22–23, 26, 78–79, 122–26; HUD, *Fifth Annual CBDG Report* (1980), 10:1–4; Quigley, "A Decent Home: Housing Policy in Perspective," 79–80; Mandelker, *Reviving Cities with Tax Abatement*, 3; Kenneth Finegold, Laura Wherry, and Stephanie Schardin, "Block Grants: Historical Overview and Lessons Learned," Series on New Federalism, A-63 (Urban Institute, 2004), at http://www.urban.org/url.cfm?ID=310991.

65. "Program Gave City Officials, Residents a Say in Spending," *SLPD*, 8 December 1991, 18A; (quote) Donald Spaid to Conway (6 September 1977), box 4, ser. 3, Conway Papers; "Opportunity Denied: St. Louis Uses Money Targeted for Housing for the Poor to Aid Wealthier Neighborhoods," *SLPD*, 8 December 1991, 1A.

66. (Schoemehl quoted) "Opportunity Denied: St. Louis Uses Money Targeted for Housing for the Poor to Aid Wealthier Neighborhoods," *SLPD*, 8 December 1991, 1A; "City Shifts Focus of HOME Aid: Federal Funds Go to Middle Class," *SLPD*, 19 December 1989, 1A; "KC Gets Less U.S. Money, Builds More Housing," *SLPD*, 11 December 1991, 18A.

67. Carl Fox to CDA (10 April 1978), box 4, ser. 3; Legal Services of Eastern Missouri, "Formal Objections to St. Louis City Year VI Block Grant Application" (1979), box 1, ser. 3, both in Conway Papers; "CDBG Housing Working Paper" (18 September 1977), folder 6; "Community Development: Where Has All the Money Gone?" (1978), folder 6; "Community Development Block Grants" (1977), folder 6; "Central Richmond Heights" file, folder 31, all in ACORN (St. Louis) Records, WHMC; HUD, *Community Development Programs: State Reports* (1988), 135–36; HUD, *UDAG First Annual Report* (1977), 91; HUD, *UDAG Second Annual Report* (1978), B14; "Opportunity Denied," 1A; "Spent Effort: City, HUD at Loggerheads over Charges of Misuses of Federal Block Grant Funds," *SLPD*, 9 December 1991, 1A.

68. Julie Goshorn, "In a TIF: Why Missouri Needs Tax Increment Financing Reform," *Washington University Law Quarterly* 77 (1999): 925–28; "Tax Increment Blighting Analysis and Redevelopment Plan for the Scullin Redevelopment Project Area" (St. Louis Economic Development Corporation, 1990), 2; Beatty, *Redevelopment in California*, 6–7; Craig L. Johnson and Kenneth A. Kriz, "A Review of State Tax Increment Financing Laws," in *Tax Increment Financing and Economic Development*, ed. Craig L. Johnson and Joyce Y. Man (Albany: SUNY Press, 2001), 35–36.

69. Mo. Chapter 99 (see sects. 805 and 810) at http://www.moga.state.mo.us/statutes/

C099.htm; "Tax Increment Blighting Analysis and Redevelopment Plan for the Scullin Redevelopment Project Area" (St. Louis Economic Development Corporation, 1990), 1; Josh Reinert, "Tax-Increment Financing in Missouri: Is it Time for Blight and But-For to Go?" *St. Louis University Law Journal* 45 (2001): 1019; Kenneth Hubbell and Peter Eaton, "Tax Increment Financing in the State of Missouri," MSCDC Economic Report no. 9073 (June 1997), 2–3; SLDC, "Keeping St. Louis in Business" (1997), 5; John Mikesell, "Nonproperty Tax Increment Programs for Economic Development," in Johnson and Man, *Tax Increment Financing and Economic Development*, 64, 68; "Missouri House Panel Targets Tax Incentives," *SLPD*, 18 September 1998.

70. Goshorn, "In a TIF," 931–4; Mo. Rev. Stat. 99.835.5 (2001).

71. Thomas F. Luce, *Reclaiming the Intent: Tax-Increment Financing in the Kansas City and St. Louis Metropolitan Areas* (Washington, D.C.: Brookings Institution Center on Urban and Metropolitan Policies, 2003); Missouri Department of Economic Development, *Tax Increment Financing in Missouri: 2004 Annual Report* (2005), at http://ded.mo.gov/cd/pdfs/2004TIFAnnual Report.pdf.

72. Goshorn, "In a TIF," 919–20; "Eureka Considers Big Break for Mall," *SLPD*, 2 September 1997, 1B; "Residents Oppose TIF Plan," *SLPD*, 10 May 1998, A6; "Developers Seek Huge Tax Breaks from Olivette," *SLPD*, 21 May 1998, D1; (quote) "A Tale of Two TIFs," *SLPD*, 20 February 2003, B6; "Rep. Stokan Targets Subsidy for Rich Areas," *SLPD*, 20 April 1998, B2; "So West County Mall Is Blighted Property?" *SLPD*, 29 July 1998, B7; "A Winner Is Declared in Suburban Mall War," *SLPD*, 3 October 1999, E1; "Opponents See Nothing to Celebrate in New Mall," *SLPD*, 22 September 2002, B1.

73. "Tax Increment Blighting Analysis and Redevelopment Plan for the Scullin Redevelopment Project Area" (St. Louis Economic Development Corporation, 1990), 2; D. J. Wilson, "Wal-Mart World," *Riverfront Times*, 20 November 2002; Linda Tucci, "City Helping Marketplace," *St. Louis Business Journal*, 27 December 1996.

74. Reinert, "Tax-Increment Financing in Missouri," 1019–20; "Missouri House OKs Legislation," *SLPD*, 22 March 2002, B3; "Blight Made Right," *SLPD*, 25 March 2002, B6; Greg Leroy, "Subsidizing Sprawl: How Economic Development Programs Are Going Awry" *Multinational Monitor* 24:10 (October 2003).

75. See Mo. Rev. Stat. 135:215; St. Louis Development Corporation summary at http://stlou is.missouri.org/sldc/busdev/eztax.html; Senate Bill 1155 (Jobs Now Act) at http://www.sen ate.mo.gov/04info/pdf-bill/tat/sb1155.pdf; "Enterprise Zones Trigger Political Dispute; Competition Keen Among Counties," *SLPD*, 6 May 1991, 1B; St. Louis Development Corporation, *SLDC*: "Keeping St. Louis in Business" (St. Louis: SLDC, 1997), 2.

76. HUD Office of Program Analysis and Evaluation, *State-Designated Enterprise Zones: Ten Case Studies* (Washington, D.C.: GPO, 1986), 126–34; "Enterprise Zones v. UDAG," *SLPD*, 8 March 1989, 2E; "Area Near Old GM Plant is Targeted," *SLPD*, 24 July 1989, 11; "Enterprise Zones Trigger Political Dispute," *SLPD*, 6 May 1991, 1B; "Enterprise Zone Near Airport Targets Ford," *SLPD*, 12 September 2003), C1; "Ferguson OKs Enterprise Zone," *SLPD*, 1 September 2003, 1.

77. (Quote) "Area Near Old GM Plant Is Targeted as First 'Satellite' Enterprise Zone" *SLPD*, 24 July 1989, 11; Peter Fisher and Alan Peters, "Tax and Spending Incentives and Enterprise Zones," *New England Economic Review* (March/April 1997), 120–23.

78. See Background documents at http://www.stlouisezone.org/about/history.htm.

Chapter 5. City of Blight: The Limits of Urban Renewal in Greater St. Louis

Earlier versions of portions of this chapter previously appeared in "Blighting the Way: Urban Renewal, Economic Development, and the Elusive Definition of 'Blight'," *Fordham Urban Law Journal* 31, 2 (January 2004): 305–37; reprinted by permission.

1. See Gordon, "Blighting the Way"; Jonathan M. Purver, Annotation, "What Constitutes 'Blighted Area' Within Urban Renewal and Redevelopment Statutes," *A.L.R.* 45,3 § 2(a)

(1972):1096; Julie A. Goshorn, "In a TIF: Why Missouri Needs a Tax Increment Financing Reform," *Washington University Law Quarterly* 77 (1999): 919, 922–26.

2. Robert Fogelson, *Downtown: Its Rise and Fall, 1880–1950* (New Haven, Conn.: Yale University Press, 2001), 320, 323 (quoting E. R. L. Gould, "The Housing Problem," *Municipal Affairs* (March 1899): 109; Jacob Riis, *How the Other Half Lives* (New York: Hill and Wang, 1957 [1890], 1–3 (quoting 1863 testimony of a New York prison official).

3. Fogelson, *Downtown: Its Rise and Fall*, 160–66, 320–56; Keith D. Revell, "The Road to Euclid v. Ambler: City Planning, State-Building, and the Changing Scope of the Police Power," *Studies in American Political Development* 13 (1999): 50, 51.

4. Mabel Walker, *Urban Blight and Slums* (Cambridge, Mass.: Harvard University Press, 1938) (quotes, 1, 2, 8); Fogelson, *Downtown: Its Rise and Fall*, 354–58; Revell, "The Road to Euclid v. Ambler," 51; Edith Elmer Wood, *Slums and Blighted Areas in the United States*, Housing Division Bulletin 1 (Washington, D.C.: GPO, 1935), 3–4; Clarence Perry, *The Rebuilding of Blighted Areas* (Chicago: Regional Plan Association, 1933), 8.

5. Fogelson, *Downtown: Its Rise and Fall*, 347–48; Walker, *Urban Blight and Slums*, 17; Mark Gelfand, *A Nation of Cities: The Federal Government and Urban America, 1933–1965* (New York: Oxford University Press, 1975), 109–11.

6. See City Plan Commission, *Urban Land Policy* (1936); City Plan Commission, *Saint Louis After World War II* (1942), 18, pl. 9.

7. Gail Radford, *Modern Housing for America: Policy Struggles in the New Deal Era* (Chicago: University of Chicago Press, 1996), 189–90, 340; 12 U.S.C. §§ 1702 et seq. (1937) (amended 1941); Fogelson, *Downtown: Its Rise and Fall*, 364–66, 378; David Beatty et al., *Redevelopment in California* (Point Arena, Calif.: Solano Press, 1991), 2–3; Jeffrey I. Chapman, "Tax Increment Financing and Fiscal Stress," in *Tax Increment Financing and Economic Development*, ed. Craig Johnson and Joyce Man (Albany: SUNY Press, 2001), 114.

8. See *Mo. Ann. Stat.* § 99.805 (West 1982) (amended 1986, 1997); Jon C. Teaford, Urban Renewal and Its Aftermath, *Housing Policy Debate* 11, 2 (2000): 443, 459; Josh Reinert, "Tax-Increment Financing in Missouri: Is it Time for Blight and But-For to Go?" *St. Louis University Law Journal* 45 (2001): 1024–25, 1046–47; Goshorn, "In a TIF," 922, 928–29; Rules of the Department of Economic Development, Division of Community and Economic Development, Enterprise Zone Program" (2001), at http://www.sos.mo.gov/adrules/csr/current/4csr/4c85–3.pdf.

9. City Plan Commission, "St. Louis Urban Redevelopment Project no. 1," (St. Louis Public Library, 1951) 14–15.

10. Alan Voorhees and Associates, "Survey and Analysis of Industrial Facilities" (1970), box 9:129, St. Louis Data Collection (SLDC) (s557), Western Historical Manuscripts Collection (WHMC), UM-St. Louis; Alan Voorhees and Associates, "Technical Report on a Residential Blight Analysis for St. Louis, Missouri" (1969), box 9:125, SLDC; Des Peres officials quoted in "Opponents See Nothing to Celebrate in New Mall," *SLPD*, 22 September 2002, B1.

11. Brief of Respondent, *Allright Parking. v Civic Plaza Redevelopment* (1975), 59180, RG 600, Supreme Court Judicial Case Files (SC Case Files), Missouri State Archives, Jefferson City.

12. Relator's Brief, *Atkinson v. Planned Industrial Expansion Authority of St. Louis* (1974), 58660, RG 600, SC Case Files.

13. Case law quoted here includes Brief of Respondent, *Annbar v. West Side Redevelopment Corporation* (1965), 51108, RG 600, SC Case Files (italics added); *Annbar Assoc. v. W. Side Redevelopment Corp.*, 397 S.W. 2d 635, 643, 646 (Mo. 1965) (citing *State v. Land Clearance Redevelopment Auth. of Kansas City*, 270 S.W. 2d 44, 53 [Mo. 1954]); Transcript on Appeal, 248, 651, *Land Clearance for Redevelopment Authority of the City of St. Louis v. St. Louis* (1954), 44430, RG 600, SC Case Files; *Schweig v. City of St. Louis and Maryland Plaza Redevelopment Corporation*, St. Louis Court of Appeals (1978) RG 600, SC Case Files; Brief of Respondent, *Atkinson v. Planned Industrial Expansion Authority of St. Louis* (1974), 58660, RG 600, SC Case Files.

14. Transcript on Appeal, 130–3, *Allright Parking v. Civic Plaza Redevelopment* (1975), 59180, RG 600, SC Case Files.

15. See dissent (O'Connor), concurring opinion (Kennedy), and opinion (Stevens) in *Susette Kelo et al., Petitioners v. City of New London et al.*, Supreme Court of the United States, no. 04–108, On Writ of Certiorari to the Supreme Court of Connecticut (23 June 2005).

16. Goshorn, "In a TIF," 922–23; Reinert, "Tax Increment Financing in Missouri," 1033–34, 1047–48; "Measuring Deterioration in Commercial and Industrial Areas" (1957), box 8:105, SLDC.

17. As of 2004, only seven states—Alabama, Arkansas, California, Massachusetts, Minnesota, Nebraska, and South Dakota—held the designation of "blighted area" to any quantifiable standard. See Ala. Code § 11–99–4 (1975); Ark. Code Ann. § 14–168–301 (Michie 2001); Cal. Health & Safety Code § 33030.1(b) (West 1999); Mass. Gen. Laws Ann. Ch. 121B, § 1 (West 2003); Minn. Stat. Ann. § 469.002 (West 2001); Neb. Rev. Stat. 13–1101 (2003); S.D. Codified Laws § 11–7-3 (Michie 2003); see also Johnson and Kriz, "A Review of State Tax Increment Financing Laws," in Johnson and Man, *Tax Increment Financing and Economic Development*, 38–39. But such standards generally only control the scale of the TIF or redevelopment region by requiring that a certain percentage of properties within the region are—in what is still a highly subjective determination—"blighted." Alabama, for example, requires that "Not less than 50 percent, by area, of the real property within the tax increment district is a blighted area and is in need of rehabilitation." Ala. Code § 11–99–4; see also Johnson and Kriz, "A Review of State Tax Increment Financing Laws," 38–39.

18. Martha Shull, "Chapter 353 Property Tax Abatements" (Missouri Division of Budget and Planning, 1981), 2–3; Alan Voorhees and Associates, "Technical Report on a Residential Blight Analysis for St. Louis, Missouri" (1969), box 9:125, SLDC; *Parking Sys., Inc. v. Kansas City Downtown Redevelopment Corp.*, 518 S.W. 2d 11, 16 (Mo. 1974); Environmental Response, "Blight? Right!" (1973), box 31:154, St. Louis League of Women Voters Records (sl234), WHMC.

19. Reinert, "Tax-Increment Financing in Missouri," 1039–42; Daniel Mandelker, Gary Feder, and Margaret Collins, *Reviving Cities with Tax Abatement* (New Brunswick, N.J.: Center for Urban Policy Research, 1980), 83–95; for the case law, see *Allright Mo., Inc. v. Civic Plaza Redevelopment Corp.*, 538 S.W. 2d 320, 324 (Mo. 1976); *Parking Sys., Inc. v. Kansas City Downtown Redevelopment Corp.*, 518 S.W. 2d 11, 15 (Mo. 1974); *Schweig v. St. Louis*, 569 S.W. 2d 215, 223 (Mo. Ct. App. 1978); *Allright Parking v. Civic Plaza Redevelopment* (1975), 59180, RG 600, SC Case Files. *Dalton* cited in Brief of Respondent (City of St. Louis), *Atkinson v. Planned Industrial Expansion Authority of St. Louis* (1974), 58660, RG 600, SC Case Files.

20. Quotes from "Analysis of Missouri's URC Law" (1975), box 16, John Poelker Papers, Washington University Archives, Clayton, Mo.; Robert Renard to Poelker (2 June 1976), box 64, Poelker Papers; Arthur Denzau and Charles Leven, "Report on Alternative Revenue Sources: Local Revenue Generation" (St. Louis Board of Education Community Advisory Committee, 1985), 5:7–8; SLDC, "Keeping St. Louis in Business," (1997), 2; Susan Kristine Walker, "The Prevalence of Blight and Brownfield Redevelopment in St. Louis" (Ph.D. dissertation, University of Missouri-St. Louis, 2003), 330.

21. Mandelker et al., *Reviving Cities with Tax Abatement*, 21; *Mo. Rev. Stat.* § 99.810 (2003); Johnson and Kriz, "Review of State Tax Increment Financing Laws," 39; Thomas Luce, *Reclaiming the Intent: Tax-Increment Financing in the Kansas City and St. Louis Metropolitan Areas* (Washington, D.C., Brookings Institution, 2003), 7; Jonathan M. Davidson, "Tax Increment Financing as a Tool for Community Redevelopment," *University of Detroit Journal of Urban Law* 56 (1979): 405, 409; Goshorn, "In a TIF," 922–23, 929–30; Fred Faust, "Businesses Angry over Use of TIF; Rival Redevelopment Plan Didn't Need Tax Subsidy," *SLPD*, 8 September 1996, 1E.

22. *Allright Mo., Inc. v. Civic Plaza Redevelopment Corp.*, 538 S.W. 2d 320, 322 (Mo. 1976); *Parking Sys.*, 518 S.W. 2d at 13; George Lefcoe, "Finding the Blight That's Right for California Redevelopment Law," *Hastings Law Journal* 52 (2001): 995–96, 1003–5; quote from A. T. Redevelopment Coprp. Proposal (April 1975), box 16, Poelker Papers.

23. Dan Mihalopoulos, "West County Mall Wins Initial Backing," *SLPD*, 21 November 19907, 1C; Goshorn, "In a TIF," 938–42; Faust, "Businesses Angry," 1E; (quote) "A Tale of Two TIFs," *SLPD*, 20 February 2003, E6; Reinert, "Tax-Increment Financing in Missouri," 1045–46; "Developers Make Pitch for Tax Breaks," *SLPD*, 14 November 1997, C9; *JG St. Louis W. Ltd. Liab. Co. v. Des Peres*, 41 S.W. 3d 513, 514–20 (Mo. Ct. App. 2001); "Blight and the Galleria," *SLPD*, 24 April 2002, (quote) B6; "End the Tax Giveaway," *SLPD*, 25 November 1989, 2B.

24. (Quotes) Purver, "What Constitutes Blighted Area'," 3; Wood, *Slums and Blighted Areas*, 3; Perry, *The Rebuilding of Blighted Areas*, 8; Lefcoe, "Finding the Blight," 994, 1008; Voorhees and Assoc., "Technical Report."

25. *Mo. Rev. Stat.* § 99.805 (3). For interpretation and discussion of the statute, see Goshorn, "In a TIF," 929 n. 53; Reinert, "Tax Increment Financing in Missouri," 1033–34. See also *Oberndorf v. Denver*, 900 F.2d 1434, 1439 (10th Cir. 1990); Purver, "What Constitutes 'Blighted Area'," 3; *99 Cents Only Stores v. Lancaster Redevelopment Agency*, 237 F. Supp. 2d 1123, 1131 (C.D. Cal. 2001).

26. *JG St. Louis W. Ltd. Liab Co. v. Des Peres*, 41 S.W. 3d 513, 518 (Mo. Ct. App. 2001).

27. See Gordon, "Blighting the Way," 325–26.

28. Margaret Collins, *Chapter 353: A Policy Study for Existing and Future Application* (St. Louis Community Development Agency, 1978), 20–23; City Plan Commission, *Blighting Study for Downtown St. Louis* (1970); Mandelker et al., *Reviving Cities with Tax Abatement*, 74; (Baer quote) Robert Olson, "Critical Analysis of Missouri's URC Law" (1975), box 16, Poelker Papers.

29. "East St. Louis Development on Hold," *SLPD*, 3 May 2001, 1.

30. "Businesses Angry over Use of TIF," *SLPD*, 8 September 1996, 1E.

31. Stevens opinion in *Susette Kelo et al., Petitioners v. City of New London et al.*, Supreme Court of the United States, No. 04-108, On Writ of Certiorari to the Supreme Court of Connecticut (23 June 2005).

32. *Oberndorf v. Denver*, 900 F. 2d 1434, 1438–40 (10th Cir. 1990); *Berman v. Parker*, 348 U.S. 26, 35 (1954); Purver, "What Constitutes 'Blighted Area'," § 3; Lefcoe, "Finding the Blight," 1023–25.

33. See Transcript on Appeal, 7–8, *Schweig v. City of St. Louis and Maryland Plaza Redevelopment Corporation*, St. Louis Court of Appeals (1978), RG 600, SC Case Files.

34. (Quote) "Ferguson OKs Enterprise Zone; Plan Would Give Tax Breaks to Attract Industry," *SLPD*, 1 September 2003, 1.

35. The literature on economic development incentives is vast and varied. The earliest efforts are traced in James Cobb, *The Selling of the South: The Southern Crusade for Economic Development, 1936–1980* (Baton Rouge: Louisiana State University Press, 1982); and their spread across the rest of the country in Peter Eisinger, *The Rise of the Entrepreneurial State: State and Local Economic Development Policy in the United States* (Madison: University of Wisconsin Press, 1988). For surveys of recent patterns, see Peter Fisher and Alan Peters, "The Failures of Economic Development Incentives," *Journal of the American Planning Association* 70, 1 (2004); Greg LeRoy, *The Great American Jobs Scam: Corporate Tax Dodging and the Myth of Job Creation* (San Francisco: Berrett-Koehler, 2005); Joyce Y. Man, "Effect of Tax Increment Financing on Economic Development," in Johnson and Man, *Tax Increment Financing and Economic Development*, 101–22.

36. Mandelker et al., *Reviving Cities with Tax Abatement*, 33–36.

37. East-West Gateway Coordinating Council, Transportation Task Force, Background Paper (September 1972), box 8:191, RCGA Records; "A Tale of Two TIFs," *SLPD*, 20 February 2003, B6.

38. "Comments on 353 Report" (n.d.), box 1, ser. 3, John Conway Papers, Washington University Archives, Clayton, Mo.; Ken Langsdorff to Dale Ruthsatz (6 November 1974), box 14, Poelker Papers; Chase Park Plaza Hotel to Carl Fox (18 July 1980), box 1, ser. 3, Conway Papers; Mandelker et al., *Reviving Cities with Tax Abatement*, 25–27.

39. "Strategy for Retaining Mallinckrodt Chemical Work's Corporate Headquarters" (November 1973); "County Rebuffs, City Woos" both clippings in box 16, Poelker Papers;

(quote) Triangle Terminal Warehouses to Poelker (26 September 1973), box 16, Poelker Papers.

40. Lefcoe, "Finding the Blight," 998–1006, 1011–18, 1029–31; Bernard Frieden and Lynne Sagalyn, *Downtown Inc.: How American Rebuilds Cities* (Cambridge, Mass.: MIT Press, 1989), 144–47; John L. Mikesell, "Nonproperty Tax Increment Programs for Economic Development: A Review of the Alternative Programs," in Johnson and Man, *Tax Increment Financing and Economic Development*, 57, 64; Goshorn, "In a TIF," 920–23; "End the Tax Giveaway," *SLPD*, 25 November 1989, 2B; "A Shell Game with Tax Money," *SLPD*, 6 October 1989, 2C; (quote) "Hostages in the Bidding Wars," *SLPD*, 15 March 1998, B2; "Blight and the Galleria," *SLPD*, 24 April 2002, B6.

41. Edith Elmer Wood, "Slums and Blighted Areas in the United States," *Housing Division Bulletin* 1 (1935): 3–16; Chapman, "Tax Increment Financing and Fiscal Stress," 114; Fogelson, *Downtown: Its Rise and Fall*, 317–19, 340, 344–46, 355, 377–78; Teaford, *Urban Renewal*, 444–45; John Quigley, "A Decent Home: Housing Policy in Perspective," in *Brookings-Wharton Papers on Urban Affairs* (Washington, D.C.: Brookings Institution Press, 2000), 74–76; Gelfand, *A Nation of Cities*, 338–39, 360.

42. Fogelson, *Downtown: Its Rise and Fall*, 318–20, 337–39, 342–58; St. Louis Area Descriptions (1937), box 110, City Survey Files, Records of the Home Owners Loan Corporation, RG 195, National Archives 2, College Park, Md.; Gelfand, *A Nation of Cities*, 207–9; (quote) James Ford to Walter Head (Anti-Slum Commission) (26 May 1948), reel 11, Harland Bartholomew Papers (Correspondence), Washington University Archives (WU).

43. See *Levin v. Bridgewater*, 274 A. 2d 1, 4 (N.J. 1971); *Cannata v. New York*, 182 N.E. 2d 395, 397 (N.Y. 1962); *Parking Sys., Inc. v. Kansas City Downtown Redevelopment Corp.*, 518 S.W. 2d 11, 15 (Mo. 1974); Brief of Appellant, *Allright Parking v. Civic Plaza Redevelopment* (1975), 59180, RG 600, SC Case Files; HBA to Arthur Blumeyer (December 1951), reel 11, Bartholomew Correspondence.

44. Minutes, LCRA Board of Commissioners (18 August 1954), box 14, ser. 1, Raymond R. Tucker Papers, WU; Frieden and Sagalyn, *Downtown Inc.*, 153; (quote) City Plan Commission, "Blighting Study: Area Bounded by Twelfth, Clark, Eleventh, and Walnut" (1969), box 9:123, SLDC; (quote) Bob Duffe to Poelker (7 September 1973), box 16, Poelker Papers.

45. See Luce, *Reclaiming the Intent*, 8–11; Goshorn, "In a TIF," 929–30; *Mo. Rev. Stat.* § 99.805(3), (5) (1982) (amended 1986, 1991, 1997); Division of Economic Development files in box 16, Poelker Papers; Lefcoe, "Finding the Blight," 1004.

46. (Quote) "Dear Neighbor" letter (February 1915), Race Relations Collection, box 1, Missouri Historical Society, St. Louis; (quote) John Clark to Harland Bartholomew (3 December 1946), box 5, ser. 1, St. Louis Urban League Papers, WU; James Ford to Walter Head (Anti-Slum Commission) (26 May 1948), reel 11, Bartholomew Papers.

47. "Visits to Eastern Insurance Companies" (December 1945), reel 11, Bartholomew Papers; (quote) Russell, Mullgardt, Schwarz, Van Hoefen, "Study for a Comprehensive Plan for Redevelopment of the Central City Area" (1953), box 8, ser. 1; *St. Louis Commerce* clipping (February 1954), box 6, ser. 1, both in Tucker Papers; (quote) "Market Analysis and Reuse Appraisal of Mill Creek Urban Renewal Area" (1956), folder 78, box 3, Roy Wenzlick Papers, WHMC; (quote) City Plan Commission, "Rebuilding Industry and Commerce in St. Louis" (1960?), box 8, ser. 1, Tucker Papers.

48. Alexander Von Hoffman, "Why They Built Pruitt Igoe," in *From Tenements to the Taylor Homes: In Search of an Urban Housing Policy in Twentieth Century America*, ed. John Bauman, Roger Biles, and Kristin Szylvain (University Park: Pennsylvania State University Press, 2000), 186–93; Lee Rainwater, *Behind Ghetto Walls: Black Families in a Federal Slum* (Chicago: University of Chicago Press, 1970), passim.

49. Comptroller General of the U.S., *Inadequate Relocation Assistance to Families Displaced from Certain Urban Renewal Districts in Kansas and Missouri* (Washington, D.C.: GPO, 1964), 5–6, 8–11;

Frieden and Sagalyn, *Downtown Inc.*, 32; civil rights leader quoted in Gary Orfield, "Federal Policy, Local Power, and Metropolitan Segregation," *Political Science Quarterly* 89,4 (1974–75): 788.

50. (Quote) "Commission on Financing Minutes (26 June 1960), box 17, ser. 3, Tucker Papers; (quote) "Economic Development Planning Analysis: DeSoto-Carr Urban Renewal Project Area" (1968), box 32, ser. 1, Alfonso J. Cervantes Papers, WU; Brief of Plaintiffs-Appellants, *Schweig v. City of St. Louis and Maryland Plaza Redevelopment Corporation*, St. Louis Court of Appeals (1978), RG 600, SC Case Files.

51. See Jeffrey Brown, "A Tale of Two Visions: Harland Bartholomew, Robert Moses, and the Development of the American Freeway," *Journal of Planning History* 4,1 (2005): 3–5; Raymond Mohl, "Stop the Road: Freeway Revolts in American Cities," *Journal of Urban History* 30,5 (2004): 683–86; for examples from other cities, see Patricia House, "Relocation of Families Displaced by Expressway Development: Milwaukee Case Study," *Land Economics* (1963): 75–78; F. James Davis, "The Effects of a Freeway Displacement on Racial Housing Segregation in a Northern City," *Phylon* 26, 3 (1965): 209–15.

52. Andrew Hurley, "Draft of Text for Historical Markers on Old North St. Louis History Trail," at http://www.umsl.edu/~ahurley/poi.htm.

53. Robert Duffe to Robert Sullivan (13 June 1958), box 13, ser. 2, Tucker Papers. See "The 'Ozark Highway' Does Affect You!" (handbill, n.d.), and letters in Highways file, both in box 12, ser. 1, Tucker Papers; EWGCC, "Missouri 755" (1973), and Schmoel to Mo. Highway Commission (16 November 1981), both in box 11, Lafayette Square Restoration Committee Records, Mercantile Library, UMSL; Harry Levins, "Interstate Highways," *SLPD*, 13 January 2004; Virgil Tipton, "The Way West: Highway 40 Grew in Fits and Starts," *SLPD*, 19 September 1994; "Review of Expressway Progress in St. Louis City and County Since 1934" (1954), box 13, ser. 1, Tucker Papers.

54. St. Louis Development Program, "Technical Program: History of Renewal" (1971), 14.

55. Comptroller General of the U.S., *Inadequate Relocation Assistance to Families Displaced from Certain Urban Renewal Districts in Kansas and Missouri*, 8–9. See also Gelfand, *A Nation of Cities*, 211–14; (quote) "Mill Creek Valley Urban Renewal Report" (n.d.), box 12:542, Freedom Of Residence (FOR), Greater St. Louis Committee Records, (sl509), WHMC.

56. Jon Teaford, *The Rough Road to Renaissance: Urban Revitalization in America* (Baltimore: Johns Hopkins University Press, 1990), 150, 155; Daniel J. Monti, *Race, Redevelopment, and the New Company Town* (Albany: SUNY Press, 1990), 42–64, 65–86, 87–107, 130–53 (quoted at 70–71).

57. *Young v. Harris*, no. 78–1896, U.S. Court of Appeals, 8th Cir., 599 F. 2d 870; 1979 U.S. App. LEXIS 14035; 13 ERC (BNA) 1313 (15 March 1979); Monti, *Race, Redevelopment, and the New Company Town*, 108–29.

58. *Young v. Harris*, no. 78–1896, U.S. Court of Appeals, 8th Cir., 599 F. 2d 870; 1979 U.S. App. LEXIS 14035; 13 ERC (BNA) 1313 (15 March 1979).

59. See "Market Analysis and Reuse Appraisal of Meacham Park Urban Renewal Area" (1959), folder 74, box 3, Wenzlick Papers; HUD memo cited in USCCR Staff Report, "Housing in St. Louis" (1970), box 3:127, FOR Records.

60. USCCR Staff Report, "Housing in St. Louis" (1970), box 3:127, FOR Records; Gary Orfield, "The Housing Issues in the St. Louis Case," Report to Judge William Hungate, U.S. District Court (St. Louis, Mo.), *Liddell v. Board of Education* (April 1981), 72; USCCR, *Hearings: St. Louis* (January 1970), 299, 577–78.

61. For these examples, see Report upon the Feasibility of Urban Renewal, North Webster Groves (1957), vol. 56, ser. 2 (Red), Bartholomew Papers; USCCR, Staff Report, "Housing in St. Louis" (1970), in USCCR, *Hearings: St. Louis* (January 1970), 560–70; "Statement of the Land Clearance for Redevelopment Authority of Olivette" (January 1970), in USCCR, *Hearings: St. Louis* (January 1970), 8–13; Orfield, "The Housing Issues in the St. Louis Case," 72; "Market Analysis and Reuse Appraisal of Meacham Park Urban Renewal Area" (1959), folder 74, box 3, Wenzlick Papers.

62. Appellant's Brief, *Brooks v. Land Clearance for Redevelopment* (1966), RG 600, SC Case Files; Elmwood Park Urban Renewal Plan (October 1964), in *Brooks v. Land Clearance for Redevelopment* (1966), RG 600, SC Case Files; Final Report of the Grand Jury of St. Louis County (January 1965), in *Brooks v. Land Clearance for Redevelopment* (1966), RG 600, SC Case Files.

63. Final Report of the Grand Jury of St. Louis County (January 1965), in *Brooks v. Land Clearance for Redevelopment* (1966), RG 600, SC Case Files; Appellant's Brief, *Brooks v. Land Clearance for Redevelopment* (1966), RG 600, SC Case Files; Transcript on Appeal, 156, *Brooks v. Land Clearance for Redevelopment* (1966), RG 600, SC Case Files.

64. Elmwood Park Urban Renewal Plan (October 1964), in *Brooks v. Land Clearance for Redevelopment* (1966), RG 600, SC Case Files; Transcript on Appeal, 317, 419–20, 679–81, *Brooks v. Land Clearance for Redevelopment* (1966), RG 600, SC Case Files.

65. Relocation Ledger (Plaintiff's Exhibit 1); Transcript on Appeal, 86, 412, 641–43; Elmwood Park Project Area: Relocation Plan (1962), all in *Brooks v. Land Clearance for Redevelopment* (1966), RG 600, SC Case Files.

66. For the Malcolm Terrace controversy, see folder 35, Kay Drey Papers, WHMC.

67. Mandelker et al., *Reviving Cities with Tax Abatement*, 45–50.

68. See LCRA file in box 15, ser. 3, Tucker Papers.

69. Martha Shull, "Chapter 353 Property Tax Abatements" (Missouri Division of Budget and Planning, 1981), 8; Collins, *Chapter 353*, 30–35; Mandelker et al., *Reviving Cities with Tax Abatement*, 32–33.

70. "Enterprise Zones Aren't the Answer," *SLPD*, 9 May 1991, 2C; (quote) "The Rip-off Zone," *SLPD*, 24 April 1992, 2C; "Enterprise Zones Trigger Political Dispute," *SLPD*, 6 May 1991, 1B; "Ferguson OKs Enterprise Zone; Plan Would Give Tax Breaks to Attract Industry," *SLPD*, 1 September 2003, 1. For a broader overview of enterprise zone performance, see Peter Fisher and Alan Peters, *State Enterprise Zone Programs: Have They Worked?* (Kalamazoo, Mich.: W.E. Upjohn, 2002).

71. Denzau and Leven, "Report on Alternative Revenue Sources: Local Revenue Generation," ES:6, V-1; Linda Tucci, "City Addicted to Abatement Exacts Heavy Toll on Schools, Study Says," *St. Louis Business Journal*, 12 January 1998, at http://stlouis.bizjournals.com/stlouis/stories/1998/01/12/story1.html (Michael Jones quoted at 1); "E. St. Louis Robs Peter to Pay Paul," *SLPD*, 4 May 1991, 3A.

72. Legislators quoted in "Enterprise Zones Trigger Political Dispute," *SLPD*, 6 May 1991, 1B.

73. Collins, *Chapter 353*, 6; Walker, *Urban Blight and Slums*, 4, 5 (quoting National Municipal League); *Mo. Rev. Stat.* § 353.020(2); *Mo. Rev. Stat.* § 99.805(5)(c) (1982) (amended 1986, 1991, 1997).

74. Mandelker et al., *Reviving Cities with Tax Abatement*, 46.

75. Denzau and Leven, "Report on Alternative Revenue Sources: Local Revenue Generation," 5:13–15, 18–19; Triangle Terminal Warehouses to Poelker (26 September 1973), box 16, Poelker Papers.

76. Shull, "Chapter 353 Property Tax Abatements," 14; "Developer Offers Plan," *SLPD*, 12 March 1991, 1; economic development director quoted in "Mediation May Be Step to Eminent Domain in Manchester," *SLPD*, 9 November 2005, B4.

77. Lehnen and Johnson, "The Impact of Tax Increment Financing on School Districts," 137–42; "City Addicted to Tax Abatement," *St. Louis Business Journal*, 9 January 1998, 1.

78. (Quote) "Shell Game with Tax Money," *SLPD*, 6 October 1989, 2C; "Cost of Galleria Expansion Studied," *SLPD*, 13 April 1989, 2; "Clayton Schools Agree to Plan for Lower Galleria Tax Losses," *SLPD*, 15 October 1989, 8C; Denzau and Leven, "Report on Alternative Revenue Sources: Local Revenue Generation," 5: 14–15; "Agreement Cuts Losses to Clayton Schools," *SLPD*, 9 April 1991, 12B; Collins, *Chapter 353*, 60.

Conclusion. Our House Revisited: The Twenty-First Century at 4635 North Market Street

1. Peter Dreier, John Mollenkopf, and Todd Swanstrom, *Place Matters: Metropolitics for the Twenty-First Century* (Lawrence: University Press of Kansas, 2001), 98–132; Thomas Sugrue, "The Geography of Fear," *The Nation* (27 February 2006), at http://www.thenation.com/doc/ 20060227/sugrue.

2. Dreier, Mollenkopf, and Swanstrom, *Place Matters*, 36–37.

3. David Rusk, *Cities Without Suburbs* (Baltimore: Johns Hopkins University Press, 2003), 8. Over the same span, the population of Greater St. Louis grew by about 50 percent (from 1.7 to 2.6 million), while its land area grew by over 150 percent (from 2,490 square miles to 6,320 square miles). See David Laslo, "A Brief Demographic and Spatial History of the St. Louis Region: 1950–2000" (Public Policy Research Center, UM-St. Louis, 2003), 1–14.

4. Transportation Research Board and National Research Council, *The Costs of Sprawl—2000* (Washington, D.C.: National Academy Press, 2002), 15–16.

5. Alfred Price, "Urban Renewal: The Case of Buffalo, NY," *Review of Black Political Economy* 19,3/4 (1991): 125ff; Meghan Stromberg, "Tough Love in Buffalo," *Planning* (October 2005): 6–9; Mark Goldman, *City on the Lake: The Challenge of Change in Buffalo, New York* (Buffalo: Prometheus, 1990), 167–75; Jon Teaford, *Rough Road to Renaissance: Urban Revitalization in America, 1940–1985* (Baltimore: Johns Hopkins University Press, 1990), 1–3, 21–22; Frank Giaratanni and David Houston, "Structural Change and Economic Policy in a Declining Manufacturing Region: Implications of the Pittsburgh Experience," *Urban Studies* 26 (1989): 550–51.

6. See, for example, Robert Self, *American Babylon: Race and the Struggle for Postwar Oakland* (Princeton, N.J.: Princeton University Press, 2003), 20–34.

7. Rolf Pendall, Robert Puentes, and Jonathon Martin, "From Traditional to Reformed: A Review of the Land Use Regulations in the Nation's 50 Largest Metropolitan Areas" (Washington, D.C.: Brookings Institution, August 2006), 12–13, 17–18, 21–22.

8. Rusk, *Cities Without Suburbs*, 53–65, 80–81.

9. See Heather Thompson, "Rethinking the Politics of White Flight in the Postwar City: Detroit, 1945–1980," *Journal of Urban History* 25 (1999): 163–98; Sherry Lamb Schirmer, *A City Divided: The Racial Landscape of Kansas City, 1900–1960* (Columbia: University of Missouri Press, 2002), 97–110; Margaret Garb, "Drawing the 'Color Line': Race and Real Estate in Early Twentieth Century Chicago," *Journal of Urban History* 32, 5 (2006): 773–87; Self, *American Babylon*, 104–5.

10. Arnold Hirsch, *Making the Second Ghetto: Race and Housing in Chicago, 1940–1960* (New York: Cambridge University Press, 1983), 15, 40–67; Thomas Sugrue, *The Origins of the Urban Crisis: Race and Inequality in Postwar Detroit* (Princeton, N.J.: Princeton University Press, 1996), 33–56, passim.

11. For examples, see Schirmer, *A City Divided*, 52–55; Hirsch, *Making the Second Ghetto*, 4–5, 17–18; Sugrue, *Origins of the Urban Crisis*, 35–36, 41–43; John Bauman, *Public Housing, Race, and Renewal: Urban Planning in Philadelphia, 1920–1974* (Philadelphia: Temple University Press, 1987), 58–59, 65–69.

12. Hirsch, *Making the Second Ghetto*, 9–10; Sugrue, *Origins of the Urban Crisis*, 44–45; Thomas Hanchett, *Sorting Out the New South City: Race, Class, and Urban Development in Charlotte, 1875–1975* (Chapel Hill: University of North Carolina Press, 1998), 6–9, 116–17; Schirmer, *A City Divided*, 2–3, 42–44.

13. Victoria Wolcott, "Recreation and Race in the Postwar City: Buffalo's 1956 Crystal Beach Riot," *Journal of American History* (June 2006): 74–80; Teaford, *Rough Road to Renaissance*, 14–15, 45–54.

14. Teaford, *Rough Road to Renaissance*, 45–54; Roger Parks and Ronald Oakerson, "Comparative Metropolitan Organization: Service Production and Government Structures in St. Louis (MO) and Allegheny County (PA)," *Publius* 23, 1 (1993): 35–37; Kenneth Heineman, "Model

City: The War on Poverty, Race Relations, and Catholic Social Activism in 1960s Pittsburgh," *The Historian* (2003): 869–73.

15. See Colin Gordon, "The Lost City of Solidarity: Metropolitan Unionism in Historical Perspective," *Politics and Society* 27, 4 (1999): 557–81; Schirmer, *A City Divided*; Sugrue, *Origins of the Urban Crisis*; Heineman, "Model City," 869–73; Self, *American Babylon*, 6–8, 35–46.

16. Self, *American Babylon*, 2–3, 242–46.

17. See Hirsch, *Making the Second Ghetto*, 102–5; Teaford, *Rough Road to Renaissance*, 1–3, 40–42; Price, "Urban Renewal: The Case of Buffalo," 125 ff.

18. Charles Shaw, "Gateway Bypass: Can St. Louis Survive in the Post-Industrial Era?" *The Next American City* 5 (July 2004), at http://www.americancity.org/article.php?id_article=37.

19. This was especially true of urban highway development. For examples see Raymond Mohl, "Planned Destruction: Interstates and Central City Housing," in *From Tenements to the Taylor Homes: In Search of an Urban Housing Policy in Twentieth Century America*, ed. John Bauman, Roger Biles, and Kristin Szylvain (University Park: Pennsylvania State University Press, 2000), 226–45; Self, *American Babylon*, 149–55; Sugrue, *Origins of the Urban Crisis*, 48.

20. See Arnold Hirsch, "Less Than *Plessy:* The Inner City, Suburbs, and State-Sanctioned Residential Segregation in the Age of *Brown*," in *The New Suburban History*, ed. Kevin Kruse and Thomas Sugrue (Chicago: University of Chicago Press), 34–35, 37–40; Price, "Urban Renewal: The Case of Buffalo," 125 ff; Sugrue, *Origins of the Urban Crisis*, 49–50; Hanchett, *Sorting Out the New South City*, 249–51; Bauman, *Public Housing, Race, and Renewal*, 35–36; Hirsch, *Making the Second Ghetto*, 13–15.

21. For these examples, see Bauman, *Public Housing, Race, and Renewal*, 43–45, 118–43, 167–74; Guian McKee, "Liberal Ends Through Illiberal Means: Race, Urban Renewal, and Community in the Eastwick Section of Philadelphia, 1949–1990," *Journal of Urban History* 27, 5 (2001): 547–83; William Jenkins, "Before Downtown: Cleveland, Ohio and Urban Renewal, 1949–1958," *Journal of Urban History* 27, 4 (2001): 471–96; Sugrue, *Origins of the Urban Crisis*, 65–88; June Manning Thomas, *Redevelopment and Race: Planning a Finer City in Postwar Detroit* (Baltimore: Johns Hopkins University Press, 1997), 45–46; Self, *American Babylon*, 140; Zane Miller and Bruce Tucker, *Changing Plans for America's Inner Cities: Cincinnati's Over-the-Rhine and Twentieth-Century Urbanism* (Columbus: Ohio State University Press, 1998), 29, 59–60; Roy Lubove, *Twentieth Century Pittsburgh: Government, Business, and Environmental Change* (New York; John Wiley, 1969), 106–41; Hirsch, *Making the Second Ghetto*, 100–134, 244.

22. Peter Dreier, "America's Urban Crisis: Symptoms, Causes, Solutions" in *Race, Poverty, and American Cities*, ed. John Charles Boger and Judith Welch Wagner (Chapel Hill: University of North Carolina Press, 1996), 80.

23. Thanks to Joel Rogers for this insight. The figures are from the Bureau of Economic Analysis, Regional Economic Accounts (http://bea.gov/bea/regional/gsp/); and from the CIA, *World Factbook 2005* (https://www.cia.gov/cia/publications/factbook/rankorder/2001 rank.html).

24. A good primer is Alan Evans, "The Pure Theory of City Size in an Industrial Economy," *Urban Studies* 9, 1 (1972): 50–79.

25. Joseph Persky and Wim Wiewel, "Central City and Suburban Development: Who Pays and Who Benefits?" (Chicago: Great Cities Institute, 1996); NRC, *The Costs of Sprawl—2000*, 13–17; Urban Land Institute, *Higher Density Development:* Myth and Fact (2005); and the research of the Center for Neighborhood Technologies (http://www.cnt.org/), including "Two Views of Cities and CO_2" at http://www.cnt.org/repository/CO2EmissionsChicago.pdf.

26. See Joel Rogers and Daniel Luria, *Metro Futures: Economic Solutions for Cities and Their Suburbs* (Boston: Beacon, 1999), 11–23; and the work of Good Jobs First, especially Greg LeRoy and Sara Hinkley, "Smart Growth and Workforce Development" (2000); and Greg LeRoy, "Talking to Union Leaders About Smart Growth" (2001), both at http://www.goodjobsfirst.org/publica tions/index.cfm.

27. Center for Neighborhood Technologies, "Housing and Transportation Cost Trade-Offs

and Burdens of Working Households in 28 Metros'' (July 2006) at http://www.cnt.org/reposi tory/H-T-Tradeoffs-for-Working-Families-n-28-Metros-F ULL.pdf ; Greg LeRoy and Karla Walter, ''The Thin Cities: How Subsidized Job Piracy Deepens Inequality in the Twin Cities Metro Area'' (Washington, D.C: Good Jobs First, 2006).

28. Richard Florida, ''The Economic Geography of Talent,'' *Annals of the Association of American Geographers* 92, 4 (2002); Florida, *The Rise of the Creative Class* (New York: Basic Books, 2002).

29. Bruce Katz, ''Six Ways Cities Can Reach Their Economic Potential,'' Living Cities Policy Overview (Washington, D.C.: Brookings Institution, 2005), 2–6; NRC, *The Costs of Sprawl—2000*, 34–37.

30. Dreier, Mollenkopf, and Swanstrom, *Place Matters*, chap. 3.

31. An argument made most eloquently by Rusk, in *Cities Without Suburbs*, 5–48. See also Elliot Sclar, ''Urban Revitalization: The Short Road to Long-Term Growth,'' in *Reclaiming Prosperity: A Blueprint for Progressive Economic Reform*, ed. Jeff Faux and Todd Schaeffer (Washington, D.C.: Economic Policy Institute, 1999), 308–9.

32. Rusk, *Cities Without Suburbs*, 89–91; Myron Orfield, *Metropolitics: A Regional Agenda for Community and Stability* (Washington, D.C.: Brookings Institution, 1997); Dreier, Mollenkopf, and Swanstrom, *Place Matters*, 177–82, 205–23.

33. See Rogers and Luria, *Metro Futures*, 12, 23–35.

34. See Peter Dreier, ''America's Urban Crisis After the LA Riots,'' *National Civic Review* 92,1 (2003); Alan Berube and Bruce Katz, ''Katrina's Window: Confronting Concentrated Poverty Across America,'' Special Analysis in Metropolitan Policy (Washington, D.C.:, Brookings Institution, 2005).

Index